Collected Papers on Money, Interest, and Monetary Policy

Collected Papers Volume 1

L. M. Bhole
Professor (Economics)
Department of Humanities and Social Sciences
Indian Institute of Technology, Bombay
Mumbai

Amani International Publishers

Bibliographic information published by the Deutsche Nationalbibliothek

The Deutsche Nationalbibliothek lists this publication in the Deutsche Nationalbibliografie; detailed bibliographic data are available in the Internet at http://dnb.d-nb.de

Manufactured in Germany

E-Mail: service@amani-publishers.com
http://www.amani-publishers.com

ISBN: 978-3-938054-17-8

Collected Papers on Money, Interest, and Monetary Policy

Dedicated To My Students

Preface

As a teacher and researcher in Economics for more than 35 years, it is a matter of satisfaction to me that, as a result of the encouragement and blessings of my teachers, affection of my students, and help of my friends, colleagues, and peers, I have been able to make some contribution to the subject of Economics in the form of a few books and a fairly good number of research papers. At this juncture of my academic career, I thought that it would be of great help and convenience if these widely scattered papers are brought together and published in a book form. When I suggested this to Mr. Peter Dudy, the Managing Director of Amani International Publishers, he appreciated the idea and undertook to implement it. The result has been the publication of the following four books: (1) Collected Papers on Money, Interest, and Monetary Policy, (2) Collected Papers on Credit and Finance, (3) Collected Papers on Gandhian Thought, (4) Unemployment, Inequality, Entrepreneurship, and Other Collected Papers.

These four volumes contain selected theoretical, empirical, and policy-oriented papers authored by myself singly or jointly with my Ph.D. students, and which have been published earlier in various academic, technical journals, and in various edited anthologies, the names of which I have gratefully acknowledged in the respective papers. I wish to thank all my co-authors – Dr. B. Kamaiah, Dr. V.J. Sebastian, Dr. Pradyumna Dash, Dr. Shreeya Pattanaik, Dr. K.V.S.S. Narayan Rao, Dr. Manoj Kumar, Dr. Jitendra Mahakud, Ms. R.V. Bhavani, Dr. Sunil Khandelwal, and Dr. Abdul Shaban – for allowing me to include our jointly-written papers in these volumes.

The papers have not been arranged chronologically. Although no particular ordering of papers could be followed, it can be said that the sequencing of papers has been, as far as possible, a themic one. While some papers have been slightly edited or revised, the most of them have been reprinted in their original form. Since many papers in these books cover different time periods during 1950 to 2005, the books provide long-term, and evolutionary or historical perspective also on the themes discussed in them. The books are primarily reference monographs, but they can be used as supplementary texts at the post-graduate level in Economics. The faculty, doctoral and post-doctoral students, and researchers in Economics and finance, and the policy makers would find the books of great interest and utility.

All the four books have been dedicated to my students who have given me their affection in a measure which can be called only as generous. I am grateful to various journals for publishing my papers many of which have been included in these volumes. I wish to thank Indian Institute of Technology, Bombay, at which I have spent almost all the years of my service, for providing excellent facilities and academic ambience conducive for being productive. I am also thankful to the Curriculum Development Programme at IIT Bombay for providing me financial assistance for preparing the manuscripts of all the four volumes. I cannot thank enough Mr.Kunjukunju for skillfully, efficiently, and painstakingly preparing the manuscripts on the word processor. I also owe sincere thanks to my friends in the Department – Dr. A. Ramanathan, Dr. K. Narayanan, Dr. C.D. Sebastian, and others – for being ever ready to willingly provide help of very many kinds, particularly the constant emotional support. I would also like to thank Mr. Peter Dudy and Amani International Publishers for doing a high quality job of publishing my books. Mr. Peter Dudy indeed showed much flexibility, understanding and cordiality which I appreciate immensely. I also thank IGEP Foundation for putting me in touch with Amani International Publishers.

The present volume on Collected Papers on Money, Interest and Monetary Policy contains twenty-two research papers on themes such as definition, measurement, and determination of money supply, demand for money or liquidity preference, determinants of short-term and long-term interest rates, administered interest rates system, structure of interest rates, impact of interest rates on investment, inflation, and business cycles, and various aspects of monetary and interest rates policy. These themes have been discussed primarily in the Indian context, but the international context also has been referred to wherever possible. The papers in the volume are highly policy-useful.

L. M. Bhole
July 2007

About the Author

Laxman Madhao Bhole is Professor in the Department of Humanities and Social Sciences, IIT Bombay. After graduating from Poona University in 1965, he obtained his M.A. in Economics from Bombay University in 1967. He obtained Ph.D. from Bombay University in 1971 and joined Sydenham College, Bombay, where he taught for two years. He joined IIT Bombay in1973 and was the Head of the Department of Humanities and Social Sciences during 1989-92. He was awarded Maharashtra Government Open Merit Scholarship, Ford Foundation Scholarship, and UGC Fellowship for pursuing his studies at various levels. He visited the Institute for Studies in Economic Development, Naples, Italy for six months on an Italian Government scholarship. Prof. Bhole has been teaching Economics for more than 35 years.

A prolific writer, Prof. Bhole has many books, and over 125 research articles published in books and reputed journals, to his credit. His Books are: (1) *Investment, Interest, and Monetary Policy in India* (1974); (2) *Impacts of Monetary Policy* (1985); (3) *Financing of the Private Corporate Sector: Trends, Issues, and Policies* (2000); (4) *Essays on Gandhian Socio-Economic Thought* (2000); (5) *Financial Institutions And Markets: Structure, Growth, And Innovations* (Fourth Ed.) (2004); (6) *Collected Papers on Money, Interest, and Monetary Policy* (2007); (7) *Collected Papers on Credit and Finance* (2007); (8) *Collected Papers on Gandhian Thought* (2007); and (9) *Unemployment, Inequality, Entrepreneurship, and other Collected Papers* (2007).

Prof. Bhole has completed sponsored research projects for the national organizations such as the Indian Council of Social Science Research, the Committee to Review the Working of Monetary System in India, the Reserve Bank of India, and Tata Economic Consultancy Services. He has successfully guided the research work for more than 25 Ph.D., 12 M.Phil., and 7 M.Tech. dissertations.

Prof. Bhole has been an Associate at the Indian Institute of Advanced Study, Shimla; a University Grants Commission Visiting Fellow at different Universities; a Guest Faculty at various Universities and Institutions; a Referee for many M.Phil. and Ph.D. dissertations, sponsored research projects, and journals; and a Member of Board of Editors of many journals. He has served on the Board of Directors of the Interconnected Stock Exchange of India, Mumbai; on the Project Selection Committee and Programmes Advisory Committee of the Shastri Indo-Canadian Institute; and on the faculty Selection Committees of various Universities and Institutions.

He was invited to attend the Citizen's World Assembly in 2001 by the Alliance For Responsible, Plural, and United World, held at Lille in France. He was also invited to attend their Annual Meeting in January 2006 by the American Finance Association.

Prof. Bhole's current areas of teaching and research interests are Gandhian Thought; Financial Markets and Institutions; and Money, Banking, and Finance. He is at present working on the book, Beyond the State and Market: A Search for Alternative Paradigm.

Contents

1. Definition, Measurement, and Determination of Money Supply 1

2. An Empirical Definition of Money: Some Factor Analytic Evidence for India 27

3. An Empirical Study of Liquidity Preference of Corporate Sector in India, 1951-1974 39

4. On the Stability of Corporate Liquidity Preference in India, 1950-51 to 1973-74 53

5. Administered Interest Rates in India 65

6. Interest Rate and Corporate Investment in India 101

7. Determinants of Interest Rates in a Deregulated Open Economy 113

8. Determinants of Long-Term Interest Rates in India During 1970s to 1990s 127

9. Domestic and External Factors in Short-Term Interest Rates Determination in India 151

10. The Structure of Interest Rates in Theory and Practice 175

11. Some Issues Concerning Interest Rates Theory and Policy 189

12. An Interest Rate Policy for Stable Economic Growth 203

13. A Critique of New Interest Rates 209

14. Recent Changes in Interest Rates Policy in India 219

15. An Appraisal of Recent Interest Rates Policy in India 229

16. Industrial Recession in India: Is Interest Rate the Cause? 253

17. Anti-Inflationary Policy in India 269

18. The Role of Interest Rate in Exchange Rate Management in India 277

Contents

19. Responsiveness of Investment and Other Expenditures to Changes in Techniques of Monetary Control in India, 1950-51 to 1977-78 295

20. Some Aspects of the Past Evolution and Future Prospects of Monetary Policy in India 309

21. International Aspects of Monetary Policy in India 317

22. Recent Changes in the Theory and Policy of Cash Reserves Ratio and Statutory Liquidity Ratio: A Critical Appraisal 337

[1]

Definition, Measurement, and Determination of Money Supply[*]

Introduction

Money is one of the important macro economic variables. Correct understanding of the role of money in economic activity hinges on defining and measuring money correctly. There has been a growing tendency both in India and abroad to conduct monetary analysis and policy in terms of empirically defined broad money and multiple measures of money. Recently, the Committee to Review the Working of the Money System also has held that M_3 is the appropriate definition of money and that the money multiplier framework is dependable for money supply analysis and control. This would give a further wrong direction to the evolution of monetary theory and monetary policy as well as their information base in India.

This paper seeks to undertake a fresh and comprehensive discussion of major issues relating the concept, measure and determination of money supply with a view to restraining the tendency mentioned above. Section I presents the context or background of this study. Section II examines which of the existing approaches to defining money is correct. Section III discusses the special economic characteristics of money, while Section IV presents a new measure of money supply for India in the light of these characteristics. Section V examines whether and how far the money multiplier theory is empirically supported in India.

I. Context or Background

The role of money in economic activity, i.e., whether and how far money matters in determining prices, output, employment, etc. has been one of the most intensely and widely debated

[*] Paper published in Economic and Political Weekly, June 6, 1987, and June 13, 1987.

topics in economic literature. If the role of money is to be properly and realistically understood, the prior and correct conceptualization of what is money and how it is to be measured is essential since the conclusions reached in economics often depend upon conceptions used. If money is not correctly defined, the role of some other economic variable(s) may get appropriated to money which, in turn, may introduce an error in the assessment of the claim about the distinctive and superior exegetic power of different macro monetary models. The choice of economic policies, policy instruments, and their effectiveness would also be affected. The issues concerning the concept, measurement, and determination of money supply have, therefore, remained as an important agenda for the researchers in economics everywhere.

It can be seen from the relevant literature that, quite often, the care is not taken to maintain a distinction between the concept of money and the measure of money. Similarly, there is no agreement as to whether the appropriate definition of money should be arrived at on *a priori* or empirical basis. Further, while some people accept the 'narrow' measure of money, some others believe in its 'broad' measure, and still some others prefer to work with multiple measures of money. The official publications in different countries publish data on a number of measures of money which are arrived at by making various permutations and combinations of different financial assets in the respective economies and which are reviewed and revised from time to time. [1] In short, the area of present inquiry is still in a state of flux; it is still riddled with a great deal of confusion and uncertainty.

In India, the evolution of thinking in this field has been influenced mainly by the works of two working groups on money supply which were appointed by the Reserve Bank of India (RBI). [2] The First Working Group (FWG) regarded 'narrow' money as the appropriate measure of money; it did not use the term money for assets other than currency, demand deposits, and other deposits, which it rightly called as near money assets in order to distinguish them from money. The Second Working Group (SWG) adopted a rather ambivalent approach in this context. While it thought that the hard core of monetary aggregates should basically continue to be those assets possessing the quality of superior liquidity arising from the conception of money as a medium of exchange and the most generally accepted means of payment available for the mediation of transactions and final settlement of claims, it also somehow came to believe that the use of a single measure of money stock for monetary analysis and policy would be inadequate and misleading, and that there is no unique measure of monetary aggregate. [3] It, therefore, proposed four measures of money, viz., M_1 to M_4. In this process, the assets such as time deposits also came to be designated as money. Both the working groups gave great importance to operational considerations such as comprehensive or extensive coverage and availability of data in defining money because, according to them, money supply could not be defined purely on *a priori* grounds.

Till SWG's recommendations were accepted, the official statistics on money supply used to be made available in tables with appropriate titles such as Money Supply with the Public, Seasonal Variations in Money Supply with the Public, and Variations in Money Supply with the Public in RBI publications. Subsequently, these tables were replaced by tables titled as

Money Stock Measures, Sources of Seasonal Variations in M_3, and Sources of Variations in M_3, respectively. Similarly, certain other important monetary statistics such as the average and marginal money multipliers, income velocity of money, etc., are now being presented with respect to M_3 only in official publications. One also finds that the analyses of interrelationships between money, prices and output in official publications and by some academic and other researchers are now being conducted are dominantly in terms of M_3 alone.

Recently, the Committee to Review the Working of the Monetary System (CRWMS), throughout its report, [4] has analysed the working of the Indian monetary system and policy as if the issue of appropriate definition and measure of money has been settled in favour of M_3 beyond any doubt. It has recommended setting up of monetary target in terms of M_3 as an instrument of monetary policy. It has also reposed faith in money-multiplier (MMT) as the theory of money supply determination and control. Thus, "we, therefore, recommend that the Reserve Bank of India adopt monetary targeting as an important monetary policy tool. Formulation of monetary policy with M_3 as the monetary variable to be targeted becomes a feasible proposition in the restructured monetary system envisage by us." [5] How one wishes that, instead of being certain about the appropriateness of M_3, the CRWMS had viewed the issue of definition and measure of money in the same way as it did in the case of deficit financing. About the money multiplier, the CRWMS has said, "A study on the behaviour of reserve money multiplier and money stock ... shows that the multiplier can be predicted ... this stability and predictability of the money multiplier imparts greater strength to monetary regulation measures aimed at influencing the course of reserve money." [6] More recently, the deputy governor of the RBI has stated, "My own personal preference is to estimate that demand function for broad money and work with a larger elasticity implicit in such a formulation than use the narrow definition of money which may have very serious definitional problems." [7] One wonders what these "serious" problems are and whether the broad money does not have far more serious definitional problems.

This somewhat lengthy tracing out of the views on money supply should show that the belief in M_3 as the appropriate measure of money and in the money multiplier theory is poised for wider acceptance in India. This, in our view, would give further impetus in the wrong direction to the evolution of monetary theory, monetary policy, and their information base in our country. Therefore, taking the views of the CRWMS as a point of departure, we undertake a comprehensive and fresh examination of many issues concerning the concept, measure, and determination of money supply in this paper.

II. Taxonomical Issues

Every economy is characterized by the existence of a large number of monetary and financial assets/liabilities [8] which differ in respect of their functions and economic characteristics. Before we proceed to determine which of these assets are money, it is necessary to emphasise here that the terms, concept of money and measure of money are distinctly separate and they are not to be used synonymously as it is often done. The statements such as "... money has been traditionally defined as the sum of currency with the public and that portion of the deposits ... which are withdrawable on demand" [9] are not accurate. The correct measure of money is impossible without the prior specification of the correct concept of money. As it has been rightly pointed out, the monetary analysis is often disoriented because of the failure to remember that defining and measuring money are not matters of expediency, and that they are not to be treated as identical issues. [10]

Three approaches are known to have been in use for defining and measuring money: *a priori* approach which is variously known as the logical or analytical or conceptual or technical or theoretical approach, the empirical approach and the operational approach. Under the first one, all the relevant functional and institutional attributes which define moneyness of the assets are systematically specified and then the measure of money is obtained by grouping together those assets which meet or satisfy these attributes. The process is clearly to develop first the concept of money which is an analytical construct of scientific nature in the sense that it can be subjected to empirically verifiable or refutable observations, and then to measure this analytical construct in order to make the theory operational. The attributes of moneyness are likely to differ in their nature, i.e., some of them can be deemed to be basic, universal, and permanent and are, therefore, emphasized, while others may be changeable over time and space and, therefore, may be regarded to be of lesser importance. In other words, in certain cases, it may be necessary to use institution and judgment in measuring money on the basis of its properties. The second and third approaches are really about only the measurement of money; they are not about the conceptualization of money. The operational approach emphasizes considerations such as the availability of data, the frequency with which data are available, whether there is a correspondence between the measure and the use of which it is to be put, etc. The empirical approach has two variants: the first one is mainly due to the monetarists and can be called the 'monetarist empirical approach' (MEA). The other one may be called the 'substitution approach' (SA). Under the latter, the degree of substitutability between the generally deemed (traditionally defined) money assets and the other assets is ascertained by finding out (a) cross-elasticities of substitution, i.e., the percentage change in narrow money per percentage change in the rate of return on each competing asset, or (b) elasticities of substitution, i.e., the percentage change in narrow money per percentage change in each competing asset. [11] Under the MEA, all the different aggregates of financial assets are designate as money and that aggregate is regarded as the best measure of money which, when introduced in certain functions such as demand for money, prices, national income, etc., gives the best results in terms of certain preconceived and preselected criteria. According to this approach, money is best measured as that sum of liquid financial assets which (a) has the highest correlation with national income, (b) has a stable and sturdy demand function, (c) represents the best target for monetary policy, and (d) produces an adequate theory of demand for money. [12]

Which one of these approaches is the correct one? Why? There is no difficulty in admitting that sometimes the operational difficulties of availability of data, etc., cannot be solved and that it may, therefore, become necessary to make a compromise in respect of inclusion or exclusion of one asset or another while measuring money. This, however, should not mean that money can be measured predominantly on operational grounds and at the cost of compromising theoretical prerequisites of money. Both the variants of the empirical approach are not dependable because the available empirical tests at their current stage of development may not be reliable, may have low power of explanation, and may hardly be able to narrow down the universe of possible aggregates and to indicate a single appropriate measure of money. Similarly, in the absence of generally agreed value as a standard for making judgment, it is not possible to claim universal superiority for one measure over the other(s) on the basis of empirical results wherein the values of parameters may not differ much for a given period and country or they may differ widely for different countries, time periods, functional forms, and models. In short, there is no determinate empirical definition of money. It has been rightly emphasized that " ... the available empirical evidence is both conflicting and difficult to interpret. Although M. Friedman had previously established that historically M_2 has exhibited the most stable relationship to GNP, more recent studies suggest that this conclusion is unwarranted ... the empirical tests of N Berkman ... show that it is impossible to identify an unique aggregate whose relationship to GNP is uniformly superior to others over different sample periods. More importantly ... the future stability of estimated empirical regularities cannot be guaranteed under alternative future monetary strategies and rules." [13]

Serious Drawbacks

In addition, MEA suffers from drawbacks which are of more fundamental and serious nature. It suffers from the circularity of thinking; it is characterized by the logical frog-leap, it has been designed to support a given monetary model of the economy; it forecloses the possibility of showing that money along does not matter; it, in effect, says that money is what money does to prove the validity of a given theory of money. In economic analysis, the purpose of empirical work is to verify the concepts and theory, and the stage of empirical work clearly comes only after the relevant concepts have already been defined. What is the role of money in economic activity? What is the role of money is economic activity? What are the determinants of demand for money? Is demand for money stable? The questions such as these cannot be empirically studied at all unless it is first conceived as to what is money and how it is t be measured. Similarly, the statistical properties of the estimated functions cannot be meaningfully interpreted unless all the variables with which functions are estimated are first defined. We know from value theory that the extent of price elasticity of demand for a commodity depends on the scope of definition of a commodity (viz., a brand of toothpaste, toothpaste, dentifrice). Do we argue here that the appropriate definition of a commodity is the one which gives the highest price elasticity? Do we define a commodity such that it produces an 'adequate theory of demand' for that commodity and there is no 'breakdown' of the concept of that commodity? To say that money is something for which demand is stable the study is to presume that money demand must be stable and sturdy, i.e., what was to be empirically tested is presumed to have been already proved. MEA is born out of the desire to prove that the monetarist model of the economy is the only valid model. But if we accept the criteria mentioned above, we can not legitimately reject the criteria, if formulated, by the proponents of some other model, say, by the Keynesians. For example, why not say that money is that aggregate of assets for which demand for money is not stable, which has high interest elasticity of demand, and which has low correlation with the national income? We then get as many appropriate definitions of money as the number of models of the economy.

In view of its palpably misleading and unscientific nature, it is surprising that so many monetary economists have so easily and widely accepted and used the notion of 'empirical definition of money'. There is no reason why money alone, among many economic variables, should enjoy the kind of convenient treatment and special status it has actually enjoyed in its definition. While studying the role and determinants of saving, investment, consumption, etc., the economists do not define, say, investment as that aggregate of real assets which best explains the national income. They do not determine the appropriateness of the definitions of the price expectations and price deflator on the basis of their performance in explaining given economic phenomena. Similarly, if money plays the most crucial role in economic activity, it must be possible to validate it by using theoretically defined and measured money in empirical functions. The operational and substitution approaches can be supplements to such a theoretical approach whose primacy should never be sidetracked. It is necessary to guard that the arguments such as "money cannot be defined purely on *a priori* grounds" do not degenerate into a position that money can be defined purely on empirical and operational grounds. The arguments that there is no compelling *a priori* reason for accepting one or other definition of money and that the problem is to choose the most appropriate definition of money for the conduct of monetary policy are not convincing because the conduct of monetary policy very much depends on the theory of monetary policy and there is no universally validated and accepted theory of monetary policy. The kind of monetary policy to be conducted first requires the settlement, *inter alia*, of the role of money in economic activity.

Theoretical Approach Essential

In short, the issue of appropriate definition of money has to be resolved theoretically. The theoretical approach is not only analytically superior but also it is capable of incorporating the effects of dynamic changes in the economic system. If, over the period of time, some assets newly come to acquire basic properties of money, they can be included in the measure of money. Such a 'broadening' of the measure of money, however, is fundamentally different from the well known convenient 'broadening' contained in the 'empirical definition' of money. Under the former, the researchers would be quite ready to countenance the possibility, for example, that the demand for money may not be stable even for the new extended measure of money.

Though not many, there are a few economists who also have argued in favour of the theoretical approach and against the empirical approach to defining money. Apart from Modigliani and Papademos mentioned earlier, the other important names in this connection are Mason, [14] Berkman, [15] and Lombra. [16] Mason has very forcefully and candidly argued that the empirical definition of money is a conceptual confusion; that an empirical definition of money designed to validate a monetary hypothesis precludes empirical invalidation; that it is the anti-thesis of scientific procedure; that it confuses empirical verification with hypothesisation and precludes the progression from hypothesis to theory; that conceptualization and definition must precede hypothesisation, and conceptualization must precede definition in order to produce a testable hypothesis capable of empirical verification as a theory. [17]

III. Appropriate Definition and Measure of Money

In order to be able to define and measure money theoretically, we first discuss below the major special functional and institutional characteristics which determine the moneyness of assets. This discussion closely follows Douglas Fisher's very good survey of the views of many monetary theorists on the nature of money. [18]

Different economists have emphasized different attributes as being of crucial importance in defining money. Irving Fisher thought 'general acceptability in exchange' to be the most important attribute of money. It is very closely linked with money's function as a direct medium of exchange or a medium of transactions balances. Sometimes, a distinction has been made between the terms, 'medium of exchange' and 'ultimate means of payment' or 'ultimate means of settlement of transactions'. The latter two terms are wider than and inclusive of the former. Money must be the 'ultimate or perfect means of payment.' Since instruments such as trade credit, credit card, etc., are not generally acceptable and are only temporary means of procurement without being the means of final settlement of payment or completing the transactions, they cannot be regarded as money. [19] I Fisher and CAE Goodhart have maintained that even demand deposits are not generally acceptable ultimate means of payment on par with currency. It is the institutional buttressing of providing legal tender status or adequate transmission facilities at the fixed price ratio, and the institutional force of custom which render demand deposits more or less generally acceptable medium of exchange and ultimate means of payment. Therefore, according to these authors, strictly speaking, even demand deposits are not money, although ultimately they have granted to include these deposits in the measure of money. It is important to note this position because it shows that the Modern Quantity Theorists (Monetarists) have parted Fisher's company on so fundamental and vital an issue as the definition of money.

Keynes has discussed the differentia of money in the General Theory. It is interesting to note in passing that while referring to money, he has used qualifying phrases such as 'money as we know it' or ' money to which we are accustomed'. He has talked of zero or very small elasticity of production, zero or nearly equal to zero elasticity of substitution, and fixity of supply as special characteristics of money. He has emphasized the medium of exchange and liquidity as very important properties of money. According to Keynes, money's utility is solely derived from its exchange value so that the two rise and fall *pari passu*, and that money is, in the estimation of public, *par excellence* liquid and, therefore, it alone has the capacity to satisfy liquidity preference of the public. Money is *par excellence* liquid because its yield from liquidity does not fall in response to an increase in its quantity and it has a low or negligible carrying cost. [20] From his discussion, it becomes clear that Keynes has currency in mind when he refers to money.

It may be stated here by way of elaboration that the perfect means of payment, perfect liquidity, and perfect maturity are interdependent attributes of money. In a sense, it is meaningless to talk about liquidity and maturity of money itself; these terms acquire meaning only in respect of other assets and only because of the prior definition of money as a perfect means of payment. It is common to define the degree of liquidity of assets as the ease and costlessness with which they can be converted into cash – the essentiality of conversion into cash arises because cash alone can ultimately settle transactions or debt. The implication of this argument is that since money as means of payment is the standard of measurement of liquidity and maturity of other assets including time deposits, these other assets themselves cannot be called money; they cannot be aggregated with money in a common category. If this is done, the result would be a misaggregation.

Don Patinkin, W Newlyn, B Pesek, and T Saving have emphasized the medium of exchange, being net wealth of the public, and the absence of cash or any other explicit reward as the special characteristics of money. It has been argued that a thing to be called money should be a net-worth to be society, it should not be a debt to the public, it should not earn any rate of return of interest, and it should be capable of being employed in exchange for commodities or factors of production without affecting the market for loans. Again, it is only the currency which possesses these characteristics. Even demand deposits may not be regarded as the net wealth of the society and the absence of interest payment is not their universal and permanent property.

Case of Demand Deposits

Should then demand deposits be excluded from the measure of money? In order to be able to decide about demand deposits (and saving deposits too) it is necessary to discuss further the property of absence of explicit rate of return. Such a discussion would gain in clarity and strength if it refers to certain other closely related properties also which are often mentioned while defining money. The origin of the asset (i.e., does the asset originate as a result of the placement of cash with the financial system or does it originate as a result of the working of the process of multiple credit creation?), whether the asset is a part of transactions balances or whether it is a part of saving-investment portfolio, and whether the asset supports the process of multiple credit creation or not are the characteristics which we have in mind here. It has been argued that only those assets which originate from the support the process of multiple credit creation and which are a part of transactions balances are money.

It is necessary to exercise judgment in applying the characteristics just mentioned. It is reasonable to hold that the absence of payment of interest cannot be adjudged to be the basic property of money on par with those of perfect means of payment and perfect liquidity insofar as it is subject to temporal and spatial variations. Therefore, if the asset more or less possesses the latter attributes, it can be counted as money although it may be carrying a nominal interest payment. As far as the other three properties are concerned, the final determining test is the motivation, perception, intention of the public in holding a given asset and not merely the outward form in which it is held. There are some assets which appear to be a part of saving portfolio but which people explicitly hold with a purpose to use them as payments mechanism for current and capital transactions and to meet liquidity needs rather than to earn a return; if they happen to earn some return on these assets, it may be purely a matter of institutional arrangements; the public would continue to hold them even if institutions cease to offer any return on them. The demand deposits which arise from the placement cash (and all saving deposits) belong to such a 'transactions-savings' category and are, therefore, money. On the other hand, there are certain assets (viz., time deposits) which are not normally intended to be used for transactions proposes even though institutional facilities for their quick and low-cost transfer into cash may be readily available. These assets are very definitely intended to product an optimum rate of return for their holders. They represent genuine long-term savings and are to be clearly distinguished from money. While 'transactions-savings' serve as if they themselves are cash, long-term savings have to be converted into cash before they can be used as money.

This brings us to the store of value or store of wealth function of money. It is rather unfortunate that this universally recognised function of money has been used to bedevil discussions on definition of money. It has been erroneously used to make a case for the 'broad' definition of money. It has been argued, mostly by the monetarists, that since money can act as a store of value, it is a substitute for the whole array of financial and physical assets and therefore, some of the financial assets are money. In effect, it is argued that money is wealth, there are other forms of wealth and, therefore, some of the other forms of wealth are money. This argument undoubtedly involves a very curious or queer quirk of logic and the questionable on a number of grounds. Firstly, if the basic premise in the argument is valid, we cannot conveniently include only certain financial assets such as time deposits in the measure of money; every other asset then qualifies to be called money. If so, there is no place and need for a separate macro variable of money. This may be countered by pointing out that this problem can be resolved empirically by estimating the degrees of substitution between money and other assets and only those assets which have a high degree of substitution with traditional money can be regarded as money. This also is not acceptable because there does not exist a generally agreed standard of "how high is high", and basically this is not an empirical question at all. We cannot aggregate quantities of tea and coffee and call the aggregate tea because they are close substitutes. The estimate measure of substitution in no way enlightens us whether the asset in question is substitutable for money both as a store of value and medium of exchange. This has to be determined on *a priori* basis only. Secondly, therefore, when the substitution between traditional money and other assets is considered, it ought to be ascertained whether these other assets are substitutable for money not only as a store of value but also as means of payment. In other words, in order to be eligible to be called money, the candidate assets should satisfy all the primary characteristics of money. Many of the financial assets including time deposits do not do this and, therefore, cannot be called money. While money assets are both means of payment as well as net wealth, the other assets are neither *net* wealth nor means of payment. Thus, money is *sui generic*. Thirdly, although money can be a store of value, the extent to which it does act as a store of value actually in practice is very small. Between the functions of medium of exchange and store of value, it is the former which is more widely and generally performed by money and, therefore, is, in a sense, money's primary function. Money acts more as a medium of exchange than as a store of value except in rural areas at low level of financial development; it is first and foremost a means of payment.

IV. Towards an Appropriate Money Supply Measure for India

In general acceptability, perfect means of payment, perfect liquidity and maturity, net store of wealth or value, absence of rate of return, absence of being a part of intended long-term saving-investment portfolio are the major differentia of money. Which of the assets in India possess these characteristics and should, therefore, constitute the measure of money supply? Although an indication in this respect has been given above, it is now necessary to discuss the matter in greater details in its historical perspective. The possible list of assets from which the choice is to be made is as follows:

(1) Currency (C), (2) other deposits with RBI (ODR), (3) current deposits with banks (CDB), (4) saving deposits with banks (SDB), (5) saving deposits with post-office saving banks (SDPOSB), (6) fixed deposits with banks (FDB), (7) time deposits with post-offices (TDPO), (8) other deposits with post-offices (ODPO), (9) national saving certificates (NSCS), (10) other certificates with post-offices (OCPO), (11) treasury bills (TBS), (12) commercial bills (CBs), (13) government bonds (GBs), (14) industrial bonds (IBs), (15) fixed deposits with non-banking companies (FDCOs), (16) trade credit (TC), (17) unutilized credit limits (UCL), and (18) industrial shares (IS).

Now, there is a complete agreement among economists that the currency meets all the attributes of money perfectly well. Currency is, therefore, money *par excellence*. Current deposits generally and mostly possess properties of money: the relaxation in the rigour of application of these properties in their case is not of serious nature. There is a well-established consensus in favour of including CDB in the measure of money. There is also a good consensus that assets nine to eighteen can not be included as a part of money supply. It is the assets four to eight which belong to the area of doubt and about which the decision needs to be taken.

Treatment of SDB

Should all SDB be excluded from money supply or should all of them be included? Or, should only a part of them be included? If yes, what should be the basis of division? Normally, the total exclusion of SDB from money supply has not been suggested. The two working groups referred to earlier had recommended that the portion of SDB which is 'withdrawable without notice' should be treated as demand deposits and money. The RBI used to do this till August 16, 1978. When treated in this way, the demand deposit component of SDB used be, on the average, about 85 per cent. With effect from 1978, the RBI began to count 'the portion of SDB on which banks did not pay interest' as demand deposits. As a result, the demand deposit component of SDB declined, on the average, to about 60 per cent. The implicit view in this change of method is that in defining money, the absence of interest payment is a more important criterion than that of liquidity. In view of our earlier discussion, this position is highly questionable.

It has been suggested that while SDB in rural and semi-urban areas should be treated as time deposits because they represent savings, those in urban and metropolitan centres should be treated as demand deposits since they are likely to be used predominantly as transactions balances. [21] It is difficult to believe that all SDB in rural and semi-urban areas represent genuine long-term savings. If it was so, people would have held time deposits with banks and post-offices instead of saving deposits. The study of debits to deposit accounts with banks has not revealed that the deposit-turnover rate for saving deposits is lower in rural areas than in urban areas. [22]

In the light of our discussion of differentia of money, we think that instead of dividing SDB on the basis of any of the criteria just mentioned, all SDB should be treated as money. [23] The rules of operating saving deposits accounts are very liberal and there is a general belief among the public that these accounts, in practice, can be operated without any restrictive conditions. The public treats their saving deposits as transactions balances; it determines the level of these accounts in the light of current and anticipated short-term needs for cash.

Treatment of SDPOSB

The SDPOSB are at present excluded from the (narrow) measure of money. The FWG has recommended their exclusion "more or less for the same reasons for which time deposits are excluded. The postal saving deposits are more analogous to time deposits in as much as they originate from the placement of cash and do not act as a basis for credit creation." [24] This is questionable on grounds of inconsistency, etc. Firstly, there is no reason why the FWG should have compared SDPOSB with time deposits instead of saving deposits with banks. Secondly, the property of 'being primary deposits' is common to both SDB and SDPOSB and since the FWG included the (part of) former in money supply, it was inconsistent not to have included the latter. Thirdly, being the basis of credit creation is not a fundamental and necessary property of money. The cash in hand with the public also does not act as the basis for credit creation but we do not exclude it from money supply on that account. When a given asset does not act as the basis for credit creation, it does not contribute to 'further' or 'multiple' credit creation; this, however, does not preclude it from performing the function of money in the initial stage also.

The SWG also did not include SDPOSB in M_1; instead it created a new measure (M_2) to accommodate them. The understanding and perception of SWG about the properties of SDPOSB should have really led it to include them in M_1 but it curiously chose not to do this advancing operational difficulties as the reason. It is very obvious that operational problems, if they exist, would remain in the case of M_2 also. In reality, it appears that information problems with respect to post-office organization cannot be greater than those with respect to rural branches of banks. In any case, operational considerations cannot be the main determining factor in this context, and necessary steps can and ought to be taken to get over whatever operational difficulties may exist.

In our view, SDPOSB should form a part of money supply. They are very similar to SDB. They are withdrawable on demand by using either the withdrawal slips or cheques or both and the withdrawal rules have been liberalized over the period of time. As the SWG has state, "... conceptually from the point of view of 'liquidity' these deposits can be compared to demand liability portion of savings deposits with banks". [25] The withdrawal ratio (defined as withdrawals as percentage of receipts of deposits in a given year) in the case of SDPOSB was between 81 to 103 during 1970-71 to 1981-82, while it was between 3 to 59 and 0 to 26 for post-office time deposits and certificates, respectively. The very high withdrawal ratio of SDPOSB indicates that they are held primarily as transactions balances.

Treatment of FDB and TDPO

As stated earlier, by invoking the store of value function of money, time deposits are very often treated as money. We think that FDB and TDPO do not possess any of the special characteristics of money except the store of value and, therefore, they are best excluded from the volume of money supply. The FWG had excluded time deposits from money supply and had called them near-money assets. This was an analytically sound treatment of time deposits. The SWG however deviated from it insofar as it has given time deposits a status of money and created a new measure of money (M_3) to include them. Incidentally, in view of very similar nature of time deposits with banks and post-offices, SWG has unnecessarily excluded time deposits with post-offices from M_3 and created a separate money measure (M_4) to accommodate them.

Empirically, subject to our view that measures of substitution cannot by themselves prove that time deposits are money, the available evidence abroad and in India very clearly shows that time deposits are a very poor substitute for assets agreed to be money. Silber has found that the elasticity of substitution between demand deposits and time deposits was only about -0.115 for the American economy. Teign and Goldfeld have found that the cross-elasticity between demand deposits and time deposits was quite low. Similarly, Gramlich and Kalchbrenner have shown that cross elasticities for demand deposits with respect to the time deposit rate, and savings and loan rate were only -0.097 and -0.023, respectively. [26]

For India, Singh, Shetty and Venkatachalam, based on quarterly data for the period 1970-71 to 1981-82, have found that the elasticity of currency and demand deposits with respect to three-year time deposit rate was only -0.0041 to -0.25 and -0.33 respectively. [27]

For the purpose of this paper, we estimated cross-elasticity of currency (C), CDB, SDB, and SDPOSB with respect to 12-month fixed deposit rate (TDR) for the period 1956-57 to 1981-82, and with respect to average fixed-deposit rate (ATDR) for the period 1970-71 to 1981-82 by using linear and double log-linear functional forms. It was found that time deposit rate had a perverse (positive) sign in all functions without a single exception in both the time periods. Sensing that this could be due to the presence of the trend element, the double-log functions were recomputed by introducing the time variable (T) and by using the step-wise regression technique. The results of this exercise are reproduced in Table 1.

Table 1: Cross Elasticities of Certain Financial Assets

1) C = 7.555	–	0.322 TDR +	0.099 T;	$R2 = 0.989$;
		(0.118)	(0.005)	
		(2.73)	(21.09)	D W = 0.435
2) CDB = 6.546	–	0.695 TDR +	0.154 T;	$R2 = 0.967$;
		(0.312)	(0.012)	
		(2.228)	(12.435)	D W = 0.316
3) SDB = 5.371	-	0.329 TDR +	0.186 T;	$R2 = 0.994$;
		(0.172)	(0.997)	
		(1.913)	(26.57)	D W = 0.436
4) SDPOSB = 5.683	–	0.037 TDR +	0.083 T;	$R2 = 0.998$;
		(0.058)	(0.002)	
		(0.638)	(36.08)	D W = 1.669
5) C = 8.248	–	0.271 ATDR +	0.117 T;	$R2 = 0.990$;
		(0.118)	(0.005)	
		(2.053)	(23.4)	D W = 1.252
6) CDB = 7.531	–	0.171 ATDR +	0.185 T;	$R2 = 0.998$;
		(0.102)	(0.004)	
		(1.676)	(46.25)	D W = 2.593
7) SDB = 7.663	-	0.246 ATDR +	0.213 T;	$R2 = 0.998$;
		(0.112)	(0.004)	
		(2.196)	(53.25)	D W = 2.012
8) SDPOSB = 7.024	–	0.134 ATDR +	0.088 T;	$R2 = 0.988$;
		(0.114)	(0.005)	
		(1.175)	(19.04)	D W = 2.44

Equations 1 to 4 in Table 1 are for the period 1955-56 to 1981-82 and equations 5 to 8 are for the period 1970-71 to 1981-82. The figures in the first and second rows under each equation are standard errors and t-ratios, respectively. Although sometimes marred by the presence of serial correlation, these results clearly show that after the elimination of trend, the rate of interest has the correct sign in all equations. This reversal of the sign of rate of interest, the first choice of the time variable in all functions in step-wise estimation, very high level of r^2 due to time variable and very high significance level of coefficient of determination of time variable in all functions unmistakably confirm the presence of strong trend element in variables. Although the time deposit rate of interest has the correct sign after the elimination of trend, the size of its elasticity coefficient is very small in almost all equations and its significance level also is mostly low. Thus, there is strong empirical evidence against conferring the status of money on time deposits on the basis of cross-elasticity test.

Origins of Broad Money and Multiple Money Aggregates

Before we proceed to present the new framework, it would be instructive to understand how the notions of broad money and multiple measures of money might have become the part of literature on money.

With the passage of time, many innovations in respect of financial instruments, practices and institutions have occurred in various economies. The economists have studied the implications of these financial innovations for the role of money and monetary policy. The works of Gurley and Shaw and Radcliffe Committee, for example, are relevant in this connection. These works, in turn, spawned many empirical studies to search for appropriate definition and measure of money. The result has been the adoption of multiple measures of money. However, this result has been rather unfortunate and unintended. The early writers on financial innovations were not really making a case for redefining and remeasuring *money per se.* Their work was really meant to show that money proper or money alone has a limited role to play; that monetary policy should not focus attention only on commercial banks, and only on money as target/indicator of policy. It argued for recognizing the complex realities of the financial and monetary sectors and for devising appropriate indicators, instruments, and actions by monetary authorities. The famous Radcliffe Committee statement that what matters is overall liquidity in the economy and not money supply alone at once reflects two positions: that money alone does not matter, and that there is no need to broaden money. It suggests the appropriateness of the traditional definition of money and the need for incorporating diversifications and innovations in and complexities of the financial system through the nexus of liquidity and the structure of multiple yields and prices.

It is quite well known that the notion of broad money has been popularized mostly by the monetarists. There is direct and indirect evidence to show that in the beginning the monetarists believe in the 'narrow' definition of money but as the monetarist propositions came to be questioned seriously on both theoretical and empirical grounds, they improvised at a later stage the concepts of broad and empirical definitions of money to be able to hold on to their tenets. In "Studies in Quantity Theory of Money", money was defined as "... claims or commodity units that are generally acceptable in payments of debt at a fixed nominal value." [28] In the same book, Cagan has stated that because money serves as a ready purchasing power for contingencies, the nominal amount that individual wants to hold at any moment depends on the value of money, and he has used only quantity of hand-to-hand currency as the quantity of money for his empirical analysis. [29] Similarly, while examining the optimum quantity of money, Friedman has clearly stated, "the direct counterpart of the money in our analysis is 'high-powered' money - total currency. This total is non-interest bearing and, in effect, currently all fiat ... If the legal prohibition of interest payment on demand deposits were fully effective ... then demand deposits also would be non-interest bearing assets ... However, this is a big if ... As an arbitrary compromise, let us treat half of demand deposits ... (to be) equivalent to non-interest bearing money. This gives a maximum estimate of the quantity of 'money' of about ten weeks' personal disposable income." [30] The indirect evidence is in the form of internal inconsistencies which later starkly emerged in monetarist analysis as a result of the shift in their position on definition of money. The monetarist positions on exogeneity of money and money multiplier are inconsistent with their belief in broad money. The time deposits component of broad money is very obviously determined by the saving investment decisions of the spending units and it cannot be controlled by the Central Bank alone through the control of reserve money only.

Thus, the evolution of the concept of broad money has been motivated by the biased thinking. It is instructive to note that the opening passage of the book, Monetary Statistics of the United States has emphasized that the purpose of which its authors were developing the definition of money stock was to be able to predict changes in the prices and nominal income in the US. The process of reverse logic and biased analysis is too plain here to need further comment.

New Framework and Measure of Money for India

The major points which emerge from the entire foregoing analysis can now be stated as follows:

(a) We should cease to use terms such as narrow money and broad money in the interest of terminological accuracy and conceptual neatness, clarity, and distinctiveness. The notion of broad money is to be discarded because it is the result of biased thinking and it is based on the erroneous and unscientific empirical approach to defining money. Similarly, the practice of thinking and working with multiple money aggregates is erroneous, confusing and misleading. There cannot be multiple measures of *money*, there can be only a single analytically or conceptually sound measure of money. There are no compelling theoretical reasons to continue to operate with either the broad measure of money or multiple measures of money.

(b) The measure of money for India to be denoted by M should include currency, current deposits with banks, saving deposits with banks, saving deposits with post-office saving banks, and other deposits with the RBI.

(c) The role of financial assets other than those just mentioned also cannot be ignored; the analysis of economic activity would be incomplete unless the role of the whole complex of other financial assets is also taken into account. However, we must explicitly and clearly recognize these other assets to be different from *money* and, therefore, revive the old practice of designating them as near-money assets. These assets can be grouped in one or more aggregates to be called Near Money Aggregates (NMAs) on the basis of their liquidity, maturity, marketability, risk, etc. We tentatively suggest two such aggregates - NMA1 and NMA2 - for India. NMA1 would include fixed deposits with banks and time deposits with post-offices. NM2 would include NMA1 and other deposits with post-offices.

(d) It has been pointed out by some economists that there is a substantial loss of useful information about components and there is sometimes a danger of misaggregation of dissimilar assets when we work with higher order aggregates. We fully share this viewpoint. It is, therefore, suggested that in addition to data on M and NMAs, the monetary authorities should make full, detailed, regular, and timely statistics on their each individual component available to the public.

This new framework has neither 'serious definitional' problems nor would it result in an 'inadequate' and 'misleading' monetary analysis and policy. In fact, it is the use of 'broad' definition of *money* and multiple measures of *money* which results in misleading and inconsistent monetary analysis. For example, to regard time deposits as money is to wipe out the distinction between two major concepts in economics namely, long-term genuine saving and money. The widely used IS-LM model requires analytically separate concepts of saving, investment, and money. The 'broadening' of money definition tends to render such theoretical tools of economic analysis difficult to handle. Further, it causes confusion in economic analysis because while it blurs the distinction between Keynesian and Monetarist approaches, it enables the latter to claim a greater explanatory power. To elaborate, it is possible that the higher order aggregate such as M_3 may explain variations in economic activity better but this better explanation is not really due to money; it is due to money plus something else. If it is desired to know relative explanatory powers of various approaches to monetary analysis, it is better not to merge or mix-up the key concepts in those models at the empirical level. If the theory which claims the volume of money to be central pivot of the market economy is to be validated, it must be possible to achieve this in terms of theoretically correct definition of money. To resort to the notions of 'broad money', 'empirical definition of money', and 'multiple measures of money' for such a purpose may be construed as an indirect admission of the inadequacy of that theory.

The framework presented here is preferable to the one currently in vogue in India because the four existing measures of money are not internally consistent. The current (i) M_1 includes demand deposit component of SDB but excludes that of SDPOSB; M_2 includes all SDPOSB

Table 2: New Money and Near-Money Aggregates for India, 1950-51 to 1981-82

Year	M (Rs. Crore)	NMAI (Rs. Crore)
1950-51	2221	250
55-56	2523	366
56-57	2695	547
57-58	2829	748
58-59	3016	971
59-60	3229	958
60-61	3481	975
61-61	3676	1051
62-63	3996	1142
63-64	4479	1267
64-65	4831	1450
65-66	5494	1788
66-67	5941	1961
67-68	6413	2257
68-69	7148	2600
69-70	7981	3028
70-71	8495	3152
71-72	10154	4503
72-73	11577	6015
73-74	13479	7139
74-75	14633	8779
75-76	16614	11459
76-77	19491	14200
77-78	23321	17082
78-79	28178	20421
79-80	32835	24486
80-81	39337	28389
81-82	43920	32961

SOURCE:
RBI, "Statistical Tables Relating to Banks", "Report on Currency and Finance", and *Bulletin*, various issues of each.

but excludes time deposits component of SDB; (iii) M_3 includes time deposit component of SDB but excludes SDPOSB which were included in M_2; and (iv) M_4 includes time deposits with banks but not with post-offices. In the light of the views of SWG (a) that liquidity is the major attribute to be used for classifying assets, (b) that SDPOSB are as liquid as demand liability portion of SDB, and (c) that money stock measures M_1 to M_4 should comprise assets with the descending order of liquidity, the existing measures of 'money' can be said to be internally inconsistent.

Tables 2 and 3 present information on the new measure of money supply in India. It will be seen that the volume of M has increased from Rs.2,221 crore in 1950-51 to Rs.43,920 crore in 1981-82. The annual average rate of growth in M was 2.72 per cent during 1950-51 to 1955-56 and 7.81 per cent, 8.30 percent, 10.59 percent, 13.0 percent and 17.58 per cent, respectively in each successive quinquennium thereafter. The new M has been around 130 per cent and 70 per cent of the existing M_1 and M_3, respectively.

Table 3: Structural Composition of New Money Measure (Percentage)

Year	C	CDB	SDB	SDPOSB	M
	M	M	M	M	NMAI
1950-51	63.35	20.53	6.70	8.33	880.0
55-56	62.27	17.84	7.88	11.65	689.0
60-61	60.27	17.21	9.77	12.38	357.0
65-66	55.23	17.78	14.96	11.72	307.0
70-71	51.59	18.09	18.14	11.65	270.0
75-76	40.35	24.00	26.44	8.88	145.0
80-81	34.12	25.36	33.67	5.93	139.0
81-82	32.99	26.60	34.71	5.35	133.0

SOURCE: Same as for Table 2.

It should be observed that the structural composition of money supply in India has undergone certain major changes over the past 30 years. The share of currency in money supply has declined very substantially from 63 per cent in 1950-51 to 33 per cent in 1981-82; the major part of this decline has occurred since the beginning of 1970s. On the other hand, the share of SDB has increased substantially from 7 per cent to 35 per cent; the major part of this increase again has occurred after 1970-71. While the share of CDB has increased, that of SDPOSB has declined slightly. There has been a very fast growth of near-money assets vis-à-vis money assets. The latter as percentage of the former has declined from 880 per cent to 133 per cent over the period under discussion.

V. Determination and Control of Money Supply

After having examined comprehensively various issues involved in defining and measuring money supply, the present section briefly discusses whether variations in money supply are fully under the control of the Central Bank and whether the Central Bank can control them via any single variable such as the reserve money. Specifically, it finds out whether there is enough empirical evidence in favour of money multiplier theory (MMT) to make it a major tool of money supply analysis and control in the Indian milieu.

Money supply changes in India have been discussed mostly within the framework developed by the RBI. The bank conducts money supply analysis in terms of what can be called 'component factors' wherein the relative contribution of banking, government, commercial, and foreign sectors and their constituents to changes in currency, bank money, bank credit, foreign exchange, etc., is analysed. The RBI framework is neutral or eclectic in respect of various existing monetary models. It came under severe criticism in the middle of 1970s when the MMT came to be advanced as a superior theory of money supply analysis. In the course of controversy which then arose, while the RBI approach was labeled, 'merely accounting or ex-post', 'empirically meaningless', 'without substantive content', 'without explanatory or predictive power', 'tautological, empty, faulty', etc., the MMT was called, 'mechanistic', 'simplistic', 'theoretically unsatisfactory', 'useless in practice', 'a partial explanation', etc. [31] Recently, attempts have been made again by the CRWMS and others [32] to project MMT as the dependable policy tool.

In this debate the case both against the RBI analysis and in favour of the MMT has been overstated. There is nothing in the RBI analysis which is antithetical to the MMT. It presents very much necessary and useful information for the structural and behavioural analysis of the money supply determination and control, and for the money multiplier analysis too. It enables us to understand the origins, composition and relative importance of all changes in money supply. It is because of its basic usefulness that its total abandonment or drastic modification has never been suggested by anybody; only some minor changes such as the alteration in the nomenclature, elaboration and bifurcation of certain items, etc., in it have been suggested even by the advocates of MMT.

The MMT can be said to have two versions: the simple or narrow or parsimonious, and the full or complex one. The usefulness and dependability of the MMT is determined by which of these versions is employed. In its second version, the theory is very elaborate and takes into account all the major behavioural and institutional complexities of the relevant variables in the monetary system and, therefore, has a good explanatory power and policy usefulness. But unfortunately, this version is not much in vogue. It is the first version which is popular and which is mostly referred to in the literature and while making policy recommendations. In this version, either immediately after or in the very midst of the process of mentioning complex relationships, certain convenient and unrealistic assumptions are introduced which wish away those complexities. As a result, the theory is deliberately reduced to an extremely parsimonious arithmetic formula containing barely minimum relationships.

The main elements of the MMT in its narrow version are the following: The determinants of money supply are the high-powered money (H) and money multiplier (m). The m is endogenously determined by the decisions of the 'public' and banks which are reflected in variations of currency, reserve, time deposits, etc, ratios. However, the behaviour of these ratios and, therefore, the behaviour of m can be assumed to be stable and predictable. Consequently, H is left out to be the only key determinant of variations in money supply and it is necessary and sufficient to control H in order to control money supply. It is further assumed that the economic and institutional factors which may affect H are unimportant and H is fully under the control of the Central Bank, i.e., it is assumed that H is exogenously determined. It then follows that money supply is exogenously determined. Thus, "The key to the controlled variations of money supply is the control of high powered money (H). This is based on the first approximation assumption that either m remains constant or it varies in a highly predictable manner ... the most predictable course for monetary control left with the authorities is the control of H* ... The strategy, very simply stated is control H to control M ... variations in M are largely a function of the variations in H." [33]

The MMT in this form is not at all dependable and useful; it is in no way superior to the RBI framework; and it is not at all necessary also to simplify the task of controlling money supply in this manner.

There is no strong, certain, consistent and unquestionable evidence in favour of narrow money multiplier theory to make it a major tool of money supply analysis and control in India. The double-log money supply function estimated by using quarterly data for the period 1970-71 to 1980-81 has shown that the elasticity of money supply with respect to H and currency ratio (representing m) was 0.776 and -0.454, respectively, [34] suggesting clearly that H is not the only determinant of M and that the effect of variations in m is not all that insignificant. In our earlier study of the factors of money supply determination, we have shown that it is unlikely that money supply in India can continuously be controlled in a predictable and precise manner through the inverted pyramid of credit. We have found that the coefficients of determination between the growth rates of M_1 and M_2 on the one hand and that of the reserve money on the other were 0.615 and 0.581, respectively during 1960-1980. [35]

Table 4 contains useful information on annual rates of change in new M, H, m, the ratio between rates of change in M and H, and the values of the marginal money multiplier for the period 1956-57 to 1981-82.

It plain from Table 4 that except in certain years, there has not been a close correspondence between the variations of M and H. The column four clearly brings out that the ratio between the rates of changes of M and H has been seldom close to one; it has fluctuated in a very wide range of 70 to 338 per cent. The correspondence between M and H has very significantly declined since the beginning of 1970s. Thus, as the currency component of money supply has declined, the relationship between the M and H has become all the more unstable. The wide fluctuations in H also indicates the lack of perfect control of authorities of H.

Table 4: Rates of Change in New M, H, m; and Marginal Money Multiplier in India, 1956-57 to 1981-82

	M Per Cent	H Per Cent	M Per Cent	1 ÷ 2 Per Cent	Δ M/Δ M
Year	(1)	(2)	(3)	(4)	(5)
1956-57	6.82	3.48	3.22	195.69	2.965
57-58	4.97	4.35	0.59	114.09	1.786
58-59	6.61	6.67	-0.06	99.14	1.558
59-60	7.06	9.80	-0.02	72.06	1.132
60-61	7.80	5.79	1.90	134.71	2.066
61-61	5.60	5.12	0.46	109.45	1.711
62-63	8.71	7.94	0.71	109.61	1.720
63-64	12.09	10.16	1.75	118.90	1.879
64-65	7.29	6.06	1.69	120.23	2.083
65-66	13.72	9.07	4.26	151.27	2.474
66-67	8.14	7.36	0.73	110.61	1.886
67-68	7.94	5.78	2.04	137.38	2.360
68-69	11.46	10.55	0.83	108.64	1.904
69-70	11.65	8.73	2.69	133.53	2.359
70-71	6.44	9.14	-2.47	70.45	1.278
71-72	19.53	11.79	6.92	165.62	2.931
72-73	14.01	12.09	1.71	115.86	2.193
73-74	16.49	20.70	-3.54	79.68	1.527
74-75	8.56	1.76	6.68	485.62	9.015
75-76	13.54	4.00	8.49	338.45	5.758
76-77	17.35	23.44	-4.96	74.04	1.588
77-78	19.65	14.64	4.37	134.24	2.741
78-79	20.83	25.34	-3.61	82.14	1.751
79-80	16.53	20.05	-2.93	82.42	1.693
80-81	19.80	14.11	4.97	140.35	2.799
81-82	11.65	8.92	2.53	130.68	2.736

SOURCE: Same as for Table 2.

The average money multiplier has increased from 1.4573 to 2.1463 during 1957-1982. The column three shows that it has fluctuated considerably, particularly since 1965-66. The level of marginal money multiplier also has varied considerably; the range of its variations was 1.132 to 9.015.

If H is the single most important determinant of money supply and if m is almost constant, the coefficient of H in money multiplier function should be very close to one. In order to see whether it is so for India, we have estimated double-log average and marginal money multiplier fluctuations by using the new measure of money supply.

Table 5

1) $C = 0.763$ +	$0.947\ H + 0.019\ T$;	R2 = 0.998;
	(0.073) (0.007)	
	(12.97) (2.6)	D W = 1.45
2) $\Delta M = 3.42$ +	$0.302\ \Delta M + 0.111\ T$;	R2 = 0.967;
	(0.083) (0.013)	
	(3.638) (8.672)	D W = 2.503
3) $M = 5.946$ +	$0.353\ H + 0.103\ T$;	R2 = 0.998;
	(0.078) (0.011)	
	(4.526) (9.809)	D W = 2.724
4) $\Delta M = 5.065$ +	$0.258\ \Delta H + 0.144\ T$;	R2 = 0.897;
	(0.105) (0.028)	
	(2.464) (5.143)	D W = 2.454

Equations 1 and 2 in Table 5 relate to the period 1956-57 to 1981-82 while equations 3 and 4 are for the period 1970-71 to 1981-82. [36] In all equations, as expected, H has the right sign and its coefficient is statistically quite significant. It is, however, important to note that the size of elasticity coefficient of H is not as high as implied in the MMT except in equation one. The results for the second period very clearly highlight that as the currency component in money supply has declined, the size and significance of coefficient of H has declined. Looked at differently, this means to talk of H as a determinant of M is not really meaningful; H being a part of M, the explanatory power of MMT would vary along with changes in the structural composition of M. These results show that MMT is merely an identity; it is not a behavioural function

To conclude, the earlier and new evidence in this paper clearly show that it would not be in the interests of the effectiveness of monetary policy to depend on the narrow money multiplier framework for controlling money supply variations in India. As we have shown earlier, the regulation of government market borrowings, deficit financing, foreign exchange assets, and availability of bank credit by fiscal and monetary authorities would have a high degree of success in controlling money supply. [37]

Notes and References

1. One may obtain an idea about the measures in vogue in different countries from BRYANT, R. C., "Money and Monetary Policy in Interdependent Nations", The Brookings Institution, Washington, DC, 1980, pp. 23-38; BERGSTRAND, J. H., 'Money, Interest Rates, and Foreign Exchange Rates as Indicators of Monetary Policy', *New England Economic Review*, Federal Reserve Bank of Boston, November-December 1985.
2. See RESERVE BANK OF INDIA, (First) Working Group, "Analysis of Money Supply in India – I and II" in RBI Report of the Second Working Group on Money Supply in India: Concepts, Compilation and Analysis, Bombay, 1977; and RBI Report of the Second Working Group on Money Supply in India, op. cit.
3. RESERVE BANK OF INDIA, Report of the Second Working Group on Money Supply, op.cit, p.7. The ambivalent position of the SWG is reflected also in the fact that it has presented the analysis of sources of change in money supply in respect of what it has called M_1 only; no analysis has been presented by it in respect of, say, M_3.
4. RESERVE BANK OF INDIA, Report of the Committee to Review the Working of the Monetary System, Bombay, 1985.
5. Report of the Committee to Review the Working of the Monetary System, op.cit., p. 302.
6. Report of the Committee to Review the Working of the Monetary System, op.cit., pp. 103-104.
7. RANGARAJAN, C., 'Money, Output, and Prices', S.K. Muranjan Memorial Lecture, 1985-86, December 6, 1985, p. 13.
8. One can look at the problem of measuring money from the side of either the assets or liabilities.
9. Report of the Committee to Review the Working of the Monetary System, op.cit., p. 96.
10. LOMBRA, R. E., 'Monetary Control: Consensus or Confusion', in Federal Reserve Bank of Boston, "Controlling Monetary Aggregates", Ill., Boston, 1980, pp. 273 and 277.
11. See COATS, Jr. W. L., and KHATKHATE, D. R. (eds.), "Money and Monetary Policy in Less Developed Countries", Pergamon, New York, 1980, p. 12.
12. See FRIEDMAN, M., and MEISELMAN, D., "The Relative Stability of Monetary Velocity and the Investment Multiplier in the US, 1897-1958", in Commission on Money and Credit, Englewood Cliffs, 1963; FRIEDMAN, M., and SCHWARTZ, A. J., "Monetary Statistics of the United States: Estimates, Sources, Methods", National Bureau of Economic Research, New York,

1970; Laidler, D.W., 'The Definition of Money: Theoretical and Empirical Problems', *Journal of Money, Credit and Banking*, August 1969.

13. Modigliani, F. and Papademos, L., 'The Structure of Financial Markets and the Monetary Mechanism', in Federal Reserve Bank of Boston, op.cit., pp. 113-114.
14. Mason, W. E., 'The Empirical Definition of Money: A Critique', *Economic Inquiry*, December 1976.
15. Berkman, N. G. 'Abandoning Monetary Aggregates', in Federal Reserve Bank of Boston, op.cit.
16. Lombra, R. E., op.cit.
17. Mason, W. E., op.cit., pp. 532-533.
18. Fisher, D., "Monetary Theory and the Demand for Money", Martin Robertson, London, 1978, chapter 2 (pp. 8-40).
19. See Bhole, L. M., "Impact of Monetary Policy", Himalaya Publishing House, Bombay, 1985, pp. 203-204.
20. See Keynes, J. M., "The General Theory of Employment Interest and Money" Macmillan, London, 1961, pp. 229-234.
21. Rao, J. C., 'Money and Prices: An Empirical Study of the Indian Experience, 1970-1982', Reserve Bank of India, *Occasional Papers*, June 1983, p. 3.
22. Reserve Bank of India, 'Debits to Deposit Accounts with Banks', *Bulletin*, January 1978.
23. Gupta also has argued that it is best to treat all savings deposits of banks as demand deposits for purposes of measuring money. See Gupta, S.B., "Monetary Planning for India", Oxford University Press, Bombay, 1979, p. 177.
24. Reserve Bank of India, Working Group, op.cit., p. 68.
25. Reserve Bank of India, Report of the Second Working Group, op.cit., p. 12.
26. Quoted in Feige, E. L., and Pearce, D. K., 'The Substitutability of Money and Near-Monies: A Survey of the Time Series Evidence', *Journal of Economic Literature*, June, 1977, p. 463.
27. Singh, A., Shetty, S. L., and Venkatachalam, T. R., 'Monetary Policy in India: Issues and Evidence', Supplement to the Reserve Bank of India, *Occasional Papers*, June 1982, pp. 87 and 102.
28. Friedman, M. (ed), "Studies in the Quantity Theory of Money", University of Chicago Press, Chicago, 1956, p. 5.
29. Cagan, P., 'The Monetary Dynamics of Hyper Inflation', in Friedman, M. (ed.), op.cit., pp. 26-27.
30. Friedman, M., "The Optimum Quantity of Money and Other Essays", Macmillan, London, 1959, pp. 41-42.
31. Gupta, S. B., 'Factors Affecting Money Supply – Critical Evaluation of Reserve Bank's Analysis', *Economic and Political Weekly*, January 24, 1976, and "Monetary Planning for India", op.cit.; Mujumdar, N. A., 'Money Supply Analysis – Mechanistic and Economic Explana-

tions', *Economic and Political Weekly,* February 28, 1976; SHETTY, S. L., and others, 'Money Supply Analysis – Further Comments', *Economic and Political Weekly,* April 10, 1976.

32. RANGARAJAN, C., and SINGH, A., 'Reserve Money: Concepts and Policy Implications for India', Reserve Bank of India, *Occasional Papers,* June 1984.

33. GUPTA, S. B., "Monetary Planning for India", op.cit., pp. 65 and 95-96.

34. SINGH, A., SHETTY, S. L., and VENKATACHALAM, T. R., op.cit., p. 83.

35. BHOLE, L. M., "Impact of Monetary Policy", op.cit., pp. 199-200.

36. The variable T representing the trend element was introduced on the basis of earlier experience. The step-wise estimation procedure and the significance level of the coefficient of T have confirmed the presence of trend element in this case aso.

37. BHOLE, L. M., op.cit., pp. 189-200.

[2]

An Empirical Definition of Money: Some Factor Analytic Evidence for India[*]

Introduction

Most of the studies on the demand for money in India have not paid due attention to the definition of monetary aggregates to be used therein. It has been the practice in the literature to define money *a priori* as an aggregate of a set of liquid assets. In their anxiety to arrive at stable functions, researchers have concentrated mainly on the choice of appropriate scale and opportunity cost variables, the functional form etc., and neglected the empirical problems associated with the choice and combination of liquid assets to represent money stock. This paper, therefore, aims at filling this gap by examining the appropriate money stock to be used as a dependent variable in the context of money demand function in India.

The notion of an empirical definition of money, according to Mason (1976), represents a conceptual confusion. That is, it confuses the *concept* and the *quantity* of money. It may be noted that the empirical method determines not the concept of money but the money stock. There has been a debate among economists about the way money stock is to be defined – as to what liquid financial assets and in what combination should constitute money stock. The difference of opinion is basically either due to the difference in their theoretical conception of money or due to disagreement in identifying the observable counterparts for money, or both. Quantity theorists define money in the "narrow" sense as the sum of currency with the public and the demand deposits of the banking sector. Under this conception, money is viewed as a medium of exchange. Pesek and Saving (1967) also argue that the proper definition of money should be the money defined in the "narrow" sense, though the line of argument is different.

[*] Paper published jointly with B. Kamaiah in Malayan Economic Review, April 1982.

Modern Quantity Theorists (see FRIEDMAN (1963, p. 650)) take a broader view of money by including time deposits also into the fold, emphasizing that money is a 'temporary abode of purchasing power'. Gurley and Shaw (1956) argue in favour of the inclusion of the liabilities of the non-bank financial intermediaries into the definition of money supply.

If the definition of money is confined to "narrow" money, then the theory of the demand for money is reduced to the theory of the demand for an asset that is a generally acceptable medium of exchange. Laidler (1969) argues "the theory of the demand for money is not simply a theory of means of exchange. The transactions demand for money fits this description well enough, but the theory of the speculative demand for money does not. The latter ... is a theory of the demand for an asset whose capital value does not fluctuate with the rate of interest. Time deposits are just as good as demand deposits from this point of view as indeed are deposits of mutual savings banks etc. The question as to how to define money overlaps heavily with another important issue – whether transactions motives alone are sufficient to enable one to produce an adequate theory of the demand for money". The foregoing discussion reveals that the definition of money is not independent of the theory of the demand for money. Hence, money should be defined according to the purpose to which it is put.

The inclusion of time deposits or savings deposits into the fold of money cannot be done automatically unless these deposits are very close substitutes for money. Automatic inclusion may give rise to problems of mal-aggregation. In most of the cases, it may not be possible to theorize *a priori* about the motives for holding money balances – transactions or speculative – and the definition of money on *a priori* grounds, therefore, becomes difficult. An alternative way is to define money as the collection of liquid assets with the most stable demand function, the available evidence shows that most often, more than one definition of money gives rise to a stable function. Under these circumstances it may be difficult to theorize about the motives for the holding of money and to define it at the empirical level.

Various approaches have been employed in the literature to arrive at an empirical money stock. These include (a) Friedman-Meiselman dual criteria (b) The technique based on measuring the nearness of near monies (c) discriminant analysis of time-series characteristics and (d) factor analytic technique. [1]

Friedman-Meiselman (1963) define money as a sum of liquid financial assets which explain nominal income best. Their criteria (hereafter abbreviated as F-M criteria) are (1) that the sum of assets should have the highest correlation with national income and (2) that the correlation with income of the sum of assets should be higher than that of any of its individual components. Chetty (1969) has pointed out that F-M criteria regard the various liquid assets either as perfect substitutes or as completely unrelated to money. Therefore the all-or-nothing approach in defining money on F-M lines may not be very useful. Using the substitutability of money and near money assets, Chetty has derived an adjusted money stock series. McKim (1962) has applied discriminant analysis and worked out an empirical money definition for the US economy. Factor analytic technique is suggested and applied by Koot (1975). The technique involves a two-stage procedure. In the first stage, a set of liquid assets is considered simultaneously to determine relationships among the assets, and factors are extracted based on the inter-correlations among the assets. In the second stage, F-M criteria are applied to the factor results. In this paper, this methodology is used to find out an empirical money definition for India.

Empirical Money Definition in India

The Reserve Bank of India (RBI) formed a working group (Analysis of Money Supply in India) in 1961 to study the problems of the definition of money supply. The group felt that money supply cannot be defined on purely *a priori* or theoretical grounds. The definition had to be operational and should correspond to the use to which the concept was to be put. At the theoretical level, the group favoured the role of money both as a liquid asset and as a medium of exchange. Accordingly, money supply was defined as a composite of currency with the public and demand deposits with the banking sector plus "other deposits" held with the RBI. The group did not favour the inclusion of time deposits and savings deposits with the post offices. The reasons given were that these deposits were essentially an instrument of saving rather than a medium of exchange, and originated from cash deposits at the bank or cheques drawn on demand deposits.

The second working group (1977) has opined that "the use of a single measure of money stock (as suggested by the first working group) for monetary analysis and policy could be inadequate and at times misleading", and therefore, highlighted the need to take a disaggregated view by favouring a variety of aggregates. Subsequently the group has recommended four monetary aggregates – M_1, M_2, M_3 and M_4 which are defined as follows:

$$M_1 = CU + OD$$
$$M_2 = M_1 + SD$$
$$M_3 = M_1 + TD$$
$$M_4 = M_3 + SD$$

Where,

CU : Currency with the public
DD : Demand Deposits with the banking sector
TD : Time Deposits with the banking sector
SD : Savings Deposits with the post offices
OD : Other Deposits with the RBI

These aggregates (M_1 to M_4) provide a broad spectrum of money definitions on the basis of the varying degrees of liquidity. The working group has considered the near-money assets such as deposits with nonbank companies, unutilized credit limits, trade credit etc., as potential candidates for being included in money supply. But the group found these assets "eventually unacceptable either because of basic conceptual ineligibility or operational difficulties" (1979, p. 19). The purpose of providing the variety of aggregates is to facilitate further monetary analysis. However, the group has not gone further in establishing the relative merits of one aggregate over the others using appropriate methodologies.

In the literature concerning India not many empirical studies in this direction are available. Recently Shergill (1980) has employed F-M criteria on annual observations for the period 1950-51 to 1972-73 for defining money supply. Though this study, to some extent, could solve the problem of appropriate scale variable (by using three different proxies for the income variable) based on the institutional realities, it still has the limitation of ignoring the lead-lag relationship of money with income [2] on the lines of Kaufman (1969). However, Shergill's study could not arrive at any conclusion. Owing to the inherent limitations, [3] it is felt that F-M criteria alone may not be sufficient. Any statistical procedure which takes care of the inter-correlations among the assets, instead of treating them as either perfect substitutes or no substitutes, is believed to provide a better methodology. Hence the factor analysis technique is chosen here.

Factor Analytic Technique

Factor analysis is a multivariate statistical technique which attempts to account for the correlation pattern among a set of observable variables in terms of a minimal number of unobservable variables called factors. A factor model may be given by

$$Z_j = \sum_{i=1}^{m} a_j F_i + \varepsilon_j \qquad i = 1, 2, \ldots n \qquad (1)$$

$$m \leq n$$

where Z_j is the jth observed variable in standard form, F_i is the ith hypothetical factor, a_{ji} are the factor loadings i.e., loading of the jth response of the ith factor, ε_j is the error term. The factors F_i would explain the greater part of the variance in all the observed variables Z_j.
The total variance of a variable accounted for by the combination of all common factors is usually referred to as communality (h_j^2) of a variable. In symbols,

$$h_j^2 = \sum_{i=1}^{m} a_j^{\ 2}$$

The variance accounted for by a factor i, (V_i^2) is the sum of the squares of the loadings of that factor. In symbols,

$$V_i^2 = \sum_{i=1}^{n} a_j^{\ 2}$$

This is equal to the respective eigen-value.
This determination of communalities is one of the most difficult and ambiguous tasks in factor analysis. One of the main characteristics that differentiate one factoring method from the other is the procedure used for estimating communalities.

Factor analysis may be carried out with the help of a three-step procedure.

Step 1: The preparation of the correlation matrix of the given set of varieties.
Step 2: Extraction of the initial factors – the exploration of possible data reduction.
Step 3: Rotation to a terminal solution – the search for simple and interpretable results.

The final step needs some explanation. The factors extracted initially may not be unique, i.e., one factor solution can be transformed into another without violating the basic assumptions or the mathematical properties of a given solution. In other words, there are many statistically equivalent ways to define the underlying dimensions of the same set of data. In such cases the researcher shall be in a dilemma about the choice of the factor solution from among a set of solutions, each telling something different from the others about the structure of the same data. Therefore, to arrive at a terminal solution – a solution satisfying the theoretical and practical needs of the researcher – factor rotation is resorted to.

Factor rotation can be done in two ways - (1) orthagonal rotation and (2) oblique rotation. In the former, factors are uncorrelated while in the latter correlated. There is no reason to favour one method over the other. The choice should be made depending on the situation. Orthogonal factors are mathematically simpler while oblique factors are empirically more realistic. But in dealing with socio-economic phenomenon, the choice of oblique rotation seems to be more appropriate.

Many factoring methods are available in the literature. These include (1) principal factoring without iteration, (2) principal factoring with iteration, (3) Rao's canonical factoring, (4) alpha factoring, (5) image factoring etc. For a detailed discussion, see Harman (1960) and Morrison (1967). In this study, two factoring methods are used. They are (a) principal factoring with iteration and (b) Rao's canonical factoring. For a brief description of the two methods, see Kim (1975).

Empirical Results

In this study annual observations from 1956-57 to 1976-77 are used owing to the unavailability of quarterly data on Gross National Product (GNP). Four liquid assets are chosen. These are (1) currency with the public (Cu), (2) demand deposits with the banking sector (DD), (3) time deposits with the banking sector (TD), and (4) savings deposits with the post offices (SD). This study has not covered near-money assets. The analysis was carried out on the first differences of the variables with a view to reducing the problem of auto-correlation, if any, in the error term of the model given in equation (1).

Factors are extracted using two methods, viz. (1) principal factoring with iteration, and (2) Rao's canonical factoring. Also, oblique rotation is employed to obtain final factor solutions.

Since there are only four variables, which are very much intercorrelated (see Table 1), it was possible to extract only one significant factor. Factor loadings were used to assess the contribution of individual assets in an empirical definition of money. Then F-M criteria were used on factor scores as well as on six alternative money definitions to examine whether factor results provide a stable money definition. The six monetary aggregates (in first differences) on which F-M criteria were used are defined as follows:

$\Delta M_1 = \Delta Cu + \Delta DD$ $\Delta M_3 = \Delta M_1 + \Delta TD$ $\Delta M_5 = \Delta Cu + \Delta TD$

$\Delta M_2 = \Delta M_1 + \Delta SD$ $\Delta M_4 = \Delta M_3 + \Delta SD$ $\Delta M_6 = \Delta Cu + \Delta SD$

Why Factor Analytic Technique?

The reasons are as follows: (1) The technique has the advantage of taking into account the inter-correlation pattern of the given liquid assets. The results of final factor solution yields factor loadings and factor scores which are directly interpretable. Scores on significant factors represent observations on money stock and the weights which go into the generation of factor scores are considered to reflect the importance of the assets in the monetary aggregate. (2) This technique overcomes the problem of the choice of the scale variable. (3) Unlike other techniques, (4) there are no data limitations.

Interpretation of Results

The results appear in six tables. In Table 1, the correlation matrix concerning Cu, DD, TD and SD is given. The magnitudes of the off-diagonal elements of the matrix reflect the statistical closeness of the assets considered. Table 2 gives the factor loading matrix using principal factoring with iteration and oblique rotation, since there are only four variables, it was possible to extract only one significant factor. The factor loadings are the standardized multiple regression coefficients of the liquid assets on the generated factor. From the factor loadings it is evident that all the financial assets – Cu, DD, TD and SD – have one common source of variation. It is also evident from the table that Cu and DD have factor loadings higher than those of TD and SD. The eigen-value (3.8524) signifies the amount of variance accounted for by the factor F_1. This factor explains the variations in four assets at a fairly high level.

Table 1: Assets Correlation Matrix

	Cu	DD	TD	SD
Cu	1.0000	0.9773	0.9636	0.9804
DD		1.0000	0.9960	0.9384
TD			1.0000	0.9198
SD				1.0000

(Cu: Currency with the public, DD: demand deposits, TD: Time Deposits, SD: savings deposits with the post offices. Data refer to 1956-57 to 1976-77, and are annual observations).

Table 2: Factor Loadings Obtained Using Principal Factoring with Iteration

Rotation: Oblique

Assets	Factor loadings (a_{jr}) F_1	Communalities h_j^2
Cu	0.9972	0.9945
DD	0.9934	0.9869
TD	0.9771	0.9548
SD	0.9572	0.9163
Eigen value	3.8524	
PCT of variance	100.00	
Cumulative PCT	100.00	

(Convergence required five iterations, eigen-value indicates the variance accounted for by the factor (F_1); PCT of variance is the proportion of common variance accounted for by the factor (F_1); the total variance of a variable accounted for by the combination of all factors (here, only one) is called the communality of the assets).

Table 3: Factor Loadings Using Rao's Canonical Factoring

Rotation: Oblique

Assets	Factor loadings (a_{jr}) F_2	Communalities h_j^2
Cu	0.9872	0.9745
DD	0.9884	0.9768
TD	0.9808	0.9620
SD	0.9624	0.9263
Eigen value	82.3865	
PCT of variance	100.00	
Cumulative PCT	100.00	
X^2 (Chi-square)	57.65	
Dof (degree of freedom)	2	

(Convergence required more than twenty five iterations).

Table 3 gives the factor loadings and communalities obtained by using Rao's canonical factoring and oblique rotation. Results of this method more or less exhibit the same pattern as in Table 1, except for a higher eigen-value. All the variables load heavily on a single factor (F_2). Table 4 presents the weights for Cu, DD, TD and SD. These weights are used for generating factor scores for the factors F_1 and F_2. The factor scores concerning F_1 indicate the Cu and DD have positive and higher weights than those of TD and SD. Similarly in the case of factor scores concerning F_2 factor, Cu and DD have weights higher than the weights for TD and SD. But the latter carry a negative sign. It may not be possible to draw a conclusion based on weights for both the factors put together. A separate analysis makes it clear that Cu and DD weigh relatively high in the factor scores of the factors F_1 and F_2, which, in turn, represent a monetary aggregate.

Table 4: Matrix Giving Weights for the Assets for the Generation of Factor Scores for Factors F_1 and F_2

Asset	F_2	F_2
Cu	0.9952	0.3017
DD	1.7831	0.3016
TD	-1.2997	0.2409
SD	-0.4982	0.1616

Table 5: Correlation Coefficients of Assets and the Six Money Definitions

with GNP Assets/Aggregates	Lead/Lag			
	0	-1	-2	+1
ΔCu	0.7013	0.4371	0.3780	0.5318
ΔDD	0.6606	0.6909	0.6800	0.5508
ΔTD	0.2853	0.1843	0.1796	0.1129
ΔSD	0.6230	0.6415	0.3913	0.5510
$\Delta M_1 = \Delta Cu + \Delta DD$	0.7741	0.6928	0.5911	0.5881
$\Delta M_2 = \Delta M_1 + \Delta SD$	0.7695	0.6589	0.5828	0.5744
$\Delta M_3 = \Delta M_1 + \Delta TD$	0.7059	0.6860	0.6128	0.5743
$\Delta M_4 = \Delta M_3 + \Delta SD$	0.7073	0.6721	0.6155	0.5690
$\Delta M_5 = \Delta Cu + \Delta TD$	0.7124	0.6568	0.5640	0.5758
$\Delta M_6 = \Delta Cu + \Delta SD$	0.7711	0.4167	0.3646	0.5047

(First differences of the variables were used to obtain above results).

Table 5 gives the results for F-M criteria. Six alternative definitions of money are considered. Since this is an annual study only a lag of two periods and a lead of one period are considered in order to study the stability of the results. [5] In this table, the correlations of various financial assets and monetary aggregates (M_1 to M_6) with Gross National Product are given. Results show that the monetary aggregate bearing the highest correlation with GNP varies with the leads and lags of the components of the aggregates. The M_1 aggregate with no lag and with no lead has the highest correlation coefficient with GNP. The M_6 aggregate with a two period lag has the lowest correlation coefficient with GNP. And with one period lead, the M_1 aggregate has the highest coefficient. From these results, the M_1 aggregate appears to be a better aggregate by F-M criteria.

Table 6: Correlation Coefficients between GNP and the Factor Scores on F_1 and F_2

Factor	Lead/Lag			
	0	-1	-2	+1
F_1	.7231	.7294	.7043	.7123
F_2	.7429	.7581	.7435	.7146

Table 6 shows the correlations between GNP and the factor scores for various leads and lags. The idea behind applying F-M criteria to factor scores subject to leads and lags is to see whether factor scores provide a stable monetary aggregate. The results of this table show that the correlation coefficients do not vary widely. The weights which have generated these stable scores reveal the importance of various liquid assets. Since Cu and DO have higher weights, an aggregate consisting of these would turn out to be a better empirical money definition. This result agrees with the result obtained by the author using the canonical-correlation approach in the sample period 1950-51 to 1975-76 (see KAMAIAH et al (1980)).

Concluding Remarks

The results of this study favour a money definition which mainly consists of currency with the public and the demand liabilities of the banking sector. This "narrow" money definition supports the observations of the first working group on money supply in India, constituted by RBI in 1961. However, this result does not agree with the definition of Friedman and Meiselman, who favour the inclusion of time liabilities also. The reasons could be the divergent behaviour in the transactions of the household and business sectors in India, underdeveloped cheque-drawing habit, and other institutional differences. The general conclusion of this study is that "narrow" money should be paid more attention in studies on money demand functions and monetary policy.

Notes and References

1. Since the emphasis in this paper is different, the relative merits and demerits of the various techniques are not discussed in detail here.

2. Kaufman (1969) has shown that money definition is sensitive to lead-lag relationships between money and income under F-M criteria. Also see Hulett (1970).
3. These limitations include the extreme assumption about the substitutability of assets, ignoring the role of opportunity cost variable etc.
4. For instance, the unavailability of data on the rate of interest on savings deposits with the post offices for some years in the beginning of the sample period, disallows us the use of utility maximization techniques proposed by Chetty (1969).
5. However, the selection of lead and lag lengths involves some arbitrariness.

6. Chetty, V. K., "On Measuring the Nearness of Near-Money," *American Economic Review*, Vol. 1, LIX, No.3, June, 1969.
7. Friedman, M. and Meiselman, D., "The Relative Stability of Monetary Velocity and the Investment Multiplier in the US, 1897-1958" in *Commission on Money and Credit, Stabilization policies*, (Englewood Cliffs, 1963).
8. Friedman, M. and Schwartz, A. J., *A Monetary History of the United States 1867-1960*, (Princeton: Princeton University Press, 1963).
9. Gurley, J. G. and Shaw, E. S., *Money in a Theory of Finance* (Washington: The Brookings Institution, 1960).
10. Harman, H. H., *Modern Factor Analysis* (University of Chicago Press, Chicago, 1960).
11. Hulet, D.T., "More on an Empirical Definition of Money: Note" *American Economic Review*, Vol. LX, No. 2, May, 1970.
12. Kamaiah, B. and Bhole, L. M., "On an Empirical Definition of Money: A canonical Correlation Approach," unpublished paper, 1980.
13. Kaufman, G. G., "More on an Empirical Definition of Money" *American Economic Review*, Vol. LIX, No. 1, March 1969.
14. Kim, Joe-on "Factor Analysis" in *Statistical Package for Social Sciences*, (McGraw-Hill Book Company, 1975), second edition.
15. Koot, R. S., "A Factor Analytic Approach to an Empirical Definition of Money", *The Journal of Finance*, Vol. XXX No. 4, September, 1975.
16. Liberman, C., "Transactions vs Asset Demand Approach to the Empirical Definition of Money", *Economic Inquiry*, Vol. XVII, No. 2, April 1979.
17. Laidler, D. W., "The Definition of Money: Theoretical and Empirical Problems", *Journal of Money, Credit and Banking*, 1 August, 1969.
18. McKim, B. T., *Income Velocity and Monetary Policies in the United States: 1951-60*, unpublished doctoral dissertation University of Iowa, 1962.
19. Mason, W. E., "The Empirical Definition of Money: A Critique," *Economic Enquiry*, Vol. XIV, No. 4, December 1976.
20. Morrison, D. F., *Multivariate Statistical Methods*, (McGraw-Hill Book Company, New York, 1967).

21. PESEK, B. P. and SAVING, T. R., *Money, Wealth and Economic Theory,* (Macmillan, New York, 1967).

22. SHERGILL, H., "On an Empirical Definition of Money Supply for India," *Margin,* Vol. 12, No. 2, January, 1980.

23. *Money Supply in India: Concepts, Compilation and Analysis:* Report of the Second Working Group (Bombay, Reserve Bank of India, 1977).

[3]

An Empirical Study of Liquidity Preference of Corporate Sector in India, 1951-1974[*]

Introduction

Knowledge of the factors actually determining the demand for money by different sectors in a given economy is helpful in the correct formulation of monetary policy. We have a number of studies on demand for money using data from U.S.A. and U.K. There is a need to examine the monetary experience of developing countries like India so as to gain a better insight into the working of monetary mechanism in a wider geographical and institutional setting. Further, the existing studies of demand for money have concentrated their attention mainly on the behaviour of household sector or the entire economy, and have mostly neglected the behaviour of corporate sector. [1] The present study is intended to fill partly this double gap in the existing literature on demand for money by undertaking to investigate empirically in the determinants of demand for money by the corporate sector in India. The issues which have been examined in this paper are:

(i) Among income and wealth, what is the appropriate constraint on money balances, and what is the magnitude of elasticity of this appropriate constraint with respect to the demand for money?

(ii) What is the role of interest in the demand for money function?

(iii) What is the relative importance of short-term and long-term interest rates in explaining the demand for money?

[*] Paper published in the *Indian Economic Journal*, July-September 1979; and in the *Indian Journal of Economics*, April 1978.

(iv) What are the other important factors which explain the variations in the demand for money by the Corporate Sector?

(v) What is the appropriate definition of money?

The paper is divided in four sections. The theoretical underpinnings of the corporate demand for money are discussed in Section I. Sections II and III present the definition of variables and empirical evidence, respectively. Section IV reports the main findings.

Section I

Theoretical underpinnings of Corporate Demand for Money in Developing Countries

Theory of demand for money has been discussed well in Friedman (4), Meltzer (12), Orr (15), Heston (7), Pearson Hunt (17) and others. It is therefore possible to be brief in setting out theoretical specifications of demand for money function here. It would be necessary to highlight more only the peculiarities of Indian economy in the present context.

All activities of the firm are goal-directed. It is assumed that all decisions of the firm, including those concerned with the management of money, are taken to maximize profits. Now the firm maintains certain money balances because thereby it earns what is known as 'convenience yield' (2, p. 12) in the form of not being forced to borrow and repay continuously in order to meet all the payments. It is also convenient to hold part of these money balances in the form of cash to minimize the risk of insolvency during the period of 'float', i.e., the time required for banks having firm's deposit account to realize the proceeds of cheques deposited with them by the firm concerned (17, p. 93). As per the accepted theory, the actual level of firm's money holdings would be positively related with its volume of transactions. However, it is interesting to note how the differences in institutional arrangements and practices in developed and developing countries have a bearing on the level of money balances, and the cash component thereof held by firms in these respective countries. In a country like U.S.A. there exist assets like tax anticipation certificates, commercial paper of sales finance companies which are regarded particularly suitable as 'temporary abodes of purchasing power' by the U.S. firms. There are also repurchase agreements with the Government bond dealers in that country. All this is quite suitable for reducing the firms' transactions and precautionary money balances in U.S.A. (22). In a developing country like India where financial markets still lack such sophisticated developments, and where easily convertible income-yielding assets are rare; the firm's demand for money is likely to be higher than that in U.S.A.

Similarly, in U.S.A. and U.K. where transactions are mediated predominantly through cheques, While the fear that banks may not make funds available during 'float' would necessitate firm's holding of certain amount of cash, the practice of commercial banks in these countries of giving credit to the payees before cheques are debited into the accounts of the issuers might enable the firm to maintain lower cash balances than dictated by the fear mentioned above. In developing countries, on the other hand, where banking habits and banking facilities are relatively much less developed even in the organized sector, and where the above mentioned practice of giving credit to payees does not exist, the firm's level of cash holdings can be accepted to be higher than in developed countries.

Although holding of money offers convenience yield and other benefits, it also involves opportunity cost in the form a return foregone on the best alternative income-yielding asset to cash. Assuming that the rate of interest represents the opportunity cost of holding money, the rise (fall) in the rate of interest would induce a fall (rise) in the level of firm's money holding. This negative relationship between the rate of interest and demand for money would be relatively stronger at the higher level of interest rates than at their lower level. When interest rates rise, firms would economize on their money balances by way of reducing operating cash requirements, better forecasting of cash flows and nurturing alternative sources of liquidity (17, p. 102). It would however, not be possible for the firms to hold all their transactions and precautionary needs in the form of income-yielding assets because the latter are not perfect substitutes for money, and because their conversion entails transactions costs.

What is the role of speculative motive in determining the volume of money balances of the firm? According to Keynesian analysis, the demand for money for the speculative purpose varies inversely with the rate of interest (8, Chap. 15). It has been rightly argued that in case of business firms, speculative motive of this type, i.e., arising from expected changes in interest rates is of secondary importance (23, p. 407). This is specially true of developing countries. In India for instance where Government bonds are mainly held by the Central Bank and commercial banks, it is not really an important financial asset used for speculative purpose by the household and corporate asset holders. The widening of the band of *only financial assets* for the purpose under discussion also does not really improve the matter because there do not exist in developing countries many other financial instruments, nor is the holding of assets like variable dividend securities and industrial debentures widespread among the public in these countries. [2] However, speculative activity engendered by expected changes in prices of real assets like stocks of commodities, land, etc., is more prevalent in these economies. Therefore, in the discussion of business firms' demand for money, it becomes necessary to include real assets as being competitive with the holding of money. The inventories of raw materials and finished products remains one of the best real assets chosen by firms for the purpose of speculation. In the period of rising prices, holding of inventories becomes all the more attractive for the speculative purpose. There is evidence to show that in India, where prices have been rising quite rapidly over a long period of time, the part of inventory accumulation by the joint-stock companies has been with a view to profit from the future changes in prices of commodities (1, Chap. 3).

The foregoing suggests that the holding of inventories for speculative purpose will be negatively related with the firm's holding of money balances. Heston (7, pp. 76-77) has argued that inventory accumulation for normal business purposes also will show inverse relationship with the holding of cash and Government securities, because in an expansionary phase, inventory accumulation would take place by means reducing holdings of money balances and Government securities. Thus the total inventories can be expected to be negatively related with the liquid assets of the firm. The inverse relationship or inventories would be stronger with M_3 than M_1 and M_2 as defined in Section II. This is because gains from inventory accumulation are likely to be g4reater than those on Government holdings in a period of rising prices and business expansion, while there would be limitations on reducing cash and bank balances below a certain level for the purpose of holding commodity stocks.

Friedman, Nadiri (14), and others have stressed the role of changes in the price level as a determinant of demand for money. In India, where the money has been experiencing inflationary pressures for quite a long period of time, this factor is all the more relevant in studying the demand for money function. The firm's demand for nominal money balances and the rice level are expected to be positively to be positively related because of the working of 'real-balance' effect, and the increase in the size of transactigon when prices go to (3, pp. 17-18).

The actual money holdings of the manufacturing concern are also dependent upon its ability to use its liabilities for meeting the need for money. For example, the availability of trade credit and the ready access to bank credit would influence the management's assessment of the firm's need for money balances in a given period of time. Similarly, money holdings of the manufacturing firm are influenced also by its current asset like bills receivable. In order to assess the magnitude of the influence of trade payables and receivables on the firm's demand for money, the net receivables is to be introduced as one of the arguments in the demand function for money. When net receivables increase, it is most likely that the firm would finance them by reducing its money balances and other liquid assets like Government securities.

In addition to the five factors mentioned heretofore – the size of transactions, the rate of interest, prices, inventories, and net receivables – which would be empirically tested with regard to their respective magnitude of influence on the firm's demand for money, the reference must be made to one more factor which has been missed by monetary theorists, but which has been emphasized by financial management experts as having significant influence on the level of firm's money holdings in a given period. It has been argued (17, p. 95) that in advanced economies the need to hold 'compensating balances' with the banks for the purposes of building up favourable banking relationship, and reducing the cost of servicing their accounts tends to push up the level of money balances held by the firms. While it is doubtful as to how far this factor works in developing economies, it may be believed that firms' need for money balances would be reduced in India on account of a high degree of integration between manufacturing and financial sectors through interlocking directorship, etc. Similarly, under the systems of cash credit and overdraft privileges, unutilized credit lines have been quite common in case of many Indian companies. It has been estimated that in India, at the end of June 1974, while the credit limits sanctioned aggregated to Rs.12,880 crores, the actual utilization of credit limits granted was only 57% (18, p. 12). Whenever the firms are reasonably sure that they have much a kind of banking relationship as will enable them to raise money quickly whenever needed, or if they have a line of credit (ordinary or committed) with the banks, their actual holdings of money balances would be at lower levels in the absence of such factors. [3]

The Form of Equation

Having discussed the factors influencing the demand for money, formally the corporate sector's demand for money function in log-linear terms as tested in this paper can be written as:

$$\text{Log } M_t = a + b_1 \log S_t + b_2 \log R_t + b_3 \log P_t + b_4 \log IN_t + b_5 \log NR_t + U_t$$

Where M = Money balances, narrow M_1 or broad M_2 broader M_3; S = sales income; R = rate of interest, short term RT or long term RD; P = price level, general level of prices P, or expected prices EP; IN = inventory holdings; NR = net receivables; [4] t is time subscript; U_t is an error term; and $b_1 \ldots b_5$ are the respective elastics of each independent variable with respect to demand for money, and are expected to carry the following signs: $b_1 > 0$, $b_2 < 0$, $b_3 > 0$, $b_4 < 0$, $b_5 < 0$; a is the intercept.

Section II

Definition of Variables and Description of Data

(A) In order to find out empirically the magnitude of elasticities of the variables discussed in the previous section, the definitions and measures of those variables adopted for the purpose of this study are discussed below.

(1) Money

The debate on the concept of money and its empirical content still remains inconclusive. In the literature on demand for money, while some economists (12) have preferred a narrower definition of money which includes currency and demand deposits with banks, (usually denoted by M_1), others (4) have found reasons to use a wider definition of money which includes currency, demand deposits and time (including savings) deposits (usually denoted by M_2). On the basis of his review of theoretical developments and empirical results, Laidler had to conclude that stable demand functions for money defined both to include and exclude time deposits may be identified for U.S. economy (11, p. 523).

We think that if one is interested in studying the demand for money by the household sector, it would be more correct to use the narrower definition of money. The households' demand for money transactions and speculative purposes is more likely to take the form of currency and demand deposits rather than time deposits. Among the existing assets there are some which are deemed by public to be suited as a genuine savings medium, while there are others which are regarded as suitable by the public either for smoothening out transactions cycles or for converting them sooner or later into other mediums of savings. It is well-known that according to Cambridge quantity theorists, K has been defined as that proportion of income (or planned transactions) which people want to keep in the form of real money balances. Keynes regarded this transactions approach to the demand for money to be incomplete and added the asset demand for money, i.e. "the possibility that people may choose to hold money as an asset instead of other liquid assets when their prices were expected to fall" (21,

p. 78, emphasis original). It should be noted that an asset demand for money is the amount of non-income earning medium of exchange ***temporarily*** held with an intention to convert it into an income-earning asset(s) and it is ***not*** the money held over a fairly long period of time in the form of an income-earning asset as such. Further, when we try to decide whether a particular asset is money or not on the basis of its quality of liquidity, it should be remembered that the liquidity of the asset does not depend only on its *inherent* quality of a quick and costless conversion into means of payments, [5] but also on whether public *intends* to use that asset as a 'temporary abode of purchasing power' for satisfying transactions, precautionary and speculative motives, or whether it *intends* to hold it as a form of personal wealth to be used for fairly *remote* requirements. For the reasons just mentioned, just as that part of income which is held in the form of liquid assets like bonds, shares, etc. is not regarded as part of money, the part of income held in the form of time deposits cannot be included as part of money. In developing countries particularly, time deposits constitute a genuine savings medium which offers security of the principal, security of return, regularity of return – the advantages highly valued by most of the people even in cities. Therefore time deposits are rarely likely to be used for the purpose of speculation born of expected changes in interest rates and prices. [6]

While the above-mentioned remarks remain true for the household sector, one is justified in including time deposits in the definition of money for studying the demand for money function of the business sector. For the business sector, even time deposits are generally held to bridge the gap between receiving and making payments. If the investment opportunities with a good prospective rate of return arise, the firm would quite willingly reduce its holdings of time deposits in order to benefit from the better business prospects. This outcome is likely to materialize all the more if there is an increase in interest rates in the economy, for the latter involves increase in the cost of finance for the firm. Accordingly, the following three definitions of money have been tested in this paper:

(i) M_1 : cash and other (than fixed deposits) Bank balances.
(ii) M_2 : cash and all (including fixed deposits) bank balances.
(iii) M_3 : Cash, all bank balances and investment in Government and semi-Government securities.

(2) Size of Transactions

In studies on demand for money, a considerable attention has been paid to finding out the right measure of the variable of the size of transactions or the level of operations as a determinant of demand for money. The question which has been raised is, whether it is the income or wealth which is the correct measure of the variable under consideration? Therefore current sales-income (S), output (O) and total assets (TS) were alternatively used to represent the size of transactions variable in the initial analysis, while only sale-income was used at an advanced stage.

(3) Interest Rate

Both the long-term and short-term interest rates were used to find out the interest elasticity of demand for money. While the short-term interest rate was represented alternatively by the prime lending rate of the State Bank of India, (RS), and the (ii) Treasury Bill rate (RT); the long-term rate of interest was represented alternatively by (i) the industrial debenture yield (RI), and (ii) government bond yield (RG) in the initial stage of analysis. At this stage of analysis, year to year changes in the industrial debenture yield were also introduced as a measure of the expectations regarding future changes in the rate of interest. [7] At the advanced stage of experimentation, only the industrial debenture yield and the Treasury bill rate were used.

(4) Prices

Two measures were used to represent the prices variable. The first was the Index of Wholesale Prices (P) (1961-62 = 100). Another was year to year changes in the Index Number of Wholesale Prices (EP) for representing the expectations in regard to appreciation or depreciation of the value of money.

(5) Inventories

The level of total inventories (IN) included inventories of raw materials, goods in process, finished goods, and others.

(6) Net Receivables

The difference between the accounts receivable and accounts payable in each year was used to represent this variable.

(B) Data

The data used for our analysis relate to the functioning of the sample of non-financial, non-government Medium and Large Public Limited Companies in India during 1950-51 to 1973-74. The yearly figures for variables 1, 2, 5 and 6 mentioned above were obtained from the consolidated balance-sheets of the joint stock companies published by the Reserve Bank of India (RBI) (19). Medium and Large Public Limited Companies have been defined by RBI as those with paid-up capital of more than Rs.5,00,000 each. The sample of Medium and Large Public Limited Companies selected by the RBI constituted around 80 per cent of all non-financial, non-Government Public Limited Companies in India, in terms of their paid-up capital. The necessary figures for variables 3 and 4 were obtained from the other publications of the RBI (20).

As quarterly data was not available, we had to be satisfied with the use of annual figures. Similarly, as it was assumed that one year is a sufficiently long period for completing the adjustment between the dependent variable and independent variables, lagged analysis was not conducted.

Section III

Empirical Evidence

The main results of the specifications of Section I are reproduced in Table 1. For lack of space, all the simple regression equations and many of the experimental multiple regression lines which we fitted to our data have not been reproduced here. However, the important points which emerge from *all* the equations are stated below:

(i) There is no unequivocal choice in favour of either of different measures - sales, output, total assets - of the size of transactions as a determinant of demand for money. While the coefficient of determination is slightly higher for sales and output respectively, the regression coefficient is shown to be slightly higher for assets compared to that of sales and output respectively.

(ii) The income-elasticity of demand for money is greater than unity for all three definitions of money. The magnitude of income-elasticity of money is the highest for M_3, followed by that of M_2 and M_1 in that order. However, statistically, while the regression coefficient of sales income is statistically significant at one per cent probability level for M_1 it is significant only at 5 percent level of probability for M_2 and M_3. The magnitude of elasticities of coefficients, and their margin of error as indicated by values of F-ratios show that income is more important than interest in determining corporate demand for money.

While Kisselgoff (10) also found income-elasticity of demand for money to be greater than unity for large U.S. manufacturing companies, Heston (7) reported income-elasticity to be less than unity for money balances also for large U.S. Corporations. For Government securities, however, Heston obtained greater than unitary income-elasticity.

(iii) The regression coefficients of the rate of interest have the expected negative sign. However, it is the long-term rather than the short-term rate of interest which performs better as an explanatory variable both when narrow and wide definitions of money are used as dependent variable. This result is comparable with the findings of Nadiri (14), Friedman (4) and Khan (9) on this point for the developed countries. The regression coefficient of the short-term rate of interest is statistically insignificant throughout. The magnitude of the long-term interest rate elasticity of the demand for money is the highest (-0.60803) for M_1, followed by that of M_2 (-0.56755), and M_3 (-0.47899) in the same order. Statistically, while the regression coefficient of the long-term rate of interest is significant at 5 per cent probability level for M_1, it becomes insignificant for M_2 and M_3 respectively. This may be construed to mean that the elasticity of demand for money with respect to even the long-term rate of interest is not statistically strong enough to count in policy decisions. Since the issue is important, it is worthwhile to examine the performance of the long-term interest rate in the following equations fitted by us to our data before reaching the final conclusion.

$$M_1/S = 0.07129 - \underset{(0.00082)}{0.00603}\ RD \qquad (1)$$

$$F = 53.719$$

$$R^2 = 0.70945;\ N = 24$$

$$M_2/S = 0.7986 - 0.00549$$
$$(0.00111)$$
$$F = 24.219$$
$$R^2 = 0.52473;\ N = 24 \qquad (2)$$

Where M_1/S is the ratio of cash and other (than time deposits) bank balances to sales; M_2/S is the ratio of cash and all bank balances to sales; RD is industrial debentures yield; figures in brackets indicate standard error of respective regression coefficient; and F is the F-ratio for respective regression coefficient.

It is obvious from equations (1) and (2) that when the demand for money divided by sales is regressed on the rate of interest for a period 1950-51 to 1973-74, the latter becomes statistically significant at 1 per cent level of probability. [8] Thus the long-term interest rate is shown to play a significant role in determining business demand for money in India although the power of predictability of estimates seems to be rather weak due to the presence of margin error to which interest rate coefficients are subject in multiple regression equations.

While comparing the performance of the rate of interest, it can be said that the magnitude of interest-elasticity (between -0.60803 to -0.47899) obtained by us accords well with the values of interest rate coefficients obtained in many of studies of U.S.A. and U.K. Further, the fact that interest-elasticity of demand for money is reduced when expanded definition of money is used supports the view held by many in developed countries that lumping of time deposits with the money stock obscures their movements based on changes in the interest rate (see 21, p. 88).

(iv) The price variable as measured by the level of general prices has a correct sign, and is statistically significant as 1 percent probability level. The price elasticity of demand for money varies between 0.71 to 1.13. It is shown to be almost as important as income as a determinant of demand for money. This result is in the same line as those obtained by Nadiri for U.S. manufacturing sector, and by Friedman for the U.S. Economy. The magnitude of price-elasticity of demand for money is the highest for M_3 followed by that of M_2 and M_1 in that order.

(v) The variable expected changes in prices performs badly. Although it has a correct sign in almost all the combinations of variables, it is statistically insignificant throughout.

(vi) The regression coefficient of inventories has expected negative sign throughout, and it is statistically significant at 5 per cent probability level in some combinations, and at 10 per cent probability level in others. The elasticity of the demand for money with respect to inventories is the highest when money is defined as M_3, followed by the elasticities for M_2 and M_1 in that order. This suggests that the Government securities are liquidated to accumulate inventories when such accumulation becomes profitable. Our evidence accords well with Heston's findings that securities and cash are negatively related to inventories, and that it is

Table 1: The Determinants of Liquidity Preference of Corporate Sector in India, Sample Period 1950-51 to 1973-74 (Logarithms)

Sl. No.	Dependent variable	a	Independent Variables					R^2
1	$M_{1(t)}$	-1.16278	1.40504 S_t (0.67022) (4.395)	-0.60803 RD_t (0.35179) (2.987)	+0.80441 P_t (0.38815) (4.295)	-1.32664 IN_t (0.82349) (2.595)	+0.05658 NR_t (0.05553) (1.038)	0.74318
2	$M_{1(t)}$	-1.21737	1.76022 S_t (0.70066) (6.311)	-0.03427 RT_t (0.21759) (0.025)	+0.71681 P_t (0.44690) (2.573)	-1.89789 IN_t (0.81476) (5.426)	+0.04679 NR_t (0.05972) (0.614)	0.70096
3	$M_{1(t)}$	-0.30761	1.01955 S_t (0.71120) (2.055)	-0.56514 RT_t (0.38738) (2.128)	+0.01806 EP_t (0.02816) (0.411)	-0.43101 IN_t (0.77191) (0.313)	+0.10858 NR_t (0.05991) (3.285)	0.68900
4	$M_{1(t)}$	-0.54462	1.49267 S_t (0.72785) (4.206)	-0.14594 RT_t (0.21990) (0.440)	+0.01041 EP_t (0.02976) (0.122)	-0.10520 IN_t (0.68628) (2.593)	+0.08845 NR_t (0.06207) (2.031)	0.66053
5	$M_{2(t)}$	-1.89857	1.72706 S_t (88559) (3.807)	-0.56755 RD_t (0.46483) (1.491)	+1.14687 P_t (0.51287) (5.000)	-1.65965 IN_t (1.08810) (2.326)	-0.00385 NR_t (0.07338) (0.003)	0.80053
6	$M_{2(t)}$	-1.94994	2.12156 S_t (0.88499) (5.747)	-0.15532 RT_t (0.27483) (0.319)	+0.97403 P_t (0.56447) (2.978)	-2.14334 IN_t (1.02910µ) (4.338)	-0.01056 NR_t (0.07543) (0.020)	0.78754
7	$M_{2(t)}$	-0.69914	1.18457 S_t (0.96989) (1.523)	-0.49466 RD_t (0.52284) (0.895)	+0.01719 EP_t (0.03801) (0.205)	-0.38436 IN_t (1.04182) (0.136)	+0.06486 NR_t (0.08085) (0.644)	0.74770

Table 1 (Continued)

8	$M_{2(t)}$	-1.06108	1.76773 S_t (0.93086) (3.606)	-0.31803 RT_t (0.281237) (1.279)	+0.00588 EP_t (0.03806) (0.024)	-1.05954 IN_t (0.87771) (1.457)	+0.04087 NR_t (0.07938) (0.265)	0.75272
9	$M_{3(t)}$	-1.67511	1.86285 S_t (0.96526) (3.724)	-0.47899 RD_t (0.50665) (0.894)	+1.32274 P_t (0.55901) (5.599)	-2.14628 IN_t (1.18600) (3.275)	+0.01432 NR_t (0.07988) (0.032)	0.65469
10	$M_{3(t)}$	-1.71867	2.22703 S_t (0.94693) (5.531)	-0.19226 TD_t (0.29406) (0.427)	+1.13169 P_t (0.60398) (3.511)	-2.52992 IN_t (1.101113) (5.279)	+0.00987 NR_t (0.080071) (0.015)	0.64696
11	$M_{3(t)}$	0.24403	1.22004 S_t (1.03826) (1.381)	0.42321 RD_t (0.556552) (0.560)	+0.04043 EP_t (0.04111) (0.967)	-0.67461 IN_t (1.12687) (0.358)	+0.10663 NR_t (0.08745) (1.487)	0.57036
12	$M_{3(t)}$	-1.81474	2.16739 S_t (0.96184) (5.078)	+1.348999 RT_t (0.66983) (4.056)	-0.00943 P_t (0.04414) (0.046)	-2.68405 IN_t (1.16340) (5.323)	-0.00354 NR_t (0.09298) (0.001)	0.63846

NOTATION:

M_1, M_2, M_3 as defined in Section I; S = sales-income; RD = long-term interest rate; RT = short-term interest rate; P = price level; t = time subscript; EP = Experted price; IN = inventories; NR = Net receivables; While figures in the first row of brackets under each equation are the standard errors of respective regression coefficients, those in the second row of brackets are the F-ratios connected with respective regression coefficients. F-ratios rather than t-ratios are presented because our results were obtained by using Statistical Package for the Social Sciences, A System of Computer Programmes authored by Norman Nee, D.H. Bent, and C.H. Hull, and published by McGraw-Hill, New York, 1970.

securities rather than cash which absorb most of the shocks from short-term adjustments in the current assets (7, p. 104).

(vii) The regression coefficient of net receivables has a wrong sign, i.e., positive in almost all the combinations of selected variables; and it is statistically insignificant whenever it has expected negative sign. Heston's evidence on this point is at variance with ours. He finds persistent negative relationship between cash and securities respectively and net receivables; and this relationship is found to be stronger for securities than for cash (7, pp. 95-96).

(viii) The values of R^2 are quite high and they are significantly different from zero at high probability levels. The five selected variables explain 74 per cent, 80 per cent, and 65 per cent variation in M_1, M_2 and M_3 respectively (see Equations 1, 5 and 9 in Table 1).

Section IV

Summary and Main Findings

In this paper we conducted an empirical investigation into the determinants of demand for money by the corporate sector in India by using ordinary least-square estimation procedure. The data used for the empirical testing was obtained from the balance sheets of the medium and large public limited companies in India. The period of study falls between 1950-51 and 1973-74.

It was found that the income-elasticity of demand for money was reasonably high indicating the significant role of interest rate in demand for money function. It was the long-term rather than the short-term rate of interest which was found to explain better the variations in cash and other liquid assets of the business firms. The price-elasticity of demand for money was shown to be around one, and the explanatory power of the price variable was shown to be as great as that of sales income. Inventories were negatively related to the demand for money however defined, but the elasticity of demand for money with respect to inventories was the highest when money was defined as M_3. Net receivables performed very poorly as an explanatory variable in the demand for money function.

Thus the sales-income, prices, the rate of interest and inventories explained the major portion (65 to 80 per cent) of variations in the demand for money by the manufacturing concerns in India. The evidence in this paper on income-elasticity, and price-elasticity of corporate demand for money falls in Friedmanian line of evidence on this subject. With regard to appropriate definition of money, the magnitudes of income-elasticity, price-elasticity, inventories-elasticity and the coefficients of determination suggest that *for the corporate sector* the broader definition of money (M_2) gives a better fit than the narrower definition of money (M_1). The magnitude of interest-elasticity however is greater for M_1 than for M_2. Thus the evidence in this paper on the appropriate definition of money mainly supports Friedman's analysis, but it also contains something to support partly Meltzer's thinking on this point. Finally, there was not much to choose among income and wealth as determinants of demand for money by the corporate sector.

Notes

1. Here the notable exceptions are the studies of Kisselgoff (10) Miller M. and Orr D. (13), Heston, A.W. (7) Nadiri (14), and Orr D. (15).

2. It seems that in the recent past, companies' investment in the securities of other companies have markedly increased.

3. This needs to be qualified by saying that this is likely to be more true in normal trade situations than in the highly expansionary period in which the 'the fringe of unsatisfied borrowers' tends to widen. In such a period, reserved borrowing capacity may not serve as a substitute for actual money balances.

4. For detailed discussion of definitions of variables and alternative ways of measuring them, see Section II of this paper.

5. In any case, time deposits do not sufficiently advance notice if the depositor wishes to use them for making payments before the end of their maturity period; and such a step also involves costs in the form of earning lower than the contracted interest rate.

6. In India even part of the currency has been held by the public not as a temporary abode of purchasing power in order to bridge the gap between receiving and making payments, but for the purpose of providing for old age or providing for future generation. The *time span* over which the cash is held is very much longer than what would be the case if that cash was the part of demand for money. Therefore at least conceptually, it would not be strictly correct to include the entire volume of currency and notes as part of money for studying the demand for money. Due to the practical difficulties of finding out such a proportion however, this point may be slurred over in empirical estimation of the demand function for money.

7. Some authors have used current values of the variables concerned to approximate their expected values (see 14, p. 181).

8. The use of the same form of equation by this author yielded similar results for the period of 1950-51 to 1965-66 (see 1, pp. 119-121.

References

1. BHOLE, L.M., *Investments Interest, and Monetary Policy in India*, University of Bombay, Bombay, 1974.
2. DUESENBERRY, J. S., "The Portfolio Approach to the Demand for Money and Other Liquid Assets," *The Review of Economics and Statistics* (Supplement), February 1963.
3. Fleming Miles, *Monetary Theory*, Macmillan, London, 1972.
4. FRIEDMAN, M., "The Demand for Money: Some Theoretical and Empirical Results," in his *The Optimum Quantity of Money and Other Essays*, Macmillan, London, 1969.
5. FRIEDMAN, M., 'Interest Rates and the Demand for Money," in his *The Optimum Quantity of Money and Other Essays*, Macmillan, London, 1969.

6. GUPTA, S. B., "On the Transactions Demand for Money to Hold," *The Indian Economic Journal,* April-June 1972.

7. HESTON, A.W., "An Empirical Study of Cash, Securities and Other Current Accounts of Large Corporations," in Hester, D.D., and Tobin, J. (Eds.), *Studies of Portfolio Behaviour,* John Wiley and Sons, New York, 1967.

8. KEYNES, J. M., *The General Theory of Employment, Interest and Money,* Macmillan, London, 1936.

9. KHAN, M. S., "The Stability of the Demand for Money Function in the United States, 1901 to 1965," *Journal of Political Economy,* November-December 1974.

10. KISSELGOFF, A., "Liquidity Preference of Large Manufacturing Corporations (1921 to 1939)," *Econometrica,* October 1945.

11. LAIDLER, D., "The Definition of Money, Theorwetical and Empirical Problems," *Journal of Money, Credit and Banking,* August 1969.

12. MELTZER, A. H., "The Demand for Money: The Evidence from the Time-Series," *Journal of Political Economy,* June 1963.

13. MILLER, A. H., and Orr, D., "A Model of the Demand for Money by Firms", *Quarterly Journal of Economics,* August 1966.

14. NADIRI, M. L., "The Determinants of Real Cash-Balances in the U.S. Total Manufacturing Sector," *Quarterly Journal of Economics,* May 1969.

15. ORR, D., *Cash Management and Demand for Money,* Praeger, London, 1970.

16. PATINKIN, D., *Money, Interest and Prices,* Harper and Row, New York, 1965.

17. Pearson Hunt and Others, *Basic Business Finance,* Irwin, Illinois, 1966.

18. RESERVE BANK OF INDIA, *Report of the Study Group to Frame Guidelines for Follow-up of Bank Credit,* Bombay, 1975.

19. RESERVE BANK OF INDIA:

(i) *Financial Statistics of Joint-Stock Companies in India,* 1950-51 to 1962-63, Bombay, 1967.

(ii) *Financial Statistics of Joint-Stock Companies in India,* 1960-61 to 1970-71, Bombay, 1975.

(iii) "Finances of Medium and Large Public Limited Companies, 1973-74," in *RBI Bulletin,* September 1975.

20. Reserve Bank of India: Various Issues of (i) *Report on Currency and Finance* and (ii) *RBI Bulletin.*

21. TEIGN, R. L., "The Demand for and Supply of Money", in SMITH, W. L. and TEGIN, R. L. (eds.), *Readings in Money, National Income and Stabilization Policy,* R. D. IRWIN, Illinois, 1970.

22. TOBIN, J., "The Interest-Elasticity of Transactions Demand for Cash," *Review of Economics and Statistics,* August 1956.

23. VAN HORNE, J. C., *Financial Management and Policy,* Prentice Hall, New Jersey, 1971.

[4]

On the Stability of Corporate Liquidity Preference in India, 1950-51 to 1973-74[*]

Introduction

The stability aspect of the Corporate Money Demand Function (or liquidity preference) is crucial for the framing and implementation of the financial policies for the corporate sector. Several studies – temporal as well as cross-sectional – have appeared in the literature investigating into the major determinants and the related aspects of the liquidity preference. Notable among them, concerning India, are the works of Sarvane (1971), Avadhani (1971), Balbir Singh (1972), Bhole (1978), and Prasad and Sampath (1979). A survey of these works shows that there are two major methodological defects. First, stability aspect has been discussed using the test given by Chow (1960). The limitation of this test is the *apriori* knowledge about the time point to split the whole sample period into two 'regimes'. When theory fails to provide such information, the use of this test becomes limited. Second, these studies have arbitrarily decided the functional form in favour of linear, log-linear, or semi log-linear forms. In other words, no attempt seems to have been made to *estimate* the functional form. Imposition of *apriori* form may lead to functional mis-specification, and consequently, testing the stability of a mis-specified form may lead to conclusions which are not appropriate.

Therefore, the objective of the paper is to test for the stability of corporate money demand function by taking care of the two limitations given above: For this purpose, the recursive residual test due to Brown, Durbin and Evans (1975) is used on a generalised functional form which has been estimated using Box-Cox power transformation. Also, a comparison of the results of linear, semi log-linear and generalised forms is made. The rest of the paper is divided

[*] Paper published jointly with B. Kamaiah in *Margin*, April 1981.

into three sections. Section I deals with the details of the functional specification used, Section II gives the test procedure and Section III presents the empirical results.

Section I

Based on the results of an earlier study [see Bhole (1978)], the Corporate Demand for Money (M_t) is functionally related to Sales Income (S_t), Industrial Debenture Yield Rate (D_t), General Level of Prices (P_t), Level of Inventory Holdings (IN_t) and Net Receivables (NR_t). Algebraically,

$$M_t = f(S_t, D_t, P_t, IN_t, NR_t, \varepsilon_t) \quad (1.0)$$

where f denotes a function, ε_t is the error term, t is time suffix. Linear and log-linear (or semi log-linear) are the popular functional forms that often appear in literature. Once f is assumed to take linear or semi log-linear form in our case, we have,

$$M_t = \alpha_o + \alpha_1 S_t + \alpha_2 D_t + \alpha_3 P_t + \alpha_4 IN_t + \alpha_5 NR_t + \mu_t \quad (1.1)$$

$$\log M_t = \beta_o + \beta_1 \log S_t + \beta_2 \log D_t + \beta_3 \log P_t + \beta_4 \log IN_t + \beta_5 NR_t + \phi_t \quad (1.2)$$

Here αs and βs are the coefficients, μ_t and ϕ_t are the error terms.

Since the exact form of f is not known *apriori*, assigning a particular form, say, linear or semi log-linear, amounts to arbitrariness. It is more appropriate if the functional form is *estimated* rather than assumed. For this purpose, the Box-Cox parametric transformation technique could be used to construct a more generalised form. The form used in this paper is given by

$$M_t^{(\lambda)} = \delta_o + \delta_1 S_t^{(\lambda)} + \delta_2 D_t^{(\lambda)} + \delta_3 P_t^{(\lambda)} + \delta_4 IN_t^{(\lambda)} + \delta_5 NR_t^{(\lambda)} + \phi_t \quad (1.3)$$

Here λis the transformation parameter, δs are the parameters, ψ_t is the error term, and $M_t^{(\lambda)}$ is the Box-Cox transform of M_t, given by

$$M_t^{(\lambda)} = \frac{M^\lambda - 1}{\lambda} \text{ f } \neq 0$$

$$= \log M_t \text{ if } \lambda = o$$

Similarly $S_t^{(\lambda)}$, $D_t^{(\lambda)}$, $P_t^{(\lambda)}$, $IN_t^{(\lambda)}$ and $NR_t^{(\lambda)}$ are defined. The parameter λ can be estimated by maximizing the concentrated likelihood function given by

$$L(\lambda) = const. - T/2 \log \hat{\sigma}^2(\lambda) + (\lambda - 1)\sum_{t=1}^{T} \log M_t$$

where L(λ) is the likelihood function, T is the sample size,

$$\hat{\sigma}^2 = \frac{1}{T}\sum_{t=1}^{T} \hat{\psi}_t^2$$

where $\hat{\bar{\psi}}_t^2$ is the estimated value of ψ in (1.3) for a specific value of λ.

The specifications in (1.1) and (1.2) are rather arbitrary in the sense that no rationale is available for justification. Therefore, they are considered to be imposed on the data. But the specification in (1.3) is chosen by the data itself. Hence, there is a strong justification for the use of specifications of the kind given in (1.3). Also (1.1) and (1.2) could be obtained as particular cases of (1.3). Hence, (1.3) is called the generalised form. In this study, the stabilities of the linear (1.1), semi log-linear (1.2) and generalized (1.3) forms are investigated using Brown, Durbin and Evans (1975) test which is given in the following section.

Section II

A number of stability tests are available in literature. Upto recently, dummy variables and F-test devised by Chow (1960), were used for testing whether a regression relationship is stable over a period of time or not. These tests require *apriori* knowledge about the point of time where the shift occurs exactly. Since economic theory often fails to identify such shifts, these tests have only limited application. The likelihood-ratio test, due to Quandt (1960) can be used to find out the extent of departures from the models at various time points. But this test is more useful when used as a supplementary one. The technique applied in this paper appears to be a better alternative in the sense that it does not require any *apriori* knowledge.

Any test intending to investigate departures from model specification should look at residuals. The plot of ordinary least squares residuals against time, or the cumulative sums of residuals against time, cannot reflect fully the sensitive movements of the model specification. Hence recursive residual approach is chosen to be a better alternative.

Let us consider the basic regression model

$$Y_t = X_t \beta_t + \mu_t \,,\ t = 1, 2, \dots n \qquad (2.1)$$

where Y_t is the (txl) vector of observations on the dependent variable, X_t is the (txk) matrix of observations on the k independent variables, β_t is a (kxl) vector of parameters, μ_t is a (txl) vector of observations on the error term. The suffix 't' is used for β (also) to indicate the possibility of its varying over the given on' time periods. Let us assume

(1) that the regression relationship in equation (2.1) has an intercept term.

That is, if $X_t = \begin{pmatrix} x_1^T \\ x_1^T \\ \vdots \\ x_t^T \end{pmatrix}$ and

$\bar{x}_1 = x_{ij}$ i = 1, 2, … n; j = 1, 2, … k, $k \leq n$, then

$\bar{x}_j = 1$ for all i = 1, 2, …, and j = 1.

(2) X_n is of order n x k and of rank k.

(3) $\bar{x}_j$ are non-stochastic for all j = 1, 2, … n and j = 1, 2, … k

(Here X_i^T means the transpose of X*i*)

The error term μ_t is assumed to be normally distributed with mean zero and variance σ_t^2, t = 1, 2, ... n. Now, the null hypothesis of constancy of regression relationship, H_o (say) may be written as

$$H_o : \beta_1 = \beta_2 = \ldots = \beta_n = \beta \text{ (say)}$$
$$\sigma_1^2 = \sigma_2^2 \ldots = \sigma_n^2 = \sigma^2$$

Here we are concerned more with detecting differences among βs than among σs.

Let β_{t-1} be the least squares estimate of β based on the series of observations from period 1th rough t-1. Then the prediction error, for the period t is

$$e_t = Y - x_t^T \hat{\beta}_{t-1} \qquad (2.2)$$

The recursive residual is defined as

$$\bar{e}_t = e_t / \left[+ x_t (X_{t-1} X_{t-1})^{-1} x_t^T \right]^{1/2} \qquad (2.3)$$

where X_{t-1} contains only the first t-1 rows of X_n. For a set of n given time series observations, there will be (n-k) xl vector of residual.

It can be shown that the residual $(\bar{e}_t$: t = k + 1, k + 2, … n) are normal independent variables with mean zero and variances $\sigma^2_{\bar{e}_{k-1}}, \sigma^2_{\bar{e}_{k-2}}, \cdots \sigma^2_{\bar{e}_n}$.

The next step is to define a statistic S_t :

$$S_t = \sum_{k+1}^{t} \bar{e}_t^2 \Big/ \sum_{k+1}^{n} \bar{e}_t^2$$

t = k + 1 … n

It is very clear that S_t is the ratio of the sum of squares of one-period prediction residuals from k + 1 period to the t period, to the sum of squares of one period prediction errors from the k + 1 to the nth period. The values of S_t will, therefore, lie between zero and unity as indicated below:

$$S_t = 0 \text{ if } t < k + 1$$
$$= 1 \text{ if } t = n$$

Under the null hypothesis H_o, S_t have a Beta distribution with mean (approximate) value given by

$$E(S_t) = (t - k)/(n - k)$$

where 'E' denotes the mathematical expectation. This indicates that the plot of S_t against t should lie along with its mean path. For a two-sided test of hypothesis, a linear confidence internal for S_t is constructed. Accept H_o if the sample values of S_t lie in the interval Co ± (t-k) / (n-k), where C_o are distributed as Pyke's modified Kolmogorov-Smirnov statistic. The values for C_o at. various significances levels can be obtained from Durbin (1969, Table-1) by entering the table at m = (n-k)/2 when (n-k) is even, and interpolating linearly between

$$m = 1/2 (n - k) -1/2 \text{ and } m = ½ (n - k) + 1/2$$

when (n - k) is odd.

Section III

This is a time series study based on twenty four annual observations from 1950-51 to 1973-74 of non-financial, non-Government Medium and Large Public Limited Companies in India. The variables are defined as follows:

(1) M_{1t} = Narrow money = Cash and Bank Balances (other than fixed deposits)
(2) M_{2t} = Broad money = Cash and all bank balances, including fixed deposits
(3) S_t = Sales Income
(4) P_t = Wholesale Price Index (1961-62= 100)
(5) D_t = Debenture yield rate
(6) IN_t = Level of inventories of raw materials, goods in process, finished goods etc.
(7) NR_t = Net receivables defined as the difference between accounts receivable and payable in each year.

In Table 1, results for three functional forms 'viz.' linear, semi log-linear and generalised forms are given. The reason for selecting semi log-linear form (for comparison sake) instead of log-linear form that the explanatory variable 'Net Receivables (NR_t)' has negative values as observations for some of the values in the given sample period. The values of transformations parameters (for the generalised forms) are (-)0.8 and (-)0.4 for M_1 and M_2 definitions of money respectively. For further details see Kamaiah *et al* (1980).

Stability of (LF 1), (LF 2), (SLF 1), (SLF 2), (GF 1), (GP 2) has been tested and the results are given in Tables 2 and 3. Table 2 gives the values of S_t for all the functional forms. Table 3 gives the lower and upper bound values for two levels of significance (0.05 and 0.01). The values of S_t are expected to lie between the lower and upper bounds. In case the values lie; outside the interval, it indicates structural shifts at those points. The values of C_0 (see Section II) are 0.39922 and 0.31325 for 0.01 and 0.05 levels respectively. These values are used in calculating the lower and upper bound values for S_t. Table 4 gives the details of the structural shifts of various functional forms money definition-wise. This table is prepared on the basis of the comparison of results given in Tables 1 and 2. The results reveal that the generalised forms have not undergone any structural shifts. It is also clear that the money demand function based on M_1 definition of money has fewer structural shifts than the function based on M_2 definition of Money.

The available empirical work on corporate liquidity preference in India have analysed the stability aspect with the help of arbitrary functional forms and less sophisticated stability tests. Since there was no explicit rationale for preferring a particular form, the chances of the available models of being mis-specified were not ruled out. The conclusions concerning the stability of mis-specified forms would be misleading. Under these circumstances, it may be safer first to search for an appropriate functional form that suits the data, and then go for examining the stability. Since the present study is carried out keeping in view the problems of a mis-specified form and the need for a relatively better stability test, a study of this kind is very much relevant in Indian context.

Conclusion

Based on the empirical results obtained by using the recursive residual stability test, it may be concluded that the corporate money demand function for the given sample period is stable in its generalized form and exhibits structural shifts in linear and semi log-linear forms. Since it was proved that linear and semi log-linear forms are not appropriate in the given sample period, it may be concluded that the corporate money demand function is stable during 1950-51 to 1973-74.

Table 1: Results of Corporate Money Demand Function for Various Functional Forms

Eqn. No.								
Linear Form:								
(LF1)	M_{1t}	= 7.4873	+ 0.0261 SI_t (1.4286)	(-)0.9908 D_t (2.2348)	+0.04601 P_t (1.7902)	(-)0.0580 IN_t (0.7667)	(-)0.0793 NR_t (1.7152)	R^2 = 0.87
(LF2)	M_{2t}	=10.5950	+0.0305 SI_t (0.92)	(-)1.8324 D_t (0.292)	+0.0485 P_t (1.6471)	(-)0.01202 IN_t (0.088)	(-)0.1840 NR_t (2.2085)	R^2 = 0.92
Semi Log-Linear Form: All the variables on both sides of (SLF1) and SLF2) are in logarithms except NR_t :								
(SLF1)	Log M_{1t}	=(-)1.8035	+1.3776 log S_t (2.2030)	(-)0.2422 log D_t (0.6853)	+0.6501 log P_t (1.7778)	(-)1.3842 log IN_t (1.9267)	(-)0.1458 log NR_t (2.3554)	R^2 = 0.78
(SLF2)	Log M_{2t}	=(-)2.7267	+1.3776 log S_t (1.8025)	(-)0.2040 log D_t (0.4375)	+0.8046 log P_t (1.6676)	(-)1.3343 log IN_t (1.4075)	(-)0.1616 log NR_t (1.9786)	R^2 = 0.83
Generalized Form:								
(GF1)	$M_{1t}^{(-0.8)}$	=(-)19.0487	+19.2874 $S_t^{(-0.8)}$ (2.3186)	(-)0.5408 $D_t^{(-0.8)}$ (0.2035)	+5.4233 $P_t^{(-0.8)}$ (1.8774)	(-)8.5401 $N_t^{(-0.8)}$ (2.1783)	(-)0.0578 $R_t^{(-0.8)}$ (2.1989)	R^2 = 0.88
	$M_{2t}^{(-0.4)}$	=(-)6.9313	+4.6659 $S_t^{(-0.4)}$ (1.8180)	(-)0.0338 $D_t^{(-0.4)}$ (0.0971)	+2.1666 $P_t^{(-0.4)}$ (1.862)	(-)3.0137 $N_t^{(-0.4)}$ (1.5850)	(-)0.1254 $R_t^{(-0.4)}$ (1.7994)	R^2 = 0.79

Table 2: . S-Values for M_1 and M_2 Definitions of Money for Linear, Semi Log-Linear and Generalised Functional Forms

Period	Serial No. of observation	Linear form		Values of S_t $(0 < S_t < 1)$			
		M_1	M_2	Semi Log-linear form		Generalised form	
				M_1	M_2	$M_1(\lambda = -0.8)$	$M_2(\lambda = -0.4)$
1957-58	8	0.00315	0:00001	0.00364	0.00013	0.04772	0.00311
58-59	9	0.02299	0.00301	0.01919	0.00198	0.23567	0.03304
59-60	10	0.03533	0.00393	0.03258	0.00312	0.25374	0.03977
60-61	11	0.05090	0.05159	0.06031	0.09771	0.39410	0.05710
61-62	12	0.05133	0.06321	0.06199	0.09797	0.55027	0.16695
62-63	13	0.06647	0.08063	0.07138	0.10795	0.58250	0.18198
63-64	14	0.07214	0.08071	0.08019	0.10801	0.58647	0.18452
64-65	15	0.15136	0.10539	0.13870	0.12547	0.70460	0.23378
65.66	16	0.21256	0.10808	0.16234	0.12559	0.79513	0.32822
66-67	17	0.30932	0.14977	0.22932	0.14925	0.83750	0.42961
67-68	18	0.34354	0.15167	0.26719	0.14993	0.86149	0.49176
68-69	19	0.40360	0.15990	0.33217	0.15817	0.86775	0.50400
69-70	20	0.75099	0.26580	0.66507	0.25885	0.88540	0.53963
70-71	21	0.76276	0.43953	0.74232	0.43217	0.92299	0.62177
71-72	22	0.80217	0.73774	0.86023	0.79104	0.96636	0.82495
72-73	23	0.81223	0.79518	0.88199	0.91095	0.99319	0.95699
73-74	24	1.00000	1.00000	1.00000	1.00000	1.00000	1.00000

Table 3: Mean, Lower and Upper Bound Values for S_t at 0.01 and 0.05 Levels

Period	Serial No. of observation	0.01 level (C_o = 0.39922)		0.05 level (C_o = 0.31325)		$E(S_t)$
		Upper bound	Lower bound	Upper bound	Lower bound	
1957-58	8	0.51033	(-)0.28811	0.42436	(-)0.20214	0.11111
58-59	9	0.56589	(-)0.23256	0.47991	(-)0.14658	0.16666
59-60	10	0.62144	(-)0.17700	0.53547	(-)0.09103	0.22222
60-61	11	0.67699	(-)0.12145	0.59102	(-)0.03548	0.27777
61-62	12	0.73255	(-)0.06589	0.64658	0.02008	0.33333
62-63	13	0.78810	(-)0.01034	0.70213	0.07563	0.38888
63-64	14	0.84366	0.04522	0.75765	0.13119	0.44444
64-65	15	0.89922	0.10078	0.81325	0.18675	0.50000
65-66	16	0.95477	0.15633	0.86880	0.24230	0.55555
66-67	17	1.01033	0.21189	0.92436	0.29786	0.61111
67-68	18	1.06588	0.26744	0.97991	0.35341	0.66666
68-69	19	1.12144	0.32305	1.03547	0.40897	0.72222
69-70	20	1.17699	0.37855	1.09102	0.46452	0.77777
70-71	21	1.23255	0.43411	1.14656	0.52008	0.83333
71-72	22	1.28810	0.48966	1.20213	0.57563	0.88888
72-73	23	1.34366	0.54522	1.25765	0.63119	0.94444
73-74	24	1.39922	0.60078	1.31325	0.68675	1.00000

Note: $E(S_t)$ indicates the Expected Value of St (i.e., the mean value of S_t)

Table 4: The Number of Structural Shifts – Money Definition and Functional Form-wise

Level of significance	Money definition	Functional form	Period of structural shift	No. of shifts
0.05	M_1	linear	1962-63 to 1968-69	6
0.05	M_2	lineal	1963-64 to 1970-71	8
0.05	M_1	semi log-linear	1962-63 to 1964-65 and 1968-69	4
0.05	M_2	semi log-linear	1963-64, 1964-65 and 1970-71	3
0.01	M_1	linear	-	-
0.01	M_2	linear	1965-66 to 1969-70	5
0.01	M_1	semi log-linear	1967-68	1
0.01	M_2	semi log-linear	1965-66 to 1970-71	6
0.01	M_1	generalized form (λ = -0.8)*	-	-
0.1	M_2	generalized form (λ = -0.4)	-	-
0.05	M_1	generalized form (λ = -0.8)	-	-
0.05	M_2	generalized form (λ = -0.4)	-	-

*λ is the value of the transformation parameter.

References

AVADHANI, V. A., "Money Demand in the Corporate Sector", *Indian Economic Journal,* Vol. XVIII, Nos. 4-5, April-June, 1971.

BHOLE, L. M., "An Empirical Study of Liquidity Preference of Corporate Sector in India, 1951-74", *The Indian Journal of Economics,* Vol. LVIII, Part IV, No. 231, April, 1978.

BOX, G. E. P. and COX, D. R., "An Analysis of Transformations", *Journal of American Statistical Association,* B24, Part ?, 1964.

BROUN, R. L., DURBIN, J. and EVANS, J. M., "Techniques for Testing the Constancy of Regression Relationship over Time", *Journal of Royal Statistical Society,* Series B, Vol. 37, No. 2, 1975.

CAMERON, N., "The Stability of Demand for Money Function, *Canadian Journal of Economics,* No. 2, May, 1979.

CHOW, G. C., "Tests of Equality Between Two Sets of Coefficients in Two-Linear Regressions", *Econometrica.* Vol. 28, July, 1960.

DURBIN, J., "Tests for Serial Correlation in Regression Analysis Based on the Periodogram of Least-squares Residuals", *Biometrika,* Vol. 56, March, 1969.

KAMAIAH, B. and BHOLE, L. M., "General Functional Forms and Corporate Demand for Money in India", *The Indian Journal of Economics,* No. 240, July, 1980.

KAMAIAH, B. and RAMANAIAH, P. "The Generalized Money Demand Function: A Theoretical Discussion", *Rajasthan Economic Journal,* Vol. 4, January, 1980.

KAMAIAH, B; Thomas Paul, M and BHOLE, L. M., "Functional Forms, Inflationary Expectations and the Demand for Money Function in India", *Artha Vikas,*July-December, 1979.

KHAN, M. S., "The Stability of the Demand for Money Function in the United States, 1901-1965", *Journal of Political Economy,* Vol. 82, 1974.

PRASAD, K. and SAMPATH, R. K. "Business Demand for Money: A Temporal Cross-Section Study of Business Firms", *Indian Economic Journal,* Vol. 27, No. 1, July-September, 1979.

QUANDT, R. E., "Tests of Hypothesis that a Linear Regression Obeys Two Separate Regimes", *Journal of American Statistical Association,* Vol. 55, June, 1960.

SARAVANE, M., *The Demand for Money – Sectoral Approach,* (New Delhi, Vikas, 1971).

SINGH, B., "A Cross-section Study of Business Demand for Money – An Indian Experience", *Indian Economic Journal,* Vol. XIV, Nos. 4-5, April-June, 1972.

ZAREMBKA, P., "Functional Form in the Demand for Money," *Journal of American Statistical Association,* Vol. 63, No. 322, June, 1968.

ZAREMBKA, P., "Transformation of Variables in Econometrics" in P. Zarembka ed., *Frontiers of Econometrics* (New York: Academic Press, 1974), Ch. 3.

[5]

Administered Interest Rates in India[*]

Introduction

The rate of interest is an important price in any economy. If it is determined mainly by the market forces, it may help in taking appropriate decisions about saving, investment, allocation of resources, financial and monetary policy, etc. However, the level and structure of interest rates in India have remained very closely regulated by the authorities. The present study examines the working of this administered system of interest rates, and discusses the issues and considerations which need to form the basis of future interest rate and monetary policies for the Indian economy. The plan of the study is as follows: In Section I, after stating the background and the content of the present system, we briefly refer to the nature, criteria, and feasibility of an alternative system of interest rates which, according to us, would be appropriate for India. Section II discusses the features and rationale of the present system by reconstructing its scope, techniques, authority, timing, and its effects on interest rates and credit control mechanism. The reasoning and empirical evidence in support of the case for an alternative system are presented in Section III. The lessons from experiences of some countries in operating the similar systems of controlled interest rates are mentioned in Section IV. Summary and conclusions are presented in Section V.

I. The Background and Anticipatory Remarks

The performance of the Indian economy during the past three decades of economic planning has been far below the needs and expectations. There has been ratcheting upwards of inflation and unemployment accompanied by near stagnation in the rate of growth. It has been

[*] Paper published in *Economic and Political Weekly*, June 22-29, 1985.

characteristic of the Indian economy that instead of experiencing 'trade offs' between different economic objectives, there has been a deterioration on all fronts. All this has happened in spite of the adoption of economic planning, and a fairly high rise in the rates of saving and capital formation. Such a poor outcome of our tryst with destiny is naturally making many a people restless and compelling them to seek solutions to the predicament just described.

To the extent the monetary and financial factors are relevant in economic development, efforts are being made to understand better the working of the Indian monetary system so that appropriate policies can be devised for maximising its contribution to the development process. Among other things, a clear consensus is now emerging in favour of the urgent need for an increase in the productivity of investment in place of the earlier emphasis on the increase in merely the quantum of investment. Everybody now appears to be concerned about the high and increasing capital-output and capital-labour ratios, widespread low rates of utilisation of the already existing production capacities, unduly long lags between investment expenditures and flows of output, arid the misuse of capital in other ways.

It is in this context that we have undertaken a comprehensive review of the working of the present interest rates policy in India in all its major aspects. Over the period of time, more and more interest rates have been brought under more and more detailed administrative and discretionary controls. As a result, the system with the following characteristics has evolved during the past many years: (i) The rates of interest have been kept at unnaturally low levels. (ii) The regulation of one interest rate has led to the regulation of another rate. In other words, a ceiling on one interest rate has begotten another ceiling. For example, the regulation of banks' lending rates has necessitated the regulation of their deposit rates; and the latter, in turn, has forced the regulation of interest rates on deposits with non-banking companies. (iii) Because the interest rates have been controlled and kept low, the need has arisen for the imposition of widespread and detailed quantitative ceilings or restrictions as a means of allocation or distribution of finance and fighting inflationary pressures. Thus, the system of administered interest rates comprises the presence of discretionary controls on the level and variations of interest rates, the maintenance of these rates at lower levels than what they would otherwise have been, and the existence of the quantitative restrictions on the disbursements of credit.

We have attempted to establish in this study a connection between this system and the financial and real performance of the Indian economy. It has been argued, with some empirical evidence, that it has resulted in an inappropriate saving and investment behaviour, maldistri6ution of financial resources, the accentuation of the problems of inflation, unemployment, etc, and the weakening of the effectiveness of monetary policy. Therefore, a case has been made for freeing interest rates from the administrative controls, and for the need to establish their appropriate level which at present would be much higher than what it has been so far. It is not a case for usurious or exhorbitantly high interest rates, but for 'appropriately' or 'correctly' high rates of interest. In doing this, we are sharing the perspective developed in this respect by Myrdal, Shaw, McKinnon, and Brahmananda, [1] and restating the case for free and higher interest rates. This restatement may be regarded as valuable and useful because it is far more comprehensive, up-to-date, and based on empirical evidence from the Indian economy as never before.

The system of administered interest rates is a special case of the wider system of prices and physical controls which have come to pervade most of the developing economies. It is hoped that our analysis would be useful in re-evaluating the utility and advisability of the continuation of these other controls also.

Before we proceed to explain our position, it is necessary to refer briefly to the criteria which can help to determine the appropriateness or otherwise of a given system of interest rates, what are the alternative systems which can take the place of the present system, and the feasibility of the system chosen from them.

In a wider sense, the objectives of economic planning should serve as good criteria for judging the suitability of any given sub-system in the economy. However, from the point of view of the immediate relevance and concern, given the capital scarcity, interest rates policy should be such (a) that savings are adequate, and they are held in forms which are conducive for both their use in the growth process and control by monetary authorities for the purpose of economic stabilisation; (b) that available savings capacity is harnessed for investment in essential and productive purposes, and the efficiency of investment is maintained consistently at a high level. Interest rates should induce socially desirable allocation of resources and pattern of investment.

Stated slightly differently, interest rates system should be such as to help the financial system to adapt flexibly to the evolution of the requirements upon it, and to meet these requirements adequately and equitably so that individual groups of borrowers and lenders are not arbitrarily discriminated and disadvantaged, all the possible economies in administrative and other costs are realized, and the opportunities for corruption and arbitrariness are absolutely minimized. [2] The system should be simple and open also.

It is possible to think of at least three types of system of free interest rates: (i) a completely *laissez-faire*, (ii) a system in which the quantity of money is closely controlled by the authorities and interest rates are left to find their own levels as advocated by the 'monetarists', and (iii) a system of 'indicative' regulation of interest rates accompanied by the minimum of discretionary controls. It is this last type which we have in mind when we argue for free and flexible interest rates system for India.

A completely *laissez-faire* system of freely floating interest rates, without any type of government. intervention in financial markets, is obviously unrealistic for India where formal economic planning has been of much higher degree and serious hue. At the same time, it is to be firmly grasped that it is equality unrealistic to expect that direct, discretionary, all-pervasive state intervention would help to deal with the imperfections in financial markets. A policy of discretionary controls to deal with market imperfections is a logical contradiction, it is a sure way of perpetuating imperfections, albeit from a different source.

The monetarists have been recommending that interest rates should be allowed to float freely in the markets, and the task of regulation should be performed by the Central Bank by fixing a monetary rule. It will be shown later how such a system is beset with certain practical operational difficulties because of which, apart from other weaknesses of the monetarist approach, the acceptance of such a system is also inadvisable.

Our plea, therefore, is for a system wherein, instead of fixing almost each and every interest rate, the authorities operate more through the instruments of monetary control – not this or that technique but a whole set of them used in a mutually reinforcing manner – such as the bank rate, open market operations, changes in the quantity of money, etc, to determine the market rates of interest and flows of money and credit. Such a system works through automatically functioning operational controls, and changes in interest rates therein are induced rather than administratively fixed. There is, as Myrdal has pointed out, a far greater use of price mechanism and a very high degree of automatism, i.e., people's behaviour is mostly guided by relative rates of cost and returns rather than administrative discretions. However, price mechanism is first adjusted, again mostly through changes in price signals under the control of authorities, so that now it provides the specific inducements and inhibitions which are 'correct' with reference to the goals and targets of economic policy. [3]

Such a system is quite feasible and in tune with the philosophy of economic planning. As, Oscar Lange has pointed out, the price system, including interest rates, is an important incentive serving to induce the private sector to do things required of it in the plan. But also in the public sector, the need for incentives exists which again requires a proper price system. [4] It may also be reminded that in the initial years of planning in our country, there was a clear preference for and emphasis on maximum reliance on the price mechanism and the minimum use of physical controls for implementing economic plans. It is, therefore, a misconception that planned or socialistic countries need to keep interest rates low and operate through a maze of discretionary controls. The over-reliance on the present system of interest rates is an aberration which definitely needs to be corrected sooner than later.

II. The Reconstruction of the Present System – Its Features and Rationale

Evolution, Scope, Techniques, etc.

A large variety of interest rates exists in any economy at any given time. For example, in India, there are deposit rates of commercial banks, co-operative banks, postal savings organisation, non-banking companies, then there are lending rates of these and term-lending financial institutions; further, there are rates on industrial and government securities. All these rates can be classified as loan rates and rates of return on savings (in case of 'direct securities', loan and savings rate are the same) or as short-term and long-term rates. Under perfect competition, the respective levels of all these rates, and the interrelationships between them (i.e., their structure) would be determined on the basis of market forces reflecting productivity of borrowed capital, risk and uncertainty, premium for abstinence and liquidity preference, maturity, time preference, etc. The various degrees of imperfections in the money and capital markets would modify the rate but they would still be determined mainly by the market forces.

Under the administered interest rates system the interest rates are fixed or made to rule at a given level through fiat or discretionary administrative controls with almost no reference to the factors embodied in the supply of and demand for funds. Such a system has now come to prevail in India, through gradual evolution over the period of time. Till about 1958, all the interest rates were more or less free; in the month of October of that year, however, a ceiling on the deposit rates of commercial banks was introduced through the voluntary agreement between some Indian and foreign banks. Under this agreement, a separate maximum rate was fixed for deposits of different maturities. Even then, there was a great deal of flexibility and variations in the deposit rates paid by different banks which were party to the agreement; the rates paid by other banks naturally differed from one another, and from the banks bound by the agreement. This system lasted for six years.

In September 1964, it was replaced by the regulation of deposit rates by the RBI in terms of the Banking Regulation Act, 1949. With this change, the system of regulation became more general and it involved, unlike previously, the fixation of both the minimum and maximum rates. Under this system which continues to prevail now also, while the maximum rate is prescribed on deposits of maturities upto 90 days, the minimum rate is prescribed on deposits of maturities beyond 90 days. In practice, the minimum and maximum rates have mostly turned out to be the fixed rates actually paid by the banks on respective maturities, i.e., no bank pays less than the maximum or more than the minimum rates stipulated by the RBI.

The deposit rates of co-operative banks came under the purview of these regulatory measures not until 1974. Since then, co-operative banks also have been paying on their deposits interest rates prescribed by the RBI. They are now allowed to pay interest rates which are higher by certain percentage point(s) (normally, one-half of one per cent) over the rates prescribed for the respective maturity of deposits of commercial banks. As a result of this policy interest rates of commercial and cooperative banks have come to be linked, and changes in them have been effected simultaneously since 1974.

The lending rates of commercial banks have also been controlled by the RBI in terms of the Banking Regulation Act, 1949 since 1960 in the form of prescribing minimum, maximum, dual, and differential interest rates. It prescribes different minimum and maximum rates depending upon the size of banks, the size and purpose of advance, the type of borrower, the nature of security, etc. Similarly, there are separate minimum rates for the general credit and the advances under the selective credit controls, respectively.

The lending rates of co-operative banks were regulated indirectly or through 'suasion' till 1980. As co-operative banks, at all levels of their three-tier structure, depend on the RBI for concessional financial resources, while they were always 'expected' to charge only the 'reasonable' rates to the borrowers from the agriculture and allied activities, in case of finance for production and marketing activities of the cottage and small-scale industries, the terms of concessional refinance stipulated certain conditions about the rates to be charged by them to these borrowers. In 1980, the loan rates of co-operative banks also came to be statutorily regulated and now all the lending rates of these banks are under the direct statutory control of the RBI.

Interest rates on deposits accepted by non-banking non-financial companies, and non-banking financial and miscellaneous companies, which were completely free till recently, have become subject to a ceiling fixed by the Government of India and the RBI, respectively with effect from the beginning of the financial year, 1981-82. There are certain notable points about this regulation. Firstly, unlike in the case of bank deposits, in place of different ceiling rates for deposits of different maturities, there is only one ceiling rate which is stipulated, and the companies are free to pay any interest rate upto the ceiling irrespective of the maturity of deposits. As a result, the companies have a greater degree of flexibility than the banks in respect of the mobilisation of deposits. Secondly, while the cost of deposit-resources of non-banking financial companies is regulated, their lending rates, unlike banks, are not subject to regulation. This also puts such companies in a favourable position *vis-a-vis* banks.

There is a ceiling on the level of call rate also which is imposed by the Indian Banks' Association since 1973. Interest rates on post-office saving bank, time, and other deposits, other small savings media, Treasury bills and government dated securities are all directly fixed by the Government of India. Interest rates on industrial debentures and dividends on preference shares are subject to a ceiling prescribed by the Controller of' Capital Issues. The loan rates of the statutory financial institutions, although not subject to any direct control, also can be said to be regulated through 'suasion'. To the extent that these institutions supply credit to the public sector, small scale units, units in the backward regions, and for other priority purposes, their interest rates are bound to be influenced by the thinking of the authorities about the 'appropriate' cost of finance; and this influence must be strong because of the government ownership of these institution. Similarly, institutions like IDBI impose ceilings on rates to be charged by the primary lenders who obtain refinance and rediscounting facilities from them. It is only the rates of return on ordinary shares and units, bazar bill rate, and hundi rate which appear to be free from any formal and direct control of the authorities in India.

Table 1: Interest Differentials in India

Rates ɑ / Year	51-52	55-56	60-61	65-66	70-71	75-76	80-81	81-82
1) TB-call money	0.17	-0.23	- 1.59	-2.76	-2.88	-5.95	- 2.52	-4.36
2) Bank rate (1 year) deposit	1.46	0.95	0.56	0.0	-0.38	1.0	1.0	1.5
3) SBI Advances (1 year) deposit	2.27	1.45	1.56	1.50	2.87	6.0	8.5	8.0
4) Bank deposit:								
i) (3-year)-(1-year)	-	-	0.25	0.25	0.50	1.0	2.0	1.5
ii) (5-year)-(1-year)	-	-	0.75	1.0	1.25	2.0	2.0	2.5
iii) (5-year)-(3-year)	-	-	0.50	0.75	0.75	1.0	0.0	1.0
5) Debenture coupon (5-year) deposit	-	-	3.0	0.0	0.75	-0.5	3.5	4.0
6) 5 to 15 years government bonds (5-year) deposit	-	-	-0.62	-1.74	-2.67	-4.25	-3.73	-4.59
7) Government bonds:								
i) Medium term/ short term	-	-	0.24	0.11	0.48	0.12	0.9	0.54
ii) Long term/ medium term	-	-	0.2	-0.19	0.57	0.0	0.69	0.81
8) IDBI 1oans-SBI advances	-	-	-	0.50	0.0	-3.0	-3.58	-2.5
9) IDBI loans-Debenture coupon	-	-	0 to -0.5	1.0	0.5	0.5 to 1.0	0.5	-1.0

NOTES: Deposits refer to commercial banks' fixed deposits; IDBI loan rate refers to its prime lending rate; TB is Treasury Bills.

Thus, almost every interest rate in India is now very closely administered in the form of fixation of either the specific, or minimum or maximum (ceiling) or dual or differential level by the government or RBI or Controller of Capital Issues or the Indian Banks' Association, etc, through the exercise of statutory powers or voluntary agreements or suasion. While the effect of such a policy on the behaviour of interest rates themselves is discussed in the following sub-section, its wider effects on the economic activity as a whole will be analysed subsequently.

Effects on Interest Rates and Credit Control Mechanism

Statistical series over a long period of time are available in India only for a few interest rates, although the situation here is probably not as bad as in many other developing countries. It may be mentioned here that the RBI used to publish only a few money rates of interest in its Annual Report on Currency and Finance till 1972-73; this practice underwent a welcome change with effect from 1974-75 when it started publishing data on many short-term and long-term interest rates in the 'Structure of Interest Rates in India' Table. But even now, this Table does not include information about interest rates on the post-office and other small savings media including provident fund, interest rates in the co-operative banking and credit structure, commercial banks' saving deposit rate, interest rate which the RBI pays on excess reserves, etc. This short-coming needs to be corrected. The behaviour of a few selected nominal and real rates of interest over the period of more than a hundred years (1870-1983) is depicted in Figures 1 and 2.

(i) It would be observed from Figure 1 that there has been quite a bit of increase in interest rates during the sub-period 1950-83, but the major part of this increase has occurred after 1974. [6] Incidentally, it may also be noted that there have been very few marked fluctuations in interest rates during this period. The American experience, [7] and our own in the past show that when interest rates are free, they tend to fluctuate much more in upward and downward directions.

An increase in interest rates just mentioned has been the result of periodic 'mark-ups' but we do not know how the authorities have, from time to time, decided upon the extent, frequency, timing, etc., of these 'mark-ups'. We do not have any enunciation from the authorities about the principles or considerations and the weightage given to them, which underlie their 'mark-up' decisions. It appears that decisions in respect of changes in interest rates are mostly being taken quite haphazardly, in an *ad hoc* manner, and inadequately. Consequently, the levels of interest rates, differences in different rates, and changes in both of these have usually not been related to the considerations of risk, liquidity, maturity, demand for and supply of funds, commodity prices, etc. The concept of adjacency of different financial assets in the sense of the existence of well-defined differentials in interest rates (returns) on them when they are arranged in the descending or ascending order on the basis of their major attributes does not appear to have much meaning in India (see Table 1). For example, it is difficult to understand why interest rates on time deposits of the same maturity with the post-offices and banks should differ much, and why such a difference, if it exists, should fluctuate greatly from year to year. The post-office deposits rates have been mostly higher than the bank deposits rates, and their difference has varied between zero to 2.0, and -0.5 to 2.75 percentage points in case of one to three-year, and five-year deposits, respectively during 1969-70 and 1981-82. Similarly, interest rates on small savings media have been higher than those on the government securities of comparable maturities. There is no reason why the coupon rates on the bonds of IDBI, IFC, EXIM Bank, etc., should be higher than those on government securities. While the lending rates of the EXIM Bank have ranged between 9 to 12 per cent, those of commercial banks have ranged between 4 to 18 per cent. The phenomenon of short-term interest rates exceeding the long-term rates unrelated to the cyclical swings in business activity is also to be explained in terms of the discretionary controls in this context.

Figure 1:
Nominal Interest Rates in India, 1870-1983

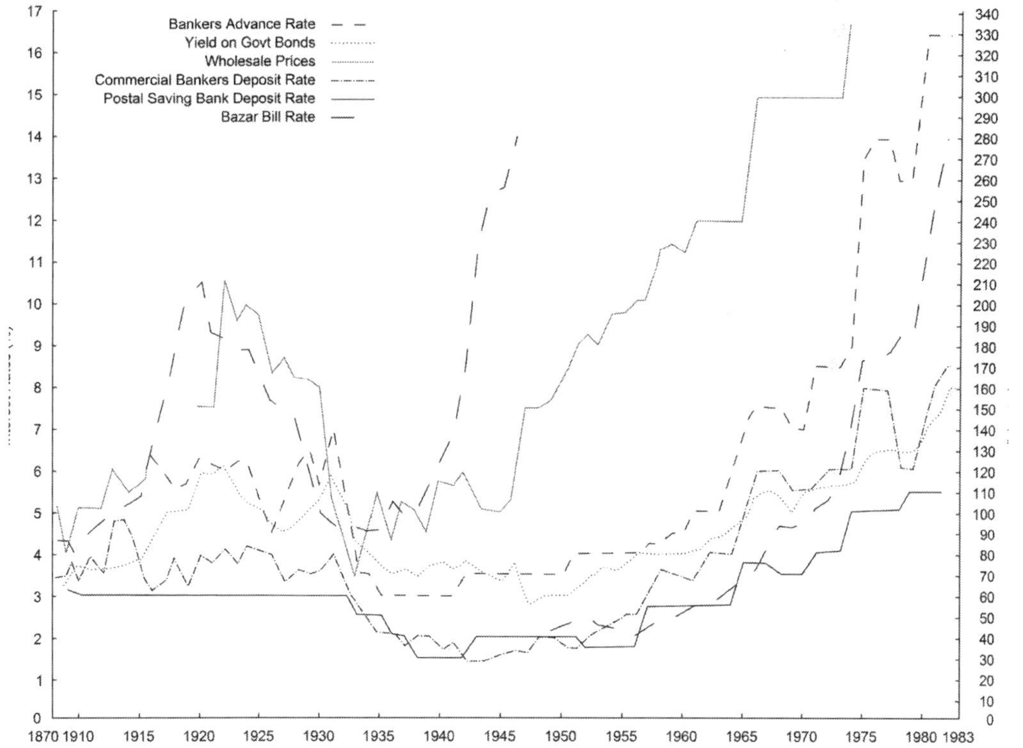

(ii) In spite of some increase, interest rates during the era of regulation can be said to have been artificially maintained at lower levels than what they otherwise would have been and what they should have been. The following theoretical and empirical evidence supports this viewpoint:

Figure 2:
Real Interest Rates in India, 1870-1983

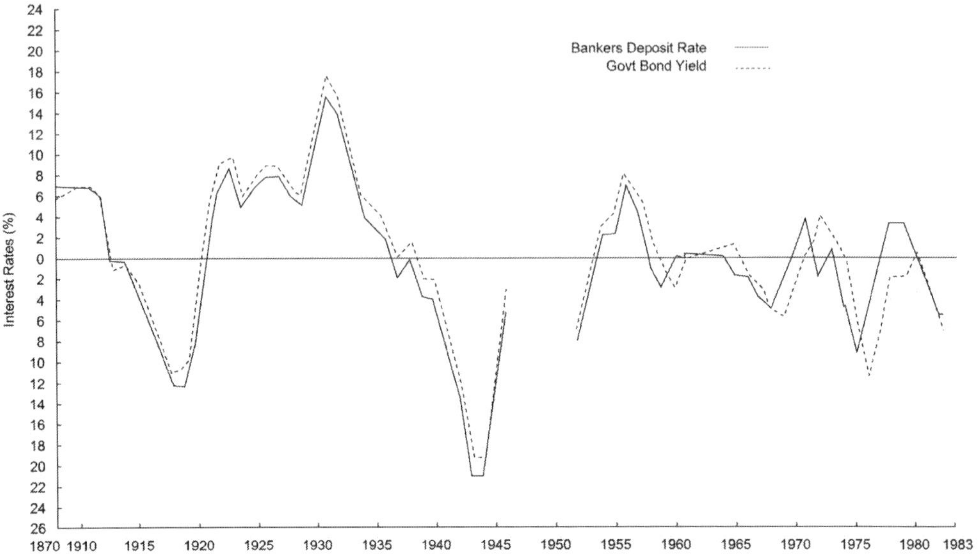

(a) The very objective of imposing discretionary controls has explicitly been to keep interest rates at lower levels as in the cases of deposit rates, rates on finance for fixed investment, rates on government debt and loans to the priority sectors, etc.

(b) Sometimes controls were introduced precisely when interest rates determined by the market forces reached the levels which were 'regarded' as 'unduly' high by the concerned authorities. In such cases, interest rates have been definitely kept at lower levels through the imposition of ceilings. For example, the call money rate. The experience in other countries such as UK and US shows that whenever the policy of pegging of interest rates was abandoned, there was a sharp increase in those rates.

(c) The rates which have not been subject or amenable to regulations have been consistently higher than the controlled rates. For example, the bazar bill rate, SBI hundi rate, and other rates in the unorganised sector of the financial markets.

(d) While judging whether interest rates in a given period are high or low, they have been very often compared with their historical level. The application of the idea of historicism to interest rates has given rise to notions such as the 'band of feasible rates', [8] or the 'gears of interest rates'. [9] It is argued that there is some 'normal' level of and changes in interest rates the idea about which can be obtained from the level of and changes in interest rates which occur in quiet times and which are consistent with the maintenance of organised markets. The rates of interest cannot rise or fall in any given period very far from this 'normal' level, except for a brief period. Some people in India have conveniently and successfully made a case for lower interest rates on the basis of such notions. They have argued that interest rates in the post-independence period have been higher than their historical level, and, therefore, they should be (further) reduced.

Table 2: Interest Rates in India and Other Countries

Country	1977			1981		
	DR	MMR	GBY	DR	MMR	GBY
1) India	9.0	10.18.	6.32	10.0	8.61	7.15
2) US	6.0	5.54	7.67	12.0	16.38	13.72
3) UK	7.0	8.06	12.73	14.0	13.29	14.74
4) Germany	3.0	4.37	6.20	7.50	12.11	10.38
5) France	9.5	9.22	9.61	9.5	15.26	15.66
6) Canada	7.50	7.33	8.70	14.66	17.72	15.22
7) Sweden	8.0	9.96	9.74	11.0	14.35	13.49
8) Italy	11.50	14.03	14.62	19.0	19.60	20.58
9) Japan	4.25	-	7.33	5.5	7.69	8.66
10) New Zealand	10.0	-	9.23	13.0	-	12.83
11) South Africa	9.0	7.87	10.96	13.50	9.80	12.56
12) Pakistan	10.0	10.87	9.27	10.0	9.27	9.40

NOTATION:
DR = Discount Rate of the Central Bank; MMR = Money Market Rate; GBY = Government Bond Yield.

SOURCE: International Monetary Fund, International Financial Statistics, various issues.

The current interest rates policy cannot be determined mainly on the basis of a historical approach because it is a static one. But even by historical standards, interest rates in India have been held at lower levels after 1950. It would be clearly observed from Figure 1 that excepting the period of 1933-50, [10] banks' advances rate, for example, has been lower during 1951-70 and only slightly higher during 1970-75 than its own level during 1870-1933. The same thing is also more or less true of other controlled rates such as banks' deposits rates, government bond yield, etc. These rates can justifiably be deemed to have been effectively still lower (than what data show) if we take into account, as we must, the fact that the expected or planned rates of economic growth and capital formation have been far higher after 1950 than in the historical period. While the rate of gross capital formation during 1861 to 1929 was about 5 to 7 per cent, [11] it was about 12 to 20 per cent during 1951-75. If the relevant factors such as the relative demand for credit and finance, the size of government borrowing programme, deficit financing, balance of payments difficulties, the rate of inflation, etc., were freely allowed to influence interest rates, the latter would have been much higher than their historical as well as current levels. Further, if the history of interest rates is important, how can we forget the history of interest rates in the unorganised and semi-unorganised sectors of the economy?

Table 3: Features of Savings Behaviour in India (Annual Averages)

Period / Feature	1951-52 to 54-55	1955-56 to 59-60	1960-61 to 64-65	1965-66 to 69-70	1970-71 to 74-75	1975-76 to 79-80
1) Net savings as percentage of NDP	5.82	8.34	10.3	11.80	14.28	19.48
2) Corporate saving						
a) as percentage of total saving	7.91	5.98	8.09	3.17	6.24	3.26
b) as percentage of NDP	0.46	0.49	0.81	0.37	0.91	0.64
3) Household saving						
a) in financial assets as percentage of NDP						
b) in physical assets as percentage of NDP	1.16	3.17	3.65	3.37	4.96	7.48
c) in currency as percentage of total household	2.96	3.31	2.78	6.14	6.23	7.47
saving	7.17	20.49	26.20	25.36	19.66	17.74

SOURCE:
RAO, V. K. R. V., "India's National Income, 1950-80", Sage Publications, New Delhi, 1983.

(e) If the interest rates are not administered, the secular and cyclical changes in the commodity prices act as a major determinant of variations in the nominal interest rates so that the real interest rates maintain appropriate positive levels. As it would be seen in Figure 2, [12] the real rates of interest in India during the post-1950 period have been mostly negative; and whenever. they were positive, they were mostly around the low level of 2 to 4 per cent per annum. [13]

It is likely to be pointed out that the real rates of interest were negative in the earlier period also when the rates were not controlled. It has to be accepted that whenever the rate of inflation has been very high (around 25 per cent and above), it has not been possible for the nominal interest rates to keep pace with such price changes even though there were no controls on their movements. This long-term experience in India suggests that the Fisher effect may not be observed in the period of hyper-inflation, and the principle stated in the previous' paragraph may be valid only in periods of normal mild inflation. Having accepted this, it may still be noted that before 1951, real interest rates were negative only during war-years; they were positive and at quite high levels (after 10 to 18 per cent) in many other years. Thus, it is possible to explain, at least partly, negative or low-positive levels of real interest rates in the planning era in terms of discretionary controls on their movements.

(f) The interest rates in India have tended to be lower than in many other countries. Subject to the imperfections of international comparison of interest rates on account of differences in the nature of financial assets, definition, financial organisation, etc., it is clear from Table 2 that interest rates in India have often been maintained at much lower levels than in capital-abundant countries such as US, UK, Canada, France, Germany, Sweden or countries with similar inflationary experience, *viz.*, Italy or countries with similar controlled interest rates systems, *viz.*, New Zealand and South Africa. In the light of this evidence, the argument sometimes heard in certain quarters that India is a country with the highest interest rates can be said to be politically motivated.

(iii) Apart from maintaining interest rates at low levels and haphazardly determined differentials, the present policy has resulted in the sacrifice of the simplicity in the working of interest rate mechanism. The authorities have had to administratively announce the fixation of an unbelievably large number and vast range of interest rates. We have not one but a band of bank rates, we also have a large number of bank deposits and advances rates directly fixed by the authorities. The interest rates structure has consequently assumed an exceedingly complex and unmanageable character – the fact which has now been admitted by the RBI itself. The so-called simplification which it introduced in March 1981 is nothing more than tinkering with the existing system 14 because it has completely retained the principle of direct fixation of almost every single interest rate in the economy.

(iv) The direct administration of interest rates has been progenitive of a complex system of quantitative credit controls or ceilings as a means of monetary policy and distribution of available finance among different borrowers, sectors, uses, etc. The controls on the price of finance have begotten controls on the quantity of finance also. From the point of view of the monetary policy, the system has been caught in a vicious circle – the discretionary controls on interest rates have led to the need for imposing quantitative credit ceilings or targets which, in turn, have resulted in the atrophy of those techniques of monetary control which are appropriate for and consistent with the competitive, efficient, and dynamic financial organisation, and this has further perpetuated the dependence on the quantitative or physical or selective or discretionary techniques of monetary control.

The Rationale of the Present System

Why have the authorities here and elsewhere imposed controls on the level and movements of interest rates? Before we discuss the considerations which prompt such an action, let it be noted that usually it is the result of a fear that otherwise interest rates would be much higher than 'desirable'. In other words, the direct regulation of interest rates is mostly resorted with a view to maintain them at low levels which, in turn, are regarded necessary for certain reasons. In such cases, the reasons for keeping interest rates low and for administering them tend to coincide.

The present day policy of controlled interest rates can be said to have been historically preceded by the anti-usury laws which either completely prohibited the charging of any interest or which sought to control it to a particular level. Such a policy was largely based on the moral and other extra-economic considerations, while the present day policy has come to depend upon quite a complex set of arguments for its introduction and continued existence.

(i) In many developing countries including India, low interest rates have been regarded desirable in order to induce a higher rate of capital formation, particularly fixed capital formation. This explains why the long-term interest rates have been kept at such low levels. The belief in the theories of economic development which gives paramount importance to the high rate of capital formation as the most critical development factor has shaped such a policy.

It is curious that while one view has argued for low interest rates for encouraging investment (which implies interest-sensitivity of investment), another view has argued for the same policy because demand for investment and bank credit is said to be inelastic to changes in interest rates. In more general terms, it has been argued that in developing countries, price incentives are weak and few people there calculate and take decisions in terms of cost and return. In such a situation, high interest rates merely lead to an increase in transactions, velocity of money, increase in difficulties of the productive sectors, particularly more vulnerable sectors such as small-scale industries, small borrowers, exports, etc, and increase in cost inflation. All this happens without curbing investment because, in sheltered markets, increased interest costs would be passed on to consumers in the form of higher prices.

(ii) The exigencies of government finance have perhaps constituted the most weighty consideration behind the actual adoption of the system of administered interest rates. In planned economies and welfare states, since the government and public sector are expected to play a very big role in economic activities, the financing needs of the government turn out to be on a huge scale. The government raises funds *inter alia* through the sale of government securities and small savings media. It is argued that if the interest rates are kept low and stable through controls, the cost of public debt would be low, and there would be a stability on the government securities market which is conducive for debt placement. Further, the Indian experience shows that under the present system, the government is in a position to manipulate rates in such a way as to induce the flow of funds in the media it desires to promote more. In the past few years, the Government of India has been paying higher interest rates on small savings than on comparable long-term marketable debt because thereby it can reduce the amount to be floated on the market which has certain inconveniences as compared with the non-marketable debt.

(iii) It is also argued that in a planned economy, the priorities and objectives of development are determined by the authorities. For example, they may desire to encourage exports, setting up of industries in backward or zero-industry areas, etc. If the course of development

Table 4: The Effect of Interest Rate on Investment Decisions in India

Sr. No.	Independent Variables										
	Intercept	AV	R	AC	PE	FE	TX	R^{-2}	DW	Functional form	Sector
1)	-2755.5	0.139*	434.8	-	-	0.686*	-	0.995	1.53	Nominal	EE
		(173.18)	(20.17)			(25.82)					
2)	1859.2	0.114*	47.15	-	-	-1.21	-	0.585	1.25	Real	EE
		(21.53)	(2.18)			(8.12)					
3)	-191.2	0.328*	109.74	-	-	0.559*	-	0.973	1.20	Nominal	PS
		(21.03)	(6.75)			(0.82)					
4)	1160.6	0.266*	-13.85	-	-	0.726*	-	0.761	1.28	Real	PS
		(21.1)	(1.4)			(3.97)					
5)	-17.87	0.032	- 0.45	684.5	-	-	0.32**	0.90	1.45	Nominal	PCS
		(1.88)	(0.15)	(2.76)			(4.1)				
6)	-1277.7	Eliminated	284.34	-	6.05	-	-	0.766	0.87	Nominal	EE
			(83.23)		(0.22)						
7)	144.94	0.021**	-10.26	-	6.68	-	-	0.12	1.74	Real	EE
		(4.28)	(0.57)		(0.21)						
8)	- 1863.5	-0.18	393.3	-	Eliminated	-	-	0.6	1.33	Nominal	PC
		(4.3)	(10:84)								
9)	217.8	0.11*	-13 .26	-	-17.64	-	-	0.09	1.33	Real	PC
		(4.4)	(0.68)		(1.22)						
10)	5.09	-0.02	-0.14	16.41	0.73*	-	-	0.44	1.74	Real	PCS
		(0.13)	(0.85)	(0.01)	(16.49)						

NOTES: Functions 1 to 5 and 6 to 10 are for total fixed investment and inventory investment, respectively; AV = Accelerator variable measured by Gross Domestic Product or Gross Public Sector Product or Sales; R = The long-term or short-term rate of interest; AC = Availability of Credit; PE = Price expectations measured by one-year lagged inflation rate; FE = Foreign exchange availability; TX = Tax factor; Figures in brackets are F-ratios; EE is Entire Economy; PS is Public Sector; PCS is Private Corporate Sector.

is to be in keeping with such priorities, the provision of credit with certainty and at low cost to the priority areas becomes necessary. This is achieved through the system of administered interest rates.

A related argument is that money and capital markets in economies like India's are characterised by varieties of imperfections. As a result, certain types of borrowers are discriminated against with regard to the availability, cost, and other terms of finance. In order to remove such discrimination against and disability of certain borrowers, the discretionary control of not only the cost but also the availability of finance becomes necessary. In a wider sense, such a policy is said to help to improve the distribution of income in favour of low-income and disadvantaged groups of society. The policies such as 'differential interest rates' have been adopted specifically for such a purpose.

(iv) Many reasons – sometimes quite contradictory to each other-have been advanced for controlling interest rates on bank deposits and advances. It is felt that if deposit rates are free, there may be unduly keen competition among banks for resource mobilisation which would increase their cost, reduce their profitability, and, in certain cases, lead to bank failures. Inter-bank agreement in India, Regulation Q in US, and inter-bank cartel in UK have been the result of such a reasoning. However, there has also been an another view that deposit rates of banks need to be regulated because otherwise they would reap exhorbitant profits by not raising these rates *pari passu* with an increase in their lending rates. The regulation Q also had the objective of limiting the expansion of bank credit which banks could bring about by the vigorous mobilisation of deposits by offering higher rates of interest.

In India, some of the reasons behind the control of deposit and lending rates of commercial and co-operative banks which have been officially mentioned [15] are: (a) To avoid unhealthy competition for both borrowing and deposit accounts. (b) To maintain a kind of uniformity of interest rates on these accounts of all types of banks. (c) To keep deposit rates in alignment with the lending rates of banks and with other market rates of interest. (d) To aid deposit mobilisation. (e) To lengthen the maturity structures of deposits by widening the spread between the long-term and short-term rates of fixing the minimum rate(s) for long-term maturities and ceiling rate(s) for short-term maturities. (f) To impinge upon both the demand for and supply of bank credit. While the prescription of minimum lending rates was meant to ensure that increases in RBI refinance/rediscount rates were transmitted to the ultimate borrowers, the ceiling rates were expected to discourage banks from borrowing more from the RBI because now they would not be in a position to transfer higher refinance cost to the borrowers. (g) To enable the authorities to avoid frequent changes in the bank rate and to achieve the results of changes in the bank rate by changing deposit and lending rates directly.

It may bear repetition to say that the case for regulation of rates being considered here involves contradictions. The deposit rates are to be allegedly regulated because the free rates would both reduce and increase banks' profitability; the regulation would both increase and decrease the deposit resources of banks; the regulation of lending rates would both ensure and hamper the transmission of higher refinance cost to the ultimate borrowers.

(v) It has been argued that when interest rates are free, changes in monetary techniques such as discount rate, open market operations, etc, might not bring about any material changes in the entire interest rates structure or they may be accompanied by undesirable movements in the market rates. It is pointed out that the authorities lack empirical evidence about the extent and direction of changes in market rates when the traditional techniques of monetary control are employed. In other words, the effectiveness and predictability of monetary measures are very limited when interest rates are free. On the other hand, if the market rates are changed directly with or without changes in the bank rate, etc, the effect of such a policy on the economic activity would be greater and more certain. In short, the administered system of interest rates allegedly enhances the predictability and efficacy of monetary policy.

We shall examine the foregoing arguments and discuss our case for free and higher rates of interest in the next section. It may only be noted here that these arguments suffer from a lack of consistency, and they largely arise from beliefs in certain theories of economic development which are quite questionable, profession of the philosophy of planning and socialism, distrust of market forces due to the alleged existence of imperfections and low price elasticities, presence pf multiple vested interests, and simply myopia.

III. The Case for an Alternative System

The reconstruction of the system of administered interest rates – designated by some as the system of "financial repression" or the one lacking "financial deepening" – has highlighted some of its defects and has indirectly shown the need for "financial reform" by replacing it with the system of free and higher interest rates. We now develop this subject further by discussing directly the beneficial effects of the alternative system on various spheres of economic activity such as the volume and pattern of savings, efficiency of the financial system, efficiency of investment and allocation of resources, efficacy of monetary policy, and by showing the weaknesses of some of the arguments which have been advanced in support of the existing system. While doing this, in addition to presenting qualitative arguments, we have attempted to furnish econometric evidence on a few major relationships or propositions posited in Shaw and Mckinnon model referred to earlier. However, given the nature of the subject-matter, the discussion has to be primarily qualitative. This has been shown by the lack of success of the attempts of Fry [16] and Galbis [17] to estimate this model for the Asian and Latin American countries, respectively. [18] In order to indicate the relevance of the econometric part of our study, it would be useful to state here for ready reference the gist of this model, and the hypotheses to be tested by us.

It has been argued that savings at a given level of income are a function of the real rate of interest, and administratively determined nominal interest rate holds the real rate below its equilibrium level. This holds saving and investment below what they would be at high real rate of interest. The ceiling on interest rates also results in non-price rationing of investible funds. The raising of nominal interest rates increases saving, investment, and the average efficiency of investment. This leads to increase in income and further increase in saving. The impacts of such a policy on growth are multiplicative. Accordingly, we shall test the following hypotheses:

(i) The rate of saving is expected to be positively related to the rate of interest. If this is empirically validated, the case for higher interest rates becomes strong provided the objective of economic policy is to increase the rate of saving.

(ii) Normally, the rate of interest is expected to be negatively related to investment. When this happens, investment decisions are taken on the basis of rational cost considerations and the efficiency of investment is high. But in the economy with the system of administered interest rates, since interest rates are kept low, they may be positively related to investment. If this is found to be true, it would mean that investment activity and the allocation of capital are not being conducted in an efficiency manner.

(iii) It follows from (ii) that the capital formation in low interest economies would be found to be playing an insignificant role in the determination of national income.

(iv) The low rates of interest result in low rates of economic growth.

Empirical results of the testing of these hypotheses would be reported at the appropriate points in the discussion of our case to which we now return.

Table 5: Capital-Output Ratios in India at Constant (1960-61 = 100) Prices

Period	Average C/O Ratio	Incremental C/O Ratio
1950-54	2.50	3.51
1955-59	2.71	4.85
1960-64	2.92	3.28
1965-69	3.43	5.41
1970-74	3.88	11.48
1975-77	4.20	6.42

NOTE: The Figures are averages for the respective periods.
SOURCE: Rao, V K R V, op cit, P 154.

Promotion of Savings

In developing countries, there is definitely a case for higher interest rates because they play an important role in raising the rate of savings, and in the institutionalisation or financialisation or activisation of those savings. The strength of this argument depends upon the magnitude of interest elasticity of savings. We, therefore, estimated a few savings functions for the entire Indian economy for the period 1951-52 to 1979-80 the two of which are reported below:

$$GSR = 5.61 + 0.0671\ GDP + 0.0048\ PCGDP^* + 0.7987\ R^* - 0.155\ PE^* + 0.187\ GSR_{-1}$$

$$(1.696) \quad (7.28) \quad (6.52) \quad (4.67) \quad (0.834) \qquad (1)$$

$$\bar{R}^2 = 0.89008;\ D\ W = 2.13469$$

$$GSR = 5.11 + 0.0042\ PCGDP^{*} + 0.7576\ R^{*} - 0.1129\ PE^{**} + 0.2868\ GSR^{**}_{-1}$$
$$(5.78) \qquad (5.749) \quad (3.022) \qquad (2.218) \qquad (2)$$
$$\bar{R}^2 = 0.88689;\ D\ W = 2.11339$$

Where, GSR is the gross saving rate; GDP is the growth rate in gross domestic product; PCGDP is the per capita GDP; R is the one-year deposit rate of interest; PE is the measure of price expectations; GSR_{-1} is the one-year lagged dependent variable; figures in brackets are F-ratios; all variables are in nominal terms; the functions are in non-logarithmic form; * and ** indicate the level of significance at 1 to 5 and 10 per cent, respectively. [19]

It would be seen that these fits are very good and the rate of interest has quite high and significant coefficient; it may be noted 'that the performance of rate of interest is better than that of income. This and the fact that the price expectations are shown to discourage savings strongly suggest the need for a higher interest rates policy in India.

It may be counter-argued that this is unnecessary in view of the good savings performance of the Indian economy in the past 30 years. The rate of gross savings has increased substantially over this period from about 10 per cent in 1951-52 to about 21 per cent in 1979-80. It may be argued that if interest rates in India are regarded to have been low, they have apparently not discouraged people from saving. We feel that this is an euphoric view of the matter, and it would be harmful if interest rates are continued to be kept low on the basis of such a reasoning. There are many other important features of savings behaviour in India which show the need for an increase in the reward for savings in future. Table 3 contains an useful information on some of these aspects of savings in India.

Firstly, it is necessary to note the time profile of an increase in the saving ratio. While it took as many as 20 years to increase by merely six percentage points during 1950-51 to 1969-70, it increased by 2.48 and 5.20 percentage points during the next two five-year periods, respectively. Thus, if we exclude the last ten years of the period under discussion, particularly the last five years which experienced a substantial increase in interest rates, the rate of growth in saving in India has been very small indeed.

The two other major factors, apart from an increase in interest rates, which have contributed to a substantial increase in the saving rate during 1970s have been the phenomenal increase in the number of bank branches and the amount of foreign remittances. From the point of view of the future, while the contribution of one of them is subject to a high degree of uncertainty and fluctuations, that of the other has almost reached its limit. Therefore, it has been rightly pointed out that we cannot take for granted the continuing increase in the rate of saving in the last quinquennial period and the establishment of a trend rate of growth which includes this period. [20] In such a situation, the offering of an attractive rate of return retains a crucial importance in the policy of promotion of savings.

Secondly, deposits with commercial and co-operative banks account for about half of total household sector savings in financial assets. Further, current account deposits constitute about 20 to 30 per cent of total bank deposits. Now, to the extent that a part [21] of the current account deposits is the result of created credit rather than genuine saving, the figures on saving ratio in India need to be adjusted downward to obtain a realistic estimate of the level of genuine savings in the country.

Thirdly, in spite of good progress in the institutionalisation of savings so far, there is still a great scope for further progress in this respect. The proportion .of household saving in the form of currency is still quite high; it has been around 18 to 26 per cent of total household saving. Similarly, the physical assets still account for about half of total household saving. If this preference for idle saving is to be reduced, the return on financial assets must become attractive both in nominal and real terms.

Fourthly, the contribution of the corporate sector in this context has been extremely poor. Its saving rate has been about 0.5 per cent, and its contribution to total saving has declined from 7.91 per cent to 3.26 per cent over the period under study. The easy availability of cheap credit from banks and term lending financial institutions has definitely been one of the important causes for this poor savings performance of the corporate sector. The estimation of the determinants of saving of the Medium and Large Public Limited Companies (equation 3) and Medium and Large Private Limited Companies (equation 4) shows that, given the profits after tax or cash flow, while the companies have disregarded interest rate (which has the wrong sign) as a relevant factor, they have changed their retention policy in the light of the availability of external funds. [22]

$$RR = 33.99 + 2.65\ PAT^{*} + 0.07\ FWI - 0.06\ ES - 0.68\ CF - 0.14\ P + 46.57\ T$$

$$(27.84) \qquad (0.931)\ R \qquad (0.23) \quad (0.10) \quad (0.64) \quad (0.34)$$

$$R^2 = 0.9645 \qquad (3)$$

$$RR = 82.52 + 11.98\ CF^{*} - 1.10\ FWI - 3.77\ ES^{*} - 0.77\ R + 0.23\ p^{*} + 2.21\ T^{*}$$

$$(14.5) \qquad (4.16) \quad (10.82) \quad (0.03) \quad (5.98) \quad (4.53)$$

$$R^2 = 0.8977 \qquad (4)$$

Where, RR is the retention ratio; PAT is profits after tax; CF is the cash flow; FWI is the investment in fixed and working capital; ES is the external sources of funds, R is the debenture yield; P is the price level; T is the time variable; figures in brackets are F-ratios; functions are in nominal non-logarithmic form; and the period of study is 1961-62 to 1974-75.

Finally, in spite of a substantial increase, can we say that the rate of saving in India has been at the required level? If it was so, there would not have been the need for so heavy and increasing dependence on foreign capital, credit creation, deficit financing, and the credit rationing on a continuous basis. It is true that a greater efficiency in the use of financial resources and physical capital would have reduced this dependence. However, as we shall show, the levei of efficiency just referred to also has been low partly on account of lower interest rates. Thus, higher interest rates become necessary both to increase (or to maintain) the rate of saving and to improve the efficiency of investment. If the former alone occurs unaccompanied by the latter, it involves a permanent sacrifice for the consumers because savings then do not contribute to the acceleration of the growth of income.

Efficiency of the Financial System

The present system has been promotive of inefficiency because the interest rate mechanism as an impersonal, neutral, and anonymous allocator of finance has been replaced by the arbitrary and discretionary means of doing the same. The command over financial resources now depends upon the ability to offer security, political pressure, the bigness of size arid ability to outmanoeuvre both other seekers of credit and credit controls, benefits to the loan officers, etc. The resources allocated in such a manner are very often used for either low-yield safe investments or for socially less useful or even detrimental purposes. There is also very often an over-capitalisation of units. The reality of this point is so well-established in India that we need not further belabour it here. The evidence accumulated by, among others, the Dutt Committee, Dehejia Committee, Thndon Committee, etc, is enough to emphasise the need to change the present system.

It is high time to realise that imperfections in markets cannot be corrected by imposing a set of other imperfections merely because the latter emanate from the authorities. The misuse of the differential interest scheme, the appropriation of credit meant for a variety of small borrowers by the big borrowers through devices such as creating fictitious or linked (captive) small units, etc., point to the dangers of non-price rationing of credit. It is acceptable that some kind of action was necessary to help farmers, small village and cottage industries, other small borrowers in the face of market imperfections. But it could have been done within the ambit of the usual legal powers of the government, through 'suasion', and through creating certain 'counterrailing' institutions which functioned on the basis of normal economic and cost considerations.

The entire array of interventions by the authorities has led to the development of an inefficient financial system in an another way also. The ceiling on the bank deposit rates has adversely affected the growth of bank deposits. If there was no large-scale expansion of bank branches, it is doubtful whether banks would have experienced the rate of growth of deposits which they actually did (between 16 to 24 per cent per year) after nationalisation. On the other hand, deposits with the non-banking companies have grown at comparable or even higher rates in many years; these deposits have grown at the annual rate of 20 to 78 per cent during 1978-82; this rate perhaps would have been still higher if there was no ceiling on the amount of deposits which each company could accept. This along with the fact that the authorities had to impose a ceiling on interest rates on company deposits also shows that the policy of regulating bank deposit rates has been wrong. The new development in the making, i.e., the entry of banks into a more complex and risky business of lease finance within the existing set-up or by setting up subsidiaries reflect banks' desire to bypass the existing regulations on them to provide funds to the corporate sector, and to benefit from the opportunities to lend at higher rates of interest.

The foregoing suggests that non-price credit rationing and ceiling on interest rates result in sub-optimal allocation of funds, the growth of financial institutions or arrangements which tend to divert the flows of funds from channels which are directly amenable to the supervision and influence of the Central Bank, reduction in the profitability of banks, [23] negation of the intentions of the authorities with regard to the sectoral distribution of credit, etc. The experience in the UK in this context has been very much similar. As pointed out by Johnson also, it is, therefore, necessary to reinstate price competition and high rates of interest on both sides of the balance sheets of banks, other financial institutions, and all the users of finance. [24]

Efficiency of Investment

Interest rates policy has a very immediate and decisive influence on the volume and efficiency of capital formation and on economic growth *via* the former. It is natural that in an inefficient financial system like India's promoted by the system of administered interest rates, the process of capital formation should have been greatly wasteful. There is much incontrovertible evidence which establishes this point.

Firstly, investment decisions in India have not been affected by interest rates in the theoretically expected manner; because of the low level of interest rates, they have been positively related to investment. Our unprecedentedly comprehensive study [25] of the interest elasticity of different components of fixed and inventory investments in seventeen industries, the private corporate and public sectors, and the entire economy, during the period 1950-51 to 1977-7826 and its' sub-periods has proved this beyond doubt. A few of a large number of investment functions estimated by us which have been presented for ready reference in Table 4 clearly show that interest rate is mostly positively related to investment, and it has been mostly insignificant statistically whenever it had the negative sign.

Secondly, it can be shown in different ways that an increase in capital formation has contributed little to fostering appropriate techniques of production and increasing labour employment; and that the creation of capital on a massive scale has not resulted in the commensurate growth of output. This is firstly reflected in the high and increasing capital-output and capital-labour ratios which prominently characterise the Indian economy. According to one estimate, the capital-labour ratio has increased from Rs. 3,185 in 1950-51 to Rs. 8,542 in 1980-81; the index of this ratio has increased from 100.0 to 268.0 during the same period. [27] Similarly, while the average capital-output ratio has increased from 2.5 during 1950-54 to 4.2 during 1975-77, the incremental capital output ratio has increased from 3.51 to 6.42 during the same period (see Table 5).

The second way of showing the wasteful use of capital in India is to study changes in its productivity and that of other factors of production. Brahmananda has estimated that the index of net output productivity of capital has declined from 100.0 in 1950-51 to 68 in 1980-

81. Further, on the basis of his study of rates of growth in total factor quantity, net domestic product, and total factor productivity in the Indian economy as a whole and in its various sectors during the planning era, he has shown that "... the contribution of improvements in total factor productivity to sectoral growth seems to have become less and less as we move from the first decade to the third decade ... both traditional and modern activities seem to be losing the productivity growth momentum. The most distressing finding is that ... registered manufacturing and mining, the two sectors on which huge amounts of capital have been invested, indicate a negative contribution from total factor productivity growth:" [28]

Table 6: The Role of Investment in the Growth of Output in India

Sr. No.	Independent Variables								
	Dependent variable	Intercept	I	MS	Time	Pop	R^{-2}	DW	Functional form
1)	NDP	4.41	Eliminated	-0.071 (2.72)	0.009* (128.4)	-	0.9911	2.13	Log-nominal
2)	PSP	4.22	-0.021 (0.05)	-0.092 (0.94)	0.006* (12.69)	-	0.8838	1.65	Log-nominal
3)	SSP	4.08	0.04 (2.62)	-0.21 (4.56)	0.01* (56.24)	-	0.9836	0.69	Log-nominal
4)	GDP	- 24.59	1.155* (8.26)	-0.322 (2.22)	-	8.27 (1.93)	0.27197	2.40	Non-log-nominal
5)	GDP	1.74	-0.418 (1.62)	- 0.011 (0.006)	-	4.15 (0.799)	-0.016	2.19	Non-log-real

NOTES:
The functions 1 to 3 and 4 to 5 are for the period 1950-51 to 1975-76 and 1951-52 to 1979-80, respectively. NDP = Net Domestic Product; PSP = Primary Sector Product; SSP = Secondary Sector Product; GDP = Gross Domestic Product; I = Investment; MS = Money Supply narrowly defined; Pop = Population; Time = Trend variable; Figures in brackets are F-ratios.

In order to clinch this issue, we have estimated the sectoral and aggregate output functions to study the contribution of capital formation to changes in output. They are reported in Table 6. Investment is shown, except in one equation, to be an insignificant or irrelevant determinant of output. It is the trend element which seems to explain variations in output in India. Incidentally, it may be noted that changes in money supply also are irrelevant in this context.

In short, investment activity in India has been taking place irrespective of changes in interest rates. The capital allocation and labour employment decisions do not seem to have been governed at all by the criterion of optimality for production, employment, etc. [29] The productivity of capital has been low in spite of a very young capital stock in the economy barring traditional industries. The present interest rate policy must share the blame for this state of affairs in our country.

The high and free rates of interest would contribute in bringing about a change in this picture. They would lead to an efficient diffusion of modern technology in the sense that the extent relative factor abundance would be taken into account when new techniques are adopted through increased investment. Interest rates have a role to play in promoting employment and appropriate technology by discouraging premature modernisation or mechanisation not only in the industrial but also in the agricultural sector. In this context, while the adverse effects of low interest rates in the industrial sector are well-received, their similar consequences in the agricultural sector tend to be overlooked. It is to be noted that just as there is a need to wean savers and investors in rural areas from assets such as gold, currency, etc, there is also a need to wean the farmers who are already well to do and also whose cash flows are improving as a result of the adoption of new seeds and fertiliser technology away from the mechanisation of agriculture which positively displaces hired labour exacerbating the problems of unemployment and underemployment, i.e., which increases the social cost. Now, higher interest rates on financial assets would help here because the farmers would then find high-yielding alternatives from outside their own enterprises.

The importance of the role of higher interest rates in allocating resources economically and using them more efficiently or productively can be guaged or appreciated from the changing attitude of the authorities in communist countries to the relevance of interest rate policy there. On the basis of his study of the working of monetary systems in these countries, Wilczynski has evidenced that in the beginning, interest rates were virtually ignored in these countries as a weapon of economic policy. Budgetary allocations of finance to enterprises were made without any charge and where interest rate was charged, it used to be very low. This led to extravagant demands for capital, widespread hoarding, and under-utilisation and a wasteful neglect of capital assets. However, the adoption of the intensive growth strategy (as distinct from the extensive one) which heavily depends upon increases in productivity of capital forced these economies to make interest rate an indispensable instrument of sound economic management. Accordingly, in the early 1960s, they introduced capital charges on enterprises and appreciably increased interest rates on saving bank deposits, consumer credit, bank credit to enterprises, and foreign credits. [30]

Efficiency of Monetary Control

From the point of view of the working of monetary policy, the case for the abandonment of the present system and the replacement of interest rates as targets/ indicators and instruments in its place rests on the following theoretical, operational, ethical and other grounds.

The monetary authorities in India have been using bank credit, money supply, bank borrowings from the RBI, seasonal return flows of funds, the growth of resources of banks and their being in 'liquidity blind', etc., as targets/indicators of monetary policy. They have not been in a position to make a conscious and active use of interest rates as targets/indicators because of the policy of administered rates. This has been inconsistent with their theoretical belief with regard to the transmission mechanism of monetary policy, [31] and it has severely undermined the effectiveness of monetary policy in India.

It may be possible to discard the use of interest rates as targets/indicators and instruments of monetary policy if one believes in the exogeneity of money supply, and if the money supply is, in fact, exogeneous. The monetarists do not, for example, bother about interest rates because they hold that the Central Bank can, by itself, completely control changes in money supply. In India, both the conditions just mentioned are not fulfilled. The monetary authorities here do not believe, and rightly so, that in the conduct of monetary policy, money supply alone matters and they can fully control its variations. Further, our empirical study of the process of money supply determination during the period of 1950-51 to 1979-80 has clearly shown that money supply in India is not at all exogeneous. [32] It has, therefore, been both logically inconsistent and wrong on the part of monetary authorities to have rendered interest rates useless as targets/indicators and instruments of monetary policy, and thereby paved the way for the inefficacy of their own policy.

Under the present system, while maintaining that it does not believe in the monetarist approach to monetary policy, in practice, the RBI perforce has been paying almost exclusive attention to money supply and bank credit as targets/indicators of monetary policy. There are reasons why this system ought to be changed if the monetary policy is to be more effective than it has been so far. Notwithstanding its importance in the Indian monetary system, the concentration of efforts to regulate mainly the bank credit has unnecessarily narrowed the ambit of monetary policy. The technique of discretionary quantitative ceilings has further narrowed down this scope because these ceilings are applicable only to certain types of bank credit to the private sector; they exclude bank credit provided for public food procurement, fertilisers and exports credit, and the Credit for all purposes by banks other than scheduled commercial banks. Under the alternative system, the policy would be more effective because changes in interest rates have a more general relevance and pervasive influence; and such changes when brought about through changes in the bank rate, open market operations, etc., would be accompanied by changes in other crucial intermediate variables such as money supply, size and composition of the government debt, etc.

Operationally, it is difficult to turn off and on the flows of bank credit (and money) instantaneously as a result of which there may be an undeterred growth of bank credit for some time even after the tight money policy is announced. This is particularly so when the cash credit/overdraft system of bank credit characterises the monetary system predominantly. Under such circumstances, there is a need for more rapid and larger increases in interest rates for the effectiveness of monetary policy. If the interest rates are also held down artificially in these circumstances, the monetary policy is bound to be ineffective as it has happened in India.

Another operational reason for freeing interest rates is that, as opposed to the quantity of bank credit (and money supply), the information about them is instantaneously available, and it is far more accurate. They, therefore, serve as excellent indicators of goings-on in the monetary system. The effective conduct of monetary policy requires that the authorities receive information on various indicators on week to week basis but at present, banking data are available to the authorities in the final accurate form after quite a significant time-lag. It is well known that these data are substantially revised even after two years or more after their first publication. With the reaching out of bank branches and the working of other financial institutions in the remote areas and given the slow communication and information processing arrangements, it has become impossible to lay hands on the relevant information with the speed required. It is, therefore, necessary to use interest rates as targets/indicators of monetary policy and to free them if they are to perform this role accurately. The experienced central bankers even in the economy such as US have made a strong plea for making a judicious use of interest rates in the conduct of monetary policy because while they are easily and accurately available, there are a number of random forces and estimating errors present in most short-period adjusted data on money and credit; and there are few weeks, even months, in which the reported movements in monetary and credit aggregates are not primarily the result of statistical 'noise'. [33]

The question of monetary control through administered *versus* free interest rate system has engaged attention of the concerned people in UK since long. A careful study of the debate on this issue in that country of the mother of central banking brings out a consensus against the system of discretionary regulation of interest rates and credit ceilings. In 1950s, the Radcliffe Committee was of the opinion that in normal circumstances credit rationing should be avoided because it is subject to substantial slippages, and it would lead to the loss of efficiency in the capital market. Recently, a number of authors [34] have argued against such a system because it is a conspicuous but uncertain way of reducing aggregate effective demand; it reduces the scope of monetary control; it does not guarantee that the rationed out units are the ones which are the least productive; and it is always likely that rationed out units would find their way around loan ceilings. It should be emphasised here with full force that the Bank of England also has always been against such a system. In its testimony to the Radcliffe Committee, it had made clear its distaste for and disinclination against the use of such a system, and it has maintained this position since then. The following quotation from the then Governor of the Bank of England ought to persuade Indian monetary authorities to review their policy of administered interest rates:

" ... quantitative restrictions should be used only when severe restraint is necessary. We are far from happy that we have had to use them so severely and so long not only because of their inherent disadvantages but also because of the strain which their prolonged use places upon the very happy cooperative as distinct from legalistic relationship which exists between Central Bank and commercial banks. It is not an economical and efficient system in which one side is continually looking for loopholes in the control and the other side continually trying to plug them. For all that, the longer ceiling restrictions are in force, the greater the strain on the system." [35]

The foregoing discussion should also show that the argument in support of the present system that it improves the predictability of the response of banks and other components of financial markets in respect of volume and terms of finance supplied by them in the event of changes in Central Bank policy does not stand scrutiny. As far as only interest rates are concerned, although it is true that they surely change when monetary policy is changed (because such changes do not depend upon indirect response-mechanism but are directly effected through fiat), the effectiveness of monetary policy is not increased because the stipulated interest rates do not adequately reflect changes/differences in relevant economic and other determinants of interest rates; and, in addition, changes in interest rates are accompanied by discretionary directives about credit disbursements which also, as shown earlier, are often determined by extra-economic considerations. If interest rates are freed and an active use of more than one technique of monetary control is made, the effect of changes in monetary policy would be greater because it would spread to the entire economic system.

It may be argued that although this is theoretically true, are there reasons to believe that the suggested mechanism of monetary control would actually work in India in this manner? There are two parts of this mechanism, the effect of changes in monetary policy instruments on market interest rates and other intermediate variables; and the effect of the latter on real variables or economic activity. Would both of these effects actually occur in Indian conditions? How widespread would they be? Would they not remain confined to the small segment of the monetary system, say the organised sector?

These are undoubtedly weighty issues and the strength of the case for the system of free interest rates depends upon their appropriate resolution. However, a number of considerations and much evidence in this regard do point towards a great potential for the success of an alternative monetary policy at the present stage of development of the Indian monetary system. We have accumulated considerable experience in the use of bank rate technique, and we do not have evidence to show that market rates would not respond to its changes if they are as bold and frequent as necessary. The government securities market in India has become quite well-developed in terms of its size, diversity of maturity structure, etc., and the Central Bank possesses enough legal powers to operate in this market. The stock of Treasury bills also happens to be significantly huge. The potential for the effective conduct of OMO also, therefore, does exist provided the objectives of debt management policy are changed which, as it will be shown shortly, is quite possible. The experience in the recent past few years of the use of Cash Reserve Ratio (CRR) technique has shown that it can be an effective tool of monetary policy. In short, unlike in the past when the RBI has ten4ed to rely very heavily on any one technique of monetary control in a given period, if more than one technique is harnessed in a well co-ordinated manner, the RBI would be in a position to influence the behaviour of intermediate variables such as market rates of interest, money supply, bank reserves, central bank refinance, etc.

Similarly, our study of the behaviour of different variables related to the aggregate effective demand has demonstrated that there is potential for transmitting the effect of monetary policy changes to economic activity also. We have already stated earlier that if the investment has not been restricted so far by changes in interest rates, it has been so because of the low level of the latter. Consumption and saving have been found to be responsive to changes in interest rates. It is often feared that the expenditure of the public sector is not responsive to monetary management. That this fear is exaggerated is indicated by the discovered. negative, although statistically insignificant, relationship between interest rates on the one hand, and government consumption expenditure and government borrowings on the other. Further, the demand by public sector enterprises to help them to reduce their debt/equity ratios, and the recent action by certain public sector trading corporations, viz., Cotton Corporation of India to reduce inventories because *inter alia* mounting interest costs have increased their operating losses certainly reflect the possibility of responsiveness of even public sector spending decisions to monetary variables. [36]

Let it be emphasised that since the Indian monetary system has become fairly well-matured and well-integrated, [37] the spread effects of the bold monetary policy changes are now going to be really wide and quick. This is true of both the 'organised' and 'unorganised' sectors. In fact, it is not really meaningful at this stage of the development of Indian economy to talk of the dichotomy of the 'organised' and 'unorganised' sector of the money market; this traditional bugbear of Indian monetary policy is now only of a historical value. The constituents of the so-called 'unorganised' sector namely, agriculture, small scale and cottage industries, other rural activities, retail trade, etc., have now become quite well-linked with the 'organised' sector through the spread of commercial and co-operative banking, operations of special financial institutions such as SFCs, SIICs/SIDCs, etc., creation of industrial estates, growth of agricultural marketing organisations such as FCI, CCI, State Marketing Federations, Monopoly Cotton Procurement, etc.

In summary, the alternative system proposed here would make monetary management in India more effective and efficient because the decisions at all different stages of the transmission process have now become amenable to the influence of policy changes.

Efficiency and Equity in Government Finances

Two major motivations for administering interest rates have been to ensure cheap availability of funds to the government, and to the 'priority sectors' and 'economically weaker and small' borrowers. The ideological form of the latter has been to state that the present system helps in bringing about equality and social justice. We deal with these aspects in this and the following sections.

The provision of cheap finance to the government is a totally unjustifiable argument for the continuation of the present system. To ensure availability of cheap credit to the government or to any borrower for that matter cannot be made the central objective or function of the Central banking policy. Further, the objective of debt raising activity of the government has to be to increase employment and output with stable prices and not to obtain command over resources at cheap cost irrespective of the consequences of such a policy. Since it is by now well established that government finances in general and debt management in particular have been the important sources of instability in the economy, and conflict with the working of monetary policy, it would be wise if the goal of holding down interest cost is not allowed to take a precedence over the other goals mentioned above. An additional reason for doing this is that the government with socialistic persuasion should not exploit its monopolistic or statutory position to appropriate, as it now does, large amount of funds at an unnaturally low cost.

Once interest rates on public debt are competitively raised, given its other investment characteristics such as safety, liquidity, etc., the government would be able to raise the major part of its financial requirements without compulsion. There would also be an increase in efficiency not only within the public sector but also in the economy as a whole because of chain effects of such a measure. The resultant increase in the debt-servicing burden should not frighten and, therefore, dissuade the government from doing this because since government debt is held mainly by government institutions, it would mean only an accounting change. Further, the government is in a position to meet this burden from borrowing ever more from the public without facing the risk of bankruptcy. But in the process, the higher rates would compel a more economical and efficient use of resources, and would also have a higher income effect.

Priority Sectors Needs

The provision of finance to priority sector borrowers is a sensitive and ticklish problem. There is no doubt that the interests of these essential but disadvantaged economic units ought to be served well by the financial system. But are higher interest rates really unsuitable for and against the interests of these borrowers? Has their disadvantage consisted in cost or availability of credit? Do they have capacity to pay higher interest rates? A dispassionate and non-ideological review of these issues would lead one to conclude that the case for higher interest rates is defensible even in this respect.

It appears to us that banks and financial institutions had been guilty of not making adequate credit available to these units rather than of charging higher interest rates to them. The objective of increasing the availability or funds to them, therefore, has been right. But, as pointed out earlier, there is really no need to adopt the measure of prescribing quantitative credit ceilings and targets to do this. The existing legal framework, moral suasion, and the minimum of directives can achieve this. This increased flow of credit, however, should be made at appropriate and not subsidised rates of interest. The higher interest rates themselves would augment the supply of funds to these borrowers *via* increase in the resources of the financial system and greater willingness of banks, etc., to lend to them. The experience in Indonesia of increasing interest rates during 1960s and 1970s has been that it led to an increase in the resources of banks which, in turn, led to their search for borrowers in the small-scale, trading, and other sectors. [38]

As to the capacity of these borrowers, the rates in the 'unorganised' sector admittedly do not reflect such capacity; they have been certainly exploitative, but is there really a need to go to the other extreme and supply funds at excessively subsidised rates? We deem such a policy to be unnecessary and unwise. It is to be noted that the capacity to pay higher rates is to be decided with reference to the rate of return not on current methods of production and cultivation but on the improved ones. Just as the high rates in the 'unorganised' sector have resulted in low investment because no worthwhile project can be implemented at such a high cost of credit, [39] the deleterious effects of low rates in the form of unproductive use of funds, encouragement of inappropriate and conspicuous technology, etc., also should not be overlooked. The best policy would be to charge interest rates between the exorbitant rates in the 'unorganised' sector and currently prevailing highly subsidised rates on institutional credit.

There are also very crucial practical considerations for abandoning the present system. Firstly, the cheap credit is being appropriated on a large scale by the untargeted groups of borrowers because of the existence of various loopholes in the system, corruption, imprecise nature of definition of small-scale units, bogus registration of small units, creation of captive small units by large units, ingenuity and influence of big units and rich farmers to obtain benefits not meant for them, etc. Secondly, in spite of the low official rates, the effective or implicit cost of credit to these borrowers in many cases actually works out to be very high indeed because they have to make underhand payments to obtain loans and the prices of goods to be purchased with sanctioned credit are 'marked up' to benefit certain functionaries and vested interests.

Income Distribution and Social Justice

This is a far more complex and wider issue but we cannot completely slur over it because the administered system of interest rates has been prominently projected as one of the means of delivering social justice. While, the discussion in the previous section (6) partly serves to indicate the weakness of this argument, the other major points are briefly discussed below.

The interest rates policy is hardly the right policy for tackling the problem of income distribution. The government budgetary policy would prove more potent in this context. Even in its supplementary role, it is the higher rather than lower interest rates which would serve the objective of income distribution better. The higher interest rates on bank deposits, small savings, provident funds, etc, would directly benefit the lower and middle income groups. In the ultimate analysis, these groups are 'surplus-spending units' to a greater extent than 'deficit-spending units' as a result of which their position is bettered more by the higher interest rates on financial savings than by the lower lending rates.

To the extent that the higher interest rates would encourage the adoption of labour intensive techniques, and since the elasticity of substitution of labour for capital is most likely to be high in developing countries, the higher interest rates policy would serve the cause of social justice better *via* the greater employment generation and consequent increase in the share of wages in national income. Moreover, to the extent that such a policy would be instrumental in curbing inflation, the lower and fixed income groups would be benefited.

The Indian economy is characterised by a plethora of price and distribution controls, the systems of industrial and import licensing, etc. These institutional arrangements have been very much loaded in favour of the well-to-do, well-connected, and the elite. Now, the possession of a licence, a quota, a permit, opens the doors of banks and financial institutions. Therefore, it is the already rich and economically powerful people who benefit from the lower interest rates. Under the present set-up, they reap double benefits-they appropriate high yielding investment opportunities, many of which are of speculative character, and they are also in a position to appropriate directly or indirectly cheap credit to finance those opportunities. In the inflationary situation, their gains have multiplied because they have benefited both as debtors and investors. In contradistinction, the poor, the low, and the middle income people have been impoverished both because of the decline in their purchasing power and low and fixed interest rates on the media of savings which are within their reach and which they prefer to hold. Thus, the case for the higher interest rates is strong from the point of view of social justice also.

IV. The Experiences of Other Countries

The adoption of the policy of low and controlled interest rates appears to be quite common in other countries also. Such a policy has existed in US, UK, Japan, Australia, New Zealand, South Africa, Malaysia, Indonesia, South Korea, Taiwan, and Latin American countries in one period or other and in one part of the financial system or other. It has taken its extreme form in the communist nations. In the non-communist world, however, the controls in India have been probably much more pervasive and direct than in other countries. The knowledge of experiences in these countries, despite the limitations to which inter-country comparisons are subject, would definitely prove instructive in formulating appropriate policy in this regard. We have, therefore, already referred to some of these experiences at the relevant junctures. Some of the other major lessons which emerge from the study of these experiences are briefly discussed below.

There does not appear to be any fixed either positive or negative-correlation between the system of interest rates and the performance of the economy with regard to saving, investment, price stability, and growth. While South Korea and Taiwan have achieved quite good results with the flexible and high interest policy, Malaysia and Singapore performed well with the low interest rate strategy. [40] Similarly, Japan has performed exceptionally well although it has been pursuing the low interest rates policy. [41] In the Commonwealth, New Zealand, Australia and UK with controls have probably done as well as the free system of Canada. [42]

But there has been unmistakably a high degree of dissatisfaction with the working of the administered rates system wherever it has been practised. Except in Japan, the good performance in such systems mentioned above has not been good enough when compared to the potential which existed in those economies. Therefore, they have either abandoned or considerably modified the administered interest rates system. The changes in the philosophy and policy in this regard which have occurred in the socialistic countries have already been referred to. Among the noncommunist world, the US abandoned the policy of supporting the government borrowing operations at fixed interest rates in 1951 through the Treasury-Federal Reserve Accord in that year; and there has been a widespread criticism of the Regulation Q in that country. Similarly, the policy of interest rates cartel, and ceilings on bank credit in UK has been under severe criticism (the dissatisfaction with it of the Bank of England itself has been shown earlier), and it was finally discontinued in 1971 under what has come to be known as the 'new approach' to monetary management propounded by the Bank of England in its document 'Competition and Credit Control'.

Japan could achieve excellent results in spite of low interest rates because of higher saving ratio and higher productivity which, in turn, were mainly due to socio-economic forces, absence of deficit financing, etc. [43] What is, however, to be noted is that the Bank of Japan has been in favour of abandoning the administered; rates system although it has not been able to do so because of government opposition to it on the basis of considerations which can easily be expected to have had a 'political' content. It has been pointed out by Patrick that the Bank of Japan preferred to have a more flexible market-determined interest rates structure, which would have resulted in raising of interest rates to a higher level than in the past. But the government insisted upon a policy of relatively low rates in order to maintain cost of exports low and to develop the long-term capital market. In spite of overall good results, such a policy has been regarded as highly misguided one because it has actually led to worsening of the balance of payments and the need for progressively tighter monetary policy during the post-war years. [44]

Among the Commonwealth countries, in New Zealand, the system is shown to have inexorably led to an increasingly complex and pervasive constraints on the financial system, and to a stifling of competition as a result of which the country suffered from the ineffective and heavily lagged responsiveness to real needs, and from the failure to curb effective demand. The situation in Australia was more or less similar till 1963-64 when the system was liberalised in the sense that interest rates were raised to a much more appropriate level and a greater use of OMO was resorted to. On the basis of a comparative study of the economies of New

Zealand, Australia, South Africa and Canada, it has been recommended that New Zealand and Australia should emulate the example of Canada and eliminate the use of direct controls on interest rates. [45]

The Latin American countries also have found that ceilings on interest rates, etc., became more and more repressive in an inflationary period; inflation required upward movement of the ceiling rate but the administratively determined increases in rates proved to be ad hoc and inadequate. The indexation of interest rates did not help for a variety of reasons. Therefore, many countries opted for the strategy of free interest rates at one point of time or the other. For example, while Uruguay and Nicaragua freed the rates in 1976, Argentina, Brazil, and Chile did so during 1967-76. [46]

V. Summary and Conclusions

We have discussed in this study the evolution of the system of low and administratively fixed interest rates and the discretionary ceilings on credit allocation, the alleged justification for the adoption of such a system, and its effects on the behaviour of interest rates, the working of monetary control, and the economic activity in India. We have shown that this system has been harmful and, therefore, it should be replaced by the alternative system of high and free interest rates with the dependence on more than one technique of monetary control used in a well co-ordinated manner. Such an alternative system would be very much conducive to increasing the rate of saving, efficiency of investment, efficiency of the financial system, efficiency of monetary control, and, as a result, efficiency of overall economic activity. The alleged justification that the vast needs of government finance, and the fulfilment of planning objectives such as meeting the financial requirements of the priority sectors and promoting equitable distribution of income require the present system of administered interest rates has been shown to be altogether unconvincing. The experiences of countries in the socialistic block, Commonwealth, Latin America, and Asia also support the case for the alternative system. There are no reasons why its adoption cannot he feasible in India.

Notes

This study was prepared for the Committee to Review the Working of the Monetary System. The author is thankful to the Committee for giving him an opportunity for working on this topic. The views expressed herein are those of the author.

1. Brahmananda, P. R., "Interest Policy in India", S K Muranjan Memorial Lecture, mimeo, 1982; McKinnon, R. I., "Money and Capital in Economic Development", The Brookings Institution, Washington, 1973; Myrdal, Gunnar, "Asian Drama", Vol. II and III, Appendix 5 and 8, Allen Lane, The Penguin Press, London, 1968; Shaw, E. S., "Financial Deepening in Economic Development", Oxford University Press, 1973.

2. National Board for Prices and Incomes, 'Borrowing and Lending', in Johnson, H G (ed), "Readings in British Monetary Economics", Clarendon Press, Oxford, 1972.
3. MYRDAL, G., op. cit., pp. 904-905.
4. Quoted by MYRDAL, G., op. cit., p. 909.
5. The description by the RBI of its own policy in this respect is confusing. Sometimes it states that it stipulated the maximum rate, at other times it states that it stipulated the minimum rate on a deposit of a given maturity. See RESERVE BANK OF INDIA, "Functions and Working", Bombay, 1983, pp. 87-91.
6. For further discussion of this point and general features of the behaviour of interest rates in India, see, BHOLE L. M., "Financial Markets and Institutions", Tata McGraw Hill Publishing Co, New Delhi, 1982, Chapter 20.
7. HOMER, S., 'Factors Determining the Secular Trend of American Interest Rates', in PROCHNOW, H. V., "The Five-Year Outlook for Interest Rates", Rand Mcnally and Co., Chicago, 1968.
8. HOMER, S., op cit.
9. HICKS, J. R., "Value and Capital", Oxford University Press, Oxford, 1939, p. 262.
10. The period of 1933-50 happens to be the phase of lowest interest rates in India which could be due to the general depression and exigencies of war finance. In the case of the banks' advances rate, there is a statistical explanation also. During 1935-50, this rate has been represented by the bank rate which is not strictly comparable with the bank rate of the Imperial Bank before 1935, and SBI advances rate after 1950.
11. GOLDSMITH, R. W., "The Financial Development of India, 1860-1977", Oxford University Press, Delhi, 1983.
12. See also, BHOLE, L. M., op cit, Chapter 20.
13. The real interest rates have been calculated as the nominal rate ± the three-year moving average of rates of change in wholesale prices (1913 = 100 for the period 1870-1946, and 1970-71 = 100 for the period 1949-83).
14. RESERVE BANK OF INDIA, "Report on Currency and Finance, 1980-81", Vol. I, p. 106.
15. RESERVE BANK OF INDIA, "Functions and Working", Bombay, 1983, pp. 87-91.
16. FRY, M. J., 'Money and Capital or Financial Deepening in Economic Developments?' in COATS, Jr, W. L., and KHATKHATE, D. R. (eds), "Money and Monetary Policy in Less Developed Countries", Pergamon Press, New York, 1980.
17. GALBIS, V., 'Money, Investment and Growth in Latin America, 1961-73', *Economic Development and Cultural Change,* April .1979.
18. Some of the equations estimated by Fry are too simplistic to be taken seriously; some of the relationships estimated by him and Galbis are not really relevant in settling the controversy of high *versus* low interest rates, *viz.*, hypotheses of complementarity between demand for money and investment, and the effect of inflation on economic growth; and notwithstanding

elaborate specifications, the estimated equations by Galbis do not contain the interest rate variable which drastically reduces the utility of his study in this context.

19. This notation is followed in all regression results in this study.

20. Rao, V K R V, "India's National Income, 1950-80", Sage Publications, New Delhi, 1983, p .136.

21. We do not know what part of current account deposits arise out of created credit but, given the fact that these deposits are mainly held by the business and industrial account-holders, it may not be wrong to assume that they arise largely out of created credit.

22. For further. discussion in this regard, see Bhole, L M, 'Retained Earnings, Dividends, and Share Prices of Indian Joint-Stock Companies', *Economic and Political Weekly*, Review of Management, August 1980.

23. It is sometimes argued that where banks are a predominant financial intermediary, interest rates ceilings are justifiable because the competitive bidding of interest rates would raise the cost for all banks without significantly improving their resource-position *vis-a-vis* each other. This is a very weak argument because it neglects the potential for the growth of other intermediaries and also the interests of savers.

24. Johnson, H. G., 'Problems of Efficiency in Monetary Management', in Johnson, H G (ed), op cit.

25. Bhole, L. M., "Responsiveness of Investment and Other Expenditures to Changes in Techniques of Monetary Control", Research Project Report submitted to the Indian Council of Social Science Research, New Delhi, July 1983.

26. The period of study for the public sector was 1960-61 to 1977-78.

27. Brahmananda, P. R., "Productivity in the Indian Economy", Himalaya Publishing House, Bombay, 1982, p. 213.

28. Brahmananda, P. R., op cit, p. 125, and p. 143.

29. Brahmananda, P. R., op cit, p. 215.

30. Wilczynski, J. "Comparative Monetary Economics", Macmillan, London, 1978, pp. 130-133.

31. For a discussion on the theory of monetary policy in India, see, Bhole L. M., Research Project Report, op cit, Chapter 2.

32. Bhole, L. M., ibid, Chapter 9.

33. Holmes, A. R., 'Operational Constraints on the Stabilisation of Money Supply Growth', and Maisel, S. J., 'Controlling Monetary Aggregates'. both in Federal Reserve Bank of Boston, "Controlling Monetary Aggregates", Boston, Massachussets, 1969, p 71, and p 152.

34. Bain, A. D., 'Monetary Control Methods in the United Kingdom', in Clayton, G., and others (eds), "Monetary Theory and Policy in the 1970s", Oxford University Press, Oxford, 1971; Karken, J., 'Appraisal of Monetary Management', in Johnson, H. R. (ed), op cit; Harrington,

R. L., 'The Importance of Competition for Credit Control', in JOHNSON, H. G., and NOBAY, A. R. (eds), "Issues in Monetary Economics", Oxford University Press, Oxford, 1974.

35. BANK OF ENGLAND, 'Monetary Management in the United Kingdom', in Johnson, H G (ed), op cit, pp. 580-81.

36. BHOLE, L. M., Research Project Report, op cit.

37. BHOLE, L. M., "Financial Markets and Institutions", op cit, Chapter 2.

38. MCKINNON, R. I., op cit.

39. BHATT, V. V., 'Some Aspects of Financial Policies and Central Banking in Developing Countries', in COATS, Jr, W. L., and KHATKHATE, D. R., op cit.

40. CHANDAVARKAR, A. G., 'Some Aspects of Interest Rate Policies in Less Developed Countries: The Experience of Selected Asian Countries', in COATS, Jr, W. L., and KHATKHATE, D. R., op cit, pp. 505-530.

41. BOLOTHO, A., "Japan: An Economic Survey, 1953-1973", Oxford University Press, Oxford, 1975.

42. TEW, J. B. H., and ARTIS, M. J., 'Monetary Policy, Part I and Part II', in BLACKABY, F. T. (ed), "British Economic Policy, 1960-74", Cambridge University Press, Cambridge, 1978; PERKINS, J. O. N., "Macro-Economic Policy: A Comparative Study", George Allen and Unwin, London, 1972.

43. BOLOTHO, A., op cit, and Lockwood, W. W. (ed), "The State and Economic Enterprise in Japan", Princeton University Press, New Jersey, 1965.

44. PATRICK, H. T., "Cyclical Instability and Fiscal-Monetary Policy in Post-War Japan", in Lockwood, W. W. (ed), op cit, pp 605-606.

45. PERKINS, J. O. N., op cit, pp 116-205.

46. GALBIS, V., "Inflation and Interest Rate Policies in Latin America, 1967-76", International Monetary Fund Staff Papers, June 1979; and JUD, G. D., "Inflation and the Use of Indexing in Developing Countries", Praeger Publishers, New York, 1978.

[6]

Interest Rate and Corporate Investment in India[*]

Introduction

A study of the relationship between the rate of interest and investment activity is significant from the point of view of economic policy. The expansion of productive capacity is absolutely necessary for increasing the volume of production which depends upon the augmentation of the stock of fixed assets as well as inventories of commodities. In short, higher rate of growth of investment is *sine qua non* of higher rate of economic growth. But if the process of acquisition of productive assets is stretched to the point where it is no longer supported by the real resources of the community, it may start a vicious circle of inflation and depression. It is therefore necessary that investment should not only not grow too less but also should not grow too much.

Now, it is the task of monetary authority to participate in the regulation of investment activity in a manner just indicated. Acquisition of physical assets presupposes the acquisition of finance. It is by controlling the movements of finance that the monetary authority can exert an influence on the investment activity. It is equipped with various techniques to do so, and the rate of interest is one of them.

It is therefore important and necessary to understand the relationship between the rate of interest and investment theoretically as well as empirically. It is the purpose of this article to present the nature of response of investment to variations in interest rates, as it was observed in the actual functioning of all the Public Limited Companies in India. The observations are based on (a) the year to year changes in the figures for investment and the interest rates; and

[*] Paper based on the Author's thesis submitted and approved for the Ph.D. degree of the University of Bombay in 1971, and published in the *Indian Economic Journal*, April-June 1972.

(b) the results obtained after using the correlation-regression technique. An attempt is also made to explain the observed relationship between the two variables under consideration. For lack of space, we had to refrain from the reproduction of data to substantiate the results presented here.

The article is divided into five sections. In section I, we have discussed the impact of changes in the rate of interest on the fixed investment of the corporate sector in India. In Section II, the relationship between the interest rate and inventory investment is discussed. In Section III, we have discussed as to how far changes in interest rates affected the supply of finance for investment in accordance with the "availability doctrine". In Section IV, the extent of the impact of interest rates on the corporate sector's portfolio selection is presented. Section V summarises the results presented in the previous sections.

I. Rate of Interest and Fixed Investment

Given the goal of the maximisation of the difference between the capitalised values of the income and cost streams associated with any investment, we can expect, *a priori*, that the rate of interest would determine the scale of investment. It can be expected to encourage or discourage capital expenditure because of its role as the cost factor as well as the discounting factor in the process of calculation of profitability of the investment projects. A rise (fall) in the rate of interest would increase (decrease) the cost of raising necessary money capital and thus earnings stream remaining equal, would reduce (increase) the profitability of investment. This may lead to a corresponding change in the decision to invest. A change in the rate of interest would change not only the cost of the project but also the present value of returns from that project. Higher the rate of interest, lower will be the present value of the prospective stream of returns over the productive life of the assets. This lower level of the present value when compared to the cost of capital (which in its turn would increase when the rate of interest would increase) would reduce the profitability of investment. This may lead to either the postponement or the curtailment or the abandonment of the planned project.

An empirical examination, however, leads one to conclude that the, rate of interest did not play any role in determining the fixed capital expenditure by the Private Corporate Sector in India during the period of 1951 to 1966. The various types of empirical evidence lead one to this conclusion. For example, the investment in fixed capital substantially increased in each successive five-year period. The yearly average rate of growth of fixed assets went up from 8.84 % during the First Five Year Plan to 13.32 % during the Second Five Year Plan, and to 11.64 % during the next Five Year Plan period. The share of fixed investment in the National Income also continuously increased during this period. While making an appraisal of the investment activity during the three Plans, the Planning Commission and the National Council of Applied Economic Research have stated that investment targets for the private sector were over-fulfilled. This over-fulfillment of the investment targets took place in precisely the same period in which the long term rate of interest also was rising continuously. This unidirectional movement of the two variables under consideration makes one tentatively believe that the rise in interest rate did not seem to have curtailed the investment in fixed capital by the corporate sector in India.

This belief was further strengthened by the results obtained by using a technique of regression. When the fixed investment (both undeflated and price-deflated) by all public limited companies in all the industries was regressed on the long term rate of interest (i.e. debenture yield), they were shown to be positively related with each other. The regression of investment on the rate of interest with one year lag; and also the use of regression equation in the logarithmic form did not change the results. In case of each of these experiments, the regression coefficient of the rate of interest had a positive sign.

Is it not possible that the above mentioned results in case of aggregate investment were due to the aggregation problem involved in such matters? The further examination of the problem showed that it was not so. The regression of fixed investment of ten individual industries like shipping, electricity generation and supply, cement, chemicals, engineering, aluminium, iron and steel, coal mining, sugar, cotton textiles, jute textiles, paper, on the rate of interest showed that in case of each of these ten industries, the regression co-efficient of the rate of interest had a positive sign without any exception. It is often maintained that the rate of interest would be more important as a determinant of investment in those industries where (a) the capital requirements are large and (b) capital is locked up for a long period of time. The regression results in case of individual industries did not bear this out.

This evidence showing the inefficacy of the rate of interest could be on account of the existence of the secular trend in the time series data used. It is possible that the trends of two time series are pronounced and moving in the same direction even though their fluctuation components are negatively correlated. In such cases, if we correlate those two time series without adjusting for trend the negative correlation coefficient between them may be lowered or may even be changed into positive coefficient. This statistical theory indicated the need for the further examination of the data. Therefore, we regressed the fixed investment by all public limited companies on the rate of interest after eliminating the secular trend in time series data. As a result, the reaction coefficient of the rate of interest did have a correct i.e., negative sign. But the magnitude of the influence of the rate of interest was shown to be rather insignificant. The partial coefficient of determination of the rate of interest was only 0.028. Moreover, the regression coefficient of the rate of interest was not statistically significant.

Thus, the rate of interest was shown to be the insignificant determinant of fixed investment during 1951-1965.

The various factors were operating during the period under consideration to make the entrepreneurs disregard the interest costs while undertaking fixed capital expenditures. Firstly, the average rates of return an investment were so remunerative as to overswamp the cost of capital consideration while taking the investment decisions. The annual average of profits after tax as percentage of net-worth was 7.8 %, 8.6 % and 9.14 % during each successive plan period respectively. There was very substantial margin between the rate of interest and the rate of return so as to render the former insignificant in investment decision process.

Secondly, during 1951-1965, there was very favourable investment climate in the sense that the future demand for the manufactured goods was almost assured. The continuous expansion in the public sector as a result of the policy of planned economic growth directly or indirectly encouraged the private sector to step-up its own investment activity far two reasons: (a) It directly guaranteed the demand far the products of those industries which were desirous of building up the capacity; and (b) The planning by committing the Government to a certain level of long run expenditures and investment, indirectly provided a general stimulus to incomes, prices and profits. In such an atmosphere of expected increasing demand and high profits, investment in fixed capital by the private sector could not be influenced by the rate of interest.

Thirdly, the organised industry in India during the period under consideration used the production technology which was unsuited to the factor endowments of this country. The predominant feature of the industrial growth during this time was the use of capital-intensive technology in the manufacturing industry. Such a use of capital intensive technology unsuited to the factor endowment in India was dictated by two factors: (a) It has been characteristic feature of India's industrialisation that almost all of its machinery and equipment have been imported from countries in which supplies of factors of production were very much different from those in India. (b) The cost of labour was also quite high. During this period the rise in money wages outpaced the rise in interest rates. As a result, in order to save the costs, the producers used more capital intensive techniques of production.

Fourthly, investment in fixed capital was unrelated to the rate of interest during the first fifteen years of planning also because quite a substantial portion of it was financed by savings abroad. It has been estimated that the external assistance in the form of aid, grants, loans from foreign Governments financed about 14 % of the gross domestic capital formation in India during 1960-63. Now, this type of external capital was supplied either free of cost or at nominal cost. For example, in 1963, about 60 % of official loans were available at the rate below 5 %. In other words, the assistance through grants and official loans was made available at less than commercial rates of interest. As far as the investment of foreign private capital in India was concerned, the rate of interest prevailing in India would hardly play any role in determining such investments. It is the difference between the expected rate of profits in India and the rate of return obtainable in home countries which would determine such investments. And India with its large and protected domestic market had been promising a high rate of profits to foreign private investors. As a result, total investment in fixed capital in India went on increasing in spite of increasing interest rates in India.

II. Rate of Interest and Inventory Investment

The responsiveness of inventory investment to changes in the rates of interest was not much different from that of fixed investment. Again, *a priori* variations in the short-term rate of interest provide a strong incentive for businessmen to vary the size of their inventories. There are various motives behind holding of stocks of goods by the businessmen. Firstly, such holding of inventories enables then to minimise the cost of procurement. If they procure goods in bulk, they can save in the cost of placing and processing orders as well as in transport and handling costs. They can also get higher quantity discounts if the goods are procured in bulk. Secondly, inventories are held to facilitate the smoothing out of production in the face of fluctuating sales. Thirdly, inventories are held in order to retain consumers' good-will. In short, entrepreneurs tend to hold large stocks of goods in order to earn what R. G. Hawtrey has called a 'convenience yield '. But the accumulation of inventories in order to earn 'convenience yield' cannot go on indefinitely because it involves certain costs like storage costs, obsolescence cost, spoilage cost, and interest cost. Therefore, ultimately the volume of inventory investment would be determined by comparing the rate of interest and the 'convenience yield'. Given the convenience yield, the rise (fall) in the market rate of interest will reduce (increase) the investment in inventories. Thus, the rate of interest will have, *a priori*, a negative influence on inventory accumulation.

However, a substantial evidence can be adduced to show that changes in interest rates did not actually affect the inventory investment of the sizeable portion of the private corporate sector in India during 1951-66. A minute study of the behaviour of inventory investment indicated the following things: (a) That there had been a substantial increase in inventory investment during each successive plan period along with the rising rate of interest. For example, the annual average of inventory investment during each successive plan period increased by Rs.29 crores and Rs.138 crores during the Second and the Third Five Year Plan periods respectively. (b) That the average rate of change of inventories during each five year period increased from one period to the next. In fact, the rate of increase of inventories during the period of stringent monetary policy (i.e. during 1960-61 to 1965-66) was substantially higher at 14.86 % than the rate of change (7.71 %) for the period 1951-52 to 1959-60. (c) That the inventory/output ratio increased together with the rate of interest in many years. (d) That the level of inventories as a percentage of National product (at current prices) increased precisely in the period in which the rate of interest was increasing fast. (e) That the situation during 1951-66 was such that the rate of interest, bank loans and inventories were rising simultaneously. The bank loans as percentage of total liabilities of all public limited companies increased from 10.70 % in 1951-52 to 17.95 % in 1965-66. If the rate of interest had been an effective instrument of credit-squeeze, such increase in bank loans would not have occurred. Further, given the fact that the bank finance was an important factor in relation to inventory accumulation in India, the failure of the rate of interest to check the expansion of bank loans signified its failure to control the inventory investment also.

The conclusion which follows from all this evidence was further substantiated by the following regression results: (a) When the total inventory investment of all public limited companies (both undefiated as well as price-deflated) was regressed on the short term rate of interest (twelve-month deposit rate of banks' or SBI advance rate, or average inter-bank call money rate, or average bazar bill rate) the regression coefficient of the rate of interest in each case had a wrong i.e. positive sign. It was possible that the wrong sign obtained at the aggregate level was because the aggregation marked the divergence among the components of the aggregate. But (b) when the stocks of raw materials and finished goods were separately regressed on the short term rate of interest, the results did not improve. Regression coefficients of the rate of interest had a positive sign showing that the rate of interest did not adversely affect the accumulation of stocks of raw materials and finished goods taken separately. (c) Another way of studying the problem in hand in disaggregation was to study the impact of variations in interest rates on the inventory investment of each individual industry. Ten industries were selected for this purpose. The results showed that the rate of interest and inventory investment in all industries, without exception, were moving in the same direction during the period under study.

One is thus led to conclude that the rate of interest did not seem to have played the expected role in determining the volume of inventory investment in the private corporate sector in India during 1951-1966.

The following factors were responsible for this result: Firstıy, there was existence of structural bottlenecks in the Indian economy. During the period under study, the foreign exchange difficulties created uncertainty of procurement of materials and spare parts to be obtained from other countries. Even with regard to nationally available materials, the supply position was difficult. One of the reasons for the difficult supply position was the inadequate, slower, and the unreliable transport system. Then the seasonal character of the Indian agriculture compelled the manufacturers to purchase raw materials whenever they were available and to store them. The uncertainty to which all these factors gave rise might have induced the manufacturers to carry larger stocks than what they would have kept in the economy free from controls and bottlenecks.

Secondly, the higher level of inventories in Indian industries during the period of rising interest rates could partly be explained by the absence of scientific management also. The training facilities in materials planning and management have been rather limited in India. There were many firms in India which did not apply their minds to the sophisticated calculations of inventory carrying cost and therefore, they were not quite aware of the cost implications of possessing large inventories.

The third important factor which can explain the poor response of inventory investment to interest rate changes was the relative movements in the rate of interest and the commodity prices. In other words, though interest rates increased during this period, they did not increase sufficiently in the sense that they did not keep pace with the increase in commodity prices. While prices were rising very rapidly, the rate of interest seems to have been limping i.e. it was rising but not quite sufficiently. Continuously rising prices might have generated expectations of further rise in prices; and these expectations might have been supported by the inflationary methods of Government finance such as deficit financing on a large scale. The speculative gains which the expectations of rising prices promised might have induced the producers to hold large stocks of commodities in spite of some increase in interest costs.

III. Interest Rate and the Supply of Finance

The discussion in the previous two sections showed that the corporate demand for investment – both fixed and inventory – was not responsive to variations in interest rates in India. But a study of relationship between the corporate investment and the rate of interest would not be complete unless we examine the reactions of the various suppliers of funds to changes in the rate of interest. As is well-known such a need was insisted upon by Robert Roosa who put forth a 'new theory' of credit control known as 'availability doctrine'. In short, he argued that changes in interest rates would be effective in regulating investment because they would affect the behaviour pattern of various suppliers of funds such that they become reluctant to meet the credit requirements of the private sector. As a result of increase in public debt and institutionalisation of savings, a slight increase in interest rates would 'lock in' the Government securities and thereby restrict the further expansion in private credit. In this context, the behaviour of the various suppliers of credit to the private corporate sector is discussed below.

The important institutions whose behaviour was studied were as follows (i) Life Insurance Corporation (LIC), (ii) State Financial Corporations, (iii) Commercial banks, (iv) Industrial Finance Corporation (IFC), (v) Industrial Credit and Investment Corporation (I.C.I.C.I.), (vi) Indigenous bankers, (vii) Managing agents and (viii) Stock market.

A study of the assets-pattern of LIC showed that its investment in Government securities as a percentage of its total assets declined from 51 % in 1958 to 41 % in 1967. The decline was all the more pronounced since March 1963. While the proportion of Government Securities declined, the proportion of loans substantially increased from 11 % in 1956 to 31 % at the end of March 1967. Thus the financial help from LIC to the corporate sector was increasing precisely in a period of increasing interest rates. This conclusion is further substantiated by the evidence on the extent of increase in the underwriting activity of the Corporation. The total amount of securities underwritten by LIC increased from Rs. 2 crores in 1957 to Rs. 26 crores in 1967.

The story was substantially the same for the SFCs. White their investment in Government securities declined considerably, their loans, advances and investment in debentures of the private sector showed quite a substantial increase.

The behaviour of the banks was not different either. A close scrutiny of the distribution of various assets of all scheduled banks in India revealed little support for the "availability doctrine". Loans, cash credit and overdrafts as percentage of total assets were shown to have increased from roughly 47 % at the end of March 1960 to about 58 % at the end of March 1966. Similarly total bank credit as percentage of their total assets increased from about 55 % to 68 % during the same period. On the other hand, banks' investment in Government securities as a percentage of their total assets declined from 35 % in 1959-60 to 24 % in 1965-66 i.e. during the period in which interest rates were scaling new highs. In other words, higher interest rates did not appear to have deterred commercial banks either from liquidating their Government securities or from expanding private credit. That the supply of money capital to at least the industrial sector was not hampered by increasing interest rates was further shown by the figures on advances of commercial banks to industry. These advances as a percentage of total advances of commercial banks increased from 36 % in 1956 to 62 % in 1966.

As far as the behaviour of the Statutory Financial Institutions and. the managing agents and the indigenous bankers was concerned, there was really no reason why they should have restricted the expansion of private credit during the period of increasing interest rate in keeping with the ideas contained in the 'availability doctrine'. The Statutory Financial Institutions were set up with the objective of meeting the private sector's need for medium and long term finance. There was little likelihood, therefore, of their denying credit to the private sector as long as it was ready to meet all their credit terms. Similarly, the indigenous bankers and the managing agents could not have been expected to provide less financial assistance to the private sector in a period of increasing interest rates. If anything, given their resources they must have increased the amount of their loans to the private sector as a result of increase in interest rates.

The effect of credit squeeze on the securities market and its consequences for company finance were almost similar. Theoretically, the increase (decrease) in the rate of interest will dampen (boost up) the security prices and thereby effect the volume of funds available from the securities market. The security prices are affected in the wake of changes in interest rates because the latter bring about a change in (a) the capitalised value of securities; (b) 'state of expectations' about the future; and (c) the 'state of credit' in the economy.

Actually, however, no consistently inverse relationship was found between the rate of interest and security prices in India. The price behaviour of three types of securities, namely, industrial debentures, preference shares and ordinary shares vis-a-vis the rate of interest was studied for the period 1951-1965. The evidence obtained showed that (i) Prices of industrial debentures and preference shares were inversely related to the rate of interest; (ii) Ordinary share prices at the aggregate level did not show such inverse relationship; and (iii) Ordinary share prices at industry level were not invariably adversely affected by a rise in the rate of interest. Where the inverse relationship was detected, there were some cases where share prices were not significantly influenced by a rise in the rate of interest.

What was more important to know was that, total capital raised through the securities market was not adversely affected by higher interest rates. While the annual average of total fresh capital issues was Rs.17 crores during 1951-55, it increased upto Rs.40 crores and Rs.77 crores during 1956-60 and 1961-65 respectively. Similarly, actual capital raised against consents as well as exemption order also increased from Rs.384 crores during 1957-61 to Rs. 467 crores during 1962-66. These figures showed that the supply of capital to the industrial sector through the stock market was not restricted by higher interest rates. The Reserve Bank of India has assessed that the amount of capital issued by public limited companies during 1961-65 was about 93 % more than the amount visualised by the Planning Commission during the same period by way of new issues of capital.

The important reason why the higher interest rates could not adversely affect the general level of prices of ordinary shares and the total amount of capital funnelled through the stock market was the support given to the market by financial institutions in the form of underwriting of and outright subscription to new issues. The functioning of the stock market during the period under consideration showed that even if increase in the rate of interest succeeds in depressing the security prices, it would not be able to restrict the flow of funds to industry, if there exist institutional investors who provide support to the new issue market. Such a support renders the new issue market less vulnerable to the stock of monetary policy.

IV. Interest Rate and Corporate Financial Pattern

A decision to invest resolves into two important aspects. Firstly, whether the firm should undertake purchases of assets at a particular time and if yes, what should be the volume of such purchases. Secondly, having decided the volume, the management has to take a concomitant decision as to what extent the various sources of finance should be utilised in order to finance the proposed capital expenditure. The purpose of this section is to discuss as to how far the interest rate influenced the financial capital structure of corporations in India.

Assuming the profit maximisation to be its goal, the corporation may be expected to raise funds through that resource-mix which would minimise the cost of capital. A rise in the cost of a particular type of capital would, therefore, induce the management to substitute that type of capital by a cheaper one. Since the rate of interest is a cost of borrowed funds, increase in the rate of interest, other thing being equal, would lead to (a) a greater retention of company's distributable income and eventual reliance on internal finance; (b) an increasing dependence on trade credit; (c) decline of cash in hand and current deposits with banks; and (d) decline in the use of debt capital compared with ownership capital.

Let us see how far shifts in the capital structures of Indian companies in the directions described above occurred during 1951-66. Firstly an examination of the balance-sheets of the public limited companies in India showed that there was no increase in their reliance on internal funds for financing their activities. For example, annual average of reserves and surplus of all public limited companies as percentage of total liabilities for the period 1951-52 to 1955-56 was 19.53 %. It declined to 16.61 % during 1956-57 to 1960-61 and was 19.39 % during the next five-year period. Variations in undistributed profits as percentage of profits after tax pointed out to the similar conclusion. The absence of any change in the retention policy of the joint stock companies during a period of rising interest rates might be due to the fact that the managements considered the maintenance of dividends rates more important. There is evidence to show that while considering what part of profits should be distributed; managements were more worried about the likely reactions of the shareholders to their policies. As a result, profit retention assumed only a residual character.

Secondly, there was no evidence to show that the corporate sector in India made use of more trade credit on account of credit squeeze during 1951-66. For example, trade dues of all public limite4 companies as percentage of total liabilities remained almost constant from year to year; the range of variation being only from 16.30 per cent to 18.56 per cent. Even if we think in terms of annual average of these percentages for each plan period, there is little evidence to show that bills payable assumed an increasing importance in the capital-structure of all public limited companies. Whatever increase in trade dues of these companies took place had been on account of their purchases. If the rise in interest rates had been instrumental in bringing about increased use of trade credit over and above that required for financing increased purchases, there should have been an observable increase in the ratio of trade dues to total purchases of the companies. But there had been no such increase.

Thirdly, there had been an expected reduction in the liquid assets holdings of the corporate sector as a result of increasing interest rates during 1951-66. The cash and bank balances as percentage of sales-income of all public limited companies declined from 4.44 % in 1955-56 to 1.91 % in 1965-66. Similarly corporate investment in Government and semi-Government securities was shown to have declined undoubtedly over the period under study. Further, total liquid assets as percentage of sales income declined from 7.5 % in 1951-52 to 3.8 % in 1960-61 and further to 2.2 % in 1965-66. That rising interest rates had been the major factor in causing this decline in the liquid assets holdings was confirmed by the regression results. When the liquidity ratio was regressed on the short-term as well as long-term rate of interest, the regression coefficients of both the types of interest rate had the negative (i.e. correct) sign; and these coefficients were statistically significant. Thus reasonably strong evidence exists to show that rise in interest rates induced the joint stock companies in India to reduce their liquid assets during the period 1951-66.

Lastly, surprisingly there was no reduction in the use of borrowed capital in comparison with ownership capital on account of increasing interest rates. The balance-sheet figures revealed that while total borrowings as percentage of total liabilities as well as of equity have definitely increased during 1950-51 to 1965-66, the equity as percentage of total liabilities has definitely decreased over the same period of time. While total borrowings as percentage of total liabilities of all public limited companies increased from 19.47 % in 1950-51 to 31.36 % in 1965-66, equity as percentage of total liabilities decreased from 56.45 % in 1950-51 to 41.38 % during 1965-66. Similarly, total borrowings as percentage of equity (i.e. debt/equity ratio) increased from 34.49 % in 1950-51 to 75.78 % in 1965-66. Thus, there is a conclusive evidence to show that the corporate capital structure in India became debt-heavy during the period of increasing interest rates.

This increase in the use of borrowed funds in spite of rising interest rates was because during the period under study, the financial assets rather than the ownership securities became more attractive for investment because the return on the former came to be higher than that an the latter. The effect of better earnings rates on the financial assets other than equities was to change the complexion of flow of funds to the industry. Investors preferred depositing their savings with financial and non-financial institutions to buying ownership securities. This shift in the preference-pattern of investors reduced the maneuverability of the corporate sector with regard to its choice of the pattern of financing its operations. Given the preference pattern of the investors, corporations devised way to meet their financial requirements in altered conditions. One of the ways was to rely increasingly an barrowed funds.

Another important factor which must have contributed to the greater reliance on debt capital was the increasing dependence of the corporate sector for their financial needs and the Statutory Financial Institutions and other financial institutions like LIC etc. These institutions generally pursue a policy of holding the exclusive or near-exclusive debt-portfolio. As a result, to the extent that the joint stock companies relied on them for financial assistance, the volume of debt was bound to increase in their capital structure.

V. Summary

We have discussed in the previous few pages as to how far variations in interest rates influenced investment behaviour of the corporate sector in India during 1950-51 to 1965-66. We found that during the period under study, the corporate investment policy in India, in *most of its aspects,* was not sensitive to changes in interest rates. Investment in fixed capital by the corporate sector was carried on unrestricted in spite of continuously rising interest rates. Similarly, accumulation of commodity stocks was not discouraged by rising interest rates. The rising rate of interest also failed to restrict the supply of finance through financial intermediaries as well as the securities market. As far as the influence on the financial-structure was concerned, rising interest rates encouraged (a) activisation of idle balances and liquidation of liquid assets; and (b) greater use of borrowed capital. However, there was no evidence to show that the higher interest rates led to a greater reliance on internal financing or on the trade credit. These findings would have been unlikely if the rate of interest had, in fact, exerted a strong and continuous influence on investment activity.

[7]

*Determinants of Interest Rates in a Deregulated Open Economy**

Introduction

The subject of interest rate has been of great interest to many since old times, and it has been referred to in religious texts also. Interest rate is a crucial or pivotal price, and its treatment has dominated the discussions of money, general prices, balance of payments, employment, business cycles, and economic growth. It connects both the monetary (financial) and real sectors of the economy.

What determines such a rate of interest? In order to be able to answer this question in a practically useful manner, two important points ought to be noted at the outset. Firstly, although economists talk of the rate of interest, actually a wide and complex variety of interest rates exist in any economy. Therefore, the question which really needs to be discussed is what determines the level and structure of interest rates? The utmost simplification possible in this context is to discuss the determination of at least two interest rates: one in the spot economy with short lending and another in the spot economy with long lending. Some progress towards understanding how the whole system of interest rates is determined may be made if one or the other of the basic rates - the short rate or the long rate - is determined (HICKS, p. 154).

Secondly, the issue of determination of interest rate is mostly discussed by assuming a closed and free market economy. However, actually, regulated closed economy, regulated open economy, and deregulated open economy also may exist, and the process of determination of interest rates would differ in these different types of economies. In the wake of a world-wide implementation of structural adjustment and stabilization programme in the recent past, the issues surrounding the determination of interest rates in deregulated open

* Paper published jointly with V.J. Sebastian in *The Indian Journal of Economics*, October 1996.

economies have come to receive considerable attention. Some of the questions which are being debated are: What is the relative role or importance of the domestic and external factors in determining interest rates in such economies? What are the respective roles of monetary policy, exchange rate, world interest rates, country risk in determining interest rates in them? How far the greater international capital market integration or the greater international capital mobility determine domestic interest rates and lead to a higher degree of interest rate parity across countries? How far interest rates in deregulated open economies can be managed by independent national interest rates policy?

It is in this context that the main objective of this paper is to discuss the determinants of interest rates in deregulated open economies with special reference to India. Section I of the paper briefly examines how far the Indian economy is an open economy. Section II presents a list of major factors which, in theory, can play an important role in determining interest rates in open economies. The next two Sections study how far interest rates in India are actually influenced by some of these factors. While Section III does so by estimating capital market integration model for India, Section IV presents certain facts regarding changes in interest rates in India during the liberalization period of 1985-95 towards that purpose. Section V presents the summary and policy implications.

I. Deregulation and Openness of the Indian Economy

After many years of licensing, physical controls, rationing, quotas, State trading, State distribution and canalization of inputs, and so on, the Indian economy began to be liberalized and deregulated around the middle of 1980's. Since then, the deregulation in various degrees is being effected in respect of general economic conditions, interest rates and other financial aspects, domestic or internal sector, and the foreign or external sector. The scope of industrial and import licensing has been drastically narrowed. While the role of public sector is being curtailed, that of private sector is being expanded. Tax reforms oriented towards liberalization are being introduced. The system of administered interest rates is being dismantled, and more and more interest rates are now being allowed to be determined by the market forces. External – or outward-growth-oriented policies are being pursued with greater vigour. The barriers or restrictions or controls or regulations on internal and foreign trade, domestic and external capital flows (receipts and payments), and domestic and foreign investments are being significantly reduced. External current account convertibility of the Indian rupee was recently formalized through declaration of Article VIII status in the IMF.

The level or degree of economy's openness also has become much higher now than before, particularly in terms of stocks and flows of international finance, though not so much in terms of trade. India's exports plus imports to GDP ratio increased only slightly from 14 percent in 1951 to 18 percent in 1992-93. This ratio is comparable with the one in USA but not in countries such as U.K., Germany, France, Canada, S. Korea, Egypt, where it has varied between 40 to 70 percent. India's GDP has been higher than her GNP; and the difference between her

GDP and GNP as a proportion of GNP, another measure of openness, has been small and it has also increased only slightly from 0.53 percent in 1951 to 1.91 percent in 1994.

The indicators of international financial utilization, participation, integration, however, show a much higher level of openness of the Indian economy. Her receipts plus payments on capital account as a proportion of GNP have increased from 2.33 percent in 1960-61 to 14.16 percent in 1992-93. The total gross external debt of India has increased sharply from Rs. 70 thousand crores in 1988-89 to Rs. 285 thousand crores in 1993-94; in relation to GDP, it has increased from 15.2 percent in 1970 to 19 percent in 1987 and 36 percent in 1993-94. The total external debt to exports ratio was 400 percent in 1993-94, and the total external debt service as a proportion of current receipts and exports was 30 percent and 43 percent, respectively in 1992-93.

There has been a significant increase in direct commercial borrowings in the private capital markets abroad by Indian financial institutions, banks, private companies, and public sector units. Many financial institutions (country funds), instruments (GDRs), Schemes (foreign institutional investors) have been introduced recently to attract funds from abroad. India's commercial borrowings, which include bank loans, securitized borrowings, and other loans, have increased sharply from Rs. 15988 crores in 1989-90 to Rs. 37279 crores in 1993-94. Similarly NRI short-term and long-term deposits have grown from Rs. 3819 crores in 1984-85 to Rs. 43807 crores in 1993-94. Thus, there has been a significant increase in the long-term, short-term, and speculative capital flows between India and the world in the recent past.

II. Theories of Interest Rates in Open Economies

The well-known theories of interest rates namely, the Classical Theory, Loanable Funds Theory, and Liquidity Preference Theory mostly explain how the equilibrium rate of interest is determined in a free and closed economy. The major determinants which emerge from them are: domestic savings, capital formation, bank credit, money supply, government debt, deficit financing, inflation rate, and financial development.

To extend this analysis and make it applicable to open economies, three other theories or hypotheses have been widely discussed in the literature. They are: (i) Uncovered Interest Rate Parity (VIP); (ii) Covered Interest Rate Parity (CIP), and (iii) Real Interest Rate Parity (RIP). They try to explain the relationships (differentials) between interest rates in different open economies by using the "law of one price" or "the concept of parity relationship" (Gupta and Gupta, pp. 4-8). Let us briefly explain these theories.

In an open economy, the opportunities to invest widen beyond national boundaries. However, the decision to invest in foreign vis-a-vis domestic assets needs to take into account the factor of exchange risk i.e. the chance that the value of the currency in which assets are denominated may fluctuate unpredictably. Due to this factor, interest rates do not equalize internationally. If domestic currency is expected to depreciate, the domestic interest rate will rise above the world interest rate to compensate investors in domestic assets. A typical investor faced with the choice between an instrument denominated in two different currencies will be concerned with the difference between interest rates on that instrument in two currencies (countries) after allowing for any expected change in the exchange rate over the maturity period of the instrument. This difference in interest rates is known as uncovered interest differential.

The uncovered interest rate parity theory states the equality between international interest rates differential and the expected rate of depreciation of domestic currency. The presence of an exchange risk premium invalidates uncovered interest rate parity condition. If investors are risk-neutral, and all of them share broadly the same expectations, the equilibrium will require that the uncovered differential is zero i.e. the gap between interest rates in two countries should be just equal to the likely change in the exchange rate over the relevant time period.

The covered or closed interest differential, on the other hand, is the differential between "offshore" and "onshore" interest rates which is hedged so as to eliminate exchange risk. Investors can insure against fluctuations in the value of currency by covering them in the forward market. The rate of return on covered foreign investment has two components: the nominal interest rate on the foreign asset and the gain (loss) from purchasing foreign currency and selling it forward. The latter is known as the forward premium (discount) or exchange gain (loss) on foreign currency.

Since covering foreign investment results in the possible exchange gain (loss) apart from the interest gain, while choosing between the covered foreign investment and the domestic investment, one must choose that investment which will yield the highest return, which does not necessarily imply choosing investment with the highest interest rate. A positive (negative) value of the covered differential means that there is a differential in favour of (against) the foreign currency (domestic currency), and it suggests that there is an incentive to invest abroad (domestically).

The equilibrium in the international money market is reached when the covered interest differential is equal to zero; that is, the forward premium on a foreign currency is equal to the interest differential between domestic asset and the foreign asset. The factors such as transaction costs, cost of gathering and processing information, government regulations, capital market imperfections, and political risk differential cause significant deviations from the covered interest parity condition.

The real interest rate parity theory states that the nominal interest rates differential across countries are explained by inflation differentials across countries.

The spectrum of proximate and ultimate determinants of interest rates in the complex, uncertain, uncomfortable world of open economy is truly wide. In addition to the domestic factors mentioned earlier, the following external factors impinge on the level and structure of interest rates in the open economy: the spot and forward exchange rates and their variability; the expected depreciation (appreciation) of currencies or expected exchange rates or exchange risk; balance on trade, current, and capital accounts (balance of payments) or foreign exchange reserves; changes in international credit, capital debt flows; international capital mobility and its term-structure; foreign interest rates; foreign inflation rates; and country risk.

III. Capital Market Integration Model

To test the relative importance of domestic and external factors, we carried out a simple econometric exercise for India. To begin with, the following two interest rate regression functions were estimated with the help of quarterly data for the period, 1984: 2 to 1994: 2 (obtained from International Financial Statistics by IMF), and by using the OLS method. While equation (1) tests for the explanation of differential in nominal short-term interest rates in India and the world economy, equation (2) directly tests for the determination of nominal domestic short-term interest rate in India.

$$i - i^* = a_1 + b_1 (P - P^*) + b_2 TB + b_3 DC + b_4 BR + U_1 \quad (1)$$

$$i = a_2 + c_1 P + c_2 TB + c_3 DC + c_4 BR + c_5 i^* + U_2 \quad (2)$$

where,

i = short-term interest rate in India measured as the State Bank of India advance rate;

i^* = the short-term interest rate in USA (representing the world rate) measured as the prime lending rate of banks there;

p and p^* are inflation rates in India and USA, respectively measured as the rate of change in consumer prices in respective countries;

TB = the size of trade balance in India as a proxy for expected exchange rate;

DC = the size of domestic credit in India;

BR = Bank Rate in India;

a_1 and a_2 are intercepts, and U_1, U_2 are error terms.

The regression coefficients are expected to have the following signs:

$$b_1 \text{ and } c_1 > 0;\ b_2 \text{ and } c_2 < 0;\ b_3 \text{ and } c_3 = \text{indeterminate};\ b_4 \text{ and } c_4 > 0; \text{ and } c_5 > 0$$

As the results obtained by estimating these equations were generally poor, the analysis was extended by estimating two more following equations by using annual data and by carrying out period analysis for the years (a) 1971 to 1994; (b) 1971 to 1982; and (c) 1983 to 1994:

$$i - i^* = a_3 + d_1 (P - p^*) + d_2 ER_{i-1} + d_3 M + d_4 CR + d_5 BDR + U_3 \quad (3)$$

$$i = a_4 + e_1 ER_{i-1} + e_2 Ms + e_3 CR + e_4 BDR + e_5 i^* + e_6 p + U_4 \quad (4)$$

where,

i = Call rate in India;

i^* = Federal Funds rate in USA;

ER_{6-1} = one year lagged exchange rate as a proxy for exchange rate expectations;

M = broad money supply in India;

CR = country risk measured as debt/GDP ratio for India;

BDR = maximum bank deposit rate;

P^* = Inflation in USA;

P = inflation rate in India;

a_3 and a_4 = intercepts;

U_3 and U_4 = error terms.

The expected signs for various regression coefficients are as follows:

$d_1 > 0$; d_2 and $e_1 > 0$; d_3 and $e_2 < 0$; d_4 and

$e_3 > 0$; d_5 and $e_4 > 0$; $e_5 > 0$; $e_6 > 0$

The results of the estimation of equations 1 to 4 are presented in Table 1. The major points which emerge from all these results are given below:

(1) Estimates are not statistically robust in certain cases.

(2) Sometimes $\overline{R}^2$ was small. It varied between 0.15 and 0.792. It was above 0.5 in 5 out of 8 equations.

(3) Estimates in 3 out of 8 equations had small D.W. values showing the existence of serial correlations. In other 5 cases, D.W. Test did not show poor results.

(4) In case of estimates based on quarterly data 1984-94, Bank rate emerged as the only variable which had an expected sign and which was highly significant.

(5) In the exercise with annual data and period analysis also, maximum bank deposit Rate was mostly with an expected sign and it was highly significant in 3 out of 6 equations.

(6) It thus can be said that the domestic monetary policy has had a significant influence on domestic market interest rates in a deregulated open economy also.

(7) In the exercise with the annual data and period analysis, inflation rate was found to be a significant determinant of domestic market interest rate. This finding suggests that Fisher effect holds good for India. The hypothesis of Real Interest Parity, however, did not find much support in the whole exercise.

(8) Trade Balance as a proxy for exchange rate expectations did not perform well. A one period (year) lagged exchange rate as a proxy for exchange rate expectations had a correct sign in 5 out of 6 equations, and it was statistically significant in two equations for the period 1971-82. For the period which witnessed relatively higher levels of deregulation and opening up (1983-94), however, exchange rate had a wrong sign and it was not significant statistically.

(9) Money supply had an expected sign in 3 out of 6 equations, but was found to be insignificant statistically in all equations.

(10) Country risk measured by external debt to GDP ratio had a correct sign in 4 out of 6 equations, but it was significant only in one equation (for the period 1971-82). It did not appear to have played a part in determining domestic interest rates in the period of deregulation and openness.

(11) Our earlier study covering a longer period, 1951-52 to 1985-86 had shown that the rate of inflation, balance of payments, foreign capital flows, government market borrowings, and budgetary deficits had significant influence on interest rates (Bhole, pp. 10-13).

Table 1: Determinants of Interest Rates in India

Coefficients	1971-1994		1971-1982		1983-1994		1984: 1 to 1994: 2	
	Annual Data						Quarterly Data	
	Dependent	Var	Dependent	Var	Dependent	Var	Dependent	Var
	i-i*	i	i-i*	i	i-i*	i	i-i*	i
1) Intercept	-16.688	-10.74	-18.21	-37.04	-34.04	-15.16	-18.68	5.78
2) P-P*	-0.07 (0.18)	-	0.338 (0.289(	-	-0.434 (0.49)	-	0.08 (0.155)	-
3) TB	-	-	-	-	-	-	0.00003	-0.00003
4) ER	0.21 (0.48)	0.204 (0.240)	8.534 (15.26)	4.42 (2.04)	-0.252 (0.53)	-0.067 (0.255)	- -	- -
5) DC	-	-	-	-	-	-	0.0001 (0.0002)	0.002 (0.001)
6) M	0.26 (0.445)	-0.29 (0.199)	-1.00 (0.915)	-0.294 (0.22)	0.509 (0.68)	0.17 (0.42)	-	-
7) CR	15.35 (48.82)	16.81 (23.79)	-10.20 (82.50)	77.11 (33.44)	59.0 (50.7)	-14.52 (29.74)	-	-
8) BR	-	-	-	-	-	-	2.53	1.5
9) BDR	0.876 (0.981)	2.32 (0.52)	-3.55 (2.0)	0.09 (0.86)	3.51 (1.29)	2.58 (0.74)	-	-
10) i*	-	-0.57 (0.22)	-	-0.59 (0.21)	-	-1.43 (0.64)	-	-
11) P	-	0.373 (0.217)	-	1.04 (0.37)	-	2.59 (0.769)	-	0.07 (0.05)
12) R^{-2}	0.159	0.512	0.129	0.530	0.610	0.792	0.624	0.241
13) D.W.	0.569	1.339	1.164	2.631	1.19	2.678	0.393	0.502

Figure 1
Nominal Interest Rates in India

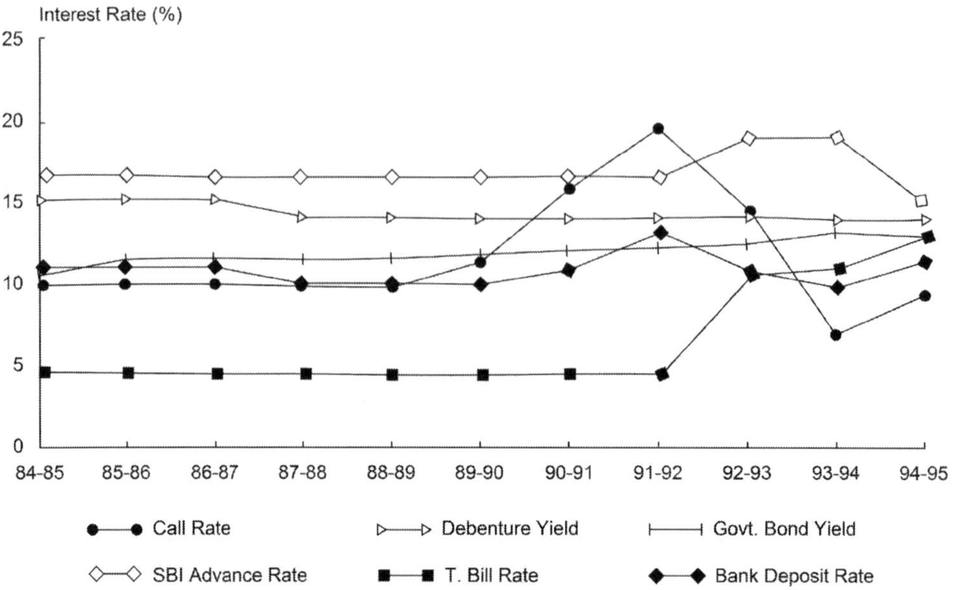

Figure 2
Ex-post Real Interest Rates in India

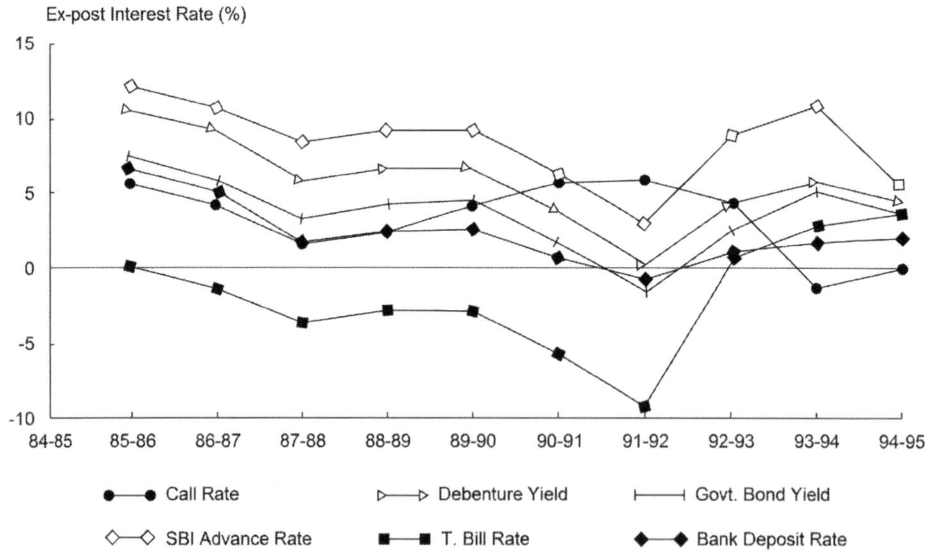

IV. Interest Rates in India during a Decade of Deregulation

It is necessary to supplement the above analysis by inquiring whether the magnitude/ direction, and nature of changes in interest rates differ significantly before and after deregulation. Tables 2 to 4 and Figures 1 to 5 present certain facts about the behaviour of interest rates in India during 1985-1995 with this purpose in mind.

Table 2 and Figure 1 show that the variability of interest rates has increased slightly after 1990-91. However, Tables 3 and 4, and Figure 2 show that no sharp increase (decrease) in interest rates has occurred during the period of deregulation and opening of the economy. Except the Treasury bill rate, an increase in all the other nominal rates has been only marginal. Similarly, the real interest rates have exhibited a mild downward movement over the past decade.

A comparison of interest rates in India and certain other countries (See Figures 3 and 4) shows that while the short-term interest rate (Treasury bill rate) in other countries has declined, it has increased significantly in India since 1991. Similarly, while the long-term rate of interest (Government bond yield) in India used to be lower than the one in other countries before 1985, it has been consistently higher thereafter. Thus, while both the short-term and long-term interest rates abroad have somewhat eased, they have somewhat hardened in India since 1990. Further, the extent of fluctuations in all the interest rates abroad has always been greater than those in India. All this suggests that interest rates in India are still determined more by domestic factors than by the world interest rates. This suggests that interest rates in India are still determined more by domestic factors than by the world interest rates.

Table 2: Nominal Interest Rates in India

Year	CR	TBR	SAR	BDR	GBY	DR
1984-85	9.95	4.60	16.5	11.0	11.0	15.0
1985-86	10.00	4.60	16.5	11.0	11.0	15.0
1986-87	9.99	4.60	16.5	11.0	11.0	15.0
1987-88	9.88	4.60	16.5	10.0	10.0	14.0
1988-89	9.77	4.60	16.5	10.0	10.0	14.0
1989-90	11.49	4.60	16.5	10.0	10.0	14.0
1990-91	15.85	4.60	16.5	11.0	11.0	14.0
1991-92	19.57	4.60	16.0	13.0	13.0	14.0
1992-93	14.42	10.68	19.0	11.0	11.0	14.0
1993-94	6.99	11.10	19.0	10.0	10.0	14.0
1994-95	9.40	13.16	15.0	11.5	11.5	15.0

NOTATIONS: CR = Call Rate; TBR = Treasury Bill Rate; SAR = SBI Advance Rate; BDR = Bank Deposit Rate; GBY = Govt. Bond Yield; DR = Debenture Rate.

SOURCE: Reserve Bank of India, Report on Currency and Finance, Various Issues.

A comparison between certain interest rates and the exchange rate in India (Figure 5) shows that while the rupee has depreciated significantly, interest rates have declined to a certain extent after 1991. Interest rates and the exchange rate had moved together in the same direction till 1991. It is likely that a sharp increase in foreign currency assets and foreign exchange reserves after 1991 has lowered interest rates via an increase in money supply after that year. To that extent, external factors can be said to have become relevant in determining interest rates in India.

Table 3: Ex-post Real Interest Rates in India

Year	CR	TBR	SAR	BDR	GBY	DR
1984-85	3.48	-1.87	10.03	4.53	4.03	8.53
1985-86	5.59	0.19	12.09	6.59	7.09	10.59
1986-87	4.17	-1.22	10.68	5.18	5.68	9.18
1987-88	1.67	-3.61	8.29	1.79	3.29	5.79
1988-89	2.32	-2.85	9.05	2.55	4.28	6.55
1989-90	4.10	-2.79	9.11	2.61	4.41	6.61
1990-91	5.59	-5.66	6.24	0.74	1.78	3.74
1991-92	5.83	-9.14	2.76	-0.74	-1.36	0.26
1992-93	4.36	0.62	8.94	0.94	2.41	3.94
1993-94	-1.36	2.75	10.65	1.65	5.08	5.65
1994-95	-0.20	3.5	5.40	1.90	3.40	4.40

Table 4: Annual Average Nominal and Real Interest Rates in India

Year	CR	TBR	SAR	BDR	GBY	DR
Nominal Rates						
1972-76	8.10	3.80	10.70	7.40	5.93	9.51
1977-81	8.66	4.60	14.60	9.00	6.53	12.11
1982-86	9.26	4.60	16.50	10.50	8.48	14.60
1987-90	10.28	4.60	16.50	10.25	11.63	14.25
1991-95	13.25	8.83	17.20	11.30	12.66	14.00
Real Rates						
1972-76	-3.88	-7.94	-1.28	-1.0	-6.04	-2.47
1977-81	0.12	-3.94	6.06	-5.18	-2.01	-2.01
1982-86	2.46	-2.21	9.69	-1.54	1.67	7.79
1987-90	3.06	-2.61	9.28	3.03	4.41	7.03
1991-95	2.84	-1.57	6.80	1.49	2.26	3.60

NOTATIONS and SOURCE (Table 3 and 4): The same as in Table 2.

Figure 3:
Short-term Interest Rates (T-Bill Rate) in UK, Japan, USA, Germany and India

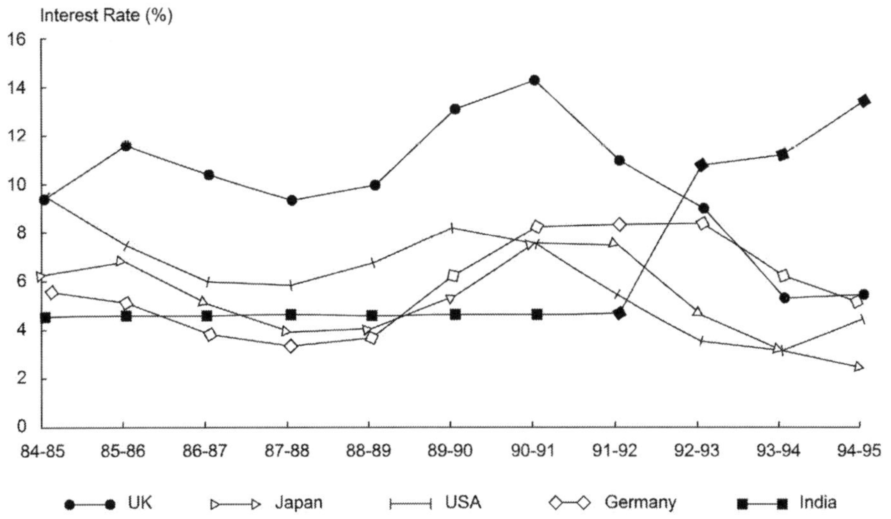

Figure 4:
Long-term Interest Rates (Govt Bond Yield) in UK, Japan, USA, Germany and India

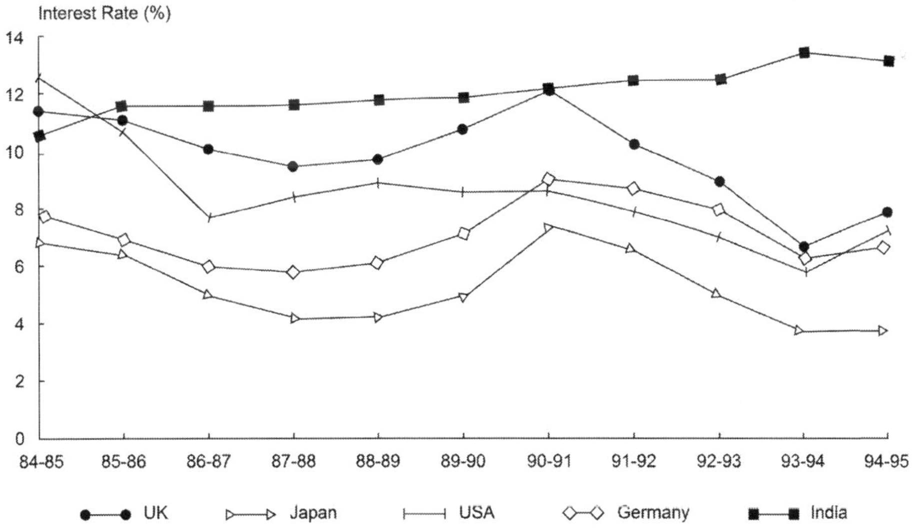

Figure 5:
Short-term and Long-term Interest Rates in India and the Exchange Rate of Rupee vis-a-vis US Dollar

V. Summary, Conclusions, and Policy Implications

The Indian economy has been increasingly deregulated and opened up in the recent past. Yet, it can be designated only as a partially deregulated partially open economy at present. Deregulation has not resulted in a full restoration of market forces; what has emerged is the "regulation responsive to market forces" or "flexible regulation". In such an economy, interest rates can be expected to be determined by exercising administrative controls in response to market conditions. The monetary authorities in India do not appear to have lost control over interest rates; they can still influence them through appropriate monetary policy. The Reserve Bank of India (RBI) can enhance the effectiveness of its policy if it could activize Bank Rate, and use the structure of interest rates as an indicator /target of monetary policy. So far, the maximum deposit rate of banks has been the most important signaling device in India.

The monetary authorities have been and will continue to determine interest rates policy in India in the light of the following factors: the inflation rate; the desire to evolve a more stable asset-liability balance in banks; the desire to ensure attractiveness of term deposits; the desire to ensure a balance and suitable margin between deposit and lending rates of banks; the exchange rate and its variability (stability); the international capital flows; and the conventional demand for and supply of loanable funds. The exchange rate plays an important role in determining particularly the interest rates on NRI deposits.

As the RBI has put it, while the monetary policy can and should influence the level of interest rates, it cannot ignore the basic demand and supply situation. It is important to note the deposit rates, though administered, followed the firming of interest rates in the money and securities markets. Eventually, as monetization of fiscal deficit is contained there would be greater scope for enlarging the money and securities markets operations of the Bank. It is through this route that more efficient interest rate policy would then emanate (RBI, 1994-95, p. 103).

References

1. BHOLE, L. M., "Some Issues Concerning Interest Rates Theory and Policy", *The Indian Economic Journal*, the Conference Volume, December 1988.
2. COPELAND, L. S. (1990), Exchange Rates and International Finance, Addison-Wesely Publishing Company, Wokingham, England, 1990.
3. GUPTA, D. D. and GUPTA, B. D., "Interest Rates in Open Economics", *Policy Research Working Paper*, The World Bank, April 1994.
4. HICKS, J. R., Value and Capital, Oxford University Press, Oxford, (1946).
5. INTERNATIONAL MONETARY FUND, International Financial Statistics, Various Issues.
6. RESERVE BANK OF INDIA, Annual Report, 1994-95.
7. RESERVE BANK OF INDIA, Report on Currency and Finance, Various Issues.

[8]

*Determinants of Long-Term Interest Rates in India During 1970s to 1990s**

Introduction

Interest rate determination is an issue that is frequently debated by economists. On the one hand, there is the classical view that equilibrium interest rate is the rate at which potential savings are equal to potential investment at full employment level. This is the real (non-monetary) theory of interest rate where quantity of money does not have any influence on interest rate (METZLER, 1955). On the other hand, there is Keynes' theory in which the rate of interest is determined by liquidity preference. It is mainly a monetary theory where there is a negative relationship between supply of money and interest rate (KEYNES, 1936). Although we talk about the rate of interest, a wide and complex variety of interest rates exist in an economy. Therefore, what determines the level and structure of interest rates? The utmost simplification possible in this context is to discuss the determination of at least two interest rates: one in spot economy with short lending and another in the spot economy with long lending (BHOLE & SEBASTIAN, 1996).

Interest rates on long-term financial assets play a central role in linking financial markets to the economy at large. Long-term interest rates have an influence on the business cycle and on capital formation and, therefore, play a central role in the transmission of macro economic policies in the economy. The extensive debate over the reasons for and implications of the apparently high level of real long-term rates in India during the post-reform period (1985-2000) attests to their practical economic significance.

* Paper published jointly with Pradyumna Dash in *Prajnan*, July-September 2003 (Vol. XXXII, No.2, 2003-04).

Tables 1 and 2 present the level of nominal and real interest rates in India during 1971-2000. The rationale behind splitting this time period between 1970-1985 and 1986-2000 is the change in the financial structure of the economy. Soon after independence, it was believed that the role of the State was essential to accelerate the process of economic growth. The philosophy of the socialist pattern of society was adopted and the government had control over many sectors, including the financial sector. Interest rates were controlled or repressed or administered and funds were made available at cheaper rates to the priority sectors. This objective gained momentum with the nationalization of banks in 1969. The banks explicitly set quantitative targets to expand their branch network in rural areas and to direct credit to priority sectors. All this lasted roughly upto the middle of 1980s.

Table 1: Nominal Interest Rates in India, 1971-2000

Interest Rates Year	Statistical Measures	Government Bond Yield (15 Years & Above)	Government Bond Yield (5-15 Years Maturity)	Government Bond Yield (1-5 Years Maturity)	IDBI Prime Lending Rate	Bank Deposit Rate (1-3 Years Maturity)
1971-1985	Mean	6.57	5.94	5.33	11.32	7.24
	Standard Deviation	1.15	1.00	0.70	2.18	1.09
1986-2000	Mean	11.28	10.48	11.94	15.22	10.18
	Standard Deviation	0.92	1.43	2.89	1.76	1.11

In the early l970s, the writings of authors such as Mckinnon and Shaw challenged the conventional wisdom of government intervention in the financial sector. In contrast to Keynesian line of thinking that interest rate has to be kept at a low level to promote investment and growth, Mackinnon and Shaw argued that the financial repression, i.e., interest rate ceilings, high reserve requirements, and regulatory credit policies discourage the development of domestic financial markets and is detrimental to economic growth. Financial liberalization leading to high interest rates was expected to channel savings to their most productive uses and generate greater efficiency in investment projects. In other words, the financial liberalization process implies a positive relationship between real interest rates and economic growth via increased savings and investments. Many studies found a direct relationship between the real rate of interest and economic growth (Lanyi and Scacaglu, 1983; Gupta, 1986; Koyck and Hooft-Welvaars, 1966; Matthews, 1960; Sen, 1971). All this led the authorities in many developing countries to remove controls on interest rates and to allow market forces to playa greater role in the process of interest rate determination.

The monetary authorities in India also took several measures to develop, integrate and enhance efficiency in the money and government securities market following the recommendations of Chakravarty Committee in 1985 and Vaghul Committee in 1987.

Table 2: Real Interest Rates in India, 1971-2000

Interest Rates Year	Statistical Measures	Government Bond Yield (15 Years & Above)	Government Bond Yield (5-15 Years Maturity)	Government Bond Yield (1-5 Years Maturity)	IDBI Prime Lending Rate	Bank Deposit Rate (1-3 Years Maturity)
1971-1985	Mean	-2.62	-3.25	-3.86	2.12	-1.95
	Standard Deviation	7.91	7.87	7.83	8.16	7.83
1986-2000	Mean	3.64	2.84	4.31	7.58	2.55
	Standard Deviation	2.93	2.35	2.40	2.58	2.69

SOURCE: Table 1, 2: Reserve Bank of India, *Handbook of Statistics on Indian Economy*, 2001, Mumbai. 2002

A multi-pronged strategy was adopted for deregulating the regime of administered structure of interest rates, removal of barriers to entry, introduction of new instruments and setting of new institutions. For instance, several new financial instruments were introduced such as Inter-Bank Participation Certificates (1988), Certificates of Deposits (June 1989), Commercial Paper (Jan 1990), and Repos (December 1992). New auction based instruments were introduced with varying maturities such as 364-day, 182-day, 91-day, 14-day Treasury Bills and the zero coupon bonds. The system of *ad hoc* Treasury Bills (with a fixed 4.6 per cent interest rate issued since July 1974 by the Central Government to the Reserve Bank) was abolished from April 1997, and the scheme of Ways and Means Advances within specified limits was introduced in its place. Currently only 91-day and 364-day Treasury Bills are issued. A ceiling of 10 per cent on call money rate imposed by the Indian Banks Association was withdrawn in 1989. The participation in the call money market was gradually widened by allowing non-banking financial institutions, non-banking finance companies, primary and satellite dealers, mutual funds, corporates (through money dealers), etc., to participate in the call money market. The Discount and Finance House of India was set-up in April 1988 and was allowed to participate in the call money market both as a borrower and lender commencing from July 1988. Setting up Securities Trading Corporation of India along with the introduction of the primary dealers system enhanced liquidity and depth in the Government securities market. Efforts like introduction of Delivery and Payment (DVP) system by the RBI (1995), introduction of screen-based trading by NSE, computerization of SGL operation, and dissemination of information by RBI on secondary market trading have resulted in considerable transparency in the trading and settlement system in the market. Foreign Institutional Investors (FIIs) were allowed to set-up 100 per cent debts funds to invest in Government (Central and State) dated securities in both primary and secondary markets. Thus, it can be said that the financial markets in India have undergone a significant change with the removal of restrictions, introduction of auction system, and freeing of interest rates since 1985.

It would be interesting to find out the implications of the above-mentioned structural shift for the determination of interest rates in India. Therefore, the purpose of this paper is to examine the role of internal and external factors in the process of determination of both long-term nominal and real interest rates in India over the past 30 years. The paper is structured as follows: Section I discusses various theories of interest rate determination and surveys the empirical literature on the determinants of long-term interest rates in India and abroad. The interest rate determination model and methodology are discussed in Section II. Section III discusses the empirical results. The conclusions are presented in Section IV.

I. Review of Literature on Interest Rate Determination

Interest rate determination is one of the most important issues that have been debated for centuries. There are many theories of interest rate determination. Fisher, Wicksell, and Keynes are some of the main contributors to the theory of rate of interests. Fisher (1930) had made a distinction between the real and nominal rate of interests. Real rate of interest is the money rate of interest adjusted for the effect of changes in the price level and is determined by the forces of productivity and thrift. Alternatively, we can say that the real rate of interest is determined at that point where savings are equal to investment. In the long-run, the real rate of interest remains unchanged as a higher rate of inflation is reflected in the higher level of nominal rate of interest. In other words, changes in money supply affect only the nominal interest rates but not the real rate of interest.

The loanable funds theory of interest rate is an extension of the classical savings and investment theory of interest rate. This theory is associated with the name of Wicksell and some other Swedish economists. According to this theory, the interest rate is, determined at that level at which demand for and supply of funds are equated. Since, besides the real factors of savings and investment, it takes into account the monetary factors of hoarding, dishoarding, and changes in bank credit in the determination of interest rate, it is said to be an improvement over the classical savings and investment theory of interest rate, Wicksell (1958) had tried to make loanable funds theory a part of general equilibrium model through his well-known dynamic analysis of the cumulative process by distinguishing the natural rate of interest from the market rate of interest. The natural rate of interest is the rate at which savings is equal to investment, and it corresponds to the marginal productivity of capital. According to Wicksell, the natural rate of interest is an unobservable variable which changes under the impact of productivity shocks, technological progress, factor endowment changes, and other real disturbances, and hence, it is unknown to the monetary authorities. On the other hand, the market rate of interest is the actual rate of interest at which banks give loans to borrowers and which they pay on deposits to the savers. The mismatch between these two interest rates results in price fluctuations. Therefore, the monetary authorities have to try to adjust the market interest rate till it becomes equal to the natural rate of interest in order to combat inflation.

Keynes in his Treatise on Money (1971) developed a theory of interest which is similar to the Wicksellian theory of interest in order to explain Gibson's Paradox, i.e., the positive relationship between price level and nominal rate of interest. According to Keynes, downward rigidity of the market interest rates and a fall in the natural rate of interest following a normal process of capital accumulation causes savings to exceed investment, and prices to fall. However, in his "The General Theory of Employment, Interest, and Money" (1936), he put forward the concept of "neutral rate of interest" which can be thought of as a variable which is consistent with the equilibrium of demand for and supply of assets at the normal rate of growth of the economy. According to Keynes, it can be called as an "optimal rate of interest". Such a neutral rate of interest, which is consistent with steady growth and steady inflation, depends on all the factors that affect aggregate supply and aggregate demand for assets including growth expectations, and the animal spirit.

But Keynes deviated completely from the classical theory while explaining the determination of market rate of interest. According to him, the rate of interest is a reward for parting with liquidity and it is determined in the money market by the demand for and supply of money. The rate of interest, therefore, is purely a monetary phenomenon. Monetary authorities can lower the rate of interest by increasing the money supply in the money market but they cannot bring it down after a certain point on account of the existence of a liquidity trap. In Keynesian model of interest rate determination, output not only affects interest rate but is also affected by the interest rate. This represents a case of joint determination of interest rate and output. Hicks (1937) had incorporated the interaction between the commodity and money markets by synthesizing the Classical and Keynesian theories of interest rates. This is popularly known as the IS-LM model of interest rate determination.

Thus, although there are many theories of interest rate determination, the most recent empirical literature on interest rates has used the loanable funds framework to study the determinants of long-term interest rates. For instance, the impact of expected inflation, ex-ante real short-term interest rate, growth rate of GDP, fiscal deficit, and capital inflows on interest rate has been studied for the US economy by using co-integration technique and Granger Causality by Cebula (1997). Another study by the same author, using the same variables and techniques, found a positive long-term relationship between the expected inflation and government deficit on the one hand, and 20-year government bond yield in UK on the other (Cebula, 1999).

To study interest rate determination in an individual country is no doubt useful, but there is also a need to extend such analysis for many countries for the following reasons: Firstly, international evidence on the determinants of interest rates can provide more information on the robustness of empirical results. Secondly, it is also useful to find out the determinants in the case of small economies in the light of growing integration of world capital markets. In this context, Nunes and Stemitsiotis (1995) have studied the influence of real short-term interest rate, expected inflation, budget deficit, public debt, and growth rate of GDP on the long-term interest rate for 10 OECD countries (US, Japan, Germany, France, UK, Canada, Belgium, Denmark, Ireland, and Netherlands) during 1970-93. They found that the real short-term interest rate, expected inflation, and budget deficit significantly influenced the nominal long-term government bond yield.

Many studies have emphasized the term structure relationship between long and short-rates. They have generally not dealt with the basic economic factors that affect the level of long-term interest rates. These studies have been interested primarily in testing the validity of the expectation theory of term structure of interest rates. A study by Goodfriend (1993) has viewed long-term bond rate as an average of expected future short-rates, which, in turn, depends on monetary policy actions and the expected trend rate of inflation, but it has not studied the impact of these economic factors on the bond rate. On the contrary, Mehra (1994) has examined the role of economic fundamentals in explaining changes in the long-term US Treasury bond rate during the 1955 Q1 to 1993 Q4. By using co-integrating regression, he has found that the bond rate is positively correlated with inflation and deficit financing.

Financial sector reforms have generally allowed interest rates to be market-determined by removing various rigidities and market imperfections which characterized the controlled regime. But this may not be true always. For instance, various reform measures were undertaken in Tunisia since 1960s to remove the negative effects of administered interest rates and to make the interest rate structure more market-determined. However, Bechri (1989) found the inertia in interest rate adjustment to changes in the rate of inflation and world interest rates, and this was due to the lack of effective action on the part of banks. He found that the Central Government, the relatively weak groups such as exporters and farmers, and the relatively more powerful groups such as industrialists and public enterprises benefited from the cheap credit. On the other hand, those groups which prefer interest rate to increase (households sector and banking institutions) have been unsuccessful in collective action and have adapted to the prevailing situation. Thus, it is to be noted that the political influences also play a significant role in the determination of interest rates or there is a political economy of interest rate determination.

Econometric models of interest rate determination usually assume that the real interest rates are stationary, i.e. they tend to return to a constant mean (hence they are called mean-reverting) although they may fluctuate. On the other hand, non-mean-reverting real interest rates would exhibit apparent changes in their mean. The real interest rates in leading developed countries such as USA, UK, Canada, Japan, Italy, and France are found to be non-stationary (Breedon, *et al*, 1999). This implies that the movement in the real long-term interest rate appears to shift in their long-run or equilibrium levels. Howe and Pigott (1991-92) have found that the increase in real long-term interest rates in US, UK, Japan, Germany, and France appears to stem largely from the increase in real equilibrium, long-term interest rate which, in turn, could be attributable to the rise in debt levels, increase in return to physical capital, and risk factors.

There is a widespread belief that the removal of capital controls resulting in free capital mobility makes the international capital market more competitive and unified. As a result, national real long-term interest rates are determined less by the national factors and more by foreign factors and there is a single world interest rate in the unified capital market. In this context, Breedon, *et al* (1999) have examined the role of debt, deficit, growth rate of GDP, real short-term interest rate at home and abroad in determining the long-term real interest rates in G-3 countries, namely, USA, Japan, and Germany during 1972: Q3 to 1988: Q4. Their findings show that interest rates in those countries were determined primarily by the domestic factors, and, therefore, the idea of the existence of a single world capital market appears to be far-fetched.

The studies on interest rate determination in India are few and far between. One such study for the period 1951-86 has shown that the factors like rate of inflation, balance of payments, government market borrowings, and budget deficits had significant effect on interest rates in India (Bhole 1988). But when the capital account is partially open, domestic interest rates are expected to be determined by both the external and internal factors. In this regard, it has been found that "the monetary authorities will continue to determine interest rates policy in India in the light of inflation rate, the desire to evolve a more stable asset-liability balance in banks, the desire to ensure attractiveness of term deposits, the desire to ensure a balance and suitable margin between deposits and lending rates of banks, the exchange rate and its variability (stability), the international capital flows, and the conventional demand for and supply of loanable funds" (Bhole and Sebastian, 1996, p. 277).

Nachane, *et al.* (1997) have used co-integration and error correction mechanism to study the impact of budget deficit and money supply on Indian short-term interest rates during April 1992 to June 1996. They found that the interest rates respond positively only to the budget deficits in India. Chakravarty (2002) used asymmetric vector autoregressive model to find out the causality between fiscal deficit and interest rate in India and found that the fiscal deficit does not induce the rise in interest rate, and the direction of causality runs from the real rate of interest to deficit. Patnaik (2001) argued that the rise in fiscal deficit will not raise the interest rates because the increase in fiscal deficit generates an equal amount of savings by increasing the level of output. Similarly, if the banks had excess reserves or there is insufficient demand for credit, the increase in fiscal deficit will not lead to high real rate of interests.

II. The Model and Methodology

On the basis of a study of theoretical and empirical literature on interest rate determination in both closed and open economies, we hypothesize that the long-term interest rates in India are influenced by real GNP (or savings and capital formation), money supply, fiscal deficit, inflation, foreign interest rates, and foreign exchange reserves (or net capital inflow).

The rationale behind this hypothesis is as follows: The gross national product affects interest rates either via investment or via savings. The former channel is widely known as the accelerator effect and the latter channel is known as thrift effect. Therefore, savings and investment can also be used as alternatives for the growth rate of GNP as determinants of interest rate. Savings by households, and private and public sectors constitute a major source of supply of long-term funds. Savings are said to have a negative impact on interest rates. The higher the savings, the lower will be the rate of interest and *vice versa*. On the other hand, gross domestic capital formation represents the investment demand. Businessmen will go on demanding long-term funds upto the point where the expected net rate of return on investment equals the rate of interest. Therefore, given the net rate of return, the gross domestic capital formation and interest rate can be expected to be positively related. The effect of GNP on interest rate, however, could be either positive or negative.

The empirical relationship between fiscal deficit and interest rate could be either positive or negative. We expect higher fiscal deficit to be associated with higher interest rates because the gap between total expenditure and total revenue in a given year would be financed by issuing bonds in the market. The higher deficit would increase net demand for funds and thereby increase interest rates. This is as per the "crowding out" relationship. However, the budget deficit may not affect the rate of interest much because of two reasons: Firstly, it could be due to the existence of the Ricardian equivalence phenomenon, according to which, if consumers anticipate the future implications of current government deficits, they would realize that the public debt being created now must be repaid in the future by an increase in taxes, and in order to increase their consumption over time, or to avoid a sharp decline in their future disposable income to pay the extra future taxes, the rational economic agents would increase their savings now. As a result, interest rates would decline or they may not be affected much when the deficit increases. Similarly, if the world capital markets are highly integrated, the budget deficit may be financed by global capital, and interest rate may not be much affected by the deficit.

What would be the effect of changes in money supply on interest rate? There are two views in this context. According to one view, an increase in money supply drives down the long-term interest rate. An increase in money supply would reduce the expected future short-term interest rates because of the expected inflationary pressure, which would make long-term securities more attractive than short-term securities, which would lead to an increase in long-term bond prices and fall in interest rates. The higher money supply and the resulting decline in interest rate is seen as a critical element in the transmission mechanism of monetary policy since it stimulates investment and consumer spending. An alternative view which has been championed by Friedman (1968 and 1969), holds that interest rates might rise in response to higher money growth because there is a rise in inflationary expectations. Friedman does not recommend an increase in money supply in order to bring interest rates down.

The world interest rates and the domestic interest rates can be expected to be positively related. It is so because in a small open economy with perfect capital mobility, a higher world interest rates would lead to capital outflow and thereby raise the domestic interest rates to contain further capital outflow. Foreign exchange reserves or net capital inflows may also influence domestic long-term interest rates. A rise in net capital inflows or foreign exchange reserves would have downward pressure on interest rates as they may reduce debt issues including government debt issues. A rise in net capital inflows or foreign exchange reserves may affect the long-term interest rates via expected changes in exchange rate also. For example, an increase in net capital inflows in a given country may lead to an appreciation in its exchange rate, which may attract greater capital inflows in that country, which may create downward pressure on its interest rates.

The nominal rate of interest is said to respond directly to the expected rate of price change. In other words, the nominal rate of interest increases due to expected rate of price increase, and it falls due to the expected rate of price decrease. It is so because when inflation is expected, lenders expect the real value of their principal and interest receipts to decline, and borrowers expect to be able to repay loans with money with lower value. Thus, under inflationary expectations, while there would be a decline in the supply of loans, the demand for loans would tend to increase. Consequently, there would be an increase in the nominal interest rates.

Based on the above-discussed rationale, the following interest rate determination function was estimated by using the OLS method:

$$I_t = C + a_1 GNP_t + a_2 GFD_t + a_3 M_t + a_4 i^*_t + a_5 FER_t + a_6 \pi^e_t + Ut_1 \qquad (1)$$

Where I = Long-term nominal interest rates, GNP = Gross National Product, GFD = Gross Fiscal Deficit, M = Money Supply (M 1), i^* = the long-term Foreign Interest Rate, FER = Foreign Exchange Reserves, π^e = Expected Inflation, and t = Time Period.

The regression coefficients in the case of nominal interest rate are expected to have the following signs:

A priori signs of a_1, a_2, and a_3 might be either negative or positive; $a_4 > 0$, $a_5 < 0$, $a_6 > 0$

The regression coefficients in the case of real interest rate are expected to have the following signs:

A priori signs of a_1, a_2, a_3 and a_6 might be either negative or positive; $a_4 > 0$, $a_5 < 0$.

Equation (1) has been used for studying the determinants of both the nominal long-term interest rate, and the real long-term interest rate. For doing the latter, the variables in equation (1) were converted into real terms by deflating them by wholesale price deflator. While studying the real interest rate determination, the researchers have not been unanimous about whether to include inflationary expectations as a relevant determinant. Some studies have completely ignored the effect of inflation on real rates (Cebula, 1987), while others (Mundell, 1963; Kolluri and Giannaros, 1987) have introduced expected inflation as an additional explanatory variable. The work by Carmichael and Stebbing (1983) also suggests that inflation variable must be included in the real interest rate determination function. The effect of rate of inflation on real interest rate might be positive or negative because an increase in expected inflation would raise the real interest rates if it increases consumption. On the other hand, an increase in expected inflation may lead to a reduction in real interest rates if it reduces the demand for real balances. Therefore, the net effect of an increase in inflation on real interest rate depends on the relative strength of the consumption and real balance effects. Following Mundell and others, we have included inflationary expectations as one of the explanatory variables in the interest rate function.

The model specified so far has been estimated by using the yearly data for three periods: 1970-2000; 1970-1985; and 1986-2000. The long-term nominal interest rate has been alternatively measured by the Central Government bond yield (with 5-years, 5-15 years, and 15 years and above maturity periods respectively), the IDBI Prime Lending Rate, and the Bank Deposit Rate (1-3 years maturity). The real interest rates are obtained by deducting the annual rate of inflation, which, in turn, is measured by the percentage change in wholesale price index (1970-71 = 100) from the respective nominal interest rate. Savings are the gross domestic savings as percentage of GNP. Capital formation is the gross domestic capital formation as percentage of GNP. GNP growth rate is used as an alternative to both savings and capital formation. Gross fiscal deficit is the total central fiscal deficit as percentage of GNP. Money supply is the growth rate of narrow money supply (M1). The world long-term interest rate is proxied by the long-term government bond yield in USA. Foreign exchange reserves and net capital inflows as percentages of GNP are used alternatively. As long-term anticipated inflation is an unobservable variable, the empirical work here uses the actual inflation rate and an average of distributed lags of current and past inflation rates alternatively as a proxy for the expected inflation. All the variables in equation (1) except the inflation rate have been transformed into real variables by deflating the nominal variables by wholesale prices.

As said above, the empirical results about the determinants of interest rate have been obtained by using the OLS method of regression. All the variables, as defined above, are expressed in logarithms. We had estimated the model by using the logarithms of the levels of variables also (the results are not reported here). The performance of the model has been relatively more robust when the data set has been in logarithms of variables in terms of percentage as defined above. The required data for the purpose of estimation have been obtained from various publications of the Reserve Bank of India and the International Monetary Fund. As it is well-known, the consistency property of this method requires that the regressors in the model are (asymptotically) uncorrelated with the error term. It may be argued that the fiscal deficit and GNP are endogenous variables, and. Therefore, they are correlated with the error term. Therefore, in order to ascertain that the variables just mentioned are not endogenous, we have used the test of exogenity which has been developed by Wu (1973), and Hausman (1978).

III. Empirical Results

The results of our empirical exercises are presented in Tables 3 to 9. The regression coefficients in Tables 5 to 9 are elasticities because, as said earlier, the estimation has been carried out after converting the variables into logarithmic form.

The Wu-Hausman statistics under the null hypothesis of exogenity have been shown in Tables 3 and 4. It was found that the growth rate of gross national product and the fiscal deficit to GNP ratio are exogenous in all equations except nominal interest rate equation during the whole time period. So the OLS results will provide consistent estimates.

The estimated Durbin-Watson statistics and Langrange multiplier test showed the absence of autocorrelation problem in all equations except the nominal interest rate equation during the whole time period. Therefore, the nominal interest rate equations were estimated by using Cochren-Orcutt method and have been presented in Tables 5, 6, 7, 8 and 9 which are now free from autocorrelation. The values of adjusted R^2 are very high in all equations. It can be observed that our model explains 44 per cent to 93 per cent of variations in the nominal long-term interest rates, and 75 per cent to 95 per cent of variations in the real long-term interest rates. Thus, apparently, the model appears to be correctly specified.

Table 3: Wu-Hausman Statistics for Testing the Exogeneity of GNP and Fiscal Deficit for the Nominal Interest Rate in Three Periods (i.e. 1970-2000, 1970-85 and 1986-2000)

Variables	Time Period	F-Statistics	Results
Government Bond Yield	1970-2000	F(2,20) = 22.74(0.00)	Rejected
(15 Years and above Maturity)	1970-1985	F(2.5) = 0.546(0.61)	Accepted
	1986-2000	F(2,6) = 6.93(0.028)	Rejected
	1970-2000	F(2,20) = 11.44(0.00)	Rejected
Government Bond Yield	1970-1985	F(2,5) = 0.118(0.89)	Accepted
(5 - 15 Years maturity)	1986-2000	F(2,6) = 1.19(0.366)	Accepted
	1970-2000	F(2,20) = 7.09(0.005)	Rejected
Government Bond Yield	1970-1985	F(2,5) = 0.405(0.687)	Accepted
(1- 5 Years Maturity)	1986-2000	F(2,6) = 0.863(0.468)	Accepted
	1970-2000	F(2,20) = 8.03(0.003)	Rejected
IDBI Prime Lending Rate	1970-1985	F(2,5) = 0.916(0.458)	Accepted
	1986-2000	F(2,6) = 0.020(0.98)	Accepted
	1970-2000	F(2,20) = 6.63(0.006)	Rejected
Bank Deposit Rate	1970-1985	F(2,5) = 0.208(0.819)	Accepted
(1 - 3 Years Maturity)	1986-2000	F(2,6) = 1.12(0.385)	Accepted

NOTE: The figures in the parentheses show the probability values.

Table 4: Wu-Hausman Statistics for Testing the Exogeneity of GNP and Fiscal Deficit for the Nominal Interest Rate in Three Periods (i.e. 1970-2000, 1970-85 and 1986-2000)

Variables	Time Period	F-Statistics	Results
Government Bond Yield (15	1970-2000	F(2,20) = 1.34(0.28)	Accepted
Years and above Maturity)	1970-1985	F(2,5) = 1.05(0.41)	Accepted
	1986-2000	F(2,6) = 2.10(0.20)	Accepted
	1970-2000	F(2,20) = 1.30(0.29)	Accepted
Government Bond Yield (5	1970-1985	F(2,5) = 1.28(0.35)	Accepted
- 15 Years maturity)	1986-2000	F(2,6) = 4.81(0.057)	Accepted
	1970-2000	F(2,20) = 1.97(0.165)	Accepted
Government Bond Yield (1- 5	1970-1985	F(2,5) = 1.13(0.39)	Accepted
Years Maturity)	1986-2000	F(2,6) = 0.943(0.44)	Accepted
	1970-2000	F(2,20) = 0.917(0.416)	Accepted
IDBI Prime Lending Rate	1970-1985	F(2,5) = 1.32(0.34)	Accepted
	1986-2000	F(2,6) = 1.38(0.32)	Accepted
	1970-2000	F(2,20) = 0.85(0.441)	Accepted
Bank Deposit Rate	1970-1985	F(2,5) = 1.00(0.431)	Accepted
(1 - 3 Years Maturity)	1986-2000	F(2,6) = 2.265(0.185)	Accepted

NOTE: The figures in the parentheses show the probability values.

The regression coefficient of the growth rate of GNP is with a positive sign in 18 out of 30 equations presented in this paper, but it is statistically significant only for nominal interest rates in the pre-reform period. On the other hand, it has a negative sign in 12 equations but it is not statistically significant in anyone of them. Therefore, on the whole one may say that there is a tendency towards increase in the long-term interest rates in India as her GNP increases. The accelerator effect appears to be playing a role in interest rate determination in India.

Both nominal and real interest rates equations were estimated by introducing savings and gross domestic capital formation to GNP ratio instead of the growth rate of GNP. But it was found (the results not reproduced here) that the coefficients of these variables were insignificant and had the unexpected signs. Such a result could have been due to high multicollinearity between savings and gross domestic capital formation. Therefore, we estimated each equation by including each of these two variables alternatively in order to know their impact on interest rates. It was found that savings to GNP ratio were negatively related with interest rate in 12 equations but their regression coefficients were statistically significant only for real interest rates in the pre-reform period. Similarly, the investment to GNP ratio had the expected sign (positive) in 13 equations but it was significant only for the real interest rates during the whole time period. The responsiveness of interest rate to the savings and investment to GNP ratio was found to be between 0.56 to 0.76 and 0.54 to 1 respectively. Thus, as expected, savings and

Table 5: Determinants of Government Bond Yield (15 Years and above Maturity)

Independent Variables	Nominal			Real		
	1970-2000	1970-85	1986-2000	1970-2000	1970-85	1986-2000
Constant	0.739	1.0005	1.54	2.46	0.345	5.86
	(2.15)	(4.24)	(3.60)	(2.17)	(0.33)	(8.44)
Growth Rate of GNP	***0.365	0.105	**0.20069	0.0008	-0.025	*0.075
	(3.57)	(1.26)	(2.39)	(0.026)	(-0.68)	(1.90)
Fiscal Deficit (% GNP)	***0.6506	**0.374	0.0378	0.1345	*-0.197	**0.145
	(6.38)	(2.06)	(0.368)	(1.10)	(-1.37)	(2.57)
Growth Rate of M_1	0.0506	-0.03018	0.1169	-0.0621	0.0067	0.0021
	(0.69)	(-0.54)	(1.24)	(-1.00)	(0.087)	(0.0420)
World Interest Rate	-0.3612	0.1813	-0.1285	***0.943	***1.10	-0.2508
	(-3.41)	(1.18)	(-1.23)	(5.99)	(8.55)	(-2.35)
Foreign Exchange Reserves (% GNP)	0.1188	-0.07166	*-0.0681	0.050	0.125	0.047
	(2.57)	(-1.03)	(1.76)	(0.85)	(1.70)	(3.37)
Rate of Inflation	-0.1018	-0.0733	0.0054	***-0.519	***-0.46	***-0.374
	(-1.23)	(-1.31)	(0.072)	(-8.71)	(-7.11)	(-13.20)
F-Statistics	F(6,23)	F(6,8)	(6,8)	F(7,21)	F(6,8)	F(6,8)
	=24.12	=9.98	=6.53	=64.53	=89.3	=55.85
Adjusted R^2	0.8	0.79	0.70	0.94	0.97	0.95
D-W Statistics	1.47	1.20	2.32	1.93	2.05	2.09

NOTES:
The values in the parentheses are the t-statistics.
***, ** and * show the level of significance at 1 per cent, 5 per cent and 10 per cent respectively.

Table 6: Determinants of Government Bond Yield (5 - 15 Years Maturity)

Independent Variables	Nominal			Real		
	1970-2000	1970-85	1986-2000	1970-2000	1970-85	1986-2000
Constant	2.61 (4.73)	0.851 (3.31)	1.96 (1.96)	1.47 (1.21)	-0.23 (-0.241)	5.46 (4.55)
Growth Rate of GNP	0.015 (0.297)	*0.144 (1.59)	0.085 (0.437)	-0.0004 (-0.011)	-0.0252 (-0.631)	0.068 (1.00)
Fiscal Deficit (% GNP)	-0.0568 (-0.531)	*0.269 (1.39)	-0.184 (-0.753)	0.0483 (0.36)	*-0.274 (-1.80)	0.101 (1.03)
Growth Rate of M_1	0.0265 (0.986)	-0.0044 (-0.073)	0.169 (0.77)	-0.0428 (-0.661)	0.0303 (0.369)	0.0049 (0.056)
World Interest Rate	-0.0859 (-0.635)	0.2019 (1.20)	-0.349 (-1.44)	***1.063 (6.26)	***1.17 (8.59)	-0.285 (-1.55)
Foreign Exchange Reserves (% GNP)	-0.009 (-0.143)	-0.033 (-0.43)	-0.0585 (-0.6491)	0.0332 (0.462)	0.155 (1.991)	0.029 (1.22)
Rate of Inflation	-0.003 (-0.092)	-0.0937 (-1.54)	0.2859 (1.62)	***-0.523 (-8.14)	***-0.46 (-6.67)	***-0.293 (-5.98)
F-Statistics	F(8,19) =52.51	F(6,8) =7.80	F(6,8) =2.89	F(7,21) =57.81	F(6,8) =85.48	F(6,8) = 11.50
Adjusted R^2	0.93	0.74	0.45	0.93	0.97	0.81
D-W Statistics	1.83	1.55	1.83	1.85	2.14	1. 71

NOTES: Same as in Table 5.

investment to GNP ratio are shown to be playing an important role in the process of interest rate determination in India.

Our results show that the nominal interest rate had increased with an increase in fiscal deficit to GNP ratio during the pre-reform period, whereas it decreased during the post-reform period. However, the fiscal deficit to GNP ratio has had a negative impact on the long-term real interest rates during pre- as well as post reform period. The sensitivity of real long-term interest rate to fiscal deficit to GNP ratio was found to be between -0.11 to -0.32. It implies that the increase in fiscal deficit to GNP ratio has not crowded out private spending in all the years in India. This result is consistent with that of many other studies (AHMAD, 1994; MAS-

CARO and METLZER, 1983; MAKIN, 1983; HOELSCHER, 1983; PLOSSER 1982 & 1987; EVANS, 1985 & 1987).

As expected, growth rate of money supply has had either negative or positive relationship with the nominal and real long-term rates of interest in India, Growth rate of money supply had a negative sign in 13 equations and a positive sign in 17 equations. But none of them were found to be statistically significant.

The results highlight a positive relationship between the world interest rate and Indian domestic interest rate. The world interest rate has a positive sign in 20 equations and they are highly significant for both nominal and real interest rates during the pre-reform and whole time periods. The elasticity of Indian interest rate to world interest rate appears to have been around 1 during the periods just mentioned. Surprisingly, however, the world interest rate is shown to have had little influence on the Indian nominal and real long-term interest rates in the post-reform period. This matter needs to be explored further.

The foreign exchange reserves to GNP ratio do not appear to have played a significant role in determining nominal or real interest rates in India. This variable had the expected sign (negative) only in 14 out of 30 equations and in most of these equations, it was not statistically significant.

In the case of nominal interest rates, the expected inflation had the expected (positive) sign in 6 out of 15 equations, out of which it was statistically significant in 4 equations, all of which pertained to the period of 1986-2000. The sensitivity of nominal interest rates to expected inflation ranges between 0.15 and 0.67. On the other hand, in the case of long-term real interest rates, the expected inflation had the expected sign (negative) in 15 out of 15 equations, and it was statistically significant in all these 15 equations. The elasticity of real long-term interest rate to inflation varied from -0.22 to -0.54. Thus, the expected inflation and the real long-term interest rates in India were found to be negatively related in all three periods studied by us. The Fisher effect, i.e. one to one correspondence between expected inflation and nominal interest rates did not hold true in India in all periods studied in this paper.

We have also applied CUSUM (Cumulative Sum) of squares test which has been developed by Brown, Durbin and Evans (1975). The CUSUM test gives a plot of the cumulative sum of squared residuals together with two critical lines. If the cumulative sum moves outside the region defined by the two critical lines, the test suggests the existence of parameter instability, i.e., there is a structural break in a given economy in a time period in which CUSUM lies outside the critical lines. We have computed the CUSUM of squares test for both nominal and real interest rates during 1970-2000, and the results are presented in Figures 1 and 2. It can be observed that while the coefficients of nominal interest rates are unstable, those of real interest rates are stable, except in the case of real government bond yield (1-5 years maturity), during the above-mentioned time period. In other words, there has been a structural change for the nominal interest rates but not for the real interest rates between the pre- and post-reform periods.

Table 7: Determinants of Government Bond Yield (1 - 5 Years Maturity)

Independent Variables	Nominal			Real		
	1970-2000	1970-85	1986-2000	1970-2000	1970-85	1986-2000
Constant	1.79 (1.68)	1.06 (3.80)	4.11 (2.49)	0.33 (0.269)	-0.537 (-0.45)	6.18 (2.29)
Growth Rate of GNP	-0.0025 (-0.026)	*0.142 (1.45)	0.17 (0.53)	-0.018 (-0.54)	-0.036 (-0.83)	-0.067 (-0.44)
Fiscal Deficit (% GNP)	0.052 (0.269)	0.109 (0.5091)	-0.433 (-1.07)	-0.0344 (-0.23)	**-0.327 (-1.98)	0.0115 (0.052)
Growth Rate of M_1	-0.0168 (-0.335)	-0.0104 (-0.158)	-0.314 (-0.87)	-0.0639 (-1.00)	0.022 (0.247)	-0.226 (-1.15)
World Exchange Rate	0.204 (0.705)	0.209 (1.14)	-0.71 4 (7.01)	***1.24 (-1. 79)	**1.20 (8.09)	-0.4185 (-1.015)
Foreign Exchange Reserves (% GNP)	0.0014 (-0.009)	-0.0274 (-0.334)	**-0.316 (-2.12)	-0.0331 (-0.38)	0.146 (1.73)	-0.034 (-0.637)
Rate of Inflation	-0.0141 (-0.225)	-0.120 (-1.82)	**0.676 (2.32)	***-0.54 (-8.45)	***-0.493 (-6.57)	**-0.217 (-1.97)
F-Statistics	F(8,19) =23.11	F(6,8) =3.86	F(6,8) =3.49	F(7,21) =57.57	F(6,8) =75.23	F(6,8) = 1.15
Adjusted R^2	0.86	0.55	0.51	0.93	0.97	0.06
D-W Statistics	1.75	1.79	1.76	1.54	1.91	1.59

NOTES: Same as in Table 5.

Table 8: Determinants of IDBI Prime Lending Rate

Independent Variables	Nominal			Real		
	1970-2000	1970-85	1986-2000	1970-2000	1970-85	1986-2000
Constant	3.08	1.20	3.49	2.32	2.63	4.34
	(5.44)	(6.16)	(4.34)	(2.50)	(3.01)	(3.36)
Growth Rate of GNP	0.008	**0.148	-0.127	0.022	0.0219	-0.07006
	(0.112)	(2.17)	(-0.81)	(0.798)	(0.688)	(-0.95)
Fiscal Deficit (% GNP)	**-0.243	0.102	**-0.431	0.0245	0.0449	*-0.1612
	(-1.88)	(0.683)	(-2.18)	(0.259)	(0.371)	(-1.53)
Growth Rate of M_1	0.022	0.0035	-0.1084	-0.0439	-0.039	-0.097
	(0.605)	(0.077)	(-0.616)	(-0.879)	(-0.598)	(-1.03)
World Interest Rate	0.041	***0.427	0.0093	***0. 739	***0.738	-0.1043
	(0.275)	(3.36)	(0.048)	(5.62)	(6.78)	(-0.527)
Foreign Exchange Reserves (% GNP)	0.007	0.017	-0.0253	0.0386	0.094	-0.0105
	(0.093)	(0.298)	(-0.349)	(0.853)	(1.51)	(-0.404)
Rate of Inflation	-0.0283	-0.1014	**0.318	***-0.398	***-0.379	***-0.314
	(-0.609)	(-2.20)	(2.23)	(-7.92)	(-6.90)	(-5.95)
F-Statistics	$F(7,21)$ = 17.09	$F(6,8)$ =20.93	$F(6,8)$ =2.90	$F(7,21)$ =58.85	$F(6,8)$ =77.82	$F(6,8)$ =8.11
Adjusted R^2	0.80	0.89	0.44	0.93	0.97	0.75
D-W Statistics	2.10	1.55	2.41	1.81	1.50	2.60

NOTES: Same as in Table 5.

Table 9: Determinants of Bank Deposit Rate (1- 3 Years Maturity)

Independent Variables	Nominal			Real		
	1970-2000	1970-85	1986-2000	1970-2000	1970-85	1986-2000
Constant	2.52 (4.29)	1.12 (3.06)	2.42 (4.61)	1.606 (1.69)	0.812 (0.816)	4.10 (4.07)
Growth Rate of GNP	* -0. 1014 (-1.40)	0.036 (.282)	0.119 (1.168)	-0.011 (-0.397)	-0.023 (-0.635)	0.016 (0.282)
Fiscal Deficit (% GNP)	*-0.187 (-1.41)	0.034 (0.1188)	***-0.446 (-3.47)	0.007 (0.067)	-0.150 (-1.089)	*-0.116 (-1.41)
Growth Rate of M_1	**0.07 (1.87)	0.048 (0.558)	-0.012 (-0.105)	-0.041 (-0.815)	-0.004 (-0.047)	-0.0355 (-0.483)
World Interest Rate	0.0802 (0.50)	**0.384 (1.60)	0.041 (0.323)	***0.907 (6.91)	***0.959 (7.71)	-0.075 (-0.487)
Foreign Exchange Reserves (% GNP)	-0.0673 (-0.893)	-0.096 (-0.888)	0.012 (0.249)	0.003 (0.057)	0.071 (1.00)	-0.0007 (-0.033)
Rate of Inflation	0.054 (1.14)	-0.069 (-0.796)	*0.156 (1.68)	***-0.491 (-10.02)	***-0.46 (-7.39)	***-0.394 (-9.57)
F-Statistics	F(7,21) = 17.34	F(6,8) =2.54	F(6,8) =8.15	F(7,2l) =73.27	F(6,8) =81.30	F(6,8) =22.31
Adjusted R^2	0.80	0.40	0.75	0.95	0.97	0.90
D-W Statistics	1.55	1.43	1.74	1. 77	1.80	1.94

NOTES: Same as in Table 5.

Figure 1:
The CUSUM of SquaresTest for Long-term Nominal Interest Rates
(The straight lines represent critial bounds at 5 per cent significance level)

Panel a:
Nominal Government Bond Yield
(15 years and above maturity)

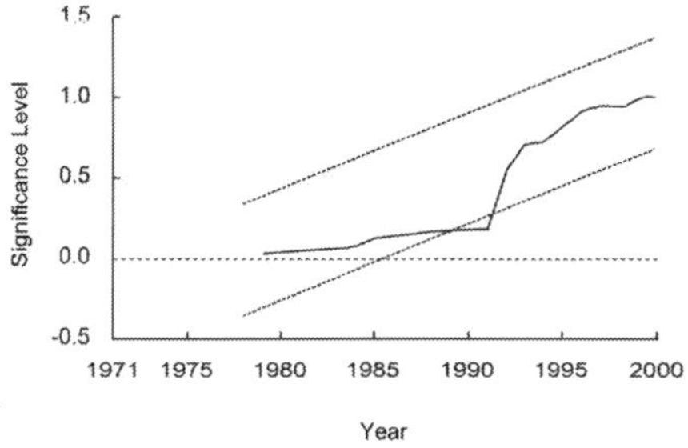

Panel b:
Nominal Government Bond Yield
(5-15 years maturity)

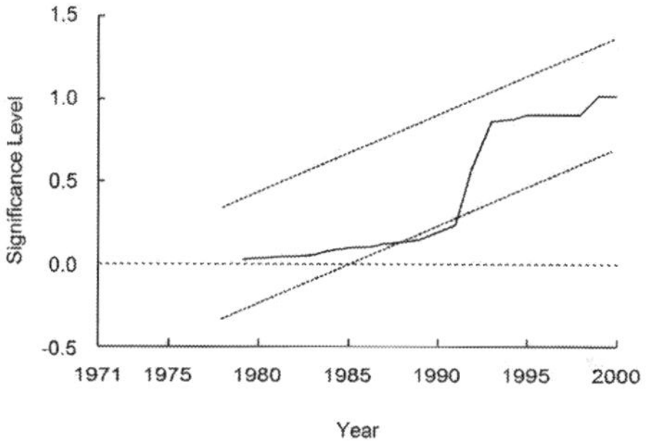

Panel c:
Nominal Government Bond Yield
(1-5 years maturity)

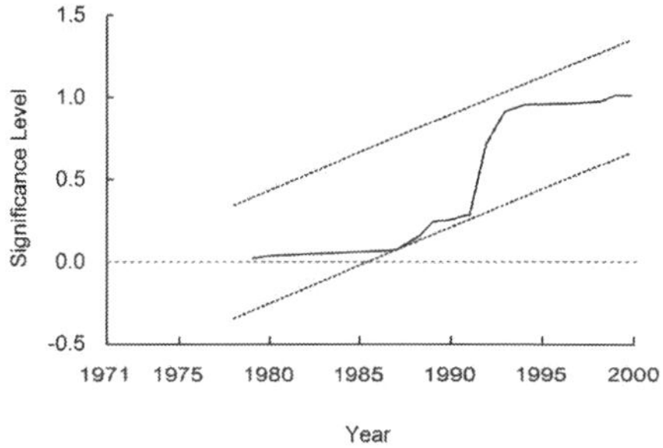

Panel d: Nominal IDBI Prime Lending Rate

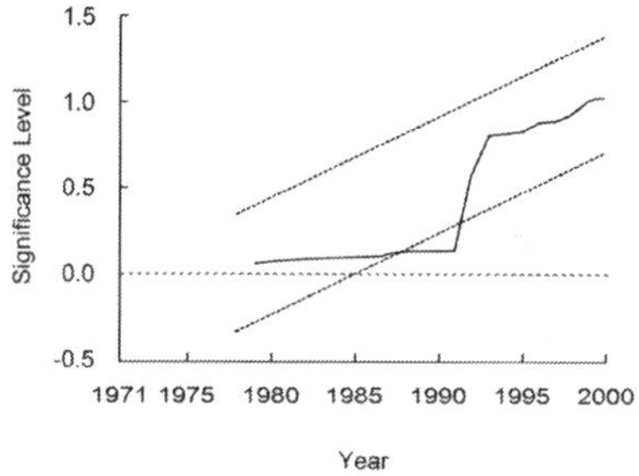

Panel e:
Nominal Bank Deposit Rate
(1-3 years maturity)

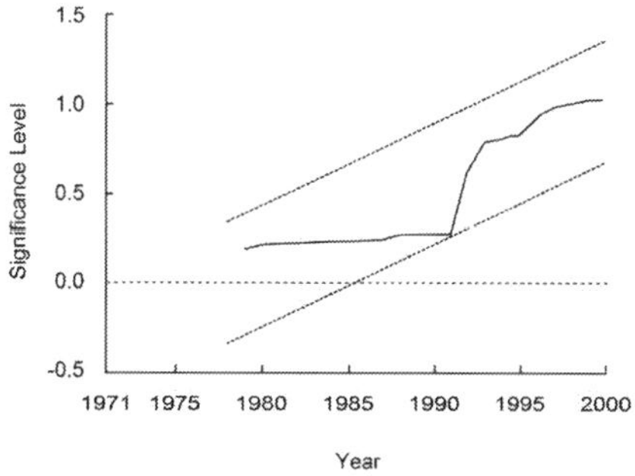

Figure 2:
The CUSUM of SquaresTest for Long-term Real Interest Rates
(The straight lines represent critial bounds at 5 per cent significance level)

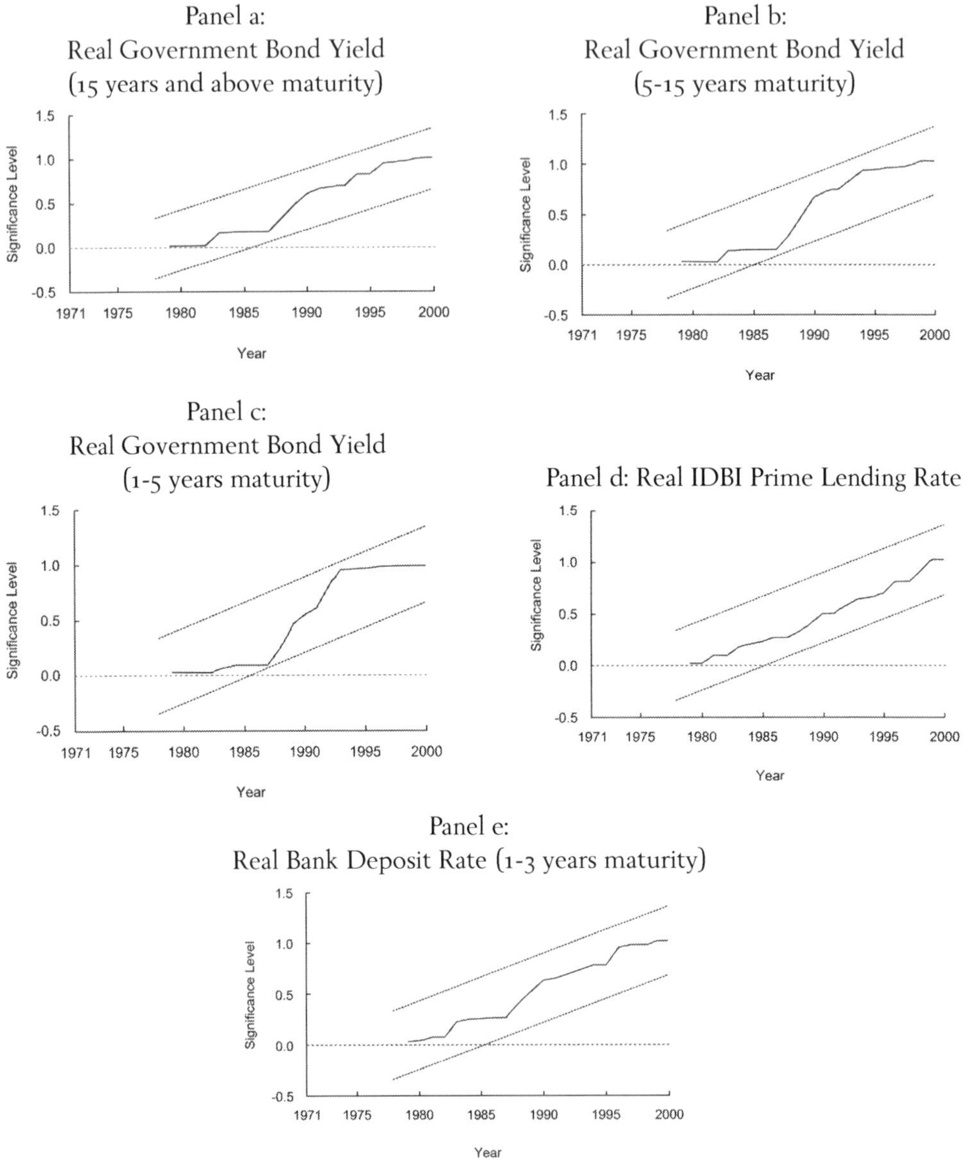

IV. Conclusions

This paper has addressed the issue as to what are the major economic determinants of long-term real as well as nominal interest rates in India during the pre- and post-reform period. The model specified to throw light on this issue has explained 44 per cent to 93 per cent of variations in the nominal interest rates, and 75 per cent to 95 per cent of variations in the real interest rates during the three periods studied in this paper. It was also found that the growth rate of GNP, fiscal deficit to GNP ratio, and world interest rate have had positive and significant effect on the long-term nominal interest rates during the pre-reform period, whereas only the fiscal deficit to GNP ratio and expected inflation appear as their significant determinants during the post-reform period. The relationship between the fiscal deficit to GNP ratio and nominal interest rate was found to be negative in the latter period. On the other hand, while the long-term real interest rates were largely influenced by the fiscal deficit to GNP ratio and world interest rate in the pre-liberalization period, they were impacted primarily by inflation and fiscal deficit to GNP ratio in the post-liberalization period. The fiscal deficit has had a negative effect on real interest rates in both these time periods.

A structural change between the pre- and post-reform periods was detected for the nominal interest rates but generally not for the real interest rates. The most important determinants of real interest rates were found to be the world interest rate and expected inflation during 1970-2000. The elasticity of the domestic interest rate to the world interest rate appears to have been about 1 during the period just mentioned.

It may be concluded that although various measures have been taken to deregulate the Indian economy since 1985, the interest rates are not yet determined mainly by the market forces. The factors like growth rate of money supply, growth rate of GNP, and world interest rate have not played much role in the process of interest rate determination during the post-reform period. The interest rates in India are still quasi-administered, or "deregulation has not resulted in the full restoration of market forces; what has emerged is the regulation responsive to market forces or flexible regulation" (BHOLE & SEBASTIAN, 1996, p. 277).

References

AHMAD, M., "The Effects of Government Budget Deficits on the Interest Rates: A Case Study of Small Open Economy", *Economia Internazialia*, Vol. 47, No.1, 1994, pp. 1-6.

BECHRI, M. Z., "The Political Economy of Interest Rate Determination in Tunisia" in K. Nabli Mustapha and Jeffery B. Nugent (eds.), *The New Institutional Economics and Development: Theory and Application to Tunisia*, Elsevier Science, New York, 1989.

BHOLE, L. M., "Some Issues Concerning Interest Rates Theory and Policy", *The Indian Economic Journal*, The Conference Volume, 1988, pp. 1-18.

BHOLE, L M, *Financial Institutions and Markets*, Third Edition, Tata McGraw Hill Publishing Company Limited, New Delhi, 1999.

BHOLE, L. M. and V. J. Sebastian, "Determinants of Interest Rates in a Deregulated Open Economy", *The Indian Journal of Economics*, Vol. 77, No. 305, 1996, pp. 261-278.

BHOLE, L. M. and P. Dash, "Industrial Recession in India: Is Interest Rate the Cause?", *Productivity*, Vol. 43, No. 2, July-Sept 2002, pp. 268-277.

BREEDON, F.; H. Brian and W. Geoffrey, "Long-Term Real Interest Rates: Evidence on the Global Capital Markets", *Oxford Review of Economic Policy,* Vol. 15, No. 2, 1999, pp.128-142.

BROWN, R. L.; J. Durbin and J. M. Evans, "Techniques for Testing the Constancy of Regression Relationship over Time", *Journal of the Royal Statistical Society,* Vol. 2, 1975, pp 149-192.

CARMICHEAL, J. and P. W. Stebbing, "Fisher's Paradox and the Theory of Interest", *American Economic Review,* Vol. 73, 1983, pp. 619-630.

CEBULA, R. J., "Federal Deficits and the Real Rate of Interest in the United States: A Note", *Public Choice,* Vol. 53, 1987, pp. 97-100.

CEBULA, R. J., "The Impact of Federal Budget Deficits on Long-Term Nominal Interest Rates in the US: New Evidence and on updating using Co-integration and Geanger Causality Tests, 1973:2-1993:3", *Economia Internazialia,* Vol. 50, No.1, 1997, pp. 49-60.

CEBULA, R. J., "Budget Deficits, Capital Flows, and Long-Term Interest Rates: CoIntegration Findings for the UK", *International Advances in Economic Research,* Vol. 5, 1999, pp. 28-43.

CHAKRABORTY, L, "Fiscal Deficit and Rate of Interest: An Econometric Analysis of the Deregulated Financial Regime", *Economic and Political Weekly,* May 11, 2002, pp. 1831-1838.

CORREIA, N. J. and L. Stemitsiotis, "Budget Deficits and Interest Rates: Is There a Link? International Evidence," *Oxford Bulletin of Economics and Statistics,* Vol. 57, 1995, pp. 425-449.

EDWARDS, S. and M. Khan, "Interest Rate Determination in Developing Countries – A Conceptual Framework", *IMF Staff Papers,* Vol. 32, 1985, pp. 377-403.

EVANS, P., "Do Large Deficits Produce High Interest Rates?", *American Economic Review,* Vol. 75, No. 1, 1985, pp. 68-87.

EVANS, P., "Do Budget Deficits Raise Nominal Interest Rates? Evidence from Six Countries", *Journal of Monetary Economics,* Vol. 20, No.2, 1987, pp. 281-300.

FINDLAY, D. W., "Budget Deficits, Short-term Real Interest Rates and the Specification of Expected Inflation: An Empirical Investigation", *Applied Economics,* Vol. 23, 1991, pp. 1147-1158.

FISHER, I., *The Theory of Interest,* New York, Macmillan, 1990.

FRIEDMAN, M, "The Role of Monetary Policy", *American Economic Review,* Vol. 58, 1968, pp. 1-17.

FRIEDMAN, M., "Factors Affecting the Level of Interest Rates", Proceedings of the 1968 Conference on Savings and Loan League, *The League,* 1969, pp. 11-27.

GOODFRIEND, M., "Interest Rate Policy and the Inflation Scare Problem: 1979 to 1992", *Federal Reserve Bank of Richmond Economic Quarterly,* Vol. 79, 1993, pp. 1-24.

GUPTA, K. L., "Financial Development and Economic Growth in India and South Korea", *Journal of Economic Development,* Vol. 11, No. 2, 1986, pp. 41-62.

HAUSMAN, J. A., "Specification Tests in Econometrics", *Econometrica,* Vol. 46, 1978, pp. 1251-1257.

HICKS, J, "Mr. Keynes and the Classics: A Suggested Interpretation", *Econometrica*, April, 1937, pp. 147-59.

HOELSCHER, M, "Federal Borrowings and Short-term Interest Rates", *Southern Economic Journal*, Vol. 50, No. 2, 1983, pp. 319-333.

HOWE, H and C Pigott, "Determinants of Long-term Interest Rates: An Empirical Study of Several Industrial Countries", *Federal Reserve Bank of New York Quarterly Review*, Winter, 1991-92, pp. 12-28.

INTERNATIONAL MONETARY FUND, *International Financial Statistics*, Various Issues.

KEYNES, J. M., *The General Theory of Employment, Interest, and Money*, Harcourt Brace and Company, New York, 1936.

KEYNES, J. M., "A Treatise on Money: The Applied Theory of Money", *The Collected Writings of John Maynard Keynes*, Vol. VI, London, Macmillan for the Royal Economic Society, 1971.

KOLLURI, B. R. and D. S. Giannaros, "Budget Deficits and Short-Term Real Interest Rate Forecasting", *Journal of Macroeconomics*, Vol. 9, 1987, pp. 109-25.

KOYCK, L. M. and Maria J t Hooft-Welvaars, "Economic Growth, Marginal Productivity of Capital, and the Rate of Interest", in F H Haan and F P R Brechling (eds), *The Theory of Interest Rates*, Macmillan, New York, 1966.

LANYI, A and R Scacaglu, "Interest Rate Policies in Developing Countries", *Occasional Papers*, No. 22, IMF. Washington D.C, 1983.

MAKIN, J., "Real Interest. Money Surprises, Anticipated Inflation, and Fiscal Deficits", *The Review of Economics and Statistics*, Vol. 65, No. 3, 1983, pp. 374-384.

MASCARO, A. and A. Metzler, "Long and Short-Term Interest Rates in a Risky World", *Journal of Monetary Economics*, Vol. 12, 1983, pp. 238-247.

MATTHEWS, R. C o, *The Rate of Interest in Growth Models*, Oxford Economic Papers, Vol. 12, 1960, pp. 417-424.

MCKINNON, R. I., *Money and Capital in Economic Development*, Brooking Institution, Washington D.C, 1973.

MEHRA, Y P, "An Error Correction Model of the Long-Term Bond Rate", *Federal Reserve Bank of Richmond Economic Quarterly*, Vol. 80, No.4, 1994, pp. 49-68.

METZLER, A, "Wealth, Saving, and Interest Rate", *Journal of Political Economy*. Vol. 59, 1955, pp. 351-365.

MUNDELL, R. "Inflation and Real Interest Rate", *Journal of Political Economy*, Vol. 70, June, 1963, pp. 280-283.

NACHANE, D. M.; A. V. Karnik and N. R. Hatekar, "The Interest Rate Imbroglio, Monetary and Fiscal Dimensions", *Economic and Political Weekly*, May 17-24, 1997, pp. 1167-1174.

NUNES, J. C. and L. Stemitsiotis, "Budget Deficit and Interest Rates: Is there a Link? International Evidence", *Oxford Bulletin of Economics and Statistics*, Vol. 4, No. 57, 1995, pp. 425-449.

PATNAIK, P., "On Fiscal Deficits and Real Interest Rates", *Economic and Political Weekly,* April 14, 2001, pp. 1160-1163. .

PLOSSER, C. I., "Government Financing Decisions and Asset Returns", *Journal of Monetary Economics,* Vol. 9, No. 3, 1982, pp. 325-352.

PLOSSER, C. I., "Fiscal Policy and Term-Structure", *Journal of Monetary Economics,* Vol. 20, No.2, 1987, pp. 343-368.

RESERVE BANK OF INDIA, "Report on Currency and Finance, 2001-02", Mumbai, 2003.

RESERVE BANK OF INDIA, "Handbook of Statistics on Indian Economy, 2002", Mumbai, 2003.

RESERVE BANK OF INDIA, "Report of the Committee to Review the Working of the Monetary System" (Chakravarty Committee Report), Bombay, 1985.

RESERVE BANK OF INDIA, "Report of the Working Group on the Money Market" (Vaghul Group Report)", Bombay, 1987.

SEN, A. K., "Interest, Investment, and Growth" in Amartya Sen (ed). *Growth Economics,* Penguin Books, Harmondsworth, 1971.

SHAW, E. S., *Financial Deepening in Economic Development,* Oxford University Press, Oxford, 1973.

WICKSELL, K., "The Influence of the Rate of Interest on Commodity Prices" in E. Lindhal (ed), *Selected Papers on Economic Theory by Knut Wicksell,* Allen & Unwin, London, 1958.

WU, D., "Alternative Tests of Independence Between Stochastic Regressors and Disturbances", *Econometrica,* Vol. 41, 1973, pp. 773-750.

[9]

*Domestic and External Factors in Short-Term Interest Rates Determination in India**

Introduction

There are many theories such as Classical Theory, Keynesian Theory, Loanable Funds Theory, and Real Business Cycle Theory of interest rate determination. Empirically, the determinants of interest rates in a given economy depend on whether the economy is closed or open, i.e., on the degree of openness of the current and capital accounts of its Balance of Payments. If a country's capital account is completely closed to the rest of the world, then the interest rates will be determined only by various domestic factors. On the contrary, if a country's capital account is fully open to the rest of the world, then the domestic interest rates will be influenced by both internal and external factors.

The Indian economy had witnessed a regime of administered interest rates structure till the middle of 1980s. But several measures were taken by the monetary authorities to develop, integrate, and enhance the efficiency in the money and government securities market following the recommendations of Chakravarty Committee in 1985 and Vaghul Committee in 1987. After 1991, a large number of financial sector reforms have been implemented in India, as in many other countries. Interest rates have been progressively deregulated as a result of which they have become largely market-determined and market-related. Similarly, various restrictions and controls on capital flows have been progressively reduced, as a result of which, the Indian financial system is said to have become much more integrated with the international financial system than before.

* Paper published jointly with Pradyumna Dash in the *Indian Economic Journal*, April-September 2004.

With such changes, the issue of interest rate determination has become increasingly more relevant and important. There is a need now to answer empirically the questions such as: which domestic market factors now determine interest rates in India, and what is the relative strength of those factors? Which external or open economy factors have a substantial and significant impact on interest rates in India? The policy makers would like to understand how far monetary policy can now influence interest rates?

It is in this context that the objective of the present Paper is to estimate empirically a model of short-term interest rates determination with the help of co-integration technique so as to identify the domestic and external determinants of short-term interest rates in India during post1991 period.

The Paper is divided in four Sections. In Section I, a brief review of some of the earlier empirical studies on interest rates determination, with a focus on Indian studies, is presented. The econometric specification of the interest rates determination model, and the estimation methodology are discussed in Section II. The results are presented in Section III. The findings and conclusions are summarized in Section IV.

I. Some Earlier Empirical Studies

The literature on interest rates is quite old and vast. The well-known theories of interest rates can be studied easily from the works by Fisher (1930), Keynes (1936), Wicks ell (1958), Hicks (1937), Metzler (1951), Mundell (1960), Goodhart (1989), Barro (1993), and so on. The aim of this Section is to review briefly only some of the relatively recent empirical studies on interest rates determination, the focus of attention being on the Indian studies.

Among these studies, Blejer (1982) has tested the validity of Uncovered Interest Parity (UIP) for Argentina during 1977-81, and has found that it cannot be rejected. It has also been found that the deviations from CIP may occur on account of various factors such as transaction costs (FRENKEL and LEVICH, 1975), taxation (LEVI, 1977), capital controls (DOOLEY and ISARD, 1980), data imperfections (MCCORMICK, 1979), and capital market imperfections (FRENKEL, 1973).

Gupta and Gupta (1994) have estimated the model of real interest rate parity to test the role of capital market integration in the process of interest rates determination in many developing and developed countries. They found that domestic monetary policy, expected change in exchange rate, and country risk influence the domestic real interest rates in developing countries. Using quarterly data during 1962-82, Edwards (1985) has developed a semi-open economy model of interest rates determination for Columbia and has found that interest rates depend on both domestic credit conditions and foreign interest rates. Edwards and Khan (1985) have also developed a model of interest rates determination for Columbia and Singapore during 1968-82 and 1976-83 respectively, and have found that interest rates in Singapore are entirely determined by the external factors, whereas in Columbia they are determined by external as well as internal factors.

Blejer and Gil Diaz (1991) found that the monetary authorities have little control over real interest rates in Uruguay. Gochoco (1991) has studied the determinants of interest rates in Philippines during January 1981 to December 1985, and found that the capital account there is quite open, and the domestic monetary policy also affects domestic interest rates indirectly. Caporale and Pittis (1997) found that the monetary policy in Germany, the expected inflation, and budget deficit significantly influence interest rates in Japan and USA respectively.

The area of empirical study of interest rates behaviour in India has remained underdeveloped on account of the prevalence of administered and semi-administered interest rates regimes over many years. Among a very few available studies, Bhole (1988) had found that the factors like expected inflation, balance of payments, government market borrowings, and budget deficit had significant effect on interest rates in India during 1951-1986. In another study, Bhole and Sebastian (1996) had found that inflation rate, the desire to evolve a more stable asset-liability balance in banks, the desire to ensure attractiveness of term deposits, the desire to ensure a balance and suitable margin between deposits and lending rates of banks, the exchange rate and its variability(stability), the international capital flows, and the conventional demand for and supply of funds were the relevant factors influencing the behaviour of interest rates in a deregulated Indian economy. Dua and Pandit (2001) have studied the determinants of short-term interest rates in India by using Co-integration and Granger causality during March 1993 to May 2000 and have concluded that there is a long-run relationship between the real interest rates, real government expenditure, real money supply, foreign interest rates, and forward premium. Nachane, et al. (1997) also have used co-integration and error correction mechanism to study the impact of budget deficit and money supply on Indian short-term interest rates during April 1992 to June 1996. They have found that the interest rates respond positively only to the budget deficits in India. Chakraborty (2002) used an asymmetric vector autoregressive model to find out the causality between fiscal deficit and interest rates in India and found that the fiscal deficit does not induce an increase in interest rates, and that the direction of causality runs from the real rate of interest to the deficit. Patnaik (2001) has argued that an increase in fiscal deficit does not increase interest rates because it generates an equal amount of savings by increasing the level of output. Similarly, if the banks have excess reserves or there is insufficient demand for credit, an increase in fiscal deficit does not lead to increase in rates of interest.

II. The Model and Methodology

On the basis of a study of theoretical and empirical literature on interest rates determination in semi-open economies, we hypothesize that the short-term interest rates in India are determined by Gross National Product, money supply, fiscal deficit, expected inflation, foreign interest rates, and forward premium (or foreign exchange reserves or net short-term capital inflows or expected changes in exchange rate).

The rationale behind this hypothesis and a priori relationships between interest rates and factors influencing them can be stated as follows: The Gross National Product (GNP) affects interest rates either via demand for real balances or via supply shocks. According to the former channel, given the level of interest rates, a higher level of income causes the demand for real balances to be higher, which causes disequilibrium in the money market. To maintain the equilibrium, interest rates have to increase. Therefore, the relationship between gross domestic product and interest rates is expected to be positive. According to the latter channel, the rates of interest are determined by the aggregate demand and aggregate supply of goods and services. For instance, given the interest rates, if the aggregate supply in an economy decreases due to any adverse factors like harvest failure, strikes, natural disasters, epidemics, and political disruptions, then there will be a decrease in aggregate demand, but the decrease in aggregate demand will be less than the decrease in aggregate supply, which, in turn, will results in net excess demand for commodities. This will make borrowings more attractive (or reduce savings) because the borrowers plan to repay their debts or build up their assets later when income is higher. As a result, interest rates will increase to bring the equilibrium in the commodity markets. Thus, the interest rates are expected to be negatively related to the output. As mentioned later, Index of Industrial Production (IIP) would be used as a proxy for GNP in this study because of the non-availability of monthly data on the GNP.

The higher fiscal deficit can be expected to be associated with higher interest rates because the gap between the Government's total expenditure and total revenue in a given month would be financed by issuing bonds in the market. The higher deficit would increase net demand for funds and thereby increase interest rates. However, it is also likely that the budget deficit may not affect rates of interest much because of two reasons: Firstly, according to the Ricardian equivalence theorem, if the consumers anticipate the future implications of current government deficits, they would realize that the public debt being created now must be repaid in the future by an increase in taxes, and in order to increase their consumption over time, or to avoid a sharp decline in their future disposable income to pay the extra future taxes, they would increase their savings now. As a result, interest rates would decline or they may not be affected much when the deficit increases. Secondly, if world capital markets are well integrated, the budget deficit may be financed by global capital; and interest rates may not be much affected by the deficit.

What can be the effect of changes in money supply on interest rates? There are two views in this context. According to one view, an increase in money supply would increase the level of income which would increase the demand for securities in financial markets and, thus, would lead to an increase in security prices and a fall in interest rates. The higher money supply and the resulting decline in interest rates is seen as a critical element in the transmission mechanism of monetary policy since it stimulates investment and consumer spending. An alternative view which has been put forth by Friedman 1968 and 1969), holds that interest rates might rise in response to higher monetary growth because there would be a rise in inflationary expectations.

The world interest rates and the domestic interest rates can be expected to be positively related because in an open economy with perfect capital mobility, higher world interest rates would lead to capital outflows and thereby raise the domestic interest rates to contain further capital outflows. Foreign exchange reserves or short-term net capital inflows may also influence domestic short-term interest rates. A rise in short-term net capital inflows or foreign exchange reserves may have a downward pressure on domestic interest rates as they may reduce debt issues, including government debt issues, and they may lead to an appreciation of the country's exchange rate which may attract further capital inflows in the country. Since the forward premium is a good approximation of changes in the future spot exchange rate, it can be used as a proxy for the latter.

In theory, the nominal rates of interest respond directly to the expected rate of price change. In other words, the nominal rates of interest increase due to expected rate of price increase, and they fall due to the expected rate of price decrease. It is so because when inflation is expected, lenders expect the real value of their principal and interest receipts to decline, and borrowers expect to be able to repay loans with money with lower value. Thus under inflationary expectations, while there would be a decline in the supply of loans, the demand for loans would tend to increase. Consequently, there would be an increase in nominal interest rates.

Based on the above-discussed rationale, the short-term interest rates determination function can be written as:

$$i_t = C + a_1 FP_t + a_2 M_t + a_4 i^*_t + a_4 GIIP_t + a_5 GFD_t + a_6 INFN_t + U_t \quad .. (1)$$

Where i = Short-term nominal interest rates represented alternatively by the call money rate, commercial paper rate, certificate of deposit rate, 91-day Treasury Bills rate, and 364-day Treasury Bill rate, FP = Forward Premium, M = Money Supply (M1), i^* = the Short-Term World Interest Rate, GIIP = General Index of Industrial Production, GFD = Gross Fiscal Deficit, INFN = Expected Inflation, C = constant, and t is time period.

Equation (1) has been used by us for studying the determinants of both the nominal short-term interest rates and the real short-term interest rates in India. The regression coefficients in the case of nominal interest rates are expected to have the following signs:

$$a_1 > 0, a_2 > \text{or} < 0, a_3 > 0, a_4 > 0 \text{ or} < 0, a_5 > 0 \text{ or} < 0, a_6 > 0$$

For estimating real interest rates determination function, the variables in equation (1) except inflation, forward premium, and Index of Industrial Production were converted into real terms by deflating them by wholesale price deflator. While studying the real interest rates determination, the researchers have not been unanimous about whether to include inflationary expectations as a relevant determinant. Some studies have completely ignored the effect of inflation on real rates (Cebula, 1987), while others (Mundell, 1963; Kolluri and Giannaros; 1987) have introduced expected inflation as an additional explanatory variable. The work by Carmichael and Stebbing (1983) also suggests that inflation variable may be included in the real interest rates determination function. The a priori effect of rate of inflation on real interest rates is difficult to state because an increase in, expected inflation would raise the real interest rates if it increases consumption or it may lead to a reduction in real interest rates if it reduces the demand for real balances. Therefore, the net effect of an increase in inflation on real interest rates depends on the relative strength of the consumption and real balance effect. Following Mundell and others, we have included inflationary expectations as one of the explanatory variables in the real interest rates function.

The regression coefficients in the case of real interest rates determination are expected to have the following signs:

$$a_1 > 0, a_2 > \text{ or } < 0, a_3 > 0, a_4 > 0 \text{ or } < 0, a_5 > 0 \text{ or } < 0, a_6 > \text{ or } < 0$$

The determinants of interest rates have been studied in this Paper by using Cointegration Analysis including Error Correction Technique, Granger Causality, and Impulse Response Technique, which is an improvement over the earlier Indian Studies in this context (HAMILTON J., 1994; GREEN, 2000). All variables are expressed in the level form. We also estimated the model by converting the variables in logarithms but the results were not robust, and, therefore, they are not reported in this Paper. The required data for the purpose of estimation have been obtained from the various publications of the Reserve Bank of India and the International Monetary Fund. The study uses monthly data for the period April 1994 to March 2004; the period before 1994 could not be covered because the monthly data for certain variables before 1994 are not available. As indicated earlier, the short-term nominal interest rate has been alternatively measured by the call money rate, the commercial paper rate, the certificate of deposit rate, the 91-day Treasury bills rate, and 364-day Treasury bills rate. The real interest rates have been obtained by deducting the monthly rate of inflation, which, in turn, is measured by the percentage change in wholesale price index (1993-94 = 100) from the respective nominal interest rates. The Index of Industrial Production (1993-94 = 100) for all commodities (GIIP) is used as a proxy for the Gross National Product because of the unavailability of monthly data for the latter. Gross fiscal deficit is the monthly Central fiscal deficit. Money supply is the growth rate of narrow money supply (M1). The world short-term interest rate is proxied by the dollar London inter-bank offer rate (LIBOR) and Fed Fund Rate. Foreign exchange reserves, short-term net capital inflow, and forward premium are used alternatively to represent one of the external factors influencing domestic interest rates. As short-term anticipated inflation is an unobservable variable, the actual inflation rate, and the average of distributed lags of current and past inflation rates have been alternatively used as proxies for the expected inflation.

The first econometric step that has been used is to test the null hypothesis that the series are random walk or non-stationary by using both Augmented Dickey-Fuller (1979) and Philips-Perron (1988) tests. If the variables were found to be non-stationary, we have tested the possibility of one or more co-integrating relationships using the Johansen and Juselius (1990, 1992) methodology in the form of two test statistics namely, the trace test and maximal eigen value test. The impact of the stationary exogenous variables on interest rates and the short-run disequilibrium has been studied with the help of error correction model (ECM) which was first used by Sargan (1984) and later popularized by Engle and Granger (1987). Granger causality has also been studied in the framework of vector error correction model (VECM) by including the error correction term in addition to lagged variables. The dynamic interaction between the variables has been captured by VECM through Impulse Response Function Analysis which traces the response of both nominal and real short-term interest rates in India to one standard deviation change in world interest rate.

Table 1 (a): Augmented Dickey Fuller (ADF) Test Statistics for Nominal Variables

Variables	With trend		Without trend	
	Levels	First differences	Levels	First differences
Call money rate	-3.56**	-	-2.51	-6.16**
Commercial paper rate	-3.41	-5.36**	-1.06	-5.20**
Certificate of deposit rate	-3.40	-6.31**	-0.99	-6.21**
91-day Treasury bills rate	-2.69	-3.67**	-1.08	-3.63**
364-day Treasury bills rate	-2.87	-3.61"*	-0.69	-3.45**
Forward premium (6 month)	-3.38	-4.90**	-2.41	-4.80**
World interest rate (6month LIBOR)	-2.11	-3.77**	-0.61	-3.72**
World interest rate (Monthly Fed Fund Rate)	-2.47	-2.87	-1.19	-2.87
Expected change in exchange rate	-2.59	-4.68**	-2.12	-4.56**
Growth rate of money supply (M1)	-0.59	-4.71**	-1.87	-4.03 * *
Fiscal deficit	-6.83**	-	-4.90	
Index of industrial production	-2.25	-5.38**	-2.25	-5.41**
Inflation	-5.48**	-	-5.41	-
Critical values (5% level)	-3.44	-	-2.88	-

NOTE:
(1) **indicates variables are stationary at 5% level.
(2) Lag length is 4.

Table 1 (b): Augmented Dickey Fuller (ADF) Test Statistics for Real Variables

Variables	With trend		Without trend	
	Levels	First differences	Levels	First differences
Call money rate	-3.86**	-	-3.51**	-
Commercial paper rate	-3.07	-5.04**	-2.36	-4.94**
Certificate of deposit rate	-2.76	-6.03 **	-2.15	-5.90**
91-day Treasury bills rate	-3.02	-4.53**	-2.80	-4.53**
364-day Treasury bills rate	-2.65	-4.72**	-2.18	4.66**
World interest rate (6month LIBOR)	-2.75	-3.51**	-2.40	-3.45**
World interest rate (Monthly Fed Fund Rate)	-2.75	-4.41**	- 2 . 4 0	-3.45**
Growth rate of money supply (M1)	-1.03	-5.31**	1.35	-5.07**
Fiscal deficit	-6.88**	-	-6.01**	-
Critical values (5% level)	-3.44	-	-2.88	-

NOTE: Same as in Table 1 (a).

Table 2 (a): Phillips-Perron (PP) Test Statistics for Nominal Variables

Variables	With trend		Without trend	
	Levels	First differences	Levels	First differences
Call money rate	-6.56**	-	-5.68**	-
Commercial paper rate	-2.81	-10.65**	-1.07	-10.61**
Certificate of deposit rate	-3.15	-13.19**	-1.94	-13.14**
91-day Treasury bills rate	-2.70	-10.74**	-1.03	-10.65**
364-day Treasury bills rate	-2.09	-8.34**	-0.27	-8.24**
Forward premium (6 month)	-3.11	-9.49**	-2.34	-9.48**
World interest rate (6month LIBOR)	-2.00	-6.75**	-0.015	-6.59* *
World interest rate (Monthly Fed Fund Rate)	-2.22	-10.10**	-0.12	-9.67**
Expected change in exchange rate	-2.27	-8.64**	-1.91	-8.61 **
Growth rate of money supply (M1)	-1.24	-14.20**	-1.67	-13.76**
Fiscal deficit	-12.52**	-	-1.28**	
Index of industrial production	-2.79	-18.28**	-2.81	-18.37**
Inflation	-10.00**	-	-9.93**	-
Critical values (5% level)	-3.44	-	-2.88	-

NOTE: Same as in Table 1 (a).

Table 2 (b): Phillips-Perron (PP) Test Statistics' for Real Variables

Variables	With trend		Without trend	
	Levels	First differences	Levels	First differences
Call money rate	-5.70**	-	-5.64**	-
Commercial paper rate	-2.69	-9.07**	-2.27	-8.99**
Certificate of deposit rate	-3.00	-10.61**	-2.69	-10.52**
91-day Treasury bills rate	-2.99	-9.02**	-2.87	-8.91**
364-day Treasury bills rate	-2.49	-8.74**	-2.19	-8.62**
World interest rate (6month LIBOR)	-2.10	-8.95**	-1.78	-8.99**
World interest rate (monthly fed fund rate)	-2.10	-8.95**	-1.78	-8.99**
Growth rate of money supply (M1)	-2.06	-9.83**	1.36	-9.66**
Fiscal deficit	-11.91**	-	-11.49**	-
Critical values (5% level)	-3.44	-	-2.88	-

NOTE: Same as in Table 1 (a).

III. Empirical Results

Tables 1 (a, b) and 2 (a, b) present the unit root test results for both nominal and real variables as per ADF and PP tests, respectively. On the basis of ADF and PP tests, the variables like commercial paper rate, certificate of deposit rate, 91-day Treasury bills rate, 364-day Treasury bill rate, forward premium, world interest rate (both LIBOR and Fed Fund Rate), growth rate of money supply, and index of industrial production are found to be non-stationary, whereas variables like call money rate, fiscal deficit, and expected inflation are found to be stationary. The plot of correlogram, i.e., the plot of the estimated autocorrelation coefficient against various lags starting from l to k of the just-mentioned variables (results not shown here) has also shown the presence of unit roots. As per the correlogram test, a variable is said to be non-stationary if the autocorrelation coefficient of that variable starts at a very high value and tapers off very slowly. So we have chosen both nominal and real commercial paper rate, certificate of deposit rate, 91-days treasury bills rate, and 364-day treasury bills rate on the one hand and their major determinants on the other to test whether any long-run relationship exist between them or not. Since the nominal fed fund rate was found to be I(2) as per the ADF statistics, we have chosen LIBOR in case of the nominal interest rate model and real fed fund rate in case of the real interest rates model.

Table 3: Cointegration LR Test Based on Maximal Eigen value of the Stochastic Matrix for Nominal Interest Rates

HO	H1	Statistics	Critical values		Results
			95%	90%	
Commercial Paper Rate = f (Forward Premium, M1, World Interest Rate, GIIP, Fiscal Deficit, Inflation) Order of VAR = 2					
r = 0	r = 1	37.27	34.40	31.73	Reject null hypothesis
r ≤ 1	r = 2	13.61	28.27	25.80	Accept null hypothesis
r ≤ 2	r = 3	9.57	22.04	19.86	Accept null hypothesis
r ≤ 3	r = 4	7.72	15.87	13.81	Accept null hypothesis
r ≤ 4	r = 5	1.51	9.16	7.53	Accept null hypothesis
Certificate of Deposit Rate = f (Forward Premium, M1, World Interest Rate, GIIP, Fiscal Deficit, inflation) Order of VAR = 2					
r = 0	r = 1	52.51	34.40	31.73	Reject null hypothesis
r ≤ 1	r = 2	15.10	28.27	25.80	Accept null hypothesis
r ≤ 2	r = 3	12.41	22.04	19.86	Accept null hypothesis
r ≤ 3	r = 4	8.51	15.87	13.81	Accept null hypothesis
r ≤ 4	r = 5	1.09	9.16	7.53	Accept null hypothesis
91-day Treasury Bill Rate = f (Forward Premium, M1, World Interest Rate, GIIP, Fiscal Deficit, Inflation) Order of VAR = 3					
r = 0	r = 1	26.60	34.40	31.73	Accept null hypothesis
r ≤ 1	r = 2	11.83	28.27	25.80	Accept null hypothesis
r ≤ 2	r = 3	9.30	22.04	19.86	Accept null hypothesis
r ≤ 3	r = 4	6.37	15.87	13.81	Accept null hypothesis
r ≤ 4	r = 5	1.97	9.16	7.53	Accept null hypothesis
364-day Treasury Bill Rate = f (Forward Premium, M1, World Interest Rate, GIIP, Fiscal Deficit, Inflation) Order of VAR = 2					
r = 0	r = 1	21.69	34.40	31.73	Accept null hypothesis
r ≤ 1	r = 2	15.90	28.27	25.80	Accept null hypothesis
r ≤ 2	r = 3	10.48	22.04	19.86	Accept null hypothesis
r ≤ 3	r = 4	7.79	15.87	13.81	Accept null hypothesis
r ≤ 4	r = 5	1.24	9.16	7.53	Accept null hypothesis

Note: r is the order of cointegration.

Table 4: Cointegration LR Test Based on Trace Statistics of the Stochastic Matrix for Nominal Interest Rates

HO	H1	Statistics	Critical values 95%	90%	Results
Commercial Paper Rate = f (Forward Premium, M1, World Interest Rate, GIIP, Fiscal Deficit, Inflation) Order of VAR = 2					
r = 0	r = 1	37.27	34.40	31.73	Reject null hypothesis
r ≤ 1	r = 2	13.61	28.27	25.80	Accept null hypothesis
r ≤ 2	r = 3	9.57	22.04	19.86	Accept null hypothesis
r ≤ 3	r = 4	7.72	15.87	13.81	Accept null hypothesis
r ≤ 4	r = 5	1.51	9.16	7.53	Accept null hypothesis
Certificate of Deposit Rate = f (Forward Premium, M1, World Interest Rate, GIIP, Fiscal Deficit, inflation) Order of VAR = 2					
r = 0	r = 1	52.51	34.40	31.73	Reject null hypothesis
r ≤ 1	r = 2	15.10	28.27	25.80	Accept null hypothesis
r ≤ 2	r = 3	12.41	22.04	19.86	Accept null hypothesis
r ≤ 3	r = 4	8.51	15.87	13.81	Accept null hypothesis
r ≤ 4	r = 5	1.09	9.16	7.53	Accept null hypothesis
91-day Treasury Bill Rate = f (Forward Premium, M1, World Interest Rate, GIIP, Fiscal Deficit, Inflation) Order of VAR = 3					
r = 0	r = 1	26.60	34.40	31.73	Accept null hypothesis
r ≤ 1	r = 2	11.83	28.27	25.80	Accept null hypothesis
r ≤ 2	r = 3	9.30	22.04	19.86	Accept null hypothesis
r ≤ 3	r = 4	6.37	15.87	13.81	Accept null hypothesis
r ≤ 4	r = 5	1.97	9.16	7.53	Accept null hypothesis
364-day Treasury Bill Rate = f (Forward Premium, M1, World Interest Rate, GIIP, Fiscal Deficit, Inflation) Order of VAR = 2					
r = 0	r = 1	21.69	34.40	31.73	Accept null hypothesis
r ≤ 1	r = 2	15.90	28.27	25.80	Accept null hypothesis
r ≤ 2	r = 3	10.48	22.04	19.86	Accept null hypothesis
r ≤ 3	r = 4	7.79	15.87	13.81	Accept null hypothesis
r ≤ 4	r = 5	1.24	9.16	7.53	Accept null hypothesis

NOTE: r is the order of cointegration.

Table 5: Cointegration LR Test Based on Maximal Eigen value of the Stochastic Matrix for Real Interest Rates

HO	H1	Statistics	Critical values 95%	Critical values 90%	Results
Commercial Paper Rate = f (Forward Premium, M1, World Interest Rate, GIIP, Fiscal Deficit, Inflation) Order of VAR = 2					
r = 0	r = 1	21.24	34.40	31.73	Accept null hypothesis
r ≤ 1	r = 2	18.15	28.27	25.80	Accept null hypothesis
r ≤ 2	r = 3	12.25	22.04	19.86	Accept null hypothesis
r ≤ 3	r = 4	6.70	15.87	13.81	Accept null hypothesis
r ≤ 4	r = 5	3.68	9.16	7.53	Accept null hypothesis
Certificate of Deposit Rate = f (Forward Premium, M1, World Interest Rate, GIIP, Fiscal Deficit, inflation) Order of VAR = 1					
r = 0	r = 1	40.70	34.40	31.73	Reject null hypothesis
r ≤ 1	r = 2	24.10	28.27	25.80	Accept null hypothesis
r ≤ 2	r = 3	14.83	22.04	19.86	Accept null hypothesis
r ≤ 3	r = 4	10.38	15.87	13.81	Accept null hypothesis
r ≤ 4	r = 5	2.85	9.16	7.53	Accept null hypothesis
91-day Treasury Bill Rate = f (Forward Premium, M1, World Interest Rate, GIIP, Fiscal Deficit, Inflation) Order of VAR = 2					
r = 0	r = 1	24.05	34.40	31.73	Accept null hypothesis
r ≤ 1	r = 2	17.07	28.27	25.80	Accept null hypothesis
r ≤ 2	r = 3	14.08	22.04	19.86	Accept null hypothesis
r ≤ 3	r = 4	7.19	15.87	13.81	Accept null hypothesis
r ≤ 4	r = 5	4.42	9.16	7.53	Accept null hypothesis
364-day Treasury Bill Rate = f (Forward Premium, M1, World Interest Rate, GIIP, Fiscal Deficit, Inflation) Order of VAR = 2					
r = 0	r = 1	19.19	34.40	31.73	Accept null hypothesis
r ≤ 1	r = 2	17.72	28.27	25.80	Accept null hypothesis
r ≤ 2	r = 3	13.38	22.04	19.86	Accept null hypothesis
r ≤ 3	r = 4	7.72	15.87	13.81	Accept null hypothesis
r ≤ 4	r = 5	4.32	9.16	7.53	Accept null hypothesis

NOTE: r is the order of cointegration.

Table 6: Cointegration LR Test Based on Trace Statistics of the Stochastic Matrix for Real Interest Rates

HO	H1	Statistics	Critical values 95%	90%	Results
Commercial Paper Rate = f (Forward Premium, M1, World Interest Rate, GIIP, Fiscal Deficit, Inflation) Order of VAR = 2					
$r = 0$	$r \geq 1$	62.05	75.98	71.81	Accept null hypothesis
$r \leq 1$	$r \geq 2$	40.80	53.48	49.95	Accept null hypothesis
$r \leq 2$	$r \geq 3$	22.64	34.87	31.93	Accept null hypothesis
$r \leq 3$	$r \geq 4$	10.39	20.18	17.88	Accept null hypothesis
$r \leq 4$	$r \geq 5$	3.68	9.16	7.53	Accept null hypothesis
Certificate of Deposit Rate = f (Forward Premium, M1, World Interest Rate, GIIP, Fiscal Deficit, inflation) Order of VAR = 1					
$r = 0$	$r \geq 1$	92.88	75.98	71.81	Reject null hypothesis
$r \leq 1$	$r \geq 2$	52.17	53.48	49.95	Accept null hypothesis
$r \leq 2$	$r \geq 3$	28.07	34.87	31.93	Accept null hypothesis
$r \leq 3$	$r \geq 4$	13.23	20.18	17.88	Accept null hypothesis
$r \leq 4$	$r \geq 5$	2.85	9.16	7.53	Accept null hypothesis
91-day Treasury Bill Rate = f (Forward Premium, M1, World Interest Rate, GIIP, Fiscal Deficit, Inflation) Order of VAR = 2					
$r = 0$	$r \geq 1$	66.83	75.98	71.81	Accept null hypothesis
$r \leq 1$	$r \geq 2$	42.77	53.48	49.95	Accept null hypothesis
$r \leq 2$	$r \geq 3$	25.70	34.87	31.93	Accept null hypothesis
$r \leq 3$	$r \geq 4$	11.62	20.18	17.88	Accept null hypothesis
$r \leq 4$	$r \geq 5$	4.42	9.16	7.53	Accept null hypothesis
364-day Treasury Bill Rate = f (Forward Premium, M1, World Interest Rate, GIIP, Fiscal Deficit, Inflation) Order of VAR = 2					
$r = 0$	$r \geq 1$	62.35	75.98	71.81	Accept null hypothesis
$r \leq 1$	$r \geq 2$	43.16	53.48	49.95	Accept null hypothesis
$r \leq 2$	$r \geq 3$	25.43	34.87	31.93	Accept null hypothesis
$r \leq 3$	$r \geq 4$	12.04	20.18	17.88	Accept null hypothesis
$r \leq 4$	$r \geq 5$	4.32	9.16	7.53	Accept null hypothesis

NOTE: r is the order of cointegration.

Johansen's maximum likelihood (ML) technique has been used to test for cointegration between domestic interest rate, forward premium, growth rate of money supply, world interest rate, industrial production, while treating fiscal deficit and expected inflation are stationary exogenous variables. The order of VAR has been chosen by using AIC, SBC, and the likelihood ratio tests, the optimal lag length was found to be different for different model which has been reported in Tables 3, 4, 5, 6. As far as the specification of the intercept and trend in the VAR is concerned, it has been found that the underlying VAR model does not contain deterministic trend but contains restricted intercepts. The maximal eigen value and the trace statistics strongly rejected the null hypothesis that there is no co-integrating relation between the variables (i.e., $r = 0$), and they showed that there is one co-integrating relationship between the variables (i.e., $r = 1$) only for commercial paper rate and certificate of deposit rate in case of the nominal interest rates and for certificate of deposit rate in case of the real interest rates (see Tables 3, 4, 5, 6). The lack of cointegration between treasury bills rates and their major economic determinants imply no long-run equilibrium relationship among the variables. Now let us move for the normalization of cointegrating vectors in the case of nominal commercial paper rate and both nominal and real certificate of deposit rates for which the long-run relationship exist.

Table 7: Co-integrating Coefficients of Nominal and Real Interest Rates

Variables	Nominal commercial paper rate	Nominal certificate of deposit rate	Real certificate of deposit rate
Constant	-2.69	0.7714	0.7194
Forward premium	0.7512	(0.0859)	0.5943
	(0.0612)	0.5860	(0.1507)
Growth rate of M I	0.3593	(0.0760)	0.1107
	(0.0551)	-0.1205	(0.1717)
World interest rate	0.6202	(0.1378)	0.7799
	(0.1074)	0.3411	(0.1338)
GIIP	0.0748	(0.0963)	0.0407
	(0.0707)	0.4017	(0.1966)
Fiscal deficit**	0.0000137	(0.0000172)	0.000019
	(0.000020)	0.00076	(0.00133)
Inflation**	0.3362	(0.1888)	0.1352
	(0.2307)	-0.0096	(0.0195)

NOTE: (a) Figures in brackets are standard errors.
(b)** Coefficients have been obtained from the error correction model.

Table 8: Tests for the Significance of Individual Coefficients for Nominal and Real Interest Rates

Tests for significance	χ^2 (Calculated)	Conclusion
Nominal Commercial Paper Rate = f (Forward Premium, M1, World Interest Rate, GIIP, Fiscal Deficit, Inflation)		
Forward premium	29.47 (0.000)	Reject zero restriction
Growth rate of M1	13.89 (0.000)	Reject zero restriction
World interest rate	10.10 (0.001)	Reject zero restriction
GIIP	0.617 (0.432)	Do not reject zero restriction
Nominal Certificate of Deposit Rate = f (Forward Premium, M1, World Interest Rate, GIIP, Fiscal Deficit, Inflation)		
Forward premium	35.10 (0.000)	Reject zero restriction
Growth rate of M1	3.88 (0.049)	Reject zero restriction
World interest rate	23.46 (0.000)	Reject zero restriction
GIIP	0.302 (0.582)	Do not reject zero restriction
Real Certificate of Deposit Rate = f (Forward Premium, M1, World Interest Rate, GIIP, Fiscal Deficit, Inflation)		
Forward premium	8.25 (0.004)	Reject zero restriction
Growth rate of M1	0.514 (0.473)	Do not reject zero restriction
World interest rate	5.33 (0.021)	Reject zero restriction
GIIP	3.70 (0.054)	Reject zero restriction

NOTE: Figures in parentheses are probability value.

The normalized co-integrating vectors for nominal commercial paper rate and certificate of deposit rate and real certificate of deposit rate have been presented in Table 7. As expected, the coefficients of external factors namely, forward premium and world interest rates respectively have positive sign for both nominal and real short-term interest rates and they are highly significant. Further, changes in the actual exchange rate as an alternative to forward premium had the correct (positive) sign and its coefficient was statistically significant (coefficients not reported here). The coefficient of the growth rate of money supply has the positive signs and is highly significant in case of all the interest rates except real certificate deposit rate but it is insignificant. An alternative specification was also attempted by including the money supply in level form but the results did not change significantly. This is similar to other findings (NACH-

ANE, et al., 1997). Similarly, there has been a positive relationship between both nominal and real interest rates on the one hand and the index of industrial production on the other.

The likelihood ratio tests for zero restrictions on the parameters are reported in Table 8. These show that the determinants like the forward premium, growth rate of money supply, and world interest rate are significant in case of both the nominal interest rates. On the other hand, the coefficient of forward premium, world interest rate, and index of industrial production are significant in case of the real certificate of deposit rate.

The impact of the stationary exogenous variables like fiscal deficit, and inflation on both nominal and real interest rates can be gauged with the help of the error correction model. The coefficients of fiscal deficit have the positive sign in the case of all the short-term nominal and real interest rates but none of them are statistically significant. This finding is similar to those reported by many other studies (AHMAD, 1994; HOLESCHER, 1983; PLOSSOR, 1982; EVANS, 1985 and 1987). The coefficients of expected inflation in the case of nominal short-term interest rates have the expected sign and are found to be statistically significant only in case of the commercial paper rate. The coefficient of the expected inflation in the case of the real interest rate has the negative sign but it is insignificant.

The coefficients of error correction term of both nominal and real interest rates in error correction model (ECM) had the correct sign (negative) and they were statistically significant in all the equations. The error correction term for both nominal and real interest rates were expected to be negative because of the anticipated negative relationship between the actual and the long-run equilibrium values of short-term interest rates. This was so because if the current short-term interest rate is higher than its long-run equilibrium value due to any shock, it should decline to its equilibrium value and vice versa. The time required for this adjustment is indicated by the magnitude of the coefficient. The higher the value of the coefficient, the faster will be the speed of adjustment and the lesser will be the time needed for adjustment and vice versa. The values of the error correction term in nominal commercial paper rate, nominal certificate of deposit rate, and real certificate of deposit rate are -0.186, -0.543, and -0.342 and their t-values are -4.11, -6.39, and -6.14 respectively.

Since the world interest rate and forward premium appear in our interest rate equation, it would be interesting to test the validity of covered interest parity theory for all nominal interest rates in a co-integrating framework. The covered interest parity theory can be said to be valid for India if the constant, the coefficients of the growth rate money supply, and of index of industrial production are zero and the sum of world interest rate and forward premium are 1. So we imposed over-identified restrictions as $C = 0$, $a1 + a3 = 1$, $a2 = 0$, $a4 = 0$. The likelihood ratio statistics for these restrictions have been presented in Table 9 which are highly significant. This indicates that the validity of covered interest parity theory is doubtful in the Indian context.

Table 9: Testing of Interest Parity Theory

	Null hypothesis	χ^2 (Calculated)	Conclusion
Commercial Paper Rate = f (Forward Premium, M1, World Interest Rate, GIIP, Fiscal Deficit, Inflation)			
CIP	C = 0, a1 + a3 = 1, a2 = 0, a4 = 0	23.19 (0.000)	Reject null hypothesis
UIP	C = 0, a1 + a3 = 1, a2 = 0, a4 = 0	20.76 (0.000)	Reject null hypothesis
Certificate of Deposit Rate = f (Forward Premium, M1, World Interest Rate, GIIP, Fiscal Deficit, Inflation)			
CIP	C = 0, a1 + a3 = 1, a2 = 0, a4 = 0	38.17 (0.000)	Reject null hypothesis
UIP	C = 0, a1 + a3 = 1, a2 = 0, a4 = 0	39.66 (0.000)	Reject null hypothesis

NOTE:
(1) CIP and UIP denote covered and uncovered interest parity theory respectively.
(2) Same as in Table 8.

Table 10: Granger Causality Tests

Null hypothesis	No.of Lags	χ^2 (Calculated)	Conclusion
Commercial Paper Rate = f (Forward Premium, M1, World Interest Rate, GIIP, Fiscal Deficit, Inflation)			
Commercial paper rate is not granger caused by forward premium	2	0.0348(0.852)	Accept null hypothesis
Commercial paper rate is not granger caused by growth rate of money supply	2	7.15(0.007)	Reject null hypothesis
Commercial paper rate is not granger caused by world interest rate	2	3.29 (0.069)	Reject null hypothesis
Commercial paper rate is not granger caused by GIIP	2	13.80 (0.000)	Reject null hypothesis
Certificate of Deposit Rate = f (Forward Premium, M1, World Interest Rate, GIIP, Fiscal Deficit, Inflation)			
Certificate of deposit rate is not granger caused by forward premium	2	14.83 (0,000)	Reject null hypothesis
Certificate of deposit rate is not granger caused by growth rate of money supply	2	22.36 (0.000)	Reject null hypothesis
Certificate of deposit rate is not granger caused by world interest rate	2	5.90(0.015)	Reject null hypothesis
Certificate of deposit rate is not granger caused by GIIP	2	27.99 (0.000)	Reject null hypothesis

NOTE: Same as in Table 8.

The above-mentioned procedures had also been followed to test the uncovered interest parity theory by replacing the forward premium rate by actual change in exchange rate as a proxy for expected change in exchange rate. The expected change in exchange rate was also found to non stationary (See Tables 1 and 2). It was found that the validity of uncovered interest parity theory is difficult to accept (See Table 9). It implies that both domestic and external factors have had significant impact on interest rate behaviour in India. Imperfect substitution of assets, trade restrictions, control over capital flows, and high risk premia may be some other possible reasons for not holding the interest rate parity conditions in India.

Figure 1:
Impulse Response of Interest Rate Changes due to one Standard Deviation Change in World Interest Rate

Panel a: Response of Nominal Commercial Paper Rate

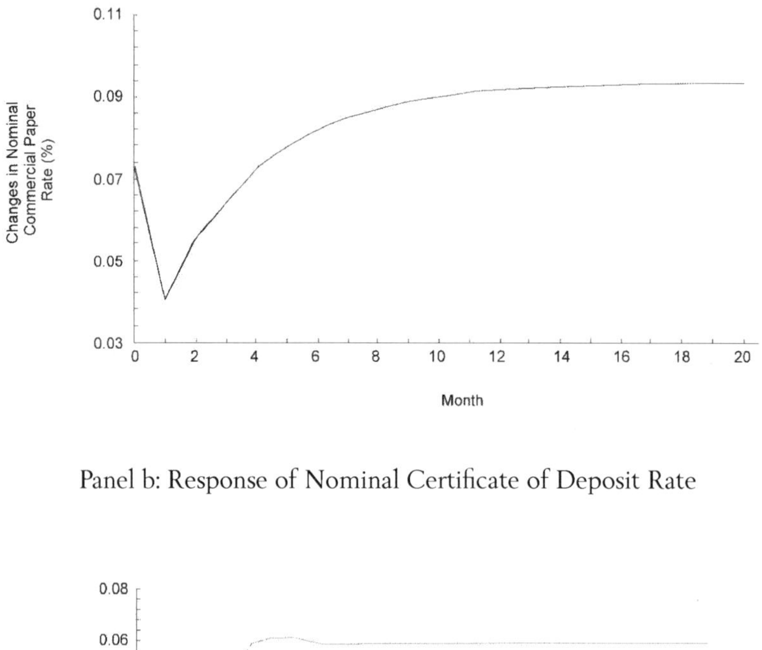

Panel b: Response of Nominal Certificate of Deposit Rate

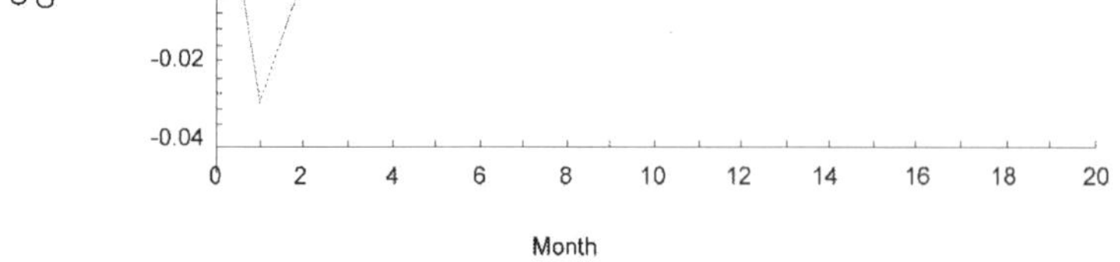

Panel c: Response of Real Certificate of Deposit Rate

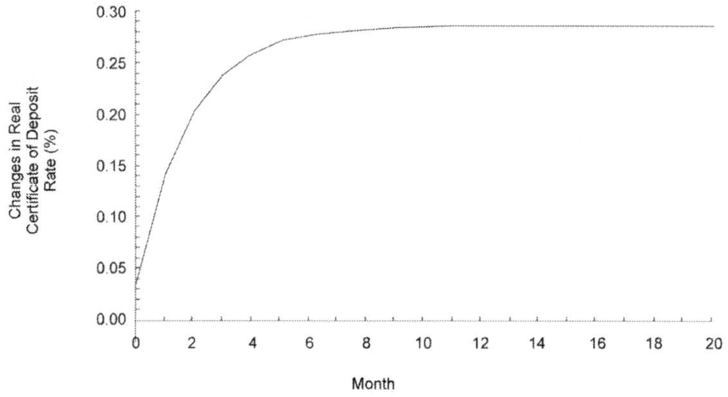

By using the error correction model, we have tested, whether the variables individually improve the forecasting performance of the model, i.e., we test if the independent variables Granger cause the interest rate. For this, we test the joint significance of the lagged variables of each variable along with the error correction term in the error correction model. This test is important because of the insignificance of some variables on interest rates equation. The results reported in Table 10 indicate that the null hypothesis of no Granger causality is strongly rejected in all the cases except the forward premium in case of the commercial paper rate. This implies that both domestic and external factors playa major role in the movement of interest rates in India.

The results of Impulse-Response Analysis are presented in Figure 1. They show the response of Indian nominal and real interest rates to a standard deviation change (around 0.2 percentage increase) in world interest rate. It is seen that a change in world interest rate caused an increase in nominal commercial paper rate till the twelfth month and certificate deposit rate till the fourth month. On the other hand, the real certificate of deposit rate in India increased continuously till the tenth month. The overall increase in nominal commercial paper rate and certificate of deposit rate due to an increase in world interest rate was found to be 0.09 and 0.06 percent respectively. On the other hand, the overall increase in real certificate of deposit rate due to an increase in world interest rate was found to be 0.28 percent.

IV. Conclusions

This Paper has attempted to identify the major economic determinants of both short-term nominal and real interest rates by using Co-integration and other technique based on vector autoregressive model in India during April 1994 to March 2004. The variables like nominal and real commercial paper rate, certificate of deposit rate, 91-day Treasury bills rate, 364-day Treasury bills rate, forward premium, growth rate money supply, world interest rate, and index of industrial production were found to be non-stationary, whereas fiscal deficit, and expected inflation rate were found to be stationary.

It was also found that there has been a long-run relationship between nominal commercial paper rate, certificate of deposit rate on the one hand, and forward premium, growth rate of nominal money supply, world interest rate, index of industrial production, fiscal deficit, and expected rate of inflation on the other. The variables like forward premium, world interest rate, and growth rate of money supply have had the positive and significant effect on both nominal commercial paper and certificate of deposit rate. Expected inflation appears to be a statistically significant determinant of only nominal commercial paper rate.

There has been a long-run relationship only between the real certificate of deposit rate on the one hand and growth rate of real money supply, fiscal deficit, forward premium, world interest rate, index of industrial production, and expected rate of inflation on the other. Real certificate of deposit rate was positively and significantly influenced by the forward premium, world interest rate, and the index of industrial production but the influence of the growth rate money supply was negative and insignificant. The lack of long-run relationship between the treasury bills rate and its major economic determinants needs to be explored separately.

The results from the error correction mechanism indicate that the nominal commercial paper rate and both nominal and real certificate of deposit rates are in general related to expected changes in exchange rate, along with the deviations from the observed long-run relationship. Further, world interest rate, forward premium, index of industrial production and growth rate of money supply have Granger caused the above-mentioned interest rates in India. The results in this paper do not support either the covered or the uncovered interest rate parity theory for India. In other words, both the internal and external factors have played an important role in the above-mentioned interest rates determination in India. Imperfect substitution of assets, trade restrictions, control over capital flows, and high risk premia may be some other possible reasons for not holding the interest rate parity conditions in India. The response of commercial paper rate and certificate of deposit rate to a change (around 0.2 percentage increase) in world interest rate was found to be permanent, i.e., their effect does not die down, but the impact on real interest rates was found to be greater than the nominal interest rate.

References

Ahmad, M. (1994), "The Effects of Government Budget Deficits on the Interest Rates: A Case Study of Small Open Economy" *Economia Internazialia,* Vol. 47, No.1, pp. 1-6.

Barro, R. J. (1974), "Are Government Bonds Net Wealth" *Journal of Political Economy,* Vol. 82, No. 4, pp. 1095-117.

Barro, R. J. (1993), Macroeconomics, John Wiley and Sons, New York.

Bhole, L. M. (1988), "Some Issues Concerning Interest Rates Theory and Policy", *The Indian Economic Journal,* the Conference Volume, pp. 1-18.

BHOLE, L. M. (2004), Financial Institutions and Markets, Fourth Edition, Tata McGraw Hill Publishing Company Limited, New Delhi.

BHOLE, L. M. and SEBASTIAN, V. J. (1996), "Determinants of Interest Rates in a Deregulated Open Economy", *The Indian Journal of Economics*, Vol. 77, No. 305, pp. 261-278.

BHOLE, L. M. and DASH, P. (2003), "Determinants of Long-Term Interest Rates During 1970s to 1990s", *Prainan*, Vol. XXXII, No.2, pp. 95-117.

BLEJER, M. I. (1982), "Interest Rate Differentials and Exchange Risk: Recent Argentine Experience" *IMF Staff Papers*, Vol. 29, pp. 270-80.

BLEJER, M. I. and DIAZ, J. G. (1986), "Domestic and External Factors in the Determination of the Real Interest Rate: The case of Uruguay", *Economic Development and Cultural Change*, pp. 589-606.

CAPORALE, G. M. and PITTIS, N. (1997), "Domestic and External Factors in Interest Rate Determination" *Applied Financial Economics*, Vol. 7, pp. 465-471.

CARMICHEAL, J. and STEBBING, P. W. (1983), "Fisher's Paradox and the Theory of Interest", *American Economic Review*, Vol. 73, pp. 619-630.

CEBULA, R. J. (1987), "Federal Deficits and the Real Rate of Interest in the United States: a Note" *Public Choice*, Vo1.53, pp. 97-100.

CHAKRABORTY, L. (2002), "Fiscal Deficit and Rate of Interest: An Econometric Analysis of the Deregulated Financial Regime", *Economic and Political Weekly*, May 11, pp. 1831-1838.

DENSLOW, D. A. and RUSH, M. (1989), "Supply Shocks and the Interest Rate", *Economic Enquiry*, Vol. 27, July, pp. 501-10.

DICKEY, D. A. and FULLER, W. A. (1979), "Distribution of the Estimators for Autoregressive Time Series with a Unit Root", *Journal of the American Statistical Association*, No. 74, pp. 427-31.

DOOLEY, M. and ISARD, P. (1980), "Capital Controls, Political Risk, and Deviations from Interest-Rate Parity", *Journal of Political Economy*, 88, 370-84.

DUA, P. and PANDIT, B. L. (2001), "Interest Rate Determination in India: The Role of Domestic and External Factors" Centre for Development Economics, Working Paper, No. 92.

EDWARDS, S. (1985), "Money, the Rate of Devaluation, and Interest Rates in a Semi open Economy" *Journal of Money, Credit, and Banking*, Vol. 17, No. 1, pp. 59-68.

EDWARDS, S. and KHAN, M. (1985), "Interest Rate Determination in Developing Countries-A Conceptual Framework" *IMF Staff Papers*, Vol. 32, pp. 377-403.

ENGLE, R. F. and GRANGER, C. W. J. (1987), "Co-integration and Error Correction: Representation, Estimation and Testing," *Econometrica*, Vol. 55, pp. 251-276.

EVANS. P. (1985), "Do Large Deficits Produce High Interest Rates?" *American Economic Review*, Vol. 75, No. 1, pp.68-87.

___ (1987), "Do Budget Deficits Raise Nominal Interest Rates? Evidence from Six Countries", *Journal of Monetary Economics*, Vol. 20, No. 2, pp. 281-300.

FINDLAY D. W. (1991), "Budget Deficits, Short-term Real Interest Rates and the Specification of Expected Intiation: An Empirical Investigation" *Applied Economics*, Vol. 23, pp. 1147-1158.

FISHER, I. (1930), "The Theory of Interest", New York, Macmillon.

FRENKEL, J. A. and Levich, R. M. (1975), "Covered Interest Arbitrage: Unexploited Profits?" *Journal of Political Economy*, Vol. 83, pp. 325-38.

FRENKEL, J . A. (1973), "Elasticities and the Interest Parity Theory", *Journal of Political Economy*, 81, pp. 741-7.

FRIEDMAN, M. (1968), "The Role of Monetary Policy" *American Economic Review*, Vol. 58, pp. 1-17.

___ (1969), "Factors Affecting the Level of Interest Rates" *Proceedings of the* 1968 *Conference on Savings and Loan legue*, The Legue, pp. 11-27.

FULLER, W. A. (1976), "Introduction to Statistical Time Series" New York, Wiley.

GOCHOCO, M. S. (1991), "Financial Liberalization and Interest Rate Determination: The Case of Philippines 1981-85", *Journal of Macroeconomics*, Vol. 2, No. 33, pp. 335-350.

GOODHART, C. A. E. (1989), Money, Information, and Uncertainty, Second Edition, The Macmillan Press Ltd., London.

GOVERNMENT OF INDIA, Economic Survey, 2002-03.

GREEN, W. H. (2000), Econometric Analysis, Fourth Edition, Prentice Hall International, Inc., Toronto.

GUPTA, D. D. and GUPTA, B. D. (1994), "Interest Rates in Open Economies: Real Interest Rate Parity, Exchange Rates and Country Risk in Industrial and Developing Countries" World Bank Policy Research Working Paper, No. 1283.

HAMILTON, J. (1994), Time Series Analysis, Princeton University Press, Princeton.

HICKS, J. (1937), "Mr. Keynes and the Classics: A Suggested Interpretation" *Econometrica*, April, pp. 147-59.

HOELSCHER, M. (1983), "Federal Borrowings and Short-term Interest Rates" *Southern Economic Journal*, Vol 50, No.2, pp. 319-333.

INTERNATIONAL MONETARY FUND, International Financial Statistics, Various Issues.

JOHANSEN, S. and JUSELIUS, K. (1990), "Maximum Likelihood Estimation and Inference on Cointegration with Applications to the Demand for Money", *Oxford Bulletin of Economics and Statistics*, 52, pp. 169-209.

JOHANSEN, S. and JUSELIUS, K. (1992), "Testing Structural Hypotheses in a Multivariate Cointegration Analysis of the PPP and UIP for UK," *Journal of Econometrica*, Vol. 53, pp. 211-44.

KEYNES, J. M. (1936), "The General Theory of Employment, Interest, and Money," Harcourt Brace and Company, New York.

___ (1923), "A Tract on Monetary Reform", London, Macmillan.

KOLLURI, B. R. and GIANNAROS, D. S. (1987), "Budget Deficits and Short-Term Real Interest Rate Forecasting", *Journal of Macroeconomics*, Vol. 9, pp. 109-25.

LEVI, M. D. (1977), 'Taxation and Abnormal International Capital Flows", *Journal of Political Economy*, 85, pp. 635-46.

LIZONDO, J. S. (1983), "Interest Differential and Covered Arbitrage" in P. A. ARMELLA, R. DORNBUSCH, and M. OBSTFELD (eds.) Financial Policies and the World Capital Market: The Problems of Latin American Countries, Chicago.

MCCORMICK, F. (1979), "Covered Interest Arbitrage: Unexploited Profits?: Comment", *Journal of Political Economy*, 87, pp. 411-17.

METZLER, L. A. (1951), "Wealth, Saving, and the Rate of Interest" *Journal of Political Economy*, 59, (2), pp. 93-116.

MUNDELL, R. (1960), "The Public Debt, Corporate Income Taxes and the Rate of Interest", *Journal of Political Economy*, Vol. 68, pp. 622-6.

MUNDELL, R. (1963), "Inflation and Real Interest Rate" *Journal of Political Economy*, Vol. 70, June, pp. 280-283.

NACHANE, D. M., KARNIK, A.V. and HATEKAR, N. R. (1997), "The Interest Rate Imbroglio Monetary and Fiscal Dimensions", *Economic and Political Weekly*, May 17-24, pp. 1167-1174.

PATTNAIK, I. and Vasudevan, D. (1999), "Interest Rate Determination: An Error Correction Model", National Council of Applied Economic Research, Discussion Paper No.3.

PATTNAIK, P. (2001), "On Fiscal Deficits and Real Interest Rates", *Economic and Political Weekly*, April 14, pp. 1160-1163.

PHILLIPS, P. C. B. and PERRON, P. (1988), "Testing for a Unit Root in Time Series Regression", *Biometrika*, No-75, pp. 335-346.

PLOSSER, C. I. (1982), "Government Financing Decisions, and Asset Returns", *Journal of Monetary Economics*, Vol. 9, No.3, pp. 325-352.

RESERVE BANK OF INDIA, Report on Currency and Finance, 2001-02, Mumbai 2003.

___ (2003), Handbook of Statistics on Indian Economy, 2002, Mumbai.

___ (1985), Report of the Committee to Review the Working of the Monetary System (Chakravarty Committee Report), Bombay.

___ (1987), Report of the Working Group on the Money Market (Vaghul Group Report), Bombay.

SARGAN, J. D. (1984), "Wages and Prices in the United Kingdom: A Study of Econometric Methodology" in K. F. WALLIS and D. F. HENDRY (Eds.), "Quantitative Economics and Econometric Analysis", Basil Blackwell, Oxford.

WICKSELL, K. (1958), "The Influence of the Rate of Interest on Commodity Prices" in E. Lindhal (Eds.), "Selected papers on Economic Theory by Knut Wicksell", Allen & Unwin, London.

WILCOX, J. A. (1983), "Why Real Interest Rates Were So Low in the 1970's", *American Economic Review*, Vol. 70, No. 1, pp. 44-53.

[10]

The Structure of Interest Rates in Theory and Practice*

Introduction

Interest rate is an important price in any economy. It has been rightly held that it is the pivot of the entire economic system and it seems to reign over the theories of money, growth, employment, general price level and balance of payments. [1] The economists conventionally conduct their economic analyses as if there is a single rate of interest in the economy. This may be due to analyses being often conducted in static or stationary framework in which only one rate of interest can exist. However, in a changing or dynamic framework and in practice, we come across the multiplicity – often of a bewildering variety – of interest rates. For example, it would be found that tables on the structure of interest rates in India occupy two to three pages in the Annual Report on Currency and Finance of the "Reserve Bank of India, and Industrial Development Bank of India Annual Report" respectively. There are some definite interrelationships among these various interest rates which are known as the spectrum or structure of interest rates.

In understanding interest rates, we ask the following three questions:

1. What determines the general level of interest rates? The Government offered a rate of 1.90 per cent in 1951 and 4.60 per cent in 1985 on its Treasury Bills. Why does the same security offer different yields at different points of time?

2. What determines the difference between long-term and short term rates i.e., what determines the term structure of interest rates? The Treasury Bill rate was 4.60 per cent in 1985 and the yield on long-term Government Securities (over 15 years) was about 6.47 to 10.0 per cent in the same year. Why do securities maturing at different dates offer different yields?

* Paper published in *Indian Journal of Economics*, October 1988.

3. What determines the general structure of interest rates? In April 1987, while the Government of India could issue lo-year bonds at the coupon rate of 10.5 per cent, the companies had to offer 14 per cent on their 7-year bonds and 14 per cent on their 3-year deposits. Why?

While there is a vast literature to explain the level of interest rates (question 1 above), the economists have paid relatively less attention to the study of structure of interest rates (questions 2 and 3 above). This latter field is regarded as rather complex, abstruse, and difficult by the students of monetary economics. The purpose of this paper is to try to aid the understanding of the structure of interest rates in theory and as it exists in practice in India. The paper is divided in four sections. In section I, the major theories of the term structure of interest rates are critically discussed. In section II, the important determinants of the general structure of interest rates are briefly discussed. In section III, we present the important features of the interest rates structure in India and point out its determinants in the light of discussion in the previous two sections. Section IV contains the major conclusions of this study.

I. Theories of the Term Structure of Interest Rates

As stated earlier, the term structure of rates refers to the relationship between different rates when all the investment characteristics [2] except the length of time to maturity of financial claims are held constant. It is the name given to the functional relation between yield to maturity and term (period) to maturity. The theories explaining this relation are discussed below.

(1) The Expectations Theory

This theory has taken two forms, restrictive and broad. In its restrictive form, it is known as the unbiased or pure expectations theory with which we will be concerned in this section. This is the best-known theory and Fisher was the first economist to develop it; Lutz, Conard, Meiselman, etc. also have made contributions to it later on. It is based on the following assumptions:

(a) There is a perfect competition in financial markets.
(b) The investors are rational i.e. they wish to maximize their holding period yield. [3]
(c) Investors have a perfect foresight, and a large enough body of investors hold uniform expectations about the future level and changes of short-term interest rates and security prices.
(d) There are no transactions costs
(e) Securities of different maturities are perfect substitutes for each other i.e. they are homogeneous.

With the help of these assumptions, it is posited that today's long-term rate is the unbiased (arithmetic or geometric) average of the current short-term rate and the successive forward or expected one-period or short-term rates during the period of long-term loan. The long-term rate will be higher than the short-term rate (i.e. the yield curve will be upward sloping

[4]) only if investors expect future short-term spot rates to be higher than the current short-term spot rate. [5] Similarly, the long-term rate will be lower than the short-term rate (the yield curve will be downward sloping) when investors expect future short-term spot rates to fall below the current short-term spot rate. If no changes in future short-term spot rates are expected, the long and short rate will be equal to each other (the yield curve will be flat). In equilibrium, short-rates can not be different from long rates because the competition equalizes yields on all possible configurations of investment over the same time span or horizon. If this condition is not fulfilled, profitable arbitrage [6] operations will ultimately bring it about. It is through variations in the price of bonds outstanding that yields calculated for the same period will be equalized for bonds with different terms to maturity.

Thus, the pure expectations theory views expectations about the future short term interest rates as the only determinant of the term structures of interest rates. These expectations determine the demand for securities which affects their prices which, in turn, determine their relative yields. The relative supplies of securities in various ranges of maturity spectrum do not change and do not affect yields as per this theory. It holds that it is not possible to influence term structure of rates by varying the supply of securities of different maturities.

While the only merit of this theory is that it has emphasized the role of expectations, it suffers from too many serious drawbacks to make it useful in explaining the interest rates structure in practice.

Firstly it totally lacks realism. Its assumptions are very restrictive and unrealistic. It cannot explain rates structure in informal and rural markets where there is no trading of securities in the manner assumed by it. Similarly, it appears to be irrelevant with regard to interest rates on bank deposits where there is no buying and selling of securities. A very practical question which can be raised is that if the expected return is the same irrespective of the maturity chosen, why do investors hold securities of different maturities? The unrealism and irrelevance of this theory is reflected also in the fact that while it implies that the Central Banks cannot affect interest rates through open market operations, in practice, Central Banks do use this technique to influence relative supplies of securities and yields on them.

Secondly, while this theory allegedly explains the long-term rate, it does not explain how short-term rates themselves are determined and how expectations about short rates are formed. Similarly, the theory is silent about the role of expectations about the future long-term rates and prices in determining the term structure of rates. It has been rightly pointed out by Dorrance and Hicks that it is much more realistic to talk of interest rates structure in terms of expectations about future long term rates since the speculators in long-term bonds must normally be concerned with their prices rather than short-term rates. By assuming that a participant in the market has expectations about the price of the long-term bond at the date when the short-term security falls due, we get along well with the simple comparison of the current short-term interest rate with the yield on the longer-term bond expected for the same time span. [7]

Thirdly, a critical reading of this theory reveals that it really states how expectations can be derived from the observed yield curve rather than how yield curve can be constructed with the help of expectations. It utilizes the currently observable yield structure to derive what current expectations of forward rates are; the theory does not use expected forward rates to explain the current level of the long-term rate. Thus, we set out to explain the term structure with the help of expectations but end up with deriving expectations with the help of term structure – a clear case of the cart before the horse. [8] It is to be noted that this theory does not say anything about what can be the shape of yield curve theoretically. It merely helps to interpret the meaning of various yield curves. It does not explain what determines the holding period also; it implicitly assumes that the holding period is independent of considerations of risk, return, liquidity etc.

(2) Liquidity Premium Theory

The main proponent of this theory is J. R. Hicks. Some people view it as an extension or modification of the pure expectation theory and, therefore, it is sometimes called a biased expectations theory. Two important characteristics of investments are the return and risk. The choice of securities depends upon the risk-return preferences of the investors. The expectations theory ignores risk and assumes that investors want to maximize return. The segmentation theory, as we are going to discuss, assumes that investors deemphasize return and try to minimize risk. The liquidity premium theory assumes that investors are risk-return traders; they do not want to maximize return whatever the risk. Similarly, they do not want to minimize risk even if it entails a very low return.

This theory also holds that long-term securities, on balance, are more risky than short-term securities. While the variance of return of capital value is greater for long-term securities than for short-term, the variance of return of interest income is greater for short-term securities than for long-term. If it is assumed that the stability of capital is valued more highly than the stability of interest, the long term securities have a net risk disadvantage. Investors will accept this additional risk only if long-term securities are priced in such a way as to offer a higher yield. In other words, because of the higher risk on long-term securities, other things being equal, the investors prefer to lend short. Borrowers, on the other hand, prefer to borrow long in order to reduce the risk of inability to meet principal payments i.e. in order to reduce the "financial risk". As stated above, because of their psychological disinclination to hold long-term securities, a positive liquidity or risk premium must be offered to induce investors to purchase long-term securities. This premium is over and above the average of the current and expected short rates. Thus, this theory implies the existence of the upward sloping yield curve more often than not.

The liquidity premium theory highlights the preference for liquidity and the desire to minimize the sum of income risk and capital risk as the additional factors determining the term structure of rates. It is more realistic because it incorporates the complexity of forces such as lenders' and borrowers' preferences, and differences in risk-return attributes of securities of different maturities. It has served a useful purpose in so far as it has exposed the fact that even in respect of securities with no default risk, the other types of risk remain present and these risks are greater, the longer the maturity period. It may, however, be added that in the context of discussing term structure of rates, liquidity premium, strictly speaking, is not a correct nomenclature because the premium which needs to be paid to lenders is for inducing them to take greater risk and not for parting with liquidity.

It is also doubtful whether the investors are really more averse to the capital risk than the income risk. One wonders whether such an assumption is really necessary. The logic of the theory of portfolio selection and the empirical evidence suggest that long-term securities have greater systematic risk [9] than the short-term securities which, rather than investor bias against capital risk, explains higher expected return on long-term securities than on short-term securities. [10]

Similarly this theory is not explicit about the cause or origin of the change in the value of the principal. Is it the change in "real value" or "nominal value" of capital which is indicated by the theory? As we know, while the real value would change due to changes in prices, the nominal value would change due to expected changes in interest rates. The theory lacks clarity in these matters. Further, by assuming that the risk (liquidity) premium will be mostly positive, the theory implies that the prices or interest rates will be mostly increasing. This is questionable.

(3) Market Segmentation Theory

The third major theory of term structure of interest rates is the market segmentation theory propounded by Culbertson. Lutz has called it the theory of risk avoidance. The theory assumes investors to be risk minimizers or risk-averters. [11] The way to minimize risk is to match maturities of assets and liabilities or to match maturities with holding periods. If a lender knows exactly how long his money will be available for investment, he can select the maturity date of the claim in such a way that he runs neither the income risk nor the capital risk. The coincidence of the maturity date of the claim with the date of his need for cash insures him against both these risks. All these results in the capital market being divided into a number of segments in which demand for and supply of bonds of each given maturity determine the rate of interest irrespective of what happens in other segments. The market segments may also be created on account of certain legal restrictions on investment selections of certain institutional investors. Of course, these segments are not totally independent of each other. Although some amount of interdependence between various segments is, admitted, this theory holds that securities in different maturity ranges, particularly more distant maturity ranges, are imperfect substitutes for each other. In other words, although the theory does not deny the possibility of some market continuity and some maturity indifference, it holds that institutions may have to be paid a differential premium to induce them to move from their preferred maturity segment. Moreover, this premium can be in either direction; it is not confined necessarily to the long side, as implied by Hicksian liquidity premium.

In such segmented markets, the term structure of interest rates is determined exclusively by the supply of and demand for securities. If on the demand side, demand for long-term capital were to predominate and on the supply side, the offer of short-term money, the long rates would come to lie above the short rates, and vice versa in the opposite case. This theory, thus, stresses the maturity structure of debt as an important factor determining the term structure of interest rates. On this theory, debt management policies of the Government and changes in the economic structure can influence the rates structure.

Although the market segmentation theory has added on important dimension to the explanation of interest rates structure, it is difficult to accept that lenders and borrowers are dominated only by the desire to avoid risk. In reality, the investors care for the return also. It is difficult to accept that an investor would select the maturity with the smallest total yield risk without comparing risks with yields, i.e. to assume that he would attempt to avoid risk at any price.

(4) Other Factors

Apart from the factors pointed out by the three theories discussed above, there are other factors which are relevant in explaining the term structure of interest rates. One such factor to which the pointed attention has been drawn by many analysts is the phenomenon of current and expected inflation. It is held that the generally ascending yield curve might be the result of inflation uncertainty. [12] The expectations theory and liquidity premium theory assume that future inflation rates are known with certainty. In reality, this is not true, and inflation uncertainty increases with the length of time in future. This inflation uncertainty causes uncertainty about interest rates. All this means that investors cannot make completely risk free investments, and the risk of investment increases as the period for which investors are required to make forward commitments of their funds lengthens. The least-risk-strategy for them is to invest in successive 1-year bonds. This means that borrowers must offer some incentive if they want investors to lend long. Thus, inflation risk renders long-term rates to be higher than the short-term rates.

The existence of transactions costs has been pointed out as another relevant factor in the present context. The impact of transactions costs on term-structure, however, has to be regarded as uncertain. This impact is the result of two opposing forces. As per the first, given the holding period, the transactions costs are lower, the longer the term to maturity because the number of transactions would be lower. [13] As per the second, the transactions costs tend to increase with the length of time to maturity because of the greater risk of long-term securities to dealers who make the market. Whether the yield curve would be downward sloping or upward sloping will depend upon the relative strength of these two forces. [14]

II. Determinants of the General Structure of Interest Rates

Although the term structure of interest rates has received the maximum (almost exclusive) attention from the monetary economists, it is to be realized that maturity is not the only dimension in understanding the structure of interest rates. Financial economists have rightly emphasized the importance of some more factors in this context. We discuss these factors briefly in this section.

(i) Default Risk

The risk is one of the most important determinants of decisions in the markets for both financial and real assets. In essence, it refers to the possibility of an adverse outcome to an event. There are many types of risk and we have already indicated how inflation risk, interest rate (capital) risk, and income risk cause differences in yields. The default risk is a major determinant of the general structure of interest rates and it refers to the possibility of the failure to meet the terms of a loan agreement, of delay in payment, of total non-payment, of partial non-payment of interest and/or principal amount. All financial assets except Government securities are subject to some degree of default risk although they differ in their degree of risk. These differences in risk levels cause differences in interest rates (yields) on financial claims. The more risky the security, the higher the interest rate it has to offer. Given the attitude of investors towards absorption of risk and given the risk in investment projects that borrowers wish to undertake, the yield on risky assets will rise to an equilibrium position which will be higher than the yield on assets that have no risk of default. The difference between these two yields is called the default risk premium. The default risk is determined by the internal financial and business position of the borrower, and the external environment or economic climate within which he operates.

(ii) Call Risk

In USA, most of the corporate bonds are issued with a clause which gives the companies an option or power to call back the bonds at a specified price before they mature. The holders of callable bonds run the risk of their bonds being called back before they voluntarily want their money back. The call practice involves certain disadvantages from the point of view of the investor. Firstly, since the call price sets a ceiling on the market price, holders of callable bonds can hope to earn only a limited amount of capital gains. Secondly, since bonds are usually called back when market yields lire low, the long-term investors have to reinvest their money at lower yields; in addition, they have to incur transactions costs for reinvestment. Thirdly, investors face a continuous overhanging uncertainty that the bond may be called back or it may not be called back. Therefore, interest rates on callable bonds will have to be higher than the rates on bonds without a call feature. The difference between the two can be called a call risk premium. [15]

In India, the practice of issuing callable bonds is not prevalent. However, the opposite practice namely, issuing bonds with buy back option has become quite widespread in the recent past. In this case, the buyers of non-convertible, debentures have the option of selling their bonds to the company at the face value whenever they want after a specified, time period. In a free market, interest rates on bonds with buy back feature can be lower than the rates on bonds without such a feature.

(iii) Marketability or Liquidity

The financial assets differ in their marketability or liquidity i.e. they offer in respect of the possibility that a significant amount of security can be sold relatively quickly without large price concessions. Other things being equal, the security which is easily marketable will carry a lower rate of interest than the one whose marketability is limited or restricted. The marketability of assets depends in part on the features of the instrument itself and in part on the nature of markets where the asset is traded. The assets which are homogeneous, which appeal to a wide variety of buyers, and which can be easily transferable without undue cost or delay have a high degree of marketability. Similarly, if the primary and secondary markets are well developed, if they have depth, breadth, and resiliency, the assets will have greater marketability. [16]

(iv) Tax Status

Tax features cause difference in yields on otherwise similar financial assets or claims. The facts that capital gains are taxed at a lower rate compared to income and that different securities differ in respect of tax exemption of interest income and principal amount of investment result in differences in interest rates on different claims.

III. Interest Rates Structure in India

Having discussed the theoretical determinants of the structure of interest rates so far, we now turn to the understanding of the nature and evolution of interest rates structure in India in the light of the foregoing discussion.

Figure 1 and Figure 2 portray the term structure and general structure of interest rates respectively in India. It can be observed that all interest rates in India have increased considerably over the period of time. The fastest increase in them has occurred during the post-1970 period. There is no doubt that the determinants which we have discussed above must have influenced the evolution of interest rates structure in India also. However, there is evidence to show that the interest rates structure in India cannot be explained primarily in terms of those factors. Any theoretical discussion of the determinants of interest rates structure is based on the assumption that interest rates are determined primarily by the market forces. But the central fact about interest rates in India is that they are administered and not determined by the market forces. Almost every single rate is directly fixed by one authority or another and the breadth and the depth of intervention by the authorities in this context have grown over the period of time. [17] This system of administered interest rates has had very important implications for the determination of the nature and evolution of the structure of interest rates in India. We wish to highlight some of these implications hereafter. [18]

Figure 1:
Term structure of interest rates (Yields on Government of India Securities)

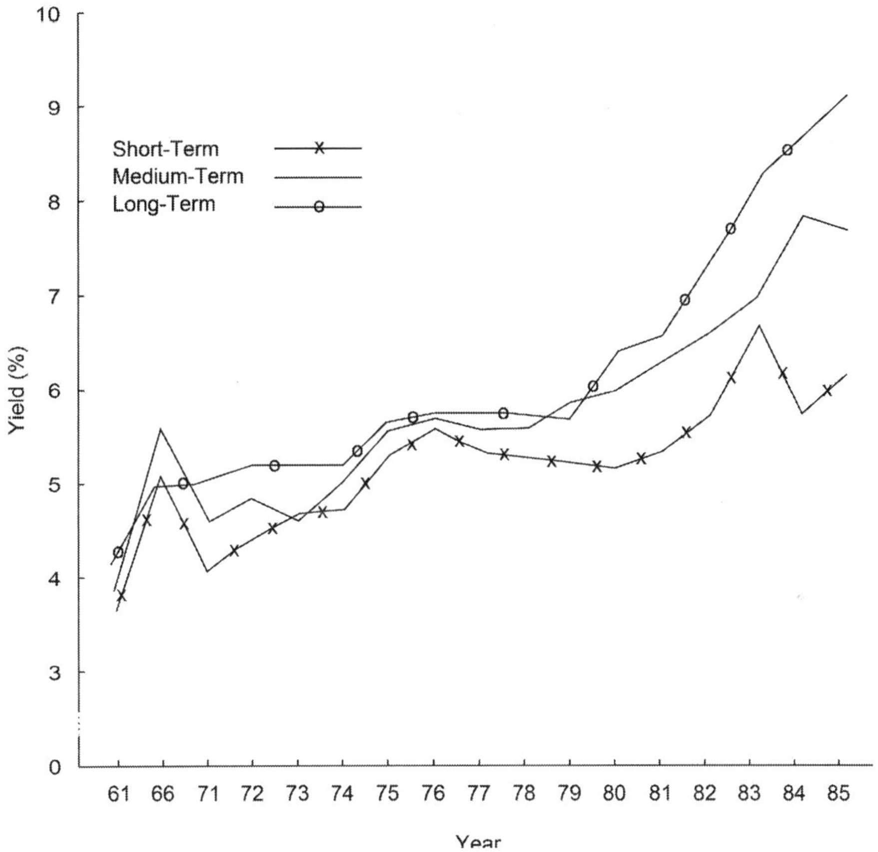

(1) The interest rates structure in India is much more complex than in other countries. Behind the general level of interest rates, there exists a large number of interest rates in each category of loans. As the Chakravarty Committee has stated, "the administered interest rates system has grown to be unduly complex and contains features which have reduced the ability of the system to promote the effective use of credit." [19]

(2) The evidence on the term structure of rates shows that the Treasury bill rate has always been lower than the Government bond yield. Normally, the yield on short-term Government securities has been lower than the yield on medium-term securities; the latter, in turn, has been lower than the yield on long-term securities. Thus, although the yield curve has generally been upward sloping, it has had a tendency to flatten out in later years. The yields on Treasury

Figure 2:
General structure of interest rates

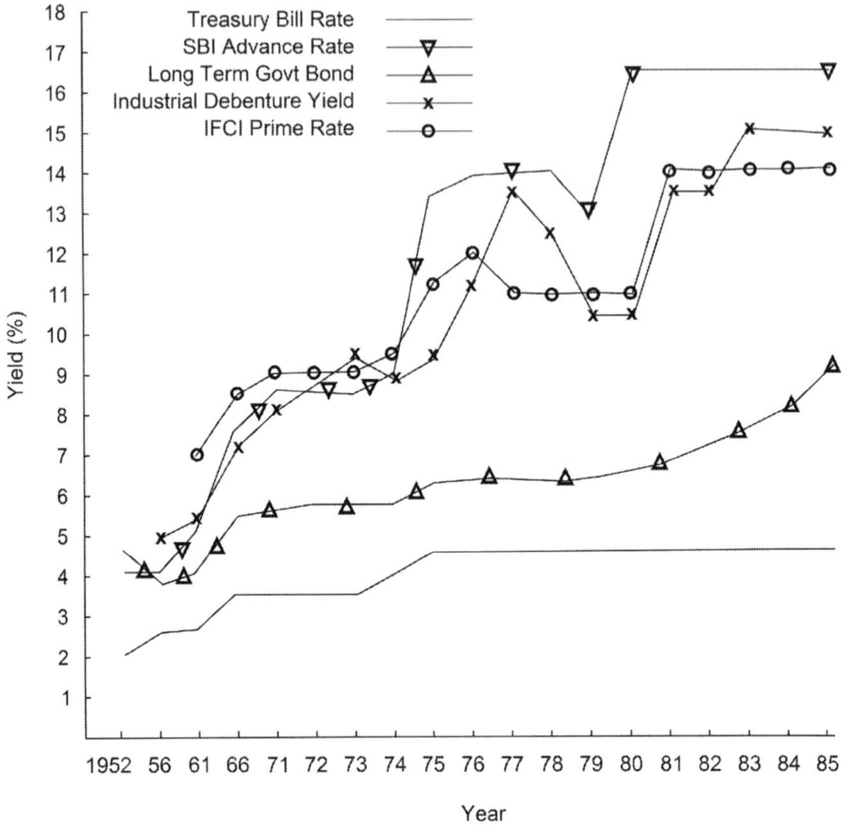

bills and bonds have been remarkably stable and they have increased much less than the other rates of interest. Given the actual inflationary experience in the Indian economy, this stability and flattening of the yield curves in India make one doubt whether the known theories of term structure have much role to play in explaining the term structure here. The policy of monetary authorities to keep the cost of Government financing low and to maintain a stable market for Government securities by undertaking appropriate support operation has resulted in stabilizing yields on them.

(3) In the entire interest rates structure, the bazar bill rate has been the highest followed by the State Bank of India (SBI) hundi rate. It is usually thought that the high degree of risk explains the level of these rates. There is a danger of over-emphasizing this factor because a deeper analysis will show that the claims in the markets under discussion are not that risky. It is the sectoral supply of and demand for funds which help to explain this structure. As lenders in the unorganized sector and rural money markets operate mostly with their own funds, and as institutional funds have not been channelized adequately into these sectors, the supply of

funds in them has been significantly short of demand for them. In other words, imperfections and monopolistic elements explain better interest rates in the unorganized sector in India.

It is to be noted in this context that the spread between the SBI hundi rate and the SBI advance rate has widened from one percentage point in early fifties to about four percentage points towards the end of seventies. Has the risk in hundi business increased over the period of time? It cannot be. It is the fact that SBI reduced its supply of funds in the hundi market after 1965 which explains better the phenomenon under discussion.

(4) In some cases, short-term interest rates have been higher than the long-term interest rates and in some other cases, the excess of long-term rates over the short-term rates has tended to diminish over the period of time. Why? Different forces have been working in different markets for funds to cause this phenomenon. In the Government securities market, the supply of long-term funds has increased over the period of time which has partly tended to reduce the long-term yields in relation to short-term yields. In the private organized sector, the long rates have risen at a slower rate than the short rates because while the cost of long-term (fixed) investment has been deliberately kept low, the cost of inventory investment has been increased faster.

(5) In general, the levels of interest rates, interest rates differentials, and changes in both of these in India cannot be said to have been predominantly determined by the considerations of risk, liquidity, maturity, demand for and supply of funds, commodity prices, etc. The concept of adjacency of different financial assets in the sense of the existence of well-defined differentials in interest rates on them when they are arranged in the descending or ascending order on the basis of their major attributes does not appear to have much meaning in India. The interest rates differentials are of *ad hoc* and haphazard nature. For example, it is difficult to understand why interest rates on time deposits of the same maturity with the post offices and banks should differ much, and why such a difference, when it exists, should fluctuate greatly from year to year. It is very easy to multiply such examples. We also find that in some cases, interest rates on conventionally risky loans (to small borrowers, unsecured personal loans, etc.) are lower than the rates on more safe and secured loans. In short, interest rates structure in India is very materially determined by the systems of differential interest rates, administered interest rates, and by the politics of ideology.

There are various theories of the structure of interest rates. Each theory concentrates attention on one factor as a determinant of the interest rates structure and as such constitutes only a partial explanation of the subject matter. Therefore, we would be able to explain interest rates structure better if we combine the insights given by each theory i.e. if we adopt an eclectic approach. If we do this, we learn that, in theory, expectations about the future short-term rates, long-term rates, and prices, supply of and demand for funds in financial markets which sometimes may be segmented, liquidity preference and risk avoidance, default risk, call risk, marketability, and tax status affect interest rates structure. However, the structure of interest rates in India cannot be wholly explained in terms of these purely economic factors. The direct fixation of rates by the authorities, the socio-economic-political objectives or considerations such as promotion of fixed investment, provision of concessional finance to the priority sectors, supply of funds to the Government sector at low cost, etc. have also to be taken into account in understanding the structure of interest rates in actual practice in India.

Notes and References

1. SHACKLE, G. L. S., "Recent Theories concerning the Nature and Role of Interest," in American Economic Association, Surveys of Economic Theory, London, 1965.
2. Maturity Period, default risk, marketability and liquidity, tax status are the major investment characteristics of financial assets or financial securities.
3. Holding period is the period of time for which the investor plans to hold or actually holds securities. It may be the same as maturity period or it may differ from the latter. If it is longer than the maturity period, the investor must reinvest; if it is shorter, he must sell the security before the maturity period is over.
4. Yield curves describe graphically the relationship between yield to maturity (shown on Y axis) and period of maturity (shown on X axis).
5. The understanding of certain terms such as current spot rate, future spot rate, forward rate, expected rate, is crucial for understanding the expectations hypothesis. Spot rate is a rate on funds for immediate delivery; it is today's rate for money to be delivered today for a specified period of time. A forward rate is today's rate for money to be delivered in the future for a specified period of time. Expected rates are normally arrived at by calculating forward rates from actual rates and by implicitly assuming that expected rates are equivalent to forward rates.
6. Arbitrage is a combination of transactions yielding an assured return. This is achieved through purchase of one security and simultaneous sale of another to give a risk free profit.
7. See LUTZ, F. A., *The Theory of Interest*, D. Reidel Co., Dordrecht, Holland, 1987, pp. 218-219.
8. HENNING, C. N., and others, *Financial Markets and the Economy*, Prentice Hall, Engelwood Cliffs, New Jersey, 1978, p. 386.
9. Systematic risk is the deviation of realized return from expected return on an efficient portfolio due to the tendency for rates of return on individual securities and portfolios to move with the rate of return on the market as a whole. In other words, it is the risk which cannot be reduced by diversifying the investment portfolio.
10. ROBINSON, R. I., and WRIGHTSMAN, D., *Financial Markets*, McGraw-Hill, New Delhi, 1981, pp. 164-165.
11. Risk averters prefer to forgo possible capital gains in order to escape capital losses and they decline possible higher returns to avoid possible lower rates.
12. ROBINSON R.I., & WRIGHTSMAN, D., op. cit., p. 165.

13. It is to be noted that the impact of transactions cost in this case will depend upon the distribution of holding periods for all investors relative to the maturity distribution of securities outstanding.
14. See VAN HORNE, J. C., *The Function And Analysis of Capital Market Rates,* Prentice Hall, Engelwood Cliffs, New Jersey, 1970, pp. 80-83.
15. See ROBINSON, R. I., and WRIGHTSMAN, D., op. cit., pp. 155-157.
16. The markets are said to have depth when there exists a large number of both sale and buy orders below and above the current market price; breadth when there exist orders to buy and sell from many different groups of investors; and resiliency when there exist new orders in big volumes when prices fluctuate.
17. For the full discussion of the system of administered interest rates, see BHOLE, L. M., "Administered Interest Rates in India," *Economic and Political Weekly,* June 22-29, 1985.
18. See also BHOLE, L. M., *Financial Markets and Institutions,* Tata McGraw-Hill Publishing Co., New Delhi, 1982, pp. 328-349.
19. RESERVE BANK OF INDIA, Report of the Committee to Review the Working of the Monetary System, Bombay, 1985, p. 173.

[11]

Some Issues Concerning Interest Rates Theory and Policy[*]

Introduction

The subject of interest rates has enthralled economists since old times, and it has been referred to in different religious texts also. It is a subject with multiple dimensions and its literature is truly vast. A large number of issues pertaining interest rates level, structure, and policy have been theoretically and empirically discussed in the literature. For example, what is rate of interest? Is it a real or monetary phenomenon? What determines the level and structure of interest rates? What is the relationship between interest rates on the one hand and investment, saving, prices, and output on the other? What is the appropriate or optimum level of interest rates? Why interest rates are administered and what are the consequences of such a policy? If interest rates are left free, would they rise and fluctuate too much and destabilise the financial system? What is and what ought to be the role of Bank rate or discount rate policy in economic management? Currently, the questions which are being prominently discussed are regarding whether the present level of interest rates in the world is too high and what explains that level? What is the impact of large public debt and deficit financing on interest rates? Are interest rates a poorer indicator of monetary policy than the supply of money? [1]

The Indian Economic Conference this year has 'Interest Rates Theory and Policy' as one of the themes for its deliberations and different scholars can discuss in depth one or more of the issues mentioned above. The present paper does not intend to analyse anyone particular issue in depth. Its scope perforce has to be somewhat wide. It is divided in four sections. In Section I, it describes certain major features of the level and structure of interest rates in India with special attention being paid to the money market rates. In Section II, the results of an exercise

* Paper published in the *Indian Economic Association Conference Volume*, December 1988.

estimating the interest rate determination function are presented. It is well-known that we have a system of administered interest in our country. Does it mean that interest rates here are completely impervious to the influence of economic factors? If no, which factors affect interest rates and to what extent? The results in section II should throw light on these questions. In Section III, we discuss the appropriate interest rates policy for India with special reference to the direction and thrust given to it by the Chakravarty Committee. Section IV contains the summary and conclusions.

I. Features of Interest Rates In India

Let it be noted at the outset that there is a bewildering variety, multiplicity, and compıcxity of interest rates in India. Abstracting from this complexity, we describe below a few important features of interest rates on the basis of statistical series of only a few major short-term and long-term rates for the period of 35 years (1951-1986). For the sake of convenience, these series have been presented as annual averages for the successive quinquenniums, along with their standard deviations and variances, in Table 1. Table 2 gives figures on ex-post real rates of interest in the similar way. Table 3 contains inter-correlation matrix among different nominal rates.

Table 1: Nominal Interest Rates in India, 1952-86, (Annual Averages, S. D., and Variance)

Period	CR	DY	GBY	SAR	BR	TBR	BDR
52-56	2.39	4.86	3.91	4.00	3.50	2.42	2.34
57-61	3.64	5.29	4.08	4.50	3.90	2.56	3.44
62 -66	4.52	6.21	4.71	6.10	5.00	2.71	4.57
67-71	4.91	8.08	5.31	7.50	5.60	3.30	5.72
72-76	8.10	9.51	5.93	10.70	7.40	3.80	6.80
77-81	8.66	12.11	6.53	14.60	9.00	4.60	7.00
82-86	9.26	14.60	8.48	16.50	10.0	4.60	8.55
52-86	5.93	8.67	5.55	9.13	6.34	3.47	5.49
S. D.	2.93	3.50	1.57	4.80	2.45	0.95	2.13
Variance	8.61	12.24	2.48	23.02	6.00	0.90	4.5

NOTATION:
CR = Call Rate; DY = Industrial Debenture Yield; GBY = Long-term Government Bond Yield; SAR = State Bank of India Advance Rate; BR = Bank Rate; TBR = Treasury Bill Rate; BDR = Bank's 1-Year Deposit Rate.

SOURCE : RBI, Report on Currency & Finance, Various Issues.

(1) A prominent fact the students would discover is that the level of all the interest rates has increased significantly and continuously although the extent of increase differs in the case

of different rates. The interest rates in 1986 were 2.5 times to 6 times their levels in 1951. Thus, while the call rate increased from 1.73 per cent in 1951-52 to 10.0 % in 1985-86, treasury bill rate increased from 1.90 % to 4.60 % over the same period of time. Whenever interest rates changed, they mostly changed in the upward direction; the movements in the downward direction were rare except in the case of call rate which has increased the most among all the rates, and, unlike other rates, it has not always hit the ceiling. This rate can be said to be the only rate which has been influenced by the market forces and its behaviour, therefore, gives us at least a partial idea about how interest rates might have behaved if they were not administered. On the other hand, the Treasury bill rate is the classic example of the administered interest rates in so far as it has increased the least and has remained remarkably stable. In fact, it has remained constant since 1974-75 in spite of so many significant changes in the financial markets and the economy as a whole.

Table 2: Ex-Post Real Interest Rates in India, 1952-86

Period	CR	DY	GBY	SAR	BR	TBR	BDR
52-56	5.05	7.62	7.32	5.92	6.22	5.15	5.14
57-61	-2.64	-0.93	-2.19	-1.78	- 2.38	-3.71	-2.83
62-66	- 1.90	0.45	-1.04	1.70	-0.76	-3.05	-1.19
67-71	-1.80	1.35	-1.41	0.78	-1.12	-3.42	-1.00
72-76	-3.88	-2.47	-6.04	-1.28	-4.66	-7.94	-5.18
77-81	0.12	-2.01	-2.01	6.06	-3.48	-3.94	-1.54
82-86	2.46	7.79	1.67	9.69	3.19	-2.21	2.91

NOTATION and SOURCE: The same as in Table 1.

Table 3: Nominal Interest Rates Correlation Matrix in India, 1952-86

Interest	CR	DY	GBY	SAR	BR	TBR	BDR
CR	1.00	0.840	0.807	0.891	0.920	0.889	0.892
DY	0.840	1.00	0.940	0.962	0.958	0.885	0.934
GBY	0.807	0.940	1.00	0.920	0.917	0.823	0.903
SAR	0.891	0.962	0.920	1.00	0.983	0.902	0.935
BR	0.920	0.958	0.912	0.983	1.00	0.920	0.943
TBR	0.889	0.885	0.823	0.902	0.920	1.00	0.921
BDR	0.892	0.933	0.903	0.935	0.943	0.921	1.00

The Bank rate has shown similar stability and stationariness. The rate of interest on Government securities also increased only a little till the end of 1970s but it has increased quite fast during 1980s. While the maximum coupon rate of interest on Government securities increase from 7.5 per cent in 1980-81 to 11.5 % in 1985-86, the long-term Government bond yield increased from 6.97 per cent in 1980-81 to 9.95 per cent in 1985-86 and 10.97 per cent in 1987-88. Interest rates on industrial debentures and bank finance have been higher than all the other interest rates throughout the entire period.

As indicated above, the variability or the amplitude of fluctuations has been different in the case of different interest rates. The standard deviation and the variance have been quite small in the cases of Treasury bill rate and the Government bond yield, but they have been very high in the cases of call rate, debenture yield, and the advance rate of the State Bank of India in their increasing order of importance in this respect. The Bank rate and the bank's deposit rate have had the similar and middle order degree of fluctuations.

(2) While the nominal rates have shown a definite upward trend, the real rates have fluctuated in a disorderly manner, and they have also been mostly either very low or negative. [2] They were positive and relatively high only during 1952 to 1956, and 1982 to 1986. The relative position of the level of certain real rates has changed over the period of time. For example, banks' real advance rate was lower than the real Government bond yield, real debenture yield, and real Bank rate respectively during 1952-56 but it has become higher than each of these rates during 1982-86. The reader can identify other similar examples from Table 2. All this suggests that the relative level and variability of real rates have been significantly influenced by the rate of inflation, variability of the rate of inflation, and the extent of change in the level of nominal rates of interest themselves.

(3) How do interest rates in India compare with the world interest rates during the recent past? As mentioned earlier, it has been argued that both short and long nominal and real interest rates have increased dramatically during 1980s and that this is a world wide phenomenon. Is this true for India also? As far as the nominal rates are concerned, except the Government bonds yields, the increase in none of the other rates was markedly or dramatically higher during 1980s than in other periods. In fact, the Bank rate, Treasury bill rate, prime lending rates of the commercial banks and term-lending financial institutions respectively remained constant, while the industrial debenture yield actually declined during 1981-88. However, all the real rates except the Treasury bill rate did increase significantly during 1980s in relation to earlier periods.

(4) In theory, the general structure of interest rates is determined by a number of factors (or the investment characteristics of the claims) such as the terms-to-maturity, risks (default, interest, inflation), tax status, call and buy-back options, liquidity or marketability, etc. The widely known theories of the structure of interest rates – Expectations Theory, Liquidity Premium Theory and Segmentation Theory – explain only the term-structure of interest rates [3] [see also paper no. 10 in this book].

Although the factors mentioned above must have had some influence on the structure of interest rates in India also, there is evidence to believe that the latter cannot be wholly or primarily explained in terms or those factors. In theory, interest rates are normally expected to be well aligned with one another in the sense that the differences (spreads) in them other than those caused by the said factors are ironed out on account of the arbitrage among alternative financial instruments, and that there is a similarity in the direction, timing, extent, frequency, etc. of their relative variations. Such a perfect alignment in the rates of interest has not been really present in India. The inter-correlation matrix in Table 3 reflects this fact to a certain extent. It is seen that while the cases of a really high correlation, say 0.95 and above, have been very few, those of a rather low correlation, say below 0.90, have been many.

To put it differently, the concept of adjacency of different financial assets in the sense of the existence of well-defined differentials in their interest rates when they are arranged in the descending or ascending order on the basis of their major attributes does not appear to have much meaning in India. It has been shown that the interest rates differentials in India are of ad hoc and haphazard nature. For example, it is difficult to understand why interest rates on time deposits of the same maturity with post-offices and banks should differ much, and why such a difference should fluctuate from time to time. We also find that in some cases, interest rates on conventionally risky loans have been lower than the rates on relatively more safe and secured loans. [4] The fact is that the socio-economic-politicaı considerations embodied in the systems of administered and differential interest rates have to be taken into account while explaining the interest rates structure in our country.

(5) Muranjan and Brahmananda have highlighted an important related feature of the interest rates structure in India. They have stressed that the short rates in our economy have peculiarly and paradoxically been higher than the long rates in the secular periods. [5] Without disagreeing with this point, it may be said that the evidence in this regard has been a mixed one. If we confine our attention here to the term structure of interest rates in the post-1950 periods [6], we would find an ascending order of interest rates on treasury bills, short-term, medium-term, and long-term government securities respectively. In other words, the yield curve for the claims on the Government has generally been upward sloping during 1951-86. It is true that it exhibited a tendency to flatten out during the latter half of the 1970s but it has resumed its upward slope during 1980s. On the contrary, the rate of interest charged by the banks on their short-term loans has usually been higher than their term-loans rate.

The evidence remains a mixed one even when we shift our attention to the general structure of interest rates. Thus, the call rate has always been lower than the industrial debenture yield and the long-term Government bond yield. The prime short-term lending rate of the commercial banks used to be lower than the industrial debenture yield till 1970-71 after which it has been higher than the latter; similarly this rate used to be slightly lower than the prime lending rate of the term lending financial institutions till 1973-74 after which it has remained higher than the latter. On the other hand, the long-term Government bond yield has been significantly lower than the short-term lending rate of the commercial banks throughout the period. In short, it is certainly true that the relationship between the short and the long rates in India has been a peculiar one, but the evidence in favour of their paradoxical relationship can be said to be only a mixed one.

(6) We now turn to the money market rates as a special case of the structure of interest rates. The call market, borrowing from RBI, Treasury bills market, and commercial bills market serve as alternative sources of funds for reserve adjustments, etc., and, therefore, the prices of funds in these markets are expected to be closely interrelated. Have the money market rates in India been so interrelated? How far have the changes in the Bank rate affected the money market rates?

Let us take the relationship between the Bank rate and call rate first. There are two viewpoints regarding their relationship in theory. One view holds that the Central Bank is a lender of last resort, and, therefore, the cost of approaching it must he higher than the cost of funds raised through other money market sources. The other view is that the Bank rate should he lower than the call rate because if it is so, there would be all incentive for the banks to borrow from the Central Bank which would increase the effectiveness of monetary policy since the Central Bank would then come to know about banks' financial conditions which would increase the scope for policy initiative.

In practice, the Bank rate in India has usually been higher than the call rate. However, as the Bank rate policy became less active and bold, the instances of the call rate exceeding the Bank rate increased in number and the extent of excess. In the past few years, the levels of both these rates have been more or less the same. The coefficient of correlation between them has been about 0.92.

The relative variations in the banks' call loans and their borrowings from the RBI as a proportion of their aggregate deposits over the period of time do not correspond with or do not reflect the above-mentioned relative movements of the call rate and Bank rate. While bank borrowings from the RBI declined from 11.19 per cent in 1971 to 1.26 per cent in 1987, the call loans increased from 0.006 % to 2.25 % over the same period of time. The decline in the borrowed reserves might have been a result of the policy of imposing quantitative ceiling on bank borrowings from the RBI. In other words, the RBI appears to have influenced the volume of borrowed reserves, and the volume and price in the call market not so much through the active and bold Bank rate policy as through quantitative credit controls. It is perhaps difficult to state that the Bank rate has led or caused the movements in the call rate in India.

The policies of paying interest on Bank reserves and pegging Treasury bill rate also have a relevance here. If interest is not paid on the bank's reserve account, banks have a relatively greater incentive to lend and borrow reserves in the call market rather than hold large excess reserves to meet possible higher reserve requirements because holding excess reserves in that case would involve (higher) opportunity cost. On the other hand, if interest is paid on the bank reserves, the tendency to hold excess reserves would be greater and the activity in the markets for call money and borrowed reserves would be relatively less. This latter policy may also induce banks to hold larger reserves than lend to priority sectors at concessional rates of interest. All this may result in the reduction of the credit multiplier. Similarly, if the treasury bill rate is pegged, the call market and rediscount market tend to become superfluous for the purpose of reserves adjustment because the banks then can use their inventory of Treasury bills for that purpose at low cost.

Now, the RBI does pay interest on the reserve accounts of the banks, and although this rate used to be lower than the call rate till the end of 1970s, it has been either equal to or higher than the call rate during 1980s. Similarly, although this rate used to be almost equal to the Bank rate for quite some time in the past, it has become higher than even the Bank rate since 1985. Further, as stated earlier, the Treasury bill rate has been pegged and it has been pegged at a low level over the past many years. It has been always lower than the Bank rate and it has been lower than the call rate also except during the first Five-Year plan. Its coefficient of correlation with the call rate and the Bank rate has been 0.889 and 0.920 respectively. This evolving structure of the money market rates is relevant in explaining the increasing but low volume of call loans, the very clear decline in bank borrowings from the RBI, and the increasing as well as high volume of reserves-all in relation to the aggregate deposits of banks during 1971 to 1987.

II. Interest Rates Determination Model

The economists are familiar with different interest rate theories such as the Classical Theory, Loanable Funds Theory, and Liquidity Preference Theory, and with the names of major interest rate theorists like Bohm-Bawerk, Wicksell, Akerman, Hayek, Walras, Fisher, Knight, Keynes, etc. One can get a very useful survey and exposition of interest rate theories in Conard, Shackle, and Lutz. [7] In theory, the pure rate of interest arises because of the productivity of capital, abstinence from consumption, liquidity preference, cost of administration of credit, etc. The list of factors or variables which may affect the rate of interest in practice can be fairly long. On the basis of a study of the theoretical and empirical literature in this context, we expect that the rate of interest in India should have been influenced by savings, capital formation, money supply government debt, deficit financing, inflation rate, and international factors embodied in the balance of payments and external capital flows.

In order to find out whether and how far the rate of interest has in fact been determined by the factors mentioned above, we estimated the following regression function with different combinations of independent variables:

$$R_t = a + b_1 GS_t + b_2 IR_t + b_3 GBD_t + b_4 M_t + b_5 GCF_t$$
$$+ b_6 FER_t + b_7 EGCF_t + U_t$$

Where, R = the rate of interest measured by the Call Rate (CR) or Industrial Debenture Yield (DY) or long-term Government Bond Yield (GBY) or State Bank of India Advance Rate (SAR); GS = Volume of Gross Domestic Savings; IR = Inflation Rate measured by the annual percentage change in the Wholesale Price Index (1970-71 = 100), GBD = Volume of Central Government's marketable internal debt plus Deficit Financing; M = Volume of Money Supply (M_1); GCF = Volume of Gross Domestic Capital Formation; FER = Volume of Foreign Exchange Reserves as a proxy for the external factors; EGCF = GCF-GS; a = intercept; U = error term; t = time subscript. The regression coefficients are expected to have the following signs:

$b_1 < 0; b_2 > 2; b_3 > 0; b_4 < 0; b_5 > 0; b_6 < 0; b_7 > 0$

All the variables are measured in the nominal values and are as annual observations. The estimates have been obtained by the OLS method. The period of estimation is 1951-52 to 1985-86. The source of data are: RBI, Report on Currency and Finance, various issues, and the Central Statistical Organisation, National Accounts Statistics, 1970-71 to 1984-85, New Delhi, January, 1987.

As mentioned above, we estimated a large number of equations with numerous combinations of variables included in the specification. All those equations cannot be reproduced here for lack of space. However, the following major findings emerged from them at different stages of our exercise:

When all the independent variables were included in the functions for our four interest rates, it was found that the saving, Government borrowing and deficit, money supply, and capital formation had the wrong sign in each of the four functions, and only the inflation rate and foreign factors performed reasonably well. This could be due to the problem of multi-collinearity as some of the variables mentioned above are obviously interrelated ciosely. Therefore another set of functions with regrouped variables was estimated; and its best-fit-subset of eight equations is reported below:

(1) $CR = 3.101 + \underset{(3.786)}{0.132}\, IR + \underset{(5.517)}{0.0008}\, GBD - \underset{(2.937)}{0.0012}\, FER - \underset{(5.598)}{0.0032}\, EGCF$

$\overline{R}^2 = 0.745;$ D.W. = 1.543

(2) $CR = 2.834 + \underset{(3.011)}{0.093}\, IR + \underset{(7.203)}{0.0005}\, M - \underset{(3.437)}{0.001}\, FER - \underset{(6.314)}{0.002}\, EGCF$

$\overline{R}^2 = 0.812;$ D.W. = 1.526

(3) $SAR = 4.416 + \underset{(3.524)}{0.164}\, IR + \underset{(3.712)}{0.0007}\, GBD - \underset{(0.286)}{0.0002}\, FER - \underset{(3.349)}{0.0025}\, EGCF$

$\overline{R}^2 = 0.831;$ D. W. = 0.994

(4) $SAR = 4.023 + \underset{(3.168)}{0.119}\, IR + \underset{(6.369)}{0.0006}\, M - \underset{(0.937)}{0.0003}\, FER - \underset{(4.592)}{0.0018}\, EGCF$

$\overline{R}^2 = 0.895;$ D.W. = 0.997

(5) $DY = 5.325 + \underset{(2.258)}{0.072}\, IR + \underset{(5.575)}{0006}\, M - \underset{(1.949)}{0.0003}\, FER - \underset{(4.636)}{0.0018}\, EGCF$

$\overline{R}^2 = 0.852;$ D.W. = 0.927

(6) $DY = 5.025 + \underset{(1.335)}{0.032}\, IR + \underset{(9.101)}{0.0005}\, M - \underset{(2.945)}{0.0007}\, FER - \underset{(5.803)}{0.0015}\, EGCF$

$\overline{R}^2$ = 0.920; D.W. = 882

(7) GBY = 4.0044 + 0.034 IR + 0.0003 GBD – 0.0003 FER – 0.0006 EGCF
(3.531) (7.141) (2.651) (3.963)
$\overline{R}^2$ = 0.930; D.W. = 1.116

(8) GBY = 3.919 + 0.021 IR + 0.0002 M – 0.0002 FER - 0.0002 EGCF
(2.418) (8.959) (2.496) (2.229)
$\overline{R}^2$ = 0.948; D.W. = 0.966

(Figures in brackets are t-values.)

It cannot be said that the fits are very good. They, however, do enable us *to* draw at least some tentative conclusions. It is seen that the adjusted R^2 is significantly high in all equations and that our model explains 75 per cent to nearly 95 per cent of variations in interest rates in India. Similarly, the variables, IR, GBD, and, FER have the correct sign and they are statistically significant within the customarily accepted bounds of significance in most of the cases. However, the variables, M, and EGCF are always with the wrong sigh, and the results are not robust in many cases in terms of the test for autocorrelation.

On the basis of all the results, we conclude that (a) the rate of inflation has been the most consistently significant determinant of the short-term as well as the long-term interest rates; (b) the changes in the quantum of the government market borrowings and the budgetary deficit have exerted positive and significant influence on interest rate, (c) the balance of payments and foreign capital flows have been relevant determining the level and changes of interest rates; and (d) it is rather surprising that interest rates do not appear to have been affected by the volume of saving, capital formation, and money supply.

III. Interest Rates Policy In India

Two major policy issues which have engaged the minds of many in this regard are about the system of administered interest rates and the appropriate level of interest rates. Should interest rates in India be freed to be determined by the market forces or not? Should they be raised or lowered? Some people have argued for the lowering of interest rates (or not raising them further) for reasons like encouraging the investment climate and the equity culture, reducing cost of production and inflation, and reducing the debt servicing burden of the Government. On the other hand, many economists from India and abroad have presented a solid case for the regime of the free and higher rates of interest for the developing countries including India [8]. We also have presented a detailed and systematic analysis of the system of administered interest rates in India in which we have discussed its origin and rationale, its ill effects on the Indian financial system, and how its abandonment would lead to a much better promotion of saving, efficiency of financial system, efficiency of investment, efficiency of monetary control, and efficiency and equity in Government finances, without sacrificing the cause of priority sectors and social justice. [9] Similarly, in a number of theoretical-cum-empirical studies, we have shown how a more bold, active, well co-ordinated, and simple dear money policy is needed for India in order to achieve the developmental objectives of growth with stability. [10]

Recently, the Chakravarty Committee [11] also has addressed itself to these issues and has made a number of very wise, useful, and important recommendations regarding them. The Committee, of course, does not visualise that the administered interest rate system can and should be completely abandoned. It, however, does hold that this system has caused an incalculable harm to the Indian financial system, and, therefore, it should be modified such that it meets the needs of the Government as a major borrower and entrepreneur, augments the pool of savings, protects the interests of small saver, increases the flexibility to effect counter-cyclical variations in interest rates, promotes more effective use of credit; etc. Accordingly, it has recommended that the ceiling on interest rates on bank loans and call loans should be abandoned and that the Treasury bill rate, yields on Government securities of all maturities, and bank deposit rates etc. should be appropriately raised so as to yield realistic and reasonable real rates of return to the holders of the claims. In its view, there is a strong case for a much greater reliance on interest rate technique for promoting the effective use of credit and for short-term monetary .management.

We feel that the Committee's argument that the higher interest rates are not really against the goal of social justice and that they in fact help small savers who are not in a position to take advantage of fiscal concessions has not received as much public attention as it deserves. It is important to note in this context that a study of the policy of imposing ceiling on deposit rates in USA has also shown that it adversely affected income distribution because the small savers lost billions of dollars in terms of interest earnings on account of such a policy. [12] All such recommendations of the Committee are meant to end an era of the weak, passive, ineffective, complicated, and economically and socially harmful interest rate policy, and, therefore, deserves to be supported by all.

There are, however, two recommendations of the Committee which concern the role of interest rates as the technique (instrument), target, and indicator of monetary policy and which need to be discussed further. As said above, the Committee does not want the system of quantitative credit controls to be completely replaced by the system of free interest rates. It visualises that interest rates technique should play a supportive and supplementary role vis-a-vis quantitative controls. The reluctance of the Committee to abandon .quantitative controls can be appreciated and is in tune with the thinking in this regard in other countries also. It may be noted that the issue under discussion has received much attention in USA and other countries and the feeling there also is that it perhaps is not possible to completely abandon quantitative credit controls and to reıy wholly on the interest rates technique only because of a number of considerations. [13]

This position cannot be rejected in toto. Yet, is it not likely that the disadvantages of the free interest rates such as a runaway increase and fluctuations in interest rates and the consequent destabilizing effects are rather exaggerated? After all, interest rates are determined by certain factors and once we identify what these factors are in a given economy, it may be possible to keep interest rates in check by regulating those factors through appropriate policy measures. In other words, if interest rates do rise phenomenally after they are freed, such an increase maybe purely temporary, and it may soon be possible to achieve the right level of interest rates through the appropriate policies. Further, the outward effects of the policy of freeing interest rates can be minimized by dismantling the system of administered interest rates slowly over an extended period of time.

The Committee has also recommended that we should formally introduce monetary targeting as the main instrument of monetary policy and the interest rates instrument should, again, play only a supplementary, supportive, subsidiary, and reinforcing role. We are sceptical about the strength of this recommendation. It is difficult to reconcile the combination of quantitative credit controls, monetary targeting, and modified free interest rates techniques with any one of the theories or approaches or transmission mechanisms of monetary policy. It is pretty certain that the monetarists would not accept such a combination. In any case, there are a number of theoretical and practical problems which beset the implementation of the policy of monetary targeting, particularly in the Indian milieu. To discuss them would need an another essay. Suffice it to say here that the experience about the policy of monetary targeting in many countries in the world appears to have greatly disillusioned the experts as well as policy makers, and the said policy is on its way out in those countries. Therefore, the emphasis on the use of monetary targeting as the prime tool of monetary policy at this juncture of the history of conduct of monetary policy in the world perhaps amounts to exercising a choice in favour of a discarded tool.

In spite of the existence of the academic and semi-official analyses in its support, the flexible, free and higher interest rates policy has not been implemented in India. The most of the recommendations of the Chakravarty Committee concerning interest rates remain unimplemented so far. The call rate, bank deposits & loan rates, etc. are still subject to a ceiling; the Treasury bill rate remains unchanged; there are no signs of the activization of the Bank rate policy; the interest rates structure is as complicated as before; the whole system of concessional interest rates remains stay put; the spread between different interest rates, particularly the bank deposits rates, continues to be haphazard, arbitrary, and anomalous. In fact during the past three years, the interest rates policy in many respects has moved in the opposite direction to what the Committee has recommended. For example, the interest rates on the whole set of saving instruments including bank deposits, and the maximum lending rates of the commercial banks were lowered in April 1987. The interest rates on Government finance have somehow been raised. But this gives an appearance that the authorities are following a policy of cheap money for the private sector and dear money for the Government sector.

IV. Summary And Conclusions

We have shown in this paper that the nominal interest rates have shown a more or less steady upward trend in India during the period of 1951 to 1986. The real rates of interest, however, have, fluctuated greatly and they have usually been very low or negative. The level and changes of real interest rates appear to have been significantly influenced by the variability of the rate of inflation and the extent of change in the nominal interest rates themselves. Unlike in other countries, there has not been any dramatic increase in the nominal interest rates in India during 1980s, although real rates were relatively much higher during this period. The structure of interest rates has been the outcome of economic factors as well as social and political considerations. The relationship between the long-term and short-term rates has been peculiar and partially paradoxical. There does not appear to be a perfect alignment in money market rates and one cannot say that the Bank rate has really led or determined the behaviour of other money market rates like the call rate, Treasury bill rate, the reserves account rate, etc. The nominal interest rate was found to be affected by the rate of inflation, the volume of public debt, and deficit financing, and the balance of payments and foreign capital inflows. It is rather curious that the volume of money supply, saving, and capital formation were shown to have had no influence on the rate of interest. There is a need for a fresh study of this point. Many studies in India have adequately and cogently established the need for and the appropriateness of the simple, free, flexible, and higher interest rates policy for India. However, such a policy remains unimplemented till now. In fact, the changes in the interest rates in the recent past have been contrary to the direction and thrust recommended by the Chakravarty Committee. Monetary targeting and quantitative controls may not be superior to the rate interest as the instrument of monetary policy.

Notes and References

1. For some of the recent studies, see BANK OF ENGLAND, "Recent Trends In Real Interest Rates", Bank of England Quarterly Bulletin, September 1986; BLANCHARD O. J., and SUMMERS, L. H., "Perspectives on High World Real Interest Rates", Brookings Papers on Economic Activity, 2: 1984; CECCHETTI, S. G., "High Interest Rates: Can Thcy Be Explained", Economic Review, Federal Reserve Bank of Kansas, City, Sept.-Oct. 1986; EVANS, Paul, 'Do Large Deficits Produce High Interest Rates", American Economic Review, March 1985; LITTERMAN, R. B., and LAURENCE, W., Money, Real interest rate, and output: A Reinterpretation of post-war US data", Econometrica, January 1985; TANZI, V., "Fiscal deficits and interest rates in the United States: An Empirical Analysis, 1960-84", IMP Staff Papers, December 1985; WEBB, R. H., "Interest Rates and Federal Deficits", Economic Review, Federal Reserve Bank of Richmond, July-August 1982; WILCOX, J. A., "Why Real Interest Rates Were So Low In The 1970s", American Economic Review, March 1983.

2. The real rates have been calculated by adjusting the Current nominal rate of interest for the current rate of inflation (Wholesale price index, 1970-71 = 100).

3. LUTZ, F. A., The Theory of Interest, D. Reidel Publishing Co., Holland, 1967; VAN HORNE, J.C., Function and Analysis of Capital Market Rates, Prentice Hall, Englewood Cliffs, New Jersey, 1970; MANKIEW, N. G., "The Term Structure of Interest Rates Revisited", Brookings Papers on Economic Activity, 1: 1986; BHOLE, L. M., "The Structure of Interest Rates in Theory and Practice", Indian Journal of Economics, October, 1988.

4. For detailed evidence and other examples, see BHOLE, L. M., Financial Markets and Institutions, Tata McGraw-Hill, New Delhi, 1982, pp. 338-345, and "Administered Interest Rates in India", Economic and Political Weekly, June 22-29, 1985, pp. 1091-1092.

5. MURANJAN, S. K., Modern Banking in India, Kamala Publishing House, Bombay 1952; BRAHMANANDA, P..R:, "Thoughts on Interest Rate Under Indian Conditions", in RBI, Recent Developments in Monetary Theory and Policy, Bombay, 1978, and "Interest Policy In India", S..K. Muranjan Memorial Lecture, mimeo, 1982.

6. For evidence in the earlier period, see BHOLE, L. M., Financial Markets and Institutions, op. cit., pp. 339-340.

7. CONARD, J. W., Introduction to the Theory of Interest, University of California Press, Berkeley, 1959; SHACKLE, G. L. S., "Recent Theories Concerning the Nature and Role of Interest", in American Economic Association, Surveys of Economic Theory, London, 1965; and LUTZ, F. A., op. cit.

8. See BRABMANANDA, P. R., op. cit.; MYRDAL, G., Asian Drama, Vol. II & III, Appendix 5 and 8; Allen Lane, The Penguin Press, London, 1958; SHAW, E. S., Financial Deepening In Economic Development, Oxford University Press, Oxford, 1973; EDWARDS, S., and KHAN, M. S., "Interest Rates Determination In Developing Countries: A Conceptual Framework", IMF Staff Papers, Sep. 1985; MOLHO, L. E., "Interest Rates, Saving and Investment in Developing Countries: A Re-Examination of the McKinnon-Shaw Hypothesis", IMF Staff Papers, March 1986.

9. BHOLE, L. M., "Administered Interest Rates In India", op.cit.

10. BHOLE, L. M., Investment; Interest, and Monetary Policy in India, University of Bombay; Bombay, 1974; and Impacts of Monetary Policy, Himalaya Publishing House, Bombay, 1985.

11. RESERVE BANK OF INDIA, Report of the Committee to Review the Working of the Monetary System, Bombay, 19385.

12. GILBERT, R. A., "Requiem for Regulation Q: What It Did, Why It Passed Away? Review, The Federal Reserve Bank of St. Louis, February 1986.

13. See FEDERAL RESERVE BANK OF BOSTON: Credit Allocation Techniques and Monetary Policy, Boston, 1973.

[12]

An Interest Rate Policy for Stable Economic Growth[*]

I. Introduction

After having experienced recessionary conditions in 1966, 1967 and partly in 1968, organised industry in India is slowly regaining its tempo of growth. The index number of industrial production registered an increase of 6 per cent in 1968 and about 8 per cent in 1969. The growth rate of industrial production in 1969 compares well with the average rate of growth of industrial production (8 to 10 per cent) during 1961-1965. If this recovery is to be maintained without substantial rise in prices, economic policy in general and monetary policy in particular will have to be appropriately geared. The purpose of this article is to suggest an appropriate monetary policy to be used during the years of the Fourth Five-Year Plan. The policy advocated here is more a sort of reminder than something quite novel.

Monetary policy for the Fourth Plan will have to be such as will facilitate the achievement of its economic goals. The magnitude of the task to be performed can be gauged by comparing these goals with those set for the Third Five-Year Plan. The comparative picture of investment, savings, employment, deficit financing and budgetary receipts corresponding to external assistance during Third and Fourth Plans can be had from Table 1.

It may be seen that the total investment to be undertaken during the Fourth Plan is a little more than double the investment undertaken during the Third Plan period. In financing this investment, the dependence on the external resources and deficit financing is to be reduced. Thus while 28.3 per cent of total outlay was financed through external aid during the Third Plan, only 16.5 per cent of total outlay is estimated to be financed by such aid during the Fourth Plan. The assumption of moderate use of external aid during the Fourth Plan is in

[*] Paper published in *Industrial India, Annual* 1970.

keeping with the mounting domestic pressures in aid giving countries and the growing realisation of the limitations of excessive dependence on external resources in our country. As to the deficit financing, the actual deficit during 1961-65 (Rs. 1133 crores) was more than double the planned for deficit (Rs. 550 crores) for the same period. The planned deficit financing during the Fourth Plan is Rs. 850 crores. In this context, there are two points to be noted for the purpose of this paper: (a) that if deficit financing remains at the estimated level, the efforts to mobilise savings will have to be greater; (b) that if the actual deficit financing exceeds the planned for deficit, the pressure on prices will be greater. Monetary policy to be followed will have to take into account these two factors. The corollary of the lesser dependence on deficit financing and external aid is the need for higher rate of domestic savings. Accordingly, the rate of savings in the Fourth Plan is to be higher than that in the Third Plan.

Table 1

(Figures in crores of rupees)

Item	Plan	
	III	IV
1. Investment	10400	22635
2. Domestic Savings (Ratio to National income)	From 8.0 % in 1960-61 to 10 % in 1965-66	From 8.8 % in 1968-69 to 13.2 % in 1973-74
3. Employment	Increased from 12.09 million in 1960-61 to15.46 million in 1965-66	Not projected
4. Deficit Financing	1133 (13.2 % of total plan outlay)	850 (5.3 % of total plan outlay)
5. Budgetary Receipts corresponding to external assistance	2423 (28.3 % of total outlay)	2614 (16.5 % of total outlay)

Implications

This comparative picture of two Five-Year Plans has the following implications: 1) That inflationary pressures may be continued to be experienced during the period of Fourth Five Year Plan. The large amount of investment expenditure will mean a pressure of demand on commodities market. This pressure is likely to be reinforced because the actual deficits may exceed the estimated deficits. This belief is based on the fact that the Fourth Plan document does not envisage any deficit by the State Governments. The recent experience about State budgets indicates that such an assumption may not be fulfilled in practice. The demand for bank credit is also expected to rise during the Fourth Plan on account of the following reasons: (a) A big Fourth Plan is likely to take a fairly large chunk of the additional resources to be mobilised by the banks. (b) The end of recession and the commencement of the Plan will generate fresh demand for credit. (c) After nationalisation, banks are required to fill credit gaps in fields hitherto left or neglected. (d) Banks will be required to finance commodity buffer stock operations. Previously, such operations were financed mainly through the budget.

All these factors indicate that the pressure .on the price front is likely to be maintained during the Fourth Plan. The recent experience shows that in spite of reasonably good harvests during the previous two years, the prices have started moving up. If this price rise continues, it will be detrimental, among other things, to our efforts to increase export earnings. As the Report of the Central Board of Directors of Reserve Bank of India for the year 1968-69 puts it, " ... yet the task of export promotion is a continuing one and its success depends *crucially* on the maintenance of competitiveness in terms of comparative costs. Any resurgence of inflationary pressures ... cannot but affect the course of exports adversely. The Fourth Plan envisages a rise of seven per cent per annum in export earnings ... A close watch on prices as well as costs is essential from this vital angle."

Upward Moving Interest Rates Structure

Therefore, it will be the task of monetary authority not to allow the price situation to go out of hand. As the pre-budget economic survey of this year puts it, "... there is a need for a credit policy which is promotional, but at the same time vigilant against *speculative pressures* and *unrewarding* uses". Monetary authority will be able to do so only if it raises the cost of credit in our country. Interest rates in our economy have remained quite low for too long a period. They have been maintained at levels comparable to those in highly developed and capital abundant countries like Japan and others. As a result, many sectors, upto this time, did not feel any need to rationalise credit use under a liberal and relatively cheap credit policy. Such a policy cannot be continued in future; and it is high time that we adjust our interest rates structure upward in an appropriate manner.

Dear money policy is necessary not only for maintaining price stability but also to mobilise more savings. The Fourth Plan document emphasizes that "in regard to the financing of the plan, emphasis is being placed on additional mobilisation of resources in a manner which will not give rise to inflationary pressures." The best way to do this is to enhance the rate of domestic savings. Stated otherwise, two things should happen in this context: (a) that total volume of savings should increase; and (b) that there should be a shift in the preference pattern of savers from physical assets to financial assets. Now during a period of continuous price rise, the total amount of savings is less and/or the Savings take the form of real assets. This suggests that in order to achieve (a) and (b) mentioned above, the rise in interest rates on savings will have to be proportionately more than the price rise. In other words, the real interest rates to be earned on savings should not be forced to such levels by rise in prices, that there remains no incentive for savings. Therefore, if savings are to increase in a period of expected price rise, the interest rates to be earned should be much higher than they are at present. Does not this assume that savings are interest elastic? Though this remains a moot point, there is following evidence to show that higher interest rates are likely to induce the savers either to save more and or to invest their savings in financial assets: (i) That net small savings increased from Rs. 75 lakhs in 1962-63 to Rs. 146 lakhs in 1965-66. According to the Report (1963-64) of the Central Board of Directors of Reserved Bank of India, one of the factors behind this rise in small savings could be a higher rate of interest. (ii) That there has been a shift in the pattern of deposits. Thus while the growth rate of demand deposits has shrunk from 22 per cent in 1963 to 16 per cent in 1965, that of time deposits has significantly increased from 2.8 per cent in 1963 to 12.3 % in 1965. Similarly, savings deposits, interest rates on which have been substantially stepped up during 1962-1965, have recorded an annual growth of 21 per cent during the same period. The most important indicator of the responsiveness of savings to interest rates is the phenomenal growth of deposits with non-banking companies (NBC) which offer attractive rates of interest. According to Reserve Bank of India survey, deposits with NBC increased from Rs. 136 crores in 1962 to Rs. 186 crores in 1964, i.e., by 37 per cent. (iii) That during a year of nationalised banking, there has been a fall in the rate of growth of deposits in spite of a substantial expansion of branches and the maintenance of National Income to the level of earlier year. Given the dire necessity of higher rate of domestic savings, this evidence suggests that attractively higher interest rates will go a long way in encouraging people to abstain from the current consumption.

Reduction in Unemployment

In addition, higher interest rates will help to reduce the unemployment in the economy by encouraging the use of such technical co-efficients of production as will suit the factor-endowment of our country. It is quite well known that Indian planning so far has expressly failed to solve the problem of labour unemployment in our nation. The backlog of unemployed work force has increased in successive plan. This was due to, at least, two reasons: (a) that the population has been increasing at a very high growth rate; and (b) that, in spite of unlimited supplies of labour in our economy, relatively greater reliance was placed on the use of capital intensive technology. This is reflected in the fact that the capital output ratio in large-scale enterprises increased from 3.11 in 1949-50 to 3.92 in 1960-61. The capital output ratio in agriculture, small enterprises, trade and transport sectors has also gone up during the same decade. The preference for the capital intensive techniques was, among other factors, due to lower cost of finance compared to that of labour. Though the policy of using capital intensive techniques must have benefited our economy in certain ways, it remains true that it resulted in building up tension consequential to the misery of unemployed people. Therefore, it is imperative now to correct this kind of imbalance by encouraging such type of technology as will employ more and more labour without injuring the growth process. We need not enter here into the controversy whether the labour intensive or the capital intensive techniques are preferable from the point of view of economic growth. This is an unsettled issue. But it can be fairly stated that, given the appropriate research, it should not be difficult to evolve the labour intensive techniques which do not hamper the growth process. Moreover, when one takes into account the danger which a large army of unemployed people poses to the very fibre of the democratic life of a nation, the case for using the labour intensive techniques gets established.

Labour Intensive Technology

Therefore, it will be the task of monetary policy to help to encourage the use of labour intensive technology during the Fourth Plan. It can move in this direction by abandoning its present liberal money policy and by enhancing the cost of capital in a manner which will compel the industries to use more labour in their production processes.

Against this plea for higher interest rates, it may be argued that it does not take into account the detrimental effects such high rates may have on investment. In other words, is it not true that higher interest rates may result in non-fulfilment of investment and National Income targets of the Fourth Plan?

In this context, it may be stated that such a danger of a fall in the growth rate of National Income on account of a restriction of investment during the period of the Fourth Plan does not really exist. It is very much unlikely that proposed higher interest rates will restrict genuinely productive investment and the investment in the priority sectors. Moreover, there already exists considerable idle capacity over a wide segment of manufacturing industry. For example, except iron and steel, capacities in almost all basic industries increased even during the period of recession, though production never kept pace with this increase in capacity. Such increase in capacity during the period of recession could be because of earlier commitments. Now, if greater care and attention is given to the efficient use of this already existing production capacity by minimising the lags in bringing capacity to full utilisation, the growth in National Income is not likely to suffer at all. In fact, Planning Commission has taken into account this factor while setting the investment targets for the Fourth Plan. Accordingly, incremental capital output ratio of 2 for Fourth Plan is lower than the average ratio of 2.4 for the first three Five-Year Plans.

Dear Money Policy

We may, therefore, conclude that the appropriate monetary policy for the Fourth Plan would be one of higher interest rates. Such dear money policy would be more effective if other tools of monetary policy such as open market operations (O.M.O.) are also properly harnessed. O.M.O. of the Reserve Bank of India (RBI) had a limited purpose so far. They were conducted mainly as an adjunct to the public debt policy of the Government of India. As a result, to maintain stability in the Government securities market and to ensure the success of the issue of Government debt were the two important goals of O.M.O. in India. These goals of O.M.O. are directly and indirectly in contradiction with the goals of dear money policy. And the failure of increases in interest rates during 1957-1965 was partly due to the way in which O.M.O. were conducted during that period. Therefore, O.M.O. will have to be a positive tool of monetary management in future. Monetary authority will have to take sufficient care so that its O.M.O. do not take away the sting of higher cost of credit.

One important way in which this can be done is to lengthen the maturity structure of the Government debt. During the past, commercial banks in India have shortened the maturity structure of their holdings of Government securities. For example, the proportion of Government securities with less than 5 years to maturity was about 50 pet cent during 1955-56. It has, in fact, increased upto 70 per cent in 1966. The proportion of securities with more than ten years to maturity has declined during the same period. When the maturity structure of the Government debt is short like this, the banks can liquidate Government securities in order to expand private credit without the fear of large capital losses. And this undermines the success of the raising of the Bank rate. Hence the need for lengthening the maturity structure of the Government debt.

Though the dear money policy along with the reforms suggested above will go a long way in achieving the national goals, it may be incapable of doing so by itself in a mixed economy like ours. It will be necessary that other tools of economic policy such as fiscal policy, commercial policy and physical controls are appropriately co-ordinated. Given such a co-ordination, the dear money policy will largely succeed in bringing about stable economic growth.

[13]

A Critique of New Interest Rates[*]

The Reserve Bank of India has reduced the deposit and lending rates of the commercial banks for the second time within a period of less than a year. The previous reduction was made in May 1977. Table 1 presents the structure of interest rates before and after these changes.

It can be observed from Table 1 that in less than a year, interest rates have been lowered by 10 per cent to 28 per cent while maintaining a façade of dear money policy by not changing the Bank rate. This article argues that there was no justification for such a drastic cut in interest rates, that the persuit a cheap money policy would act against mobilization and institutionalization of savings, interests of the small saver and the entrepreneur, generation of employment opportunities and price stability.

The empirical evidence on the responsiveness of savings and deposits to interest rates clearly establishes that the reduction in deposit rates would reduce the rate of growth of deposits and would arrest the progress of institutionalization of savings. In his comprehensive econometric study (the Falling Economy and How to Revive It), P.R. Brahmananda has found that household savings are positively related with the geometric mean of short-term and long-term interest rates, the elasticity coefficient being around 1.33. A continuous increase in deposits with non-banking companies is another type of evidence to be reckoned with in this regard.

The RBI study Group on Non-Banking Companies has emphatically stated, "... the basic reason ... for the growth of deposits of NBCs is that these companies pay higher interest rates than those paid by commercial banks". An econometric study by A.M. Khusro and N.S. Sidharthan has estimated that while interest-elasticity of total deposits is around 0.489, it is higher at about 0.542 for time deposits.

[*] Paper published in *Financial Express*, March 20, 1978.

Table 1: Interest rates Structure

Type of Deposit	Deposit rates				Short-term lending rates			Term lending rates		
	Before June 1977	After June 1977	New rates from March 1978	% reduction in new rates over those before June 1977	Prior to March 1978	New rates from March 1978	% reduction	Prior to June 1977	After June 1977	% reduction
1) Saving deposits	5.00-5.25-5.50	3.00-5.00	4.5	10-18	16.5-17.5	15.0	9.1-14.3	15.0	12.5	16.7
2) Fixed deposits:										
a) 15 days to 45 days	3	3	2.5	16.6						
b) 46 days to 90 days	3.5	3.5	3	14.3						
c) 91 days to less than 6 months	5.5	4	4	27.2						
d) 6 months to less than 9 months	6	4.5	4.5	25.0						
e) 9 months to less than 1 year	7	5	5	28.6						
f) 1 year to less than 3 years	8	6	6	25.						
g) 3 years to 5 years	9	8	7.5	16.7						
h) above 5 years	10	10	9	10.0						

SOURCE: RBI, Bulletin, Various Issues.

The latest available evidence on the behaviour of time deposits given in Table 2 corroborates what has been stated above. The growth of time deposits has slackened during the months after reduction in deposit rates effective from June 1977.

When compared to the position in the corresponding months in 1976, the rate of growth of time deposits in 1977 is much lower since the month of July. For the entire period of March 31, 1977 to January 13, 1978, increase in time deposits at Rs.2115.9 crores was lower than the increase of Rs.2119.3 crores for the corresponding period of the previous year. The Economic Survey, 1977-78, has brought out that rate of growth of time deposits declined from 25.9 per cent during March 1976-January 1977 to 20.5 per cent during March 1977-January 1978.

As a result of reduction in interest rates on time deposits, savers would be induced to hold more savings in the form of non-financial assets like land, gold and silver, which because of rising prices, offer much higher real rates of return.

The amount of demand deposits also is likely to increase because the incentive to shift into time deposits from demand deposits is reduced. This latter possibility cannot be rules out because the elasticity of demand deposits with respect to interest rate is negative.

Similarly, the rate of growth of demand deposits is shown to have increased (17.7 per cent) during March 1977-January 1978, compared to the rate (14.5 per cent) during the corresponding period of 1976-77. As relatively higher increase in demand deposits implies greater liquidity in the economy, an interest rates policy which is likely to shift the preferences of the savers in favour of demand deposits cannot be appreciated particularly in a period of existing and potential inflationary pressures.

Table 2: Behaviour of time deposits

Year / Month	1976		1977	
	Absolute increase over previous month (Rs. Crores)	% increase over previous month	Absolute increase over previous month (Rs. Crores)	% increase over previous month
May	196	2.2	247	2.1
June	270	2.9	331	2.8
July	256	2.7	292	2.4
August	237	2.4	170	1.4
September	205	2.1	73	0.6
October	179	1.8	108	0.9

SOURCE: RBI Bulletins, Oct. 1976 and Oct. 1977.

In this context, it would be incorrect to take a complacent view that the Government, by raising the level of tax-free income to Rs.5,000 in the case of contributions to LIC and the provident fund, by giving tax exemption in the case of investment in shares of new companies, etc., has taken steps to increase savings in the economy. The problem of investment in stock market securities would be taken up later.

As to LIC and provident fund investments, it has been overlooked that savings in these forms are very liquid, they bear much lower rates of return, and they also bear a higher degree of risk of depreciation in value. As a result, these forms of savings are much less popular in comparison with bank deposits.

This is evident from the fact that very few people have reached even the present ceiling of Rs.4,000 in their contributions to LIC and PF. It should not be forgotten that the decision to save is taken with an eye on both a return on savings and their liquidity. From this point of view, the reduction in deposit rates constitutes a net negative step.

The demand for lowering of interest rates was being made in certain quarters as a measure to channeling investible funds to the stock market. It was argued that the average return on shares has remained lower than the return on bank deposits, that the reduction in banks' deposit rates would we followed by reduction in interest rates on company deposits, that, as a result, both individual and institutional (LIC, UTI) investors would invest more in company shares and that this would boost the investment market. It appears that this view has prevailed in formulating the present interest rates policy.

It is maintained here that for reducing company deposits, the correct course of action would have been to increase banks' deposit rates rather than to reduce them because at lower rates paid by them, the interest differential on deposits with banks and companies is going to widen; and this would result in attracting more deposits to the companies.

It is only when bank deposit rates are raised that the differential mentioned above would be narrowed because while companies cannot raise interest rates paid by them beyond a certain limit, they need not reduce their rates along with reduction in banks' rates.

It is also maintained here that the working of the stock market over past many years suggests that there is nothing sacrosanct about diverting funds from banks to the stock market. In fact, in the Indian set-up, such a diversion of funds would mean the perpetuation of the growth of large-scale industries.

To elaborate, first, if the return on shares has been low, in a large measure it has been due to inefficiency of and the malpractices indulged in by the managements in the corporate sector. To reduce return on deposits in order to make industrial shares attractive to investors is iniquitous and is to perpetuate inefficiency and malpractices.

Secondly, the importance of the new issue market (NIM) in financing capital formation in industry has always remained marginal. NIM finances only about 15 per cent of net assets formation per year in the corporate sector. Equity capital accounts for only eight per cent of the increase in net assets.

Further, it is the bigger companies which have been obtaining more capital through NIM, while it has been playing a negligible role in financing smaller companies. It has also been observed that since 1968, it is the companies under the control of large business houses which have been the major procurers of capital through NIM. It follows that a greater flow of funds through the stock market would serve the interest of mainly large and well-established industrial companies and business houses.

If the Government's emphasis on the growth of small-scale units, and village and cotton industries is real, it should not be overlooked that the stock market is hardly a place where these units can raise funds for their needs. On the other hand, banks, through certain modifications in their attitudes, practices and policies, are much more suitable for channeling funds to these units. By reducing their deposit rates, however, the very basis of expansion of their credit i.e. deposits, is sought to be eroded.

Thirdly, Industrial securities cannot become the medium of savings to any significant extent for the small saver in urban as well as rural areas. The number of people investing in industrial securities has always remained very small. While bank deposits accounted for 32 per cent to 44 per cent of total household savings in financial assets in India during 1965-73, the share of corporate securities was hardly 0.7 per cent to 2.5 per cent during the same period.

For the small saver, bank deposits again is the ideal asset for holding their savings. By reducing deposit rates, these small savers particularly have been hit.

It is necessary to refer here to the idea of differential interest rates which has been rightly advocated by many for mobilizing savings especially in rural areas. Because of high returns on non-financial assets and high interest rates prevailing in the unorganized sector of the Indian money market, it is necessary to offer higher interest rates (than those offered in cities) on bank deposits for inculcating the banking habit in rural areas. RBI, instead of taking some such action, has erroneously chosen to reduce the existing deposit rates. This would undo what is sought to be achieved through the expansion of bank branches in rural areas and other measures.

Finally, one is skeptical about diverting funds from banks to the stock market also because the actions of commercial banks are under the direct and close supervision and regulation of the central banking authority, while the control of the stock market can be effected only indirectly which tends to lengthen the time lag involved in implementing the monetary policy.

Along with the deposit rates, commercial banks' maximum short-term and long-term lending rates were also reduced by 19 per cent to 17 per cent. This is clearly a reversal of the dear money policy which was introduced in 1973, and which was made more stringent in 1974. Does the price and monetary trends in the recent past justify such reversal?

A close scrutiny of Table 3 reveals the following facts: (i) The rate of increase of money supply which had started declining during 1974-76 began to increase during 1976-78. The money supply increased at 20 per cent in 1976-77, i.e. the highest rate in the last decade. In 1977-78, although it increased at a somewhat lower rate, it was much higher than the norm of five per cent agreed upon by the majority of economists. (ii) The rate of increase of bank credit to the commercial sector was one of the highest during 1976-77, and that the bank credit to the Government sector increased sharply during 1977-78. The average of the rates of increase of bank credit to both the sectors maintained its level during 1976-78. (iii) The rate of increase in the price level at 12 per cent in 1976-77 was very high. The decline in the price level during 1977-

78 did not warrant the liberalization of the monetary policy because the prices have reached so high a level that a fall in the prices for some time to come before they stabilize ought to be the goal of the price policy if the low-income groups are to be given a genuine relief.

Table 3: Percentage variation (over the previous year) of selected indicators)

Period	Money supply with the public	Net bank credit to the Govt. sector	Bank credit to the commercial sector	Scheduled commercial bank credit	Wholesale price index (1961-62 = 100)
1971-72	13.98	22.57	-	12.36	4.03
1972-73	15.67	20.63	18.98	16.19	9.92
1973-74	15.24	12.32	23.16	21.00	22.74
1974-75	6.53	9.27	17.98	18.42	23.13
1975-76	9.70	11.4	22.64	23.45	-3.25
1976-77	20.3	6.0	20.75	21.87	12.00
March 1976 to Jan. 1977	12.7	0.6	17.49	18.33	-
March 1977 to Jan. 1978	8.7	8.9	8.26	7.78	2.3

SOURCE: Reports on Currency and Finance and Economic Survey, 1977-78.

In short, the year 1976-77 was marked by very high rates of increase in all the indicators of the monetary policy. The budgeted deficit of Rs.1,050 crores during 1978-79 portends a highly explosive situation. Releasing both monetary and fiscal reins in the midst of past and potential high rates of increase in money supply can never serve the objective of stability. An experiment with the liberalization of the monetary policy in a similar situation in March 1968 had a disastrous effect on the economy, compelling the monetary authorities to reverse that policy in 1971.

The economic policy of the party in power enunciates, among other things, that (a) the industries in the public and private sectors should generate surpluses and use them for their expansion, and the banking system should be relieved of a need for channeling further investible funds into industry, and (b) labour-intensive industries and techniques of production should be promoted and the wasteful use of capital should be discouraged.

Will the new interest rates policy serve to achieve these objectives? When external finance is available at a lower cost, the business units are unlikely to be induced to rely more on internal funds. In India, the corporate policy with regard to profits retention is by and large, determined by the exigencies of dividend declaration. The retention of profits cannot become an active consideration unless the industrial units are required to pay on external funds interest rates which truly reflect overall paucity of capital in the economy.

The working of medium and large public limited companies shows that, in the absence of an appropriate level of interest rates, their profits retained as percentage of profits after tax has been declining (from 36 per cent in 1974-75 to 17 per cent in 1975-76), while their reliance on external funds and bank borrowings has been increasing. A further reduction in interest rates effected during the last year would most likely encourage this tendency further.

It might be misleadingly argued that cheaper credit from the banks would benefit the small industrial units and the agricultural sector also. According to the Economic Survey, 1977-78, as late as November 1977, while agriculture and small borrowers received only about 15 per cent of bank credit, the share of medium and large industry was as much as 42 per cent. It is obvious that the major beneficiary of cheaper credit is going to be the large organized industry.

Further, in the rural sector, the more important problem is that of availability of credit than that of cost of credit. The limited capital resources need to be optimally used in the rural sector as much as in the urban sector. Therefore, there was no need to blunt the instrument of interest rate as a siever of capital expenditure by reducing its level.

With regard to the use of different factors of production, there is a consensus that capital intensity of production processes, especially in the organized industry, has remained at an unduly high level and that it has been increasing from year to year. One estimate is that the real capital per worker in the manufacturing sector has been going up at a linear trend rate of 5.1 per cent per annum.

Two important factors have contributed greatly to this tendency. The relative prices of capital and labour have been weighing in favour of greater use of capital and fiscal concessions like development rebate, investment allowance, accelerated depreciation and subsidies have induced substitution of capital for labour.

In spite of the commitment by the party to withdraw such concessions for promoting the use of appropriate technology, the Government has done absolutely nothing in this regard in the latest Budget. To make matters worse, interest rates on borrowings have been reduced substantially. The continued fiscal concessions along with the cheaper capital will encourage capital deepening and create less employment opportunities in the organized industrial sector.

It may be recalled that RBI has adopted the low interest rates policy in spite of the opposition of the majority of economists to such a policy. It was being suggested by certain spokesmen of the private sector that in India while the tight money policy (implemented through selective credit controls and other physical controls like the credit authorization scheme) should be continued, the dear money policy (i.e. high interest rates) should be liberalized. Again, RBI appears to have accepted this line of thinking although it needed further examination.

The students of central banking know that the ultimate objective of monetary policy is to change the total volume of credit so as to achieve increase in production and price stability. The central bank uses the appropriate combination of general and selective credit controls to do this. Thus, the dear money also is a tool for introducing tight money policy.

In a given period of time, the volume of credit might be reduced by using physical techniques of monetary control, while maintaining the level of interest rates or by raising them slightly. In such a case, money could be tightened by pursuing the mutually conflicting policies of stricter (?) selective controls and the lowering of interest rates.

Empirically, the volume of credit coming under the net of selective credit controls constitutes only about five to eight per cent of total bank credit. Furthermore, the credit authorization scheme was liberalized in November 1975 when the minimum limit for prior authorization of RBI was raised from Rs. One crore to Rs. Two crores. Subsequently, the credit limits sanctioned by commercial banks directly have been showing a marked increase.

The working of the credit authorization scheme shows that the proportion of the amount authorized to the amount applied for increased sharply from 42 per cent in 1974-75 to 74 per cent in 1975-76. Thus, the area of control of RBI on credit expansion through so-called instruments of tight money is small, and that some of them have been liberalized in the past. Therefore, there was a case for adopting policies of both tight money and dear money, not introducing the cheap money policy.

Was there no need to reduce the cost of credit to reverse recessionary trends in Indian industry? It is true that the rate of growth of industrial production at six to eight per cent in 1977 was somewhat lower than the rate (10.6 per cent), during 1976. However, there is reason to believe that industrial production has not suffered due to the lack of adequate finance.

RBI itself has repeatedly asserted that genuine investment needs of the industrial sector have always been met by the banking sector. The Economic Survey, 1977-78, shows that rates of gross and net capital formation during 1976-77 were maintained at their respective levels in previous years. Talking particularly of industries, it stated, "there is little evidence that industrial investment in 1977-78 was running at levels lower than the previous years."

A study of fixed assets formation by medium and large public limited companies also confirms this. Term lending by the commercial banks as a percentage (eight to 10 per cent) of their total credit also has not shown any decline during the past two years. While formulating the interest rates policy, the account also ought to have been taken of the idle capacity existing in the industrial sector, indicating the scope for increasing production without raising much the amount of fixed capital expenditure.

It cannot be denied that industry needs working capital also if production is to be raised. While the genuine working capital requirements should be met by the banking sector, it should not be forgotten that the lowering of cost of credit would induce the speculative accumulation of inventories. Although inventories have increased at a lower rate of 4.5 per cent during 1975-76 in the corporate sector, there are certain disquieting features of inventory behaviour which should not have been overlooked.

First, while the stocks of raw materials declined, those of finished goods continued to increase. Second, the decline in inventories during 1975-76 could have been due to a decline in the price level during that year. The budgetary provisions like increase in excise duties, the high amount of deficit, etc. imply price expectations which would induce the speculative built-up of stocks of commodities. Third, in many of the industries, inventory levels are yet to conform to the norms laid down by the Tandon Committee. Finally, short-term bank borrowings as percentage of inventories increased from 44.4 per cent in 1974-75 to 49.5 per cent in 1975-76.

It needs to be noted that the Tandon Committee had recommended that with the passage of time, banks should provide lower and lower proportion of the working capital gap. Further, this was recommended to be achieved trough commercial banks taking a decision to that effect, and through raising the cost of credit. Obviously, the decision of RBI to reduce interest rates is against the spirit of findings and recommendations of the Tandon Committee.

An appropriate interest rates policy for India would be to abandon the practice of fixing ceilings or floors in respect of interest rates (deposits and lending) of banks. Interest rates should be allowed to find their market levels. The requirements of price stability and capital rationing demand that the interest rates structure in the organized sector is adjusted in the upward direction. This adjustment should be brought about through changes in the Bank Rate.

[14]

Recent Changes in Interest Rates Policy in India*

Introduction

The Reserve Bank of India (RBI) has recently announced certain important changes in interest rates with effect from October 9, 1991. They have evoked varied responses from different people. It is necessary to understand this policy properly, if it is not to become a victim of the pressures from various quarters. Although this policy is apparently for meeting the requirements of the current busy season, it is to be viewed as an integral part of the long-term strategy and policy framework which the RBI has been gradually evolving over the recent past in order to achieve certain objectives in our financial and economic system. It constitutes a silver lining to a largely euphoric economic policy-package introduced by the authorities in the months of June-July this year. The purpose of this paper is threefold; to describe major interest rates changes during the post-1985 period; to discuss the possible RBI perspective and intent behind its policy; and to point out some of the lacunae in this policy. The paper is divided in three sections. In Section I, important changes in interest rates policy are discussed. The rationale and shortcomings of the present interest rates policy are presented in Section II. Summary and conclusions are given in Section III.

I. Major Recent Changes in Interest Rates

From the point of view of interest rates policy, the period since 1951 can be approximately divided into three parts: (i) During 1951 to 1959, interest rates were free and flexible. (ii) During 1960-1985, they were increasingly administered. (iii) During 1986-1991, they have been partially deregulated, liberalized, made flexible, and increased.

* Paper published in *The Journal of Indian Institute of Bankers*, January-March, 1992.

The system of administered interest rates which became progressively entrenched during the second phase, resulted in many distortions and ill-effects in our economic system. According to Chakravarty Committee, the major distortions were as follows: (a) The interest rates system became unduly complex and it developed features which reduced the ability of the monetary system to promote the effective use of credit. (b) The low yields on Treasury bills and Government securities resulted in the high level of monetization of public debt and consequent monetary expansion. (c) The captive market for Government securities adversely affected the growth of capital market and profitability of banks. (d) The concessional interest rates allowed projects of doubtful viability to be undertaken. (e) The quantitative credit controls came under severe, stress in the absence of support from any price rationing mechanism. (f) The system developed inflexibility which was inimical to augmenting the pool of financial savings.

To correct these anomalies, the RBI slowly began to deregulate interest rates during the post-1985 period. It has so far introduced the following major changes in the level and structure of interest rates in our economy:

(1) The Bank rate has been raised from 10 to 11 per cent per annum with effect from July 3, 1991, and from11 to 12 per cent per annum with effect from October 9, 1991.

(2) Most of the money market rates have been deregulated. The ceiling on the call rate was withdrawn with effect from May 1, 1989. The interest rates on 182-day Treasury bills (introduced in 1986), Certificates of Deposits (introduced in June 1989), Commercial Paper (introduced in January 1990), and Inter-Bank Participations are allowed to be flexible, variable and market-determined. The 91-day Treasury bill rate is the only major money market rate which is still an administered rate now.

(3) Although interest rates on current deposits and savings deposits with banks have remained unchanged for a tong time, those on their term deposits have been moved mostly in the upward direction. In April 1985, interest rates on bank deposits with maturities between fifteen days and one year were allowed to be market-determined for a short while. In April 1987, the maximum deposit rate was reduced to 10 per cent per annum. Barring these changes, the overall policy thrust in this respect has been (a) to increase deposit rates within the framework of administered interest rates, and (b) to make short and medium-term deposits rates relatively more attractive than the long-term deposits rates. Over the past two years, while the interest rate on deposits for forty-six days to less than one year has gone up from 6 to 11 per cent per annum, the interest rate on deposits for three years and more has gone up from 10 to 13 per cent per annum. Thus, the spread between the short-term and long-term deposit rates has declined from 4 to 2 per cent per annum over the past two years (see Table 1).

(4) The lending rates of banks have been deregulated and significantly increased. In October 1988, instead of fixing a ceiling rate, the RBI fixed a minimum lending rate of 16 per cent per annum on commercial, banks loans beyond Rs.2 lakhs. Similarly, in July1989, all their term loans, which earlier carried a fixed rate of 16 per cent per annum, were subjected to a minimum rate of 15 per cent per annum, without any ceiling rate being stipulated. Further,

with effect from September 22, 1990, the distinction between interest rates on working capital finance and term loans has been done away with, except for term loans above Rs.25000 for agriculture, small industries, and transport operators with two vehicles. Effective October 9, 1991, interest rates on these term loans will be 14 per cent per annum for advances between Rs. 25000 and Rs. 2 1akhs, and 15 per cent per annum (minimum) for advances above Rs. 2 lakhs. The changes in banks' lending rates during the previous one year are reflected in Table 2.

Table 1: Interest Rates on Term-Deposits of Commercial Banks

(per cent per annum)

Maturity/w. e. f.	11.10.89	10.10.90	13.4.91	4.7.91	9.10.91
1) 46 days to less than 1 year	6	8	8	9	11
2) 1 year to less than 2 years	9	9	9	10	12
3) 2 years to less than 3 years	10	10	10	11	12
4) 3 years and above	10	11	12	13	13

Table 2: Interest Rates on Working Capital and Term Loans of Commercial Banks

(per cent per annum)

w.e.f Credit Limit (Rs.)	22.9.90	13-4-91	4-7-91	8-10-91
Upto Rs.7500	10.0	10.0	10.0	11.5
7500 – 15000	11.5	11.5	11.5	13.0
15000 – 25000	12.0	12.0	12.0	13.5
25000 – 50000	14.0	14.0	14.0	15.5
50000 – 2 lakhs	15.0	15.0	15.0	16.5
Above 2 1akhs	16.0 (minimum)	17.0 (minimum)	18.5 (minimum)	20.5 (minimum)

These rates are exclusive of interest tax of 3 per cent. Similarly, the interest rate surcharge of 25 per cent is applicable in the case of parties with cash credit/overdraft limit over Rs. 2 1akhs, if the credit is used for financing imports. It may be noted, that within one year, the minimum lending rate of banks has increased by 4 per cent points. As a result of the policy announcement in October 1991, the actual lending rates of banks are expected to increase from about 22 per cent to 25 per cent per annum.

(5) The interest rates on deposits and loans of urban (primary) co-operative banks also have been increased correspondingly.

(6) The interest rate charged by banks for public sector procurement and distribution agencies also has now been increased to 16 per cent per annum.

(7) The interest rates on the pre-shipment and post-shipment export credit were between 7.5 to 8.65 per cent per annum till April 1991; they were raised to 12.5 to 14.5 per cent per annum on August 6, 1991, and 15 to 17 per cent per annum on October 9, 1991. The export credit not otherwise specified will now be charged 20 per cent per annum, instead of 18 per cent per annum as earlier.

(8) With effect from July 4, 1991, the bills discount rate used to be 17.5 per cent per annum (minimum); it has now been raised to 19 per cent per annum (minimum) with effect from October 9, 1991.

(9) The minimum lending rate on credit against commodities coming under Selective Credit Controls (SCC) has been raised from 18.5 to 20 per cent per annum with effect from October 9, 1991.

(10) The interest rates on refinancing facilities from the RBI, which are linked to the Bank rate, have been raised by one percentage point with effect from October 9, 1991. As a result, the export credit refinance rate, standby refinance rate, discretionary refinance rate, and food credit refinance rate will now be 10.5, 14.5, 18 (minimum), and 15 per cent per annum; respectively. However, all refinance facilities other than export refinance facility have been withdrawn for the current busy season.

(11) The interest rate paid by the RBI on the cash balances maintained by banks on the incremental deposits after March 23, 1990 has been reduced from 8 to 5 per cent per annum with effect from October 9, 1991.

(12) The term lending financial institutions like the IDBI had started operating two-tier interest rates structure from August 1, 1990. They were charging the normal rate of 14 per cent per annum for the period of initial two years of the project, and a high rate of 15 per cent per annum for the period thereafter. From July 1991, these institutions have been given freedom to charge interest rates which they regard appropriate, subject to the rate of 15 per cent per annum. This rate has not been changed while announcing the October 1991 policy.

(13) From July 1991, the interest rates on the convertible and non-convertible debentures have been made free. The ruling coupon rates on the non-convertible debentures are between 15 to 18 per cent per annum at present, and they are expected to increase to 20 per cent per annum as a result of the policy announced in October 1991.

(14) The maximum rate of interest which the non-banking financial and miscellaneous companies can pay on their deposits from the public has been increased from 14 to 15 per cent per annum with effect from July 27, 1991. This means the rate which prevailed during 1982-83 to 1986-87 has now been restored.

(15) The banks are now free to determine the rates of interest they would charge on loans to individuals against shares and debentures, and on loans for consumer durables, real estate, etc. The October 1991 policy, is expected to increase these rates of interest. It is reported that

the car finance rate has increased from about 25 to about 28 per cent per annum after October 9, 1991.

(16) The interest have rates on Provident Funds, Government Securities, treasury bills, small savings media, etc. have not been changed as a part of the October 1991 policy.

II. Policy Rationale

What could be the rationale behind the current dear money policy? What lacunae do we see in this policy? We discuss these questions hereafter.

(1) *Simplification of Rates Structure:* One of the objectives of the present policy appears to be to reduce the multiplicity of interest rates and to bring about, a simplification in their structure. As said earlier, the administered interest rates system had resulted in the complex structure through the fixation of many specific interest rates on the basis of a number of loan criteria such as the size and priority nature of loans, the sectors or locations or regions of activity, the types of programmes under which the loans were provided, the income of the borrowers, etc.

Now, the efforts are being made to eliminate the criteria other than the size of loans while deciding the credit policy. The size-specific rates are meant to achieve basic societal concerns through cross subsidization of the cost of borrowings. The elimination of the distinction between the rates on working capital finance and term finance in most of the cases would also contribute to the achievement of the objective under consideration.

However, even after accepting the fact that no reform can be carried out completely in the short-run, the progress towards structural simplification can be said to have been rather faltering. There is a further scope for reducing the number of size-specific and purpose-specific interest rates fixed by the authorities.

(2) *Anti-Inflationary Measure*: The effectiveness of the economic policy to achieve given objectives depends upon the coordination between, and the unified approach of its various branches. It is well-known that the fiscal policy in India has been unduly expansionary. The enormous Government expenditure, the huge overall and revenue deficits, the large RBI credit to the Government, etc. have overheated the economy, and have created excessive liquidity and demand pressures in the system.

As a result, the price stability has been one of the major casualties in India. The rate of inflation here has been much higher than that of many other countries. This has generated strong inflationary expectations, has caused many distortions and inequities, and has adversely affected the standard of living or quality of life of the low-income and fixed-income people. It has also destroyed the competitiveness of the Indian exports in the international market. The balance of payments crisis which the country is facing now is, in. a significant way, due to the high inflationary pressures in our economy. The benefits of the recent devaluation of the Indian rupee crucially hinge upon our ability to effectively contain the price rise.

In view of all this, the RBI rightly regards price stability as the major objective which it must, and which it can help to achieve. It has, therefore, now decided to use actively and boldly the interest rates policy for the purposes of aggregate demand management, financial discipline, productivity growth, and efficiency promotion. The recent interest rates policy needs to be appreciated as a necessary anti-dote to the monetary expansion, excess liquidity, instability, inflation, and inflationary expectations generated by the profligate fiscal policy in our economy. It is, in a sense, bearing the "fiscal burden". It is to be kept in mind that in the current atmosphere of economic liberation and marketization, the technique of price controls would not be available now for the purpose of capping the price rise. The increase in interest rates has, therefore, become necessary for checking the inflation.

(3) *The Criticism Answered:* This policy has been criticised by saying that it would (a) result in cost escalation and cost-push inflation, (b) hurt business and investment activities in general and export efforts in particular, (c) affect the stock market boom and stock market activity adversely, and (d) result in wide fluctuations or high degree of instability in money market rates.

It is to be realized that the high interest rates are meant to hurt the decision makers only in the sense of forcing them to economize on the use of financial resources. The total cost of finance is a function of the volume of finance used and the rate of interest. The traders, businessmen, manufacturers, entrepreneurs, and the Government are expected to bring down their cost of finance by reducing the volume of finance used. For this, they have to increase efficiency, productivity, and capacity utilization. They have to accept the logic of the present policy of marketization and competition in its totality, and not in convenient parts only. The businessmen and their powerful organizations, used as they have been for a very long time to a highly concessional credit, are reacting to the dear money policy in a predictable manner i.e. they want to have a cake and eat it too. The higher interest rates should encourage efforts towards reducing inessential fixed investment and excessive inventories, better utilization of existing investment, and an economy in the use of funds - all this without' affecting the output adversely. No tears need to be shed if the stock market prices decline a little as a result of the current policy. It is widely accepted that the boom in share prices is primarily speculative; it has little basis in economic fundamentals.

The intent of the policy cannot be to affect the output adversely. Its thrust appears to be towards ensuring adequate availability of credit to the productive and priority sectors, albeit at a somewhat higher cost. The experience has shown that it is the adequate availability rather than the low cost of credit which is more crucial for the smooth running of the economic activity. The present policy seems to be founded on this experience. This is reflected, for example, in the fact that while raising the interest rates on export credit, the policy has sought to ensure its greater availability by liberalizing export refinance facilities.

The danger of volatility of interest rates, when they are market-determined, however, cannot be brushed aside easily. For example, the call money rate has been fluctuating in a very wide range (below 10 per cent to sometimes 100 per cent per annum) after the removal of the ceiling on it. But this needs to be understood properly. The volatility of the call rate in

India has been partly due to the fact that some banks have had an overextended credit position continuously, as a result of which they have been chronic borrowers on a large scale in the call money market. If these banks correct this situation through better portfolio management and arrive at the optimum funds positions, the call rate need not scale too high peaks as it has often been doing recently.

It is to be noted that the RBI, on its part, has been taking certain helpful policy steps to reduce the level and fluctuations in the call rate. For example, it has now allowed many financial institutions and certain other parties to participate in the call money market as the suppliers of funds. The Discount and Finance House (DFHI) also has been established to help in smoothening the flows of funds in the money market. Similarly, whenever possible, the RBI has been supplying the larger volume of refinance for this purpose either directly, or indirectly through DFHI, subject to the constraint that its refinance policy is a tool of the overall monetary policy also.

Is there a guarantee that the dear money policy will be successful in controlling the inflation? It has been sometimes pointed out that the increase in interest rates in the past few months has been, in fact, accompanied by the increase in the rate of inflation. This, however, cannot be used to question the current interest rates policy. Firstly, there are always many time lags in the working of the monetary policy. Secondly, it is necessary to think as to what would have happened in the absence of timely increase in interest rates. The manifestation of the success of dear money policy in the form of an actual decline in the rate of inflation will *inter alia* depend upon the fiscal discipline. In the face of a continuous and unbridled or excessive fiscal expansion, the success of interest rates policy will remain invisible or unmeasurable.

While the fiscal policy is inexorably pushing the economy in the grip of inflation, the other techniques of monetary policy itself are not much available for their deployment on account of various reasons. From the beginning itself, it has not been possible in India to use Open Market Operations (OMOs) for monetary management to a desired extent. The technique of Cash Reserves Ratio (CRR), which was used actively during 1970s and 1980s, cannot be used much now because the CRR has already reached the maximum level. The scope for applications of SCCs is limited, and the margin requirements under them have already reached very high levels. Thus, the increase in interest rates was unavoidable in the current state of the Indian economy.

(4) *The Issues of Equity and Disintermediation*: The two other related considerations behind the recent interest rates policy are:

(a) To establish a system of equitable rates of return available to all the savers. The Indian financial system has developed in such a way that the savers from high income groups and educated, better informed, and urban classes earn much higher effective rates of return by investing their savings in a well-diversified menu of financial assets, and by taking the benefit of multiple fiscal concessions. On the other hand, the small, ordinary, and rural savers have to be content with lower returns on' their savings because the interest rates on banks deposits - the major or the only medium available to them for investing their savings - have been kept unduly low through the system of administered interest rates. The recent interest rates policy seeks to rectify this distortion in our financial system.

(b) To arrest the decline in the share of banking system in the total volume of financial saving in the economy. The banks undoubtedly are the major and vital financial intermediaries in India; the channelization of funds through them is definitely in the interest of more effective monetary management; and bank deposits certainly happen to be a preferred medium of savings by the public. And yet, they have had to lose resources to their competitors on account of the unattractive rates of interest they have been forced to offer so far. The RBI is now rightly anxious to correct the phenomenon of "uneven playing fields" and to create "level playing fields" for banks vis-a-vis their competitors. The present interest rates policy is one of right steps in this direction.

(5) *Inadequate and Dithering Policy* : Having said this, the RBI policy in this context must be characterized as inadequate and dithering. The bank deposits rates are still administered ones. If this is thought necessary for avoiding the cut-throat competition among banks, which would adversely affect their profitability and viability, the minimum thing that needs to be done is to raise the long-term deposits rates to a still higher level than at present.

The current policy in respect of the maturity structure of bank deposits rates does not appear to be convincing. It has made short-term and medium-term rates more attractive than the long-term rates. The following two-fold reasoning behind this policy is less than convincing for the reasons given below:

(a) There are certain categories of people who are flush with liquidity, but they would invest only in liquid or short-term channels because of the nature of requirements of their business. By offering attractive rates on short-term deposits, the banks can hope to garner these funds.

In our view, even if this is true, there is no reason why it should preclude offering the higher rate of interest on the long-term deposits also. Moreover, from the point of view of stability in the overheated economy like ours, it is safer to encourage the long-term rather than the short-term media of savings.

(b) In India, the banks are primarily short-term lenders, and if their deposits are mainly long-term ones, then a "temporal gap" emerges in their' assets and liabilities. In fact, such a gap already exists, and the current policy can help to correct it.

We think that this is a rather static view of the role of banks in our economy. The message of the work of a number of Committees - Dehejia, Tandon, Chakravarty, etc. - has been that the short-term loan portfolio of the banks is to be slowly reduced in favour of the term loans for productive purposes. If the short-term deposits grow faster than the long-term deposits, there will be constraint on banks to increase their long-term loans. The better way of tackling the problem of "temporal gap" is to mobilize more of long-term deposits and to advance more of long-term productive loans.

(6) *Saving Bank and NRI Accounts:* There is a need to review the policy regarding interest rates on the saving bank and NRI accounts also. The interest rate on saving bank account has

remained low and unchanged (at 5 per cent per annum) since 1979. This again is not in the interests of the savers, particularly the small, ordinary, and rural depositors. The saving bank deposits are held by many depositors as a genuine medium of saving rather than as a medium of exchange. The RBI itself regards about 40 per cent of these deposits as time deposits as per its scheme of dividing saving deposits into demand and time liabilities. Even after taking into account the services provided by the banks to the saving deposit holders, there is a case for increasing substantially the rate of interest on these deposits, particularly in view of the inflation which has taken place in India over the past 10 years.

It is well-known that the Indian .banks pay higher rates of interest to the NRI depositors as compared to the domestic deposit holders. The maximum interest rate on Non-Resident (External) Rupee (NRE) deposits at present is 14 per cent per annum as compared to the rate of 13 per cent per annum on the domestic deposits. Similarly, it is reported that the Indian banks are offering higher rates of interest on Foreign Currency Non-Resident (FCNR) deposits as compared to the rates paid by the banks abroad. All this is unfair and unethical. Why should the NRIs alone receive the special and better deals? We do need foreign exchange, but we very much need domestic savings also. If the domestic savers had not undergone the sacrifice by giving one of the highest rates of savings in the world, our financial difficulties would have been compounded many times. To discriminate against the domestic savers, therefore, is certainly unfair and unethical.

(7) *The Profitability of Banks*: Another objective of the recent interest rates policy appears to be to help the banking system to improve its profitability and to reduce its sickness. The healthy banking system is so vital for the financial health of the entire economy that it cannot be allowed to remain unprofitable and sick for a long time. The sickness in the banking system has been due to the sickness in the business and industrial sectors, the political interference in the working of banks, and the system of administered interest rates. By removing the ceiling on the lending rates of banks, their problems in this context would be partially taken care of directly as well as indirectly; directly, by increasing their earnings on the loan portfolios, and indirectly by helping to reduce the sickness in the industrial sector.

(8) *Partial Deregulation*: Apart from the shortcomings pointed out earlier, one obvious limitation of the current policy is that the deregulation of interest rates has been only a partial one. The interest rates on Government securities, 91-day Treasury bills, company deposits, small-savings media, and bank deposits are still administered by the authorities. Thus, we now have a dual pricing policy in operation in our financial system.

The authorities had gradually tightened or firmed up interest rates on the marketable and non-marketable debt of the Government also over the past few years. However, the October 1991 policy has not changed these interest rates; nor does it give any indication whether they would be raised correspondingly in due course. Given the greater and more urgent need for the financial discipline, productivity, and cost-effectiveness in the Government finances, it is only logical and fair to expect that the interest rates on the Government debt also would be raised very soon. If that does not happen, one of the major anomalies of the administered interest rates structure, namely the Government using its powers to subsidize itself significantly in the financial markets, will re-emerge again.

III. Summary and Conclusions

Since the middle of 1980s, the monetary policy in general and interest rates policy in particular have been geared to correct the deficiencies engendered in the Indian financial system by the policy of administered interest rates. As stated in the Annual Report, 1989-90 of the RBI, the major, visible, tangible, explicit thrust or concern of the monetary policy during post-1985 period has been towards promoting efficiency, effecting appropriate structural changes, introducing greater flexibility, encouraging diversification, promoting more competitive environment, and imparting greater discipline and prudence in the operations of the financial system. The October 1991 interest rates policy is to be viewed and welcomed from this perspective. It is hoped that certain lacunae in this policy, viz., the discrimination against the long-term bank deposits, the saving bank deposits, and the domestic depositors vis-à-vis NRI depositors will be eliminated, and the interest rates on the Government debt also will be appropriately raised in the near future.

[15]

*An Appraisal of Recent Interest Rates Policy In India**

Introduction

Interest rate is a key price which is relevant for decision-making in the whole of market economy. It is a cost of credit, finance, and investment; it is also a reward for abstinence, thrift, and savings. Similarly, it is an opportunity cost of liquidity (or a reward for parting with liquidity). It connects the monetary and real sectors of the economy. The changes in the level and structure of interest rates influence the level and composition of savings and investment, efficiency of investment, the nature and extent of financial intermediation, the working of payments mechanism, distribution of credit, income, and wealth, and the health, viability, stability (volatility) of the financial institutions and markets. In other words, interest rates policy has multiple economic and social welfare consequences.

There are different views with regard to the role of finance and financial development in the process of economic development. While Keynes and others have argued that the regulated and low interest rates can be beneficial for promoting economic growth, Mckinnon (1973) and Shaw (1973) have argued for the deregulation or liberalization of the financial system and interest rates for accelerating development in the developing countries. Guided by the latter view and goaded by world financial institutions, many developing countries in the world, including India, have liberalized their financial systems in the recent past. The deregulation of interest rates has been one of the major aspects of such a financial liberalization.

* The Paper was presented at the 3rd Annual International Conference on Social Sciences held at Honolulu, USA, during June 16-19, 2004. It was jointly published with Pradyumna Dash in M. Sharma (ed.), Studies in Money, Finance, and Banking, Atlantic, New Delhi, 2005.

However, because of the multiple valid considerations and concerns which are involved in the making of interest rates policy, the deregulation of interest rates has remained a developmentally relevant and important but a controversial or a polemical subject. If the controversy of regulation vs. deregulation of interest rates is to be resolved, and if the interest rates policy is to play its legitimate role in achieving the economic and social objectives of different nations, it is essential to build and document a systematic empirical evidence on the working of interest rates policy in different countries which have deregulated their interest rates systems.

The studies by IMF (1983) and Glower (1994) have made available some such evidence in respect of Asian and other developing countries. However, we still lack enough and more recent evidence on the wider consequences of interest rates deregulation in these countries. The gap in research in India in this context has been all the greater, and there is certainly a need for studying the deregulation experience of such a major developing economy as India.

It is in this context that the present paper seeks to examine the policy of deregulation of interest rates with the special focus on soft interest rates policy pursued in India in the recent past. It discusses questions such as: whether interest rates in India should have been reduced along with their being deregulated? Should and can they be further reduced? Of late, have real interest rates in India been really high? What have been and what are likely to be the economic and social costs of the cheap money policy in India? With the help of theoretical considerations and empirical evidence, it shows how the reasons cited for lowering interest rates are not convincing, and how the soft interest rate policy can come in the way of promoting growth with stability and social justice.

The paper is divided in four Sections. In Section I, the evolution and content of present interest rates policy are briefly described. The major features of the deregulated system of interest rates are discussed in Section II. The soft interest rates policy after 1997-98 is critically examined in Section III. The summary and conclusions are presented in Section IV.

I. Evolution and Content of Present Interest Rates Policy

The period since 1951 can be divided into the following five phases of interest rates policy (system) in India:

(i) 1951-52 to 1960-61: Flexible interest rates system.

(ii) 1961-62 to 1985-86: The system of administered, regulated, and repressed or suppressed (low) interest rates.

(iii) 1986-87 to 1990-91: The beginning of liberalization or the system with inclination or intent towards liberalization and flexibility or a semi-administered system with the inching up of interest rates.

(iv) 1991-92 to 1996-97: The system of progressive deregulation and flexibility, and a significant increase in and unprecedentally high interest rates, or the phase of deregulation and dear money.

(v) 1997-98 to 2003-2004: The system of managed flexibility with nearly complete deregulation, and one of the lowest levels of interest rates in India, or the phase of deregulation and cheap money.

Interest rates in India were widely and closely administered for about a quarter century till the middle of 1980s. This policy had adversely affected savings, investment, efficiency, and growth in the Indian economy (See BHOLE, 1985).

The process of interest rates liberalization began in the middle of 1980s. Of course, freeing, deregulation, flexibility of interest rates has differed from instrument to instrument such as bank credit, bank deposits, government securities, small savings, and so on. The policy has been one of size-wise and term-to-maturity-wise differences in flexibility. For example, while the long-term deposits rates continued to be administered till April 1992, the banks were allowed to set interest rates on deposits with maturities between fifteen days and one year subject to a ceiling of 8 per cent from April 1985. However, this freedom was withdrawn from end-May 1985; the experiment proved to be short-lived because it resulted in a deposit rates war among the banks, the fear of which had been one of the reasons for adopting the system of administered interest rates (for other reasons, see BHOLE, 1985). Thus, bank deposits interest rates continued to be administered for some more time, and the deregulation policy really began with the liberalization of banks' lending rates.

In September 1991, the size-specific, usage-specific, borrower-specific, sector-specific, and programme-specific lending rates prescriptions, except for the areas like agriculture, small industries, and Differential Interest Rates Scheme (DIRS) were discontinued, and interest rates on loans above Rs. 2 lakhs were freed subject to a minimum lending rate prescribed by the Reserve Bank of India (RBI). The efforts were made to reduce significantly the multiplicity of lending rates and the complexity of interest rates structure by reducing lending categories from about 50 to about 5. The minimum lending rate prescription just mentioned was also discontinued from October 1994, and banks were given full freedom to determine their all lending rates on loans above Rs. 2 lakhs, but they were required to announce their Prime Lending Rates (PLRs). This policy continued for two years till October 1996 when banks were advised to announce the maximum spread of their lending rates over the PLR. Subsequently, each bank was permitted to operate the system of its own separate three different PLRs: general, short-term, and long-term. Now the banks and RBI are in the process of merging these bank-specific three PLRs and evolve a single PLR for the banking industry as a whole.

As described above, except for a very short interregnum of two months in April-May 1985 in the case of short-term deposit rates, interest rates on bank deposits continued to be administered till April 1992 when the process of their deregulation was started. In the beginning, the then existing maturity-wise prescriptions for interest rates on deposits were replaced by a single ceiling rate, which was subsequently varied in line with changes in the minimum lending rate. In April 1992, a single ceiling rate of 13 per cent was fixed for all deposits above 46 days maturity. This ceiling rate was reduced to 10 per cent in November 1994, and it was again raised to 12 per cent in April 1995. In October 1995, bank deposits with maturity of over two years were exempted from the prescription of the ceiling interest rate. In July 1996, deposits with maturity over one year were exempted from the ceiling rate. In April 1997, the ceiling rate for deposits of 30 days to one year was fixed at the level of Bank Rate less 200 basis points. In October 1997, deposit rates were fully deregulated by removing their linkage with the Bank Rate.

Consequently, many interest rates have now become market-determined, market-related, and flexible. However, there are still certain important interest rates in the Indian economy which continue to be administered. Interest rates on Small Savings (SS), Provident Fund (PF), and Non-Resident Indians (NRI) deposits are controlled even today. Similarly, interest rates on savings accounts with the commercial and co-operative banks also continue to be prescribed by the RBI. Further, the priority sector lending rates are also capped at PLR plus 4 per cent. Then, the RBI may soon benchmark banks' PLR to their cost of funds. As in the case of exchange rate, the monetary authorities intervene from time to time to guide interest rates movements in the country.

As a part of deregulation, the RBI has introduced the following measures to impart greater flexibility to the level and structure of interest rates in the country: (a) To encourage banks to introduce a flexible interest rates option for deposits. (b) To urge banks to review and announce the maximum spread over their PLR. (c) To ask banks to provide information on deposit rates for various maturities, the effective annualized return to depositors, and the maximum and minimum interest rates charged to their borrowers (RBI, RCF, 2001-02, p. v-2l).

II. Features of the Deregulated System

Figure 1 and Tables 1 to 3 present useful information on the changes in certain nominal and real interest rates in India during 1981-82 to 2002-03. This information and certain other facts highlight the following features of the deregulated interest rates system in India.

(i) For about 5 to 6 years in the early part of 1990s, nominal interest rates in India were characterized by both deregulation and significant upward movement. For example, in 1994-95, bank deposit rates were raised twice within a few months. Similarly, banks had increased their lending rates also. The financial liberalization had produced a dramatic increase in interest rates by 1995-96 which had persisted in 1996-97 and a part 1997-98. This was in tune with the theory of repression vs. liberalization of interest rates. It may be recalled that the theory of financial repression has made a case not only for the deregulation but also for the higher nominal interest rates so as to achieve a reasonably high level of positive real interest rates.

(ii) After 1996-97, the deregulation has been accompanied by a policy-induced significant lowering of nominal interest rates. An unprecedented decline in nominal interest rates has occurred during the past 5/6 years, and those interest rates in 2003 are about half of their level 5 years back. The nominal interest rates today have reached a level which is one of the lowest in their history. Short-term and long-term rates, deposits and lending rates, prime lending rates, interest rates on Treasury bills and bonds, industrial bond yield, interest rates on small and contractual savings, interest rates of term lending institutions have significantly declined,

Figure 1:
Nominal and Real Interest Rates in India

Panel 1: Bank Rate

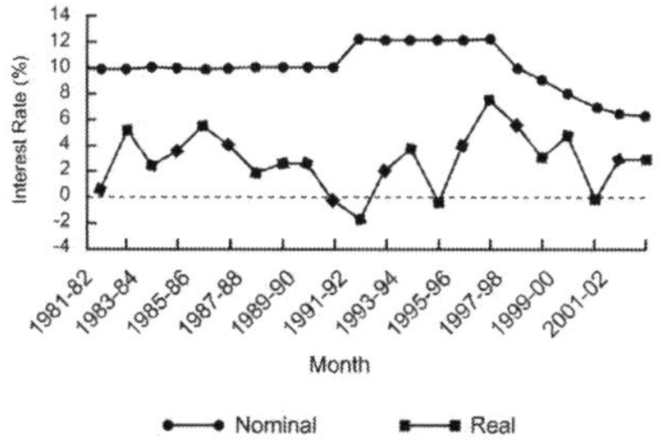

Panel 2: 91-Day Treasury Bill Rate

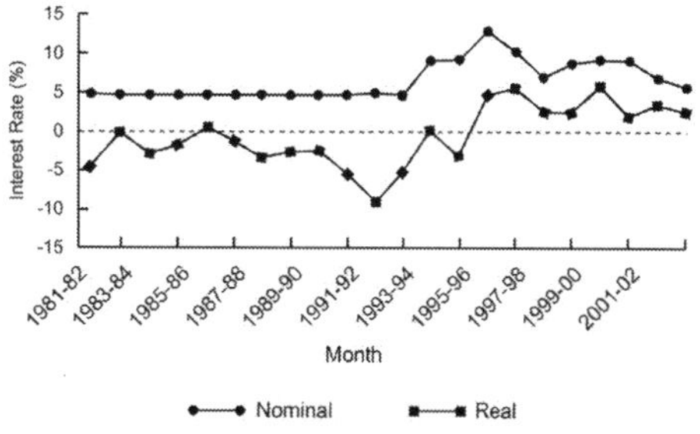

Panel 3: Bank Deposit Rate (1-3 year)

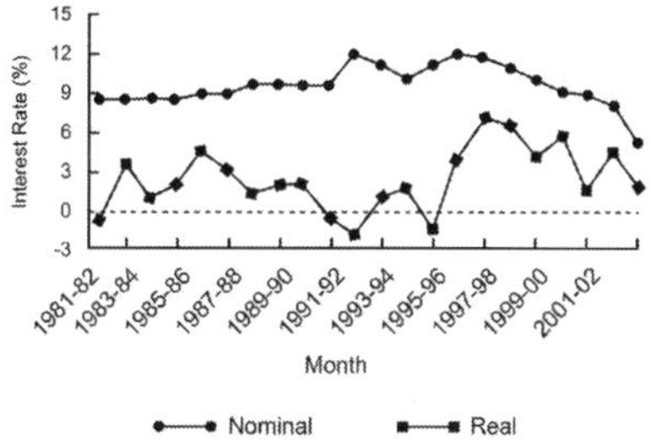

Panel 4: SBI PLR

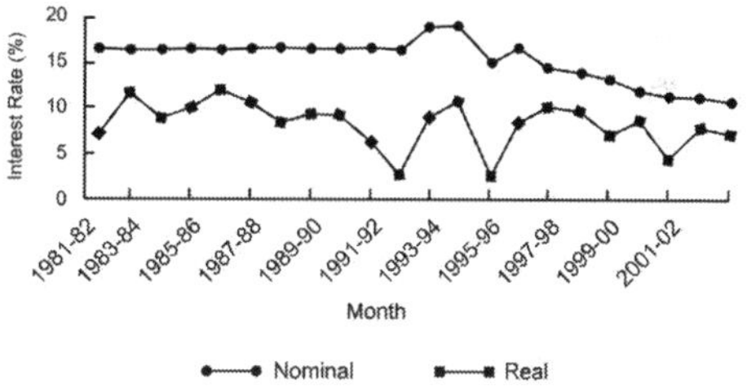

Panel 5: IDBI PLR

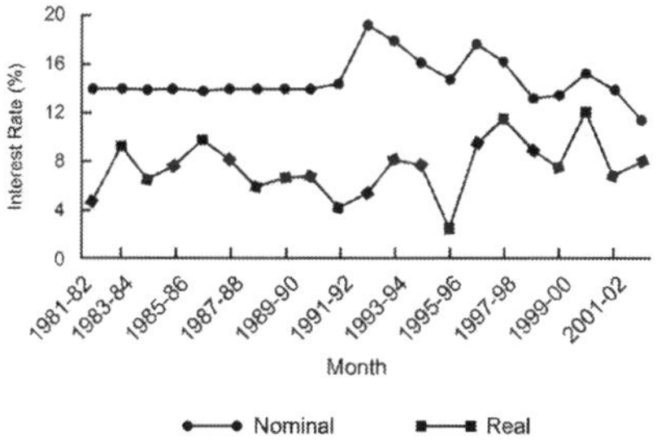

Panel 6:
Government Bond Yield (above 15 years)

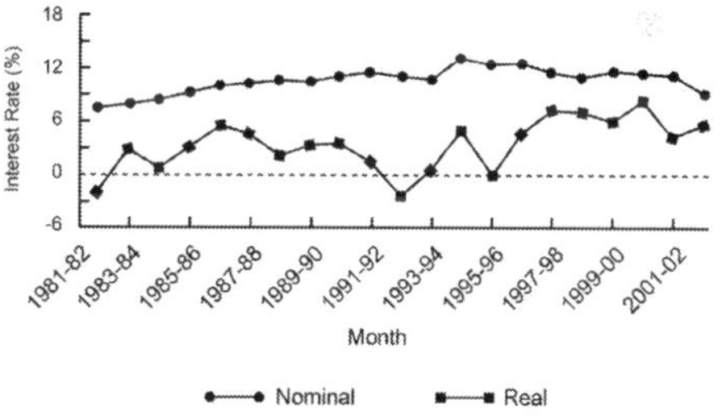

Panel 7: Maximum Post-office Deposit Rate

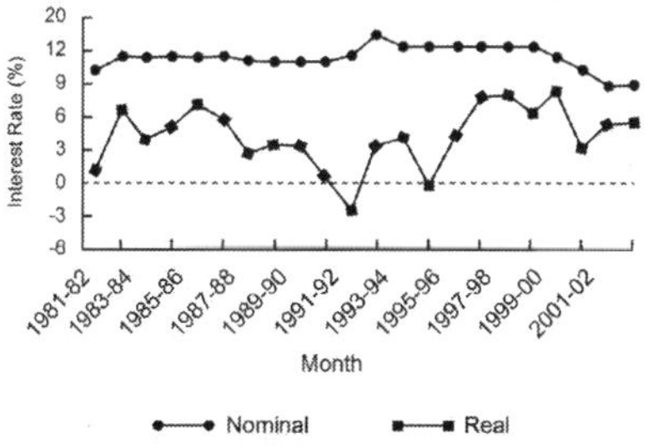

Panel 8: PF Rate

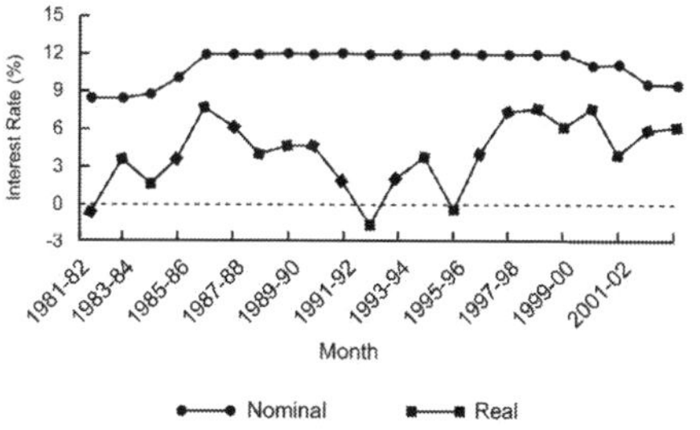

Source: RBI, Handbook of Statistics on the Indian Economy, 2002

Table 1: Level and Structure of Nominal Interest Rates in India

Year	Bank Rate	91-day Treasury Bill Rate	Bank Deposit Rate (1-3 years)	SBI PLR	IDBI PLR	Government Bond Yield (Above 15 years)	Post-office Deposit rate	PF Rate
1981-82	10	4.6	8	16.5	14	7.23	10.5	8.5
1982-83	10	4.6	8.5	16.5	14	7.23	11.5	8.5
1983-84	10	4.6	8.5	16.5	14	8.24	11.5	9.0
1984-85	10	4.6	8.5	16.5	14	9.22	11.5	10
1985-86	10	4.6	8.75	16.5	14	9.94	11.5	12
1986-87	10	4.6	8.75	16.5	14	10.19	11.5	12
1987-88	10	4.6	9.5	16.5	14	10.34	11	12
1988-89	10	4.6	9.5	16.5	14	10.55	11	12
1989-90	10	4.6	9.5	16.5	14	10.93	11	12
1990-91	10	4.6	9.5	16.5	14.5	11.45	11	12
1991-92	12	4.6	12	16.5	19	11.15	11.5 13.5	12
1992-93	12	4.6	11	19	18	10.65	12.5	12
1993-94	12	8.88	10	19	16	13.14	12.5	12
1994-95	12	9.12	11	15	15	12.62	12.5	12
1995-96	12	12.66	12	16.5	17.5	12.43	12.5	12
1996-97	12	9.95	11.5	14.5	16.2	11.60	12.5	12
1997-98	10	6.84	10.75	14	13.3	11.09	12.5	12
1998-99	9	8.55	10	13	13.5	11.73	11.5	12
1999-00	8	9.03	9	12	15.35	11.45	10.5	11
2000-01	7	8.96	8.75	11.5	14	11.24	9	11
2001-02	6.5	6.94	8	11.5	11.5	9.14	9	9.5
2002-03	6	5.81	5.12	10.75	-	-		9.5
AAR for:								
1981-86	10	4.6	8.5	16.5	14.0	8.5	11.3	9.6
1986-91	10	4.6	9.35	16.5	14.1	10.7	11.1	12
1991-96	12	7.9	11.2	17.2	17.1	11.9	12.5	12
1996-02	8.75	8.4	9.7	12.8	14.0	11.0	11.4	11.25

NOTE: AAR= Annual Average Rate.

SOURCE: Same as in Figure 1.

Table 2: Level and Structure of Real Interest Rates in India

Year	Bank Rate	91-day Treasury Bill Rate	Bank Deposit Rate (1-3 years)	SBI PLR	IDBI PLR	Government Bond Yield (Above 15 years)	Post-office Deposit rate	PF Rate
1981-82	0.7	-4.7	-0.8	7.2	4.7	-2.1	1.2	-0.8
1982-83	5.1	-0.3	3.6	11.6	9.1	2.8	6.6	3.6
1983-84	2.5	-2.9	1.0	9.0	6.5	0.7	4.0	1.5
1984-85	3.5	-1.9	2.0	10.0	7.5	2.8	5.0	3.5
1985-86	5.6	0.2	4.3	12.1	9.6	5.5	7.1	7.6
1986-87	4.2	-1.2	2.9	10.7	8.2	4.4	5.7	6.2
1987-88	1.9	-3.5	1.4	8.4	5.9	2.2	2.9	3.9
1988-89	2.5	-2.9	2.0	9.0	6.5	3.1	3.5	4.5
1989-90	2.6	-2.8	2.1	9.1	6.6	3.5	3.6	4.6
1990-91	-0.3	-5.7	-0.8	6.2	4.2	1.2	0.7	1.7
1991-92	-1.7	-9.1	-1.7	2.8	5.3	-2.6	-2.2	-1.7
1992-93	1.9	-5.5	0.9	8.9	7.9	0.6	3.4	1.9
1993-94	3.6	0.5	1.6	10.6	7.6	4.8	4.1	3.6
1994-95	-0.5	-3.4	-1.5	2.5	2.5	0.1	0.0	-0.5
1995-96	3.9	4.6	3.9	8.4	9.4	4.3	4.4	3.9
1996-97	7.4	5.3	6.9	9.9	11.6	7.0	7.9	7.4
1997-98	5.6	2.4	6.4	9.6	8.9	6.7	8.1	7.6
1998-99	3.0	2.6	4.0	7.0	7.5	5.8	6.5	6.0
1999-00	4.7	5.8	5.7	8.7	12.1	8.2	8.2	7.7
2000-01	-0.2	1.8	1.6	4.3	6.8	4.1	3.3	3.8
2001-02	2.9	3.3	4.4	7.9	7.9	5.5	5.4	5.9
2002-03	2.8	2.4	1.7	7.3	-	-	5.6	6.1
AAR for:								
1981-86	3.5	-1.9	2.0	10.0	7.5	1.9	4.8	3.1
1986-91	2.2	-3.2	1.5	8.7	6.3	2.9	3.3	4.2
1991-96	1.4	-2.6	0.6	6.6	6.5	1.4	1.9	1.4
1996-02	3.9	3.5	4.8	7.9	9.1	6.2	6.6	6.4

NOTE: (a) Real Interest rates have been arrived at by adjusting for the annual rate of change in Wholesale Price Index (1993-94=100). (b) AAR=Annual Average Rate.

SOURCE: Same as in Figure 1.

Table 3: Short-Term Interest Rates in India and Some Other Countries

Country	Short-Term Interest Rates (April)			
	2000	2002	2003	COP 2003
Developed Countries				
Australia	4.88	4.62	4.77	3.0
Britain	5.25	4.13	3.56	2.0
Canada	4.43	2.38	3.19	2.8
Denmark	5.32	3.70	2.70	1.4
Japan	0.02	0.03	0.02	0.8
Sweden	4.01	4.28	3.43	1.6
Switzerland	3.19	1.59	0.29	0.6
United States	4.17	1.82	1.16	2.2
Euro Area	4.78	3.40	2.48	1.1
Emerging Economies				
Hong Kong	4.20	2.05	1.41	3.0
India	7.71	5.84	4.94	5.1
Malaysia	3.30	3.25	3.10	5.0
South Korea	5.90	4.79	5.51	5.0
Thailand	2.50	2.25	1.75	4.2
Brazil	16.29	18.40	26.32	2.8
Chile	3.42	4.32	2.52	3.1
Mexico	13.25	5.72	5.82	2.3
Egypt	9.11	7.20	12.29	3.0
Israel	5.25	2.73	5.82	0.5
South Africa	10.70	11.20	13.75	2.8
Czech Republic	5.01	4.27	2.47	1.9
Hungary	11.30	8.45	6.50	3.6
Poland	17.14	10.18	5.63	2.6
Russia	25.00	23.00	18.00	4.0

SOURCE: Bombay Stock Exchange, *Annual Capital Market Review*, 2002-2003.

and today nominal interest rates under a deregulated system are as low as they were under the administered system.

(iii) Nominal interest rates have been reduced in spite of (a) the failure to reduce government expenditure and fiscal deficit, (b) the need for huge government borrowing programme, (c) the monetization of deficit, (d) the current account deficit, (e) the depreciation of rupee, (f) the stagnancy in savings, (g) the need for greater capital inflows, and (h) the high level of Non-Performing Assets (NPAs) across all the banks and other types of financial institutions.

(iv) It has been observed that the downward movements in nominal short-term interest rates are characterized by stickiness. In the era of soft interest rates, the yield curve should have declined, but, instead, it has flattened; the interest rates at the long end have declined more than those at the short end. For example, the spread between the over night lending rate and lo-year bench mark gilt-edged securities yield declined from about 340 basis points in 2001 to about 60 basis points in October-December 2003. Similarly, between March 2000 and March 2003, while the interest rates on bank deposits with maturity of 3 years and above declined by 425 basis points, those on deposits with maturity upto 90 days declined by only 50 to 100 basis points. The reduction in the administered interest rates on SS and PF has enabled a greater decline in the long-term deposit rates. But the factors such as the floor set by the Liquidity Adjustment Facility (LAP), and the preference for short-term deposits by banks to gain flexibility in asset-liability management have resulted in the downward stickiness of short-term deposit rates. Further, the prudential limits on call money borrowing and lending also have increased the demand for short-term bank deposits. After deregulation, banks offered higher interest rates on short term deposits than on long-term deposits in certain years. For example, in 1995, some banks offered the interest of 10 per cent per annum for deposits with maturity of 46 days to one year, 9.5 per cent on one year and upto two years, and 9.0 per cent on two years. The deregulation thus resulted in the "inversion of deposits interest rates structure", which, in turn, tended to create the "maturity gap" or "maturity mismatch" or "temporal gap" in banking, which meant that short-term deposits came to be used for long-term lending. It is to be noted that this was an altogether new phenomenon in India. During the period of administered interest rates system also, the temporal gap had existed, but it was of the opposite nature *i.e.* long-term deposits were used for short-term lending (See BHOLE, 1999, p. 155).

(v) In the deregulated framework, the "interest rates pass through" has been quite high *i.e.* the speed and extent of the response of various interest rates in the economy to the policy actions, stance, and signals from the monetary authorities have been quite great. Between 1996-97 and 2001-02, respective decline in different interest rates in basis points was as follows: Bank rate = 550; bank deposit rates = 400 to 475; SBI PLR = 500; banks' general minimum lending rate = 500; IDBI PLR = 400. It is to be noted that such a high "pass-through" has existed in spite of (a) relatively high level of NPAs pushing up the average cost of funds for banks and other financial institutions, (b) relatively high non-interest operating expense ratio (2.5 to 3 per cent of total assets) of banks, (c) relatively high risk premium component of banks' lending rate due to legal constraints and procedural bottlenecks in the recovery of dues, and (d) the large borrowing programme of the government.

(vi) The monetary authorities were conducting an appropriate interest rates policy during 1992-93 to 1996-97, but it was soon reversed, and an unprecedented reduction in interest rates has been effected by them since 1996-97 in response to the well-articulated demand, the powerful pressures exerted, and the systematic lobbying by the private corporate, big, influential borrowers, and the response to the compulsions of the government finances. The captains and various Associations of industry and business have been demanding that the gap between bank deposit rates and bank lending rates should be reduced by lowering the lending rates, that the PLR-based lending rates should be discontinued, and that the lending rates should be fixed in reference to some benchmark rate such as the rate on some benchmark securities (say, 10-year government securities rate), or some market driven rates such as MIBOR or MIFOR. It may be noted that the industry's demand for the lower lending rates has been rather insatiable. This is reflected in the fact that they were demanding a reduction in interest rates when the PLR was 18 per cent, and they are still making the same demand when the PLR is about 10.5 to 11 per cent per annum.

The authorities have shown great inclination to accept the industry's demand. They have adopted various strategies to signal and induce a substantial downward movement of interest rates. For example, the reduction in interest rates on the post-office savings accounts and PF accounts in 2001-2002, which was preceded and followed by a reduction in the Bank Rate, was meant to lead across the board reduction in interest rates in the economy. In the past, whenever the ceiling on any of the interest rates was removed, the concerned rate used to shoot up (*viz.*, short-term bank deposit rates or the call money rate). Under the present policy, this natural tendency has been ignored, and, instead, interest rates have been reduced through indirect intervention by the authorities. The changes in market forces or the economic fundamentals cannot be said to underly the current soft interest rates policy in India.

(vii) Briefly, the economic front of this political economy of interest rates reduction consists of the following arguments:

(a) Officially it has been stated that "... sustained economic growth would require a significant improvement in investment, which, in turn, would depend on ... structural reduction in inflationary expectations and real interest rates ... importance of lower real interest rates in accelerating industrial growth and boosting India's competitiveness abroad need not be over emphasized (GOI, *Economic Survey*, 2001 -22).

(b) The interest cost burden of public debt has become so heavy that government finances are in danger of becoming unsustainable; a reduction in interest rates would reduce the public debt servicing burden to a manageable level.

(c) Inflation has been brought under control as reflected in a decline or a stability in the rate of inflation in the past few years. As a result, real interest rates have become "too high" or "woefully high", which would have adverse effect on investment, growth, and economic activity. The real cost of capital has reached a rather high level in India in comparison with such a cost in global markets.

(d) According to business and industry, high cost of credit has pushed up cost of production of business units, which has injured their profit prospects and reduced their competitive strength in the international markets. Similarly, if the interest rates continue to rule high, it would be difficult to fight industrial recession successfully.

(e) Interest rates and tax-benefits-adjusted rates of return on instruments such as SS and PF are unduly high and are out of alignment with interest rates and returns on other financial instruments. This needs to be corrected. Further, high administered interest rates on SS and PF have reduced the flexibility of the monetary authorities to conduct suitable monetary policy, and they have weakened the "pass-through" effects of changes in the Bank Rate.

(f) Interest rates in USA, Japan, and some other developed nations have been continuously reduced in the recent past, and in the days of growing integration of international financial markets, it is necessary and appropriate that Indian rates also should correspondingly move southward. It is interesting that, in a way, the Chairman, Federal Reserve Board in USA, has been influencing interest rate policy in India.

III. The Appraisal of Soft-Interest Rates Policy

In this Section we examine certain major issues relating interest rate policy so as to show that the case for reduction in interest rates in India does not stand scrutiny. Tables 4 to 7 present the relevant information which underlie our arguments. The information on as many as 18 macroeconomic indicators presented in Table 4 highlights the comparative performance of the Indian economy during the two phases namely, the deregulated and high interest rates phase, on the one hand, and the deregulated and low interest rates phase, on the other. Although we would be making use of this information throughout the rest of this paper, it may be noted here at the outset that it establishes quite firmly that the overall economic performance of the Indian economy has been worse in the second phase than in the first phase. Let us now discuss in details why and how of this performance.

1. Are the Real Interest in India "Too High"?

Are real interest rates in India too high? Were not they meant to be high? If they are high, why are they high? In order to judge whether the real interest rates in India are "too high" or not, we need a standard of comparison. The Natural Rate of Interest (WICKSELL, 1958; and WILLIAMS, 2003) can be used as such a standard of comparison. However, in view of the difficulties involved in arriving at a reliable measure of the Natural Rate of Interest, the scholars have sometimes preferred to use the trend rate of growth of the economy for comparison in this context.

Now, while many real interest rates were often negative till 1982, thereafter the phenomenon of negative real rates has disappeared. It can be observed from Table 2 that most of the real interest rates were positive and at comparable levels during 1980s and 1990s. But it cannot be argued that after deregulation, they had become too high, if we compare them with the actual and planned rate of growth of the Indian economy. The average annual real growth rate in India was about 5.5 to 5.8 per cent during 1991-92 to 2001-2002 (Table 4). The Tenth Five-Year Plan expects the annual real rate of growth to be about 8.0 per cent. The RBI expects the real GDP growth rate to be 6.5 to 7 per cent in 2003-2004.

Table 4: Annual Average Growth Rates of Major Macroeconomic Aggregates (Percentage)

Indicators	1991-92 to 1996-97	1997-98 to 2001-02
Real GDP at Factor Cost	5.8	5.5
Index of Industrial Production	6.2	5.0
Savings	16.1	11.8
Investment	14.9	10.5
Exchange Rate	31.1	43.2
Total Government Expenditure	11.4	12.6
Net Market Borrowings	103.9	40.1
Inflation	9.6	4.9
Export	24.3	12.3
Total Bank Deposits	17.5	16.9
Total Bank Credit	15.9	16.2
Total Bank Credit to the Commercial Sector	16.2	14.6
Bank Credit to Small Scale Industries	13.2	9.9
Bank Credit to Medium and Large Scale Industries	15.5	11.0
Net Capital Inflows	43.9	6.4
GDP/M3	2.16	1.82
GDP/MI	6.16	6.01
GDP/C	11.11	10.54

SOURCE: Same as in Figure 1.

It means that the short-term real interest rates have been lower than the rate of economic growth. While certain long-term real rates of interest (*viz.*, IDBI PLR and SBI PLR) had been somewhat higher than the rate of growth, the same cannot be said about the long-term government bond rate. Moreover, certain long-term and short-term real interest rates have declined in 2002-03. In short, the real interest rates in India during 1992-96 had not been "too high" to have justified a substantial reduction in nominal interest rates after 1997, nor are they so high now as to require a further reduction in the nominal interest rates.

The positive and somewhat high real interest rates during 1990s have been the result of a decline in the rate of inflation; the other factors influencing them (such as high absolute size of fiscal deficit, high public debt, high NPAs and risk premium) have still not been tackled. It should not also be overlooked that the level of real interest rates in India would be somewhat lower if they are based on Consumer Price Index rather than Wholesale Price Index. Further, the realistic, hidden, and potential long-term inflation rate in India is said to be about 6 to 8 per cent. The rate of inflation has already reached the level of 7.94 per cent per annum at the end of August 2004. Similarly, given the fact that the current (relatively low) rates of inflation across many countries have generated a fear of deflation, many countries, including India, are most likely to take steps so that they do not fall in the "deflation trap" or "liquidity trap". Therefore, the expected rate of inflation has to be taken to be higher than the current rate. In short, the current level of somewhat high real interest rates in India may not be expected to continue much longer.

As pointed out by a Central Banker, high real interest rates are not something we should necessarily fear, and their current level should give little cause for concern. The stagnant saving rate might have been a contributing factor to the present level of real interest rates in India. The risk premium associated with inflation uncertainty could have caused the measured real rates to be somewhat high. The inflation uncertainty might be a reflection of the lingering memory of past inflation, the fear that the dark days of inflation may return any time, and that there may be a dramatic resurgence of inflation (Poole, 1999). The real rates may be somewhat high today, but not so long ago, they were often negative over many years. Interest rate is also a tool for controlling inflation and low interest rate policy can create favourable conditions for further inflation. The current (low) inflation rate has been partly due to recessionary conditions which are difficult to be attributed to the interest rates policy. Once the recession turns into revival and growth, the old problem of high inflation would appear and push down the real interest rates.

2. *Is Industry's Case for Lower Interest Rates Valid?*

There is enough empirical evidence to show that the corporate sector's demand for low interest rates has little rational economic basis. Let us bring together the major facts in this context:

(i) Table 5 presents percentage of interest payments to total borrowings, and sales income, respectively for 1981 to 2001 in the case of Public Limited Companies (PULCos), Private Limited Companies (PRLCos), and Foreign Companies (FCos) in India. Interest costs are not really as big a component of the sales income of the Indian corporate sector as it is made out to be; it has varied between hardly 3.19 per cent and 6.16 per cent in the case of all types of companies during 1981-82 to 2001-2002. In contrast, the interest cost to total income ratio in different countries like Belgium, Spain, France, Germany, Italy, Portugal, and UK varied between 13 to 69 per cent in 1979, 24 to 52 per cent in 1990, and 17 to 46 per cent in 1995 (BOE, 1993 & 1997).

(ii) The average effective interest cost (interest payments as percentage of total borrowings) has been about 11.12 to 13.17 per cent during 1981 to 2001, and it has continuously declined from 13.17 per cent to 11.12 per cent, from 15.36 per cent to 11.41 per cent, and from 15.09 per cent to 12.24 per cent during 1981-85 to 1996-2001 in the case of PULCos, PRLCos, and FCos, respectively. The average effective interest cost has been somewhat higher for PRLCos and FCos than that of PULCos.

Table 5: Percentage of Interest Payments to Total Borrowings and Sales Income of Three Types of Companies in India (Annual Averages)

Periods	Public limited companies		Private Limited companies		Foreign companies	
	IP/TB	IP/SAL	IP/TB	IP/SAL	IP/TB	IP/SAL
1981-85	13.17	4.62	15.36	3.51	15.09	3.19
1986-90	13.04	5.61	13.78	4.11	15.44	3.78
1991-95	12.22	6.02	13.51	4.52	15.46	4.23
1996-2001	11.12	6.16	11.41	3.41	12.24	3.69

NOTES: IP/TB = Interest Payments to Total Borrowings; IP/SAL = Interest Payments to Sales Income.
SOURCE: RBI, Company Finance, Statistics.

(iii) The corporates, particularly those with good credit quality, have always been able to push down the cost of their borrowings, and a major part of bank credit to the corporates has been at lower and middle part of the range of bank lending rates. The bank credit at interest rate of 10 per cent and above but less than 15 per cent as a percentage of total bank credit has been very high, and it has increased from 33.3 per cent in 1998-99 to 61.1 per cent in 2001-2002 (See Table 7). The cost of bank credit to the corporates has been lower than indicated here because a major part of bank credit in India (about 45 to 55 per cent) has always been in the cash credit and overdrafts. Several companies have shown significant increase in their profits after tax owing to reduction in interest rates which has occurred rapidly as compared to the corporate taxes.

(iv) Interest cost is only one among many factors that affect debt servicing burden, competitiveness, and defaults levels of the companies. In fact, corporate defaults are mostly due to bad corporate governance and not due to so-called high interest cost. It is the quality of goods, quality of management of human and material resources, customer service, and honesty which are far more important factors than interest cost in this context.

(v) If interest cost was really unaffordable or a constraining factor, the corporates would have depended on internal funds than on external borrowings much more than at present, and the recent lowering of interest rates would have led to an increase in non-food credit and corporate investment. But none of these things have occurred. The corporate capital structure "Pecking Order" in India has been different from the one in other countries. Unlike in other countries, internal funds do not hold the first rank in the sources of funds of the Indian corporates. The annual average of all internal funds as percentage of total sources of funds has declined in the case of PULCos (from 50.98 to 31.83 per cent) and PRLCos (from 42.15 to 32.14

per cent) during 1971-72 to 2001-02. On the other hand, the annual average of borrowings as percentage of total sources of funds has increased in the case of PULCos (from 21.24 to 40.51 per cent) and PRLCos (from 23.8 to 37.43 per cent) during the same period (BHOLE and MAHAKUD).

3. *The Issue of Government Finances*

One of the major motivations behind the present cheap money policy has been to reduce the cost and burden of Government finances. This, however, is inconsistent with the perspective of the expert committees (*viz.*, Chakravarty Committee, 1985) and the authorities themselves, which had emerged during 1985-1995. In those years, there was a national consensus that the government has a legitimate right to receive a part of funds mobilized by the financial system, but this should be at the market-related and reasonably high interest rates, and not at the administratively fixed low interest rates. The coupon rate on government bonds was accordingly increased in stages to a reasonably high level during those years. In 1992, an auction system for issuing government loans was introduced so that an increasing proportion of the fiscal deficit was financed by borrowings at market-related interest rates. The present low interest rates policy has reversed this approach, and the State has again been enabled to obtain cheap money through another type of captive government securities market in which banks are heavily investing because they do not have other attractive avenues for deploying their resources.

The objective of fiscal discipline or fiscal restraint is most unlikely to be served by the current policy. The burden of public debt and its servicing cannot be really reduced unless the scale of government expenditure and the volume of government borrowings are significantly reduced. But, paradoxically, these are likely to be increased rather than reduced because of the availability of cheap credit. The soft interest rates are hardly conducive for checking unplanned and unproductive government expenditure or the State profligacy.

4. *Interest Rates and Savings*

The appropriateness or otherwise of the low interest rates policy in India has to be determined in terms of its impact on the rate and composition of savings. In a capital scarce economy like India, low interest rates are economically and socially undesirable if they act as a disincentive to save. As much national self-sufficiency in savings as possible is essential for reducing the economic and political costs of capital formation, and for minimizing instability, volatility, contagion, vulnerability, and crises likely to be caused by heavy dependence on foreign capital inflows. Thus, to increase the rate of savings should be regarded as an overriding objective of the macroeconomic policy in India.

Now, an unmistakable or overwhelming long-term evidence has accumulated through the empirical studies by many scholars, which has established beyond doubt a positive relationship between the interest rates on the one hand, and total savings, financial savings, household savings, and corporate savings, respectively on the other. Let us bring together here all the relevant facts about the relationship between the interest rates and savings in India:

(a) The gross total savings rate (total savings as percentage of GDP) has remained sluggish at about 23 to 24 per cent per year during more than a decade now. The soft interest rates policy would certainly come in the way of achieving the target of gross domestic saving rate of 29.6 per cent set by the Draft Approach to Tenth Five-Year Plan (2002-2007).

(b) The annual average rate of growth of savings has declined from 16.1 per cent in 1991-97 to 11.8 per cent in 1998-2002 (See Table 4).

(c) The regression analysis by us had shown that the gross savings rate was positively and statistically significantly influenced by the rates of interest during 1951-52 to 1979-80 (BHOLE, 1985b).

(d) The Panel Data analysis of corporate savings for the period of 1966-67 to 2000-01 has shown that they are positively related to the rate of interest (BHOLE and MAHAKUD).

(e) A recent study of savings behaviour during the period 1955 to 1995 has found that the savings in India depend significantly on the rate of interest; that 1 per cent increase in the real rate of interest leads to 1.5 per cent increase in real financial savings, 1.72 per cent increase in total real private savings and 1.1 per cent increase in total nominal private savings; and that in an economy like India where savings behaviour is financial-assets-intensive, high real interest rates promote both financial and total savings (ATHUKORALA, 1998, p. 162).

(f) Our latest results from the estimation of log-real savings functions for India for the period, 1980-81 to 2001-02, reported in Table 6, clearly show that the gross total domestic savings, gross total household savings, and gross household financial savings are positively related to the rate of interest, while, the gross household real assets savings are negatively related to the interest rate.

(g) It appears that the low interest rates policy in India has tended to encourage savers to hold more of their savings not only in real assets but also in currency. It can be seen from Table 4 that the annual average of income velocity of broad money (M3), narrow money (Ml), and currency has declined from 2.16 to 1.82, from 6.16 to 6.01, and from 11.11 to 10.54, respectively between 1991-92 to 1996-97 and 1997-98 to 2001-02.

The downward movement of interest rates in India needs to be halted for attracting foreign savings also. In the recent past, the nature of foreign capital inflows has significantly changed from the official and concessional flows to the private, commercial flows through world debt and equity markets. Such inflows can be expected to take place in substantial amounts only if interest rates in India remain attractive. They can also help in ensuring that substantial capital outflows from India do not occur. The capital flows are quite responsive to variation in interest rates. The net impact of low interest rates on capital account and balance of payments is likely to be unfavourable. It is a fact that higher interest rates in India had attracted substantial amount of funds from abroad during 1990s. The annual average rate of growth of net capital inflows in India has declined from 43.9 per cent during the high interest phase to 6.4 per cent during the low interest phase (See Table 4). Similarly, low interest rates induce FII and other portfolio investments to choose compulsively equity and derivatives channels, which, in turn, increases volatility, instability, and crises in the financial system as one is observing in India in the year 2003.

Table 6: Determinants of Real Savings and Investment in India during 1980-81 to 2001-02

Dependent Variables → Independent Variables	Gross Total Domestic Savings	Gross Total Household Savings	Gross Household Financial Savings	Gross Household Real Assets Savings	Total Gross Investment
Constant	-11.67	-14.42	-16.87	-12.91	-0.721
	(-21.65)	(-17.87)	(-16.84)	(-3.82)	(-0.183)
Interest Rate	0.046*	0.0205	0.072	-0.100	0.0075
	(1.40)	(00413)	(1.16)	(-0.522)	(0.206)
Growth Rate	1.39***	1.58***	1.69***	1.45***	0.157
of GDP	(36.15)	(27047)	(23.73)	(6.53)	(0.332)
Expected Rate	0.102**	0.102*	0.142**	0.009	-
of Inflation	(2.40)	(1.60)	(1.79)	(0.070)	
Total Credit availability	-	-	-	-	0.804**
					(2.35)
Adjusted R Square	0.98	0.97	0.97	0.90	0.98
D-W Statistics	1.81	0.86	2.3	2.2	1.97
F-Statistics	526.32	298.35	227.47	48.63	277.70

NOTES:
(1) ***, **, and * show the level of significance at 1 %, 5 %, and 10 % respectively.
(2) Average of bank deposit rates (1 to 3 years maturity, 3 to 5 years maturity, and above 5 years maturity) and IDBI PLR have been used as interest rate for savings and investment function, respectively.

From this point of view, India need not follow the interest rates policies in countries such as USA and Japan closely and actively. India is not a capital-abundant country as they are. Similarly, the domestic conditions and not the international trends should receive far more weightage in formulating interest rates policy in India. It can be observed from Table 3 that there are many developed and developing countries whose interest rates are much higher than those in India. Moreover, the world interest rates have started firming up. For example, Australia, UK, and USA increased their interest rates recently.

5. *Interest Rates and Investment*

The low interest rates, in theory are supposed to encourage investment, help fight recession, revive the economy, and accelerate the rate of economic growth. In practice, such a negative relationship between investment and rate of interest are rarely been found to exist in India. On the other hand, low interest rates may have certain distortionary effects on the nature of growth in the economy. For example, they tend to tilt the factor-price ratio severely against (in favour of) labour (capital), which encourages the substitution of labour by capital and worsen the labour unemployment problem. They also tend to encourage the waste or uneconomic use of resources or the misallocation (inefficient allocation) of resources by both the government and the private sectors. In other words, low interest rates (a) may siphon off resources into uneconomic projects and push the excess-capacity-ridden industrial sector into deeper recession, (b) may result in adverse selection *i.e.* may distort investment choices or investment pattern so that projects which are actually unviable may begin to look attractive, (c) may lead to increase in speculative activity in forex, money, stock, and derivatives markets, and (d) may increase volatility in interest rates which is more harmful than high interest rates for most people, except the traders and market operators.

As in the case of savings, in the case of investment also, there are many facts, and there is much econometric evidence which point towards the inappropriateness of the present interest rates policy in India:

(a) The annual average rates of increase in investment, bank credit to large scale industries, bank credit to small scale industries, bank credit to the commercial sector, and industrial production, respectively have all been lower during the low interest rates phase than during the high interest rates phase (See Table 4). The rate of interest cannot be said to have been the cause of the current recession in India (See BHOLE and DASH, 2002). The demand for credit, and investment demand have not revived during the years of one of the lowest levels of interest rates in India. On the other hand, the softening of interest rates has adversely affected banks' willingness to lend to the business and industrial sector. A significant increase in investment in government securities by the banks in spite of a large reduction in the Statutory Liquidity Ratio (SLR) to 25 per cent is an indicator of this phenomenon. The ratio of banks' investment in government securities to their total deposits was 39.7 per cent in March 2002, 42.7 per cent in March 2003, and 45.3 per cent in October 2003.

(b) Our comprehensive studies of the interest elasticity of different components of fixed and inventory investments in the seventeen industries, the private corporate and public sectors, and the entire economy during the period 1950-51 to 1977-78 and its sub-periods have very well established that investment decisions in India have not been affected by interest rates in the theoretically expected manner *i.e.* interest rates have been mostly positively related to investment in the Indian economy (BHOLE, 1985a, and BHOLE, 1985b).

(c) The log-real investment function for the period 1980-81 to 2001-02 presented in Table 6 corroborates once again the above-mentioned empirical positive relationship between the rate of interest and investment in India.

(d) A study by Athukorala referred to earlier contains interesting findings that in India, the high real interest rate promotes private sector capital formation by facilitating the accumulation of finance necessary for undertaking investment, that 1 per cent increase in the real interest rate is associated with over 2 per cent increase in private investment, and that the cumulative net impact of the real rate of interest on investment is positive because its effect operating through financial intermediation and complementarity outweighs its cost effect (1998, p. 165).

6. *The Issue of Relative Rates of Return*

The low interest rates policy has distorted the structure of rates of return on various financial and real assets, and it has thereby distorted the pattern of investment. It has discriminated against bank deposits, Small Savings, provident Funds, other debt instruments, and in favour of equities, units, real estate, and precious metals. It has been a part of the policy in India to promote the equity culture or equity cult in the country. Investment in equities and units enjoy many attractive fiscal concessions which are not available on bank deposits and other debt instruments; there has not been any restriction any time on the rates of return earned on units and equities; there has not been any attempt any time to reduce these rates of returns which have been generally much higher than the interest rates on bank deposits; and there has been a policy preference to hold down interest rates so as to induce greater investment in units and equities.

While the business and industry, some economists, and the monetary authorities themselves have argued for the gradual reduction in interest rates, and the withdrawal of fiscal concessions on SS and PF, such measures have never been suggested by them in respect of units and equities. When the dividend rate on the Unit Trust of India (UTI) units had reached a high level of 26 per cent per year during 1992-95, the long-term bank deposit rates were hardly 10 to 11 per cent per annum. Even in the worst days of Mutual Funds (MFs) so far (2000-2003), the dividend rate on UTI units was 10 per cent as against the term deposit rates of about 5 to 6 per cent per annum. In December 2003, UTI MF declared a 100 per cent dividend on its MEP (Master Equity Plan) 1998 and MEP 1999, and this dividend is tax-free to the investors. Even investments in bond MFs have yielded double-digit returns over the last few years. The recent Union Budgets have provided for the following concessions and incentives for investment in equities and units: (a) The exemption from dividend tax for 3 years for US-64 scheme of the UTI, and all open-ended equity-oriented schemes (*i.e.* schemes with more than 50 per cent investment in equities) of the MFs; (b) the exemption from income tax for all income received in the hands of investors from the MFs, (c) the abolition of the long-term capital gains tax, (d) the withdrawal of tax on dividends in the hands of the shareholders.

Thus, the low interest rates policy in India has resulted in the misalignment of the returns on financial and real assets, and it has harmed the competitive position of banks and other deposit-accepting institutions *vis-a-vis* mutual funds and stock market. This, however, has not helped to create a robust, dynamic, and active primary stock market, to increase productive capital investment, and to enhance the economic growth.

7. *Distributional and Mass Welfare Concerns*

One of the most serious objections against the present low interest rates policy is that it has resulted in social or distributional injustice. The soft interest rates policy impacts the society at large because a major part of the population of a country is involved in at least one of the public welfare institutions like life insurance, PFs, SS, Pension Funds, trusts, charitable institutions whose financial strength and stability are adversely affected by low interest rates. A substantial reduction in interest rates on bank deposits, SS, PF, and other debt instruments has harmed the interests of the crores of people which include middle and low income savers, and those who are old, weak, poor, disadvantaged, who are in need of social help or social security or social care, and who borrow little from the financial system. While the essential expenditure such as medical expenses, house rents, educational expenses, old age home charges have gone up, interest income of this mass of people has gone down by 50 to 60 per cent in the recent past. The soft interest rates policy has tended to punish frugality and savings, and promote consumerism. To promote savings in general and financial savings in particular is a part of public or social policy. From this viewpoint, a substantial reduction in interest rates on SS and PF has penalized long-term investment and social security measures. It has also harmed the interests of banks and other financial institutions as the lenders.

In comparison, it has benefited a far less number of people who include the rich, powerful, big corporate and other borrowers, and the government. In other words, it has harmed the interests of the savers in general and small savers in particular, while it has promoted a borrower-cult in general and a big borrower-cult in particular, in so far as these entities save less and borrow more *i.e.* they are the net borrowers in the economy. Given the institutional reality in India that, in spite of the ample liquidity, banks have been reluctant to lend much to the rural, agricultural, small-scale industrial sectors, and the individual borrowers, the inequity in the distribution of benefits from the low-cost credit becomes glaring indeed. There is no doubt that there has been a geographical and size-wise concentration in bank credit disbursal. The low interest rates have substantially weakened the social objective of banks not only from their credit side but also deposits side. They have resulted in the cross-subsidization of the business and industry at the expense of individuals and households.

Table 7: Some Features of Bank Deposits and Credit

No.	Item	1998-1999	1999-2000	2000-2001	2001-2002
1.	Number of deposit accounts (Crores)	40.59	41.28	42.80	44.0
2.	Number of credit accounts (Crores)	5.23	5.43	5.24	5.63
3.	Urban and metropolitan credit accounts to total bank credit accounts (%)	25.7	26.6	30.3	28.8
4.	Credit to Urban and metropolitan accounts to total bank credit (%)	76.3	77.2	78.4	78.6

5.	Rural and semi-urban deposit accounts to total deposit accounts (%)	57.9	58.1	58.0	56.9
6.	Number of term deposit accounts with less than Rs. 1 lakh of deposit to total term deposit accounts (%)	-	-	-	93.6
7.	Amount of term deposits with less than Rs.1 lakh deposits to total term deposits (%)	-	-	-	46.8
8.	Number of credit accounts with outstanding credit limit of over Rs. 25 crores	1224	1649	2281	3076
9.	Number of accounts in (8) to total number of credit accounts (%)	Nearly zero	Nearly zero	Nearly zero	Nearly zero
10.	The amount of outstanding credit to accounts in (8) to total bank credit (%)	19.9	22.9	26.9	31.7
11.	Per cent of total bank credit at interest rate of 10 % and above but less than 12 %	3.3	7.9	17.0	24.5
12.	Per cent of total bank credit at interest rate of 10 per cent and above but less than 13 %	11.9	24.4	34.7	36.2
13.	Per cent of total bank credit at interest rate of 10 per cent and above but less than 14 %	23.6	34.7	45.6	48.0
14.	Per cent of total bank credit at interest rate of 10 per cent and above but less than 15 %	33.3	45.2	58.2	61.1
15.	Per cent of total bank credit at interest rate of less than 6 %	0,3	0.2	0.2	0.1

SOURCE: RBI, Basic Statistical Returns of Scheduled Commercial Banks in India, Various Issues.

The following facts support this viewpoint (See Table 7):

(i) The overwhelming proportion of financial savings of the household sector are held in interest-earning assets, *viz.*, PF, SS, industrial bonds, government securities, and deposits with co-operative and commercial banks, non-bank financial companies and non-bank non-financial companies. In the year 2002, while about 23.1 per cent of financial savings of the household sector was held in the form of currency, shares, debentures, units, and insurance, about 76.9 per cent of those savings was held in the form of deposits, claims on the government, PF, etc. The latest Survey (SEBI-NCAER, 2003) has shown that while the number of households investing in industrial debentures has increased from 3.7 million to 9.6 million during 1998-99 to 2000-01, that of households investing in equities has declined from 12.1 million to 6.6 million during the same period. The number of people investing in units has declined, and those who invest in units prefer bond funds.

(ii) While the number of bank deposit accounts were 40.59 to 44.00 crores, the number of bank credit accounts were only 5.23 to 5.63 crores during 1998-99 to 2001-2002. The ratio of rural and semi-urban deposit accounts to total deposit accounts was about 58 per cent during the same period.

(iii) The banks' term deposit accounts with less than Rs. 1.0 lakh of deposit each, were 93.6 per cent of total number of term deposit accounts, and they accounted for about 47 per cent of total volume of term deposits in 2001-2002.

(iv) The urban and metropolitan bank credit accounts in relation to the total number of credit accounts were 25.7 to 30.3 per cent, and they received as high as 76.3 to 78.6 per cent of total bank credit during 1998-99 to 2001-2002.

(v) Hardly about 1000 to 3000 big credit accounts with the banks in the whole economy (constituting nearly a zero per cent of the total number of bank credit accounts, and having an outstanding credit limit of over Rs. 25 crores) received about 23 to 32 per cent of total bank credit during 1999-2000 to 2001-2002.

IV. Summary and Conclusions

In this paper we have examined the interest rates policy in India during post-1991 period. The present interest rates system in India can be called a "system of managed flexibility" or a "mixed system" or a "soft interest rates system". The policy of deregulation of interest rates in India is welcome, but the wisdom of a continuous, significant, across the board reduction in interest rates which has been recently effected by the monetary authorities is questionable on empirical grounds. The reduction in interest rates has not helped to achieve the proximate (increase in savings, investment, efficient resource allocation, etc.) and ultimate (growth, social justice, and stability) developmental objectives. The regression estimates show that the higher (lower) interest rates encourage (discourage) savings but do not discourage (encourage) investment. Similarly, the soft interest rates policy has encouraged the savers to hold more of their savings in the form of currency and real assets, which is an undesirable thing to have happened. The interest rates in India cannot be reduced further without adversely affecting the multiple objectives of development. The factors such as the high carrying cost of long-term deposits and NPAs, the loading of risk premium for the future accumulation of NPAs, and the high operating cost of banks precludes further reduction in interest rates. A commercially viable and social relevant banking industry requires a halt to a further reduction in interest rates. The higher than present interest rates which are managed in a flexible manner would be the appropriate interest rates policy for India. In the coming years, it needs to serve the interests of all the stakeholders in the society.

The recent unprecedented reduction in interest rates in India has not been really the result of changes in the market forces and economic fundamentals. It has been primarily effected by the monetary authorities under the pressures from the powerful corporates who have welcomed this policy most enthusiastically, and who have been its greatest beneficiaries. This policy has hit hard the savers, particularly the small savers and the retired persons. It is meant to promote the equity cult and the big borrower cult in India. It favours the corporate and government sectors who contribute little to the national savings, while it harms the household sector which is the mainstay of savings in the economy. To be willing to pay the market-determined and the risk-related interest rates is the social responsibility of the corporate sector.

Interest rates policy in India which is oriented towards the convergence of interest rates in India and USA requires a review because these countries are so vastly different from each other. The USA has been trying to make up for its drastic fall in interest rates by attracting funds from other faltering economies such as Japan with the help of strong dollar. Such a policy is neither possible nor desirable for India.

References

ATHUKORALA, P. C. (1998), "Interest Rates, Saving, and Investment: Evidence from India", *Oxford Development Studies*, Vol. 26, No.2, pp. 153-69.

BANK OF ENGLAND (BOE) (1993 & 1997), *Quarterly Bulletin*.

BHOLE, L. M. (l985a), *Impacts* of *Monetary Policy*, Himalaya Publishing House, Mumbai.

BHOLE, L. M. (1985b), "Administered Interest Rates in India." *Economic and Political Weekly*, Vol. XX, Nos. 25 and 26, June 22-29, pp. 1089-1104.

BHOLE, L. M. (1988), "Some Issues Concerning Interest Rates Theory and Policy", *The Indian Economic Journal*, the Conference Volume, pp.1-18.

BHOLE, L. M. (1992), "Recent Changes in Interest Rates Policy in India", *The Journal of Indian Institute of Bankers*, January-March.

BHOLE, L. M. (2004), *Financial Institutions and Markets*, Fourth Edition, Tata McGraw Hill Publishing Company Limited, New Delhi.

BHOLE, L. M. and Sebastian, V.J. (1996), "Determinants of Interest Rates in a Deregulated Open Economy", *The Indian Journal of Economics*, Vol. 77, No. 305, pp. 261-78.

BHOLE, L. M. and Dash, P. (2002), "Industrial Recession in India: Is Interest Rate the Cause?" *Productivity*, Vol. 43, No.2, July-Sept. 2002, pp. 268-77.

BHOLE, L. M. and Dash, P. (2003), "Determinants of Long-Term Interest Rates in India During 1970s to 1990s", *Prajnan*, Vol. XXXII, No.2 (Forthcoming).

BHOLE, L. M. and DASH, P., "Domestic and External Factors In Short-Term Interest Rates Determination In India", Indian Economic Journal, April-September 2004.

BHOLE, L. M. and MAHAKUD, J. "Trends and Determinants of Retained Earnings of Joint Stock Companies in India: A Panel Data Analysis", Unpublished Paper (Communicated).

GLOWER, C. J. (1994), "Interest Rate Deregulation: A Brief Survey of the Policy Issues and the Asian Experience", Asian Development Bank, Working Paper.

GOVERNMENT OF INDIA, *Economic Survey*, Various Issues.

INTERNATIONAL MONETARY FUND (IMF) (1983). "Interest Rate Policies in Developing Countries", Working Paper.

MCKINNON, R. I. (1973), *Money and Capital in Economic Development.* Brooking Institution, Washington D.C.

POOLE, W. (1999), "Are Real Interest Rates too High?", Money Marketeers of New York University, New York City, Sept. 21, www.stls.frb.org/news/speeches.

RESERVE BANK OF INDIA, *Report on Currency and Finance,* Various Issues. - *Annual Report,* Various Issues.

___ *Monthly Bulletin,* Various Issues.

___ *Basic Statistical Returns* of *Scheduled Commercial Banks* in *India.* Various Issues.

___ (2003), *Handbook of Statistics on Indian Economy,* 2002. Mumbai.

___ (1985). Report of the Committee to Review the Working of the Monetary System (Chakravarty Committee Report), Bombay.

SEBI-NCAER, *Survey of Indian Investors,* SEBI, Mumbai, 2003.

SHAW, E. S. (1973), *Financial Deepening* in *Economic Development,* Oxford University Press, Oxford.

WICKSELL, K. (1936), *Interest and Prices,* (tr. of 1989 edition by R.F. Khan), Macmillan, London.

WICKSELL, K. (1958), "The Influence of the Rate of Interest on Commodity Prices" in E. LINDHAL (Ed.), *Selected Papers on Economic Theory* by Knut Wicksell, Allen & Unwin, London.

WILLIAMS, J. C. (2003), "The Natural Rate of Interest" Federal Reserve Bank of San Francisco Economic Letter, No. 2003-32, October 31.

[16]

*Industrial Recession in India: Is Interest Rate the Cause?**

Introduction

The major goals of the New Economic Policy that was introduced at the beginning of 1991 were to achieve a higher growth rate of gross domestic product (GDP) and a price stability. These objectives have been broadly achieved. However, the recession in the industrial sector in the second half of the 1990s and in the year 2001 has posed a serious threat to the credibility of economic reforms.

Many factors are said to be the causes of this recession, one of them being the existence of high real rates of interest in India. For example, it has been stated that the high real rates of interest which are in turn caused by high fiscal deficit are responsible for the current recession in India (ECONOMIC SURVEY, 2001). Many researchers and policy makers, therefore, have been pleading for the lowering of interest rates. It has been argued, on the basis of the working of stock market, that the fall in the share prices combined with high interest rates on fixed deposits has contributed to the disenchantment of the ordinary investor with share markets, and, therefore, lower interest rates are essential to revive the stock market (GOYAL, 1997). It has also been stated that the lowering of interest rates and thereby of the interest burden of the State is essential to revive investment (PATNAIK, 1999). It is in this context that the objective of this paper is to identify the causes of industrial recession in India during the second half of 1990s. It particularly attempts to reflect on whether the recession has been caused by high rates of interest and whether the low interest rates regime would help the economic revival in the country.

* Paper jointly published with Pradyumna Dash in Productivity, July-September 2002.

Table 1: Sectoral Real Growth Rates in Gross Domestic Product (GDP), 1993-94 to 2001-2002

	Percent change over the previous year								
	1993 -94	1994 -95	1995 -96	1996 -97	1997 -98	1998 -99	1999-2000(P)	2000-2001(Q)	2001-2002(A)
Agriculture and Allied Activities	4.1	5.0	-0.9	9.6	-2.4	6.1	1.3	-0.2	5.7
Industry	5.2	10.2	11.6	7.1	4.3	3.7	4.9	6.3	3.3
Services	7.6	7.1	10.5	7.2	9.8	8.3	9.5	4.8	6.5
Total GDP at Factor Cost	5.9	7.3	7.3	7.8	4.8	6.5	6.1	4.0	5.4

NOTE: P: Provisional Estimates; Q: Quick Estimates; and A: Advanced Estimates.
SOURCE: Government of India, Ministry of Finance, Economic Survey, 2001-2002.

Is there A Recession in India?

The National Bureau of Economic Research (NBER) defines recession as a significant decline in economic activity across the economy, lasting for more than a few months, visible in a decline in industrial production, employment, real income and trade. "Contraction", "slump", "downturn", are often used as synonymous with recession. According to some macroeconomists, a "recession" is a slackening of demand in any one or more industries or sectors of the economy while a "slump" is a general slow down in the tempo of the entire economy. Slump is, therefore, a wider concept that affects nearly all the segments of the economy. Recession is a state of affairs in which real income produced, real income consumed, and the rate of employment fall, and there are idle resources, unemployed workers, and unused capacity (HABERLAR, 1966).

Tables 1 to 5 and graphs 1 to 4 indicate the following points regarding the performance of the Indian economy in general and industrial sector in particular. They more or less clearly establish the fact of industrial recession in India during the later part of 1990s:

(i) The buoyancy in the growth of National Income that was witnessed after the introduction of New Economic Policy (NEP) has not been maintained during the later years of 1990s. The annual average rate of growth of real GDP was 6.35 per cent during 1997-98 to 2000-2001 compared to the rate of 7.07 per cent during 1993-94 to 1996-97 (See Table 1).

(ii) The rate of growth of industrial output has similarly declined during the 1990s; the annual average rate of growth of real industrial output at 4.8 per cent during 1997-98 to 2000-2001 was almost half of the rate of 8.52 per cent during 1993-94 to 1996-97. The annual rate of

Figure 1:
Quarterly Growth Rates of Real GDP, Q1-1997-98 to Q3 2001-02 (Base 1993-94 = 100)

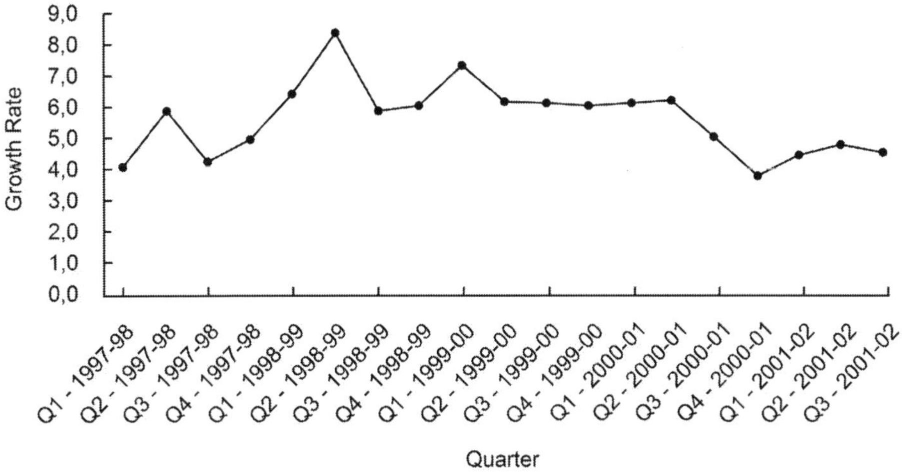

Source: Reserve Bank of India, Handbook of Statistics on Indian Economy, 2001, Mumbai, 2002.

growth of production has noticeably declined over the years in various sub-sectors of industry also. For example, the rate of growth in the manufacturing sector has declined from 14.1 per cent in 1995-96 to 5.3 per cent in 2000-2001 (See Table 2, and Figs. 2 and 3). Further, the recession has hit hard basic goods industry, consumer goods industry, capital goods industry and intermediate goods industry. The annual average growth rate of all sectors has declined during 1997-98 to 2000-2001 as compared to 1994-95 to 199697 (See Table 3).

(iii) The growth of output in the agricultural and allied activities sector also has decelerated, it has been negative in certain years, and it has been characterised by much higher degree of fluctuations during the period under discussion (See Tables 1, 6, and 7).

(iv) A number of performance indicators of the private corporate sector in India as presented in Table 4 lend further support to the view that the Indian industry has been suffering from recessionary tendencies during the latter half of 1990s. The respective annual rates of growth of production, sales, and profits have either declined or turned to be negative, and the utilisation of fixed capital has suffered a setback, which is reflected in a clear decline in the ratio of value added to fixed assets and the ratio of sales to fixed assets, respectively from 1995-96 to 1999-2000 (See Cols. 1, 2, 3, 4, 5, and 6 in Table 4). The gross profitability, net profitability, and dividend payment have also declined during the period just mentioned.

(v) The proposed investment and proposed employment given in Industrial Entrepreneur Memoranda (IEM) and Letters of Intents (LOIs) also give a fairly good idea about the industrial climate or the level of industrial activity. Table 5 shows that proposed investment as well as proposed employment has generally declined from 1995 to 2000.

Table 2: Annual Growth Rates of Industrial Production in Major Sectors of Industry, 1994-95 to 2001-02 (Percentages) (Base: 1993-94 = 100)

Year (weight)	General (100)	Mining and Quarrying (10.47)	Manufacturing (79.36)	Electricity (10.17)
1994-95	9.1	9.8	9.1	8.5
1995-96	13.0	9.7	14.1	8.1
1996-97	6.1	-1.9	7.3	4.0
1997-98	6.7	6.9	6.7	6.6
1998-99	4.1	-0.8	4.4	6.5
1999-2000	6.7	1.0	7.1	7.3
2000-2001	5.0	3.7	5.3	4.0

SOURCE: Same as in Table 1.

Table 3: Average Growth Rates of Industrial Production by Use-Based Classification (Percentages) (Base: 1993-94= 100)

Year / Sector (Weight)	1994-95	1995-96	1996-97	1997-98	1998-99	1999-2000	2000-2001
Basic Goods (35.51)	9.6	10.8	3.0	6.9	1.6	5.5	3.9
Capital Goods (9.69)	9.2	5.3	11.5	5.8	12.6	6.9	1.8
Intermediate Goods (26.54)	5.3	19.4	8.1	8.0	6.1	8.8	4.7
Consumer Goods (28.36)	12.1	12.8	6.2	5.5	2.2	5.7	8.0

Source: Same as in Table 1.

Figure 2: Monthly Growth Rates of General Index of Industrial Production, April 1995 to March 2002 (Base: 1993-94 = 100)

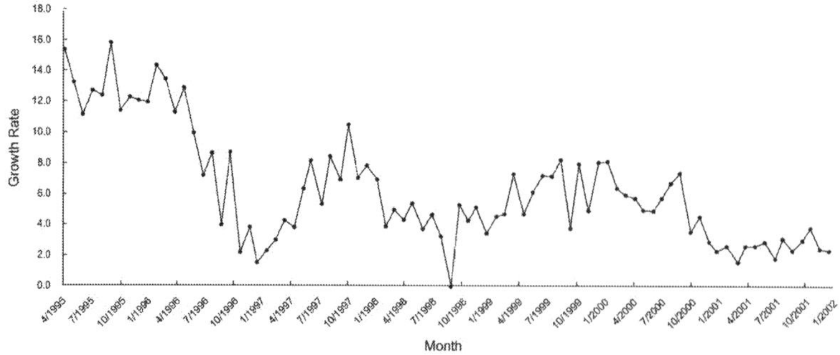

Source: Same as Fig. 1.

Figure 3:
Monthly Growth Rates of Industrial Sectors, April 1995 to March 2002 (Base: 1993-94 = 100)

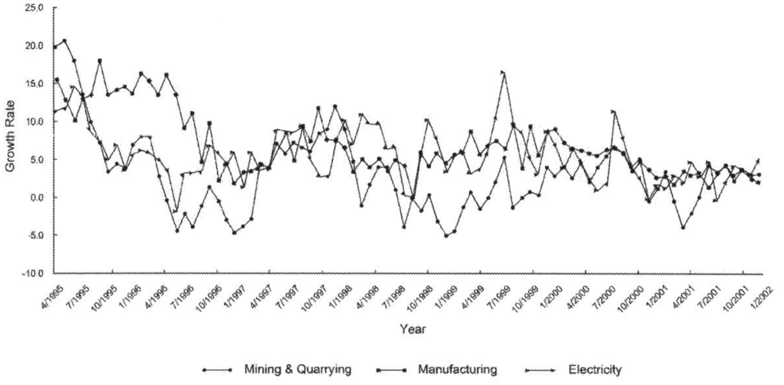

Source: Same as Fig. 1.

Figure 4:
Monthly Growth Rates of Manufacturing Production and Non-Food Credit, April 1995 to March 2002

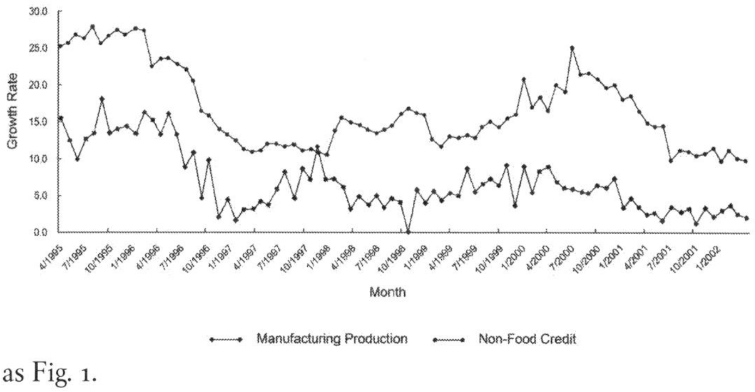

Source: Same as Fig. 1.

Causes of Industrial Slowdown

Has the industrial decline been due to higher interest rates? The relationship between the level of real interest rates and real economic growth has been discussed in academic literature especially in the less developed countries. In contrast to Keynesian line of thinking that interest rate has to be kept at a low level to promote investment and growth, it has been argued by some that the financial repression – interest rate ceilings, high reserve requirements, regulatory credit policies - discourages the development of domestic financial markets and is detrimental to economic growth. Financial liberalisation leading to high interest rates is expected to channel savings to their most productive uses and generate greater efficiency in investment projects. In other words, the financial liberalisation process implies a positive relationship between real interest rates and economic growth via increased savings and investments. Many studies have found a direct relationship between the real rate of interest and economic growth (Lanyi, A. and R. Scacaglu, 1983; Gupta, K. L, 1986; Koyck and Hooft Welvaars, 1960; Matthews, 1960; Sen, A. 1971). In the case of India also, it has been stated that "... higher real rates of interest seem to promote both financial and total savings ... financial savings promote investment through the provision of bank lending to the private sector and higher deposit rate promotes investment through facilitating self-financed capital accumulation" (Athukorala, 1998).

The positive relationship between the real rate of interest and economic growth may hold true as long as the former reflects the productivity of investment. The optimum real rate of interest in the economies growing at six to eight percent per annum should be higher than that of the advanced economies growing at two to three percent (Brahmananda, 2000). In India the real rate of interest has remained high to contain capital outflow on account of rise in risk and uncertainty in the aftermath of liberalisation. The rise in risk and uncertainty can be attributable to many factors like communal violence, rise of terrorism, political instability, the Kargil War, possibility of war between India and Pakistan etc. At any point of time, investment not only depends on real rate of interest but also on the expected profitability of investment. Keynes called the latter as the Marginal Efficiency of Capital (MEC) which is highly volatile and driven by hopes and fears, optimism and pessimism. The MEC has been fluctuating due to high risk and Uncertainty and real shocks in the Indian economy. As a result the usefulness of interest rate policy to influence the volume of investment has been limited. The Keynesian Effect has failed to operate because of the existence of liquidity trap. The nexus between money supply, inflation and income elasticity of demand for money can elucidate it. The 17.4 percent average growth rate of money supply during 1994-95 to 1999-2000 has been absorbed on account of the decline in the income velocity of money from 2.2 percent in 199495 to 1.8 percent in 1999-2000. The high growth rate of money supply has been accompanied by a low rate of inflation but has had little positive impact on the growth rate of output.

The explanation of current recession in India has, therefore, to go beyond interest rates policy. The following plausible factors can help us to understand it.

(1) The agricultural production has been highly volatile and has had a declining trend during 1990s in general and second half of the 1990s in particular as compared to 1980s (See Tables 1, 6 and 7). The impact of agricultural production on the pace of industrialisation through its linkage effect is quite well-known (Patnaik, 1994; Raj, 1994; and Vaidyanathan, 1994). In India, the consumption demand to a large extent depends on agricultural production. The agricultural sector employs 60 per cent of total labour force and contributes 26 per cent of the total gross domestic product. The causality runs from the agricultural sector to industrial sector. The expansion of agricultural sector has three advantages:(1) it creates greater employment opportunities for the rural poor; (2) it can alleviate poverty in rural areas by increasing both the availability of food as well as purchasing power; and (3) it creates a large domestic market for industrial products. The last one is probably most important so far as the linkage effect is concerned because the demand for industrial products increases with the increase in

agricultural production. It is estimated that a 10 percent increase in agricultural output would increase industrial output by 5 percent and urban workers would benefit by both increased industrial employment and price deflation (RANGARAJAN, 1988). Therefore, the industrial sector is affected severely if the agricultural sector does not grow sufficiently.

Table 4: Selected Growth Rates And Ratios of Selected Non-Government Non-Financial Public Limited Companies, 1991-92 to 1999-2000

Year	Sales %	Value of Production %	Gross Profit %	Profit after Tax %	Sales to Gross Fixed Assets %	Gross Value Added to Gross Fixed Assets %	Gross Profit to Total Net Assets %	Profit after Tax to Net Worth %	Dividends to Net Worth %
	1	2	3	4	5	6	7	8	9
1991-92	19.0	19.4	22.2	6.5	139.3	35.0	10.8	13.9	4.9
1992-93	12.2	12.6	6.6	-1.5	135.5	33.7	10.7	12.0	4.5
1993-94	15.4	12.7	22.5	68.6	123.5	30.0	9.5	9.4	3.9
1994-95	21,1	22.8	32.9	60.9	119.9	28.7	9.5	12,0	39
1995-96	23.7	24.5	23.3	23.9	120.9	29.5	10.2	14.4	4.0
1996-97	12.2	9.3	1.2	-24.6	122.7	29.9	10.9	14.4	38
1997-98	7.5	8.1	-2.8	-13.7	113.4	27.3	9.5	9.8	3.4
1998-99	7.2	6.3	-2.9	-18.6	108.7	24.3	8.0	7.6	-
1999-00	11.4	12.3	11.1	21.0	96.4	22.9	7.2	5.9	2.8

SOURCE:
(a) Reserve Bank of India, Private Corporate Business Sector in India, Selected Financial Statistics from 1950-51 to 1997-98, Mumbai, 2000.
(b) Reserve Bank of India, Monthly Bulletin, Finances of Public Limited Companies, 1999-2000, June 2001.

As far as the level of income of the farmers is concerned. it should have somewhat stabilised on account of the rise in procurement prices in spite of low agricultural production. For example, the agricultural price index as a percent of the manufacturing price index has risen from 116.4 in 1991-92 to 128.9 in 2000-01. But the increase in procurement prices is not being reflected in market priccs of agricultural commodities due to the nature of the agricultural commodity market. The benefit of the increase in procurement has not been reaching a large number of small and marginal farmers. The existence of the interlinked contracts in agricultural commodities markets force farmers (particularly small and marginal farmers) to accept a sub-optimal price that is much lower than the economic and market determined price (GANGOPADHYAY, 1994). Inter-linkages arise out of the agrarian contracts between credit, factor, and product markets. For example, a farmer is said to be adversely affected by factor-product market interlinkage if he borrows from a large farmer and is forced to sell his product at a price much below the existing market price. Similarly, geographically segmented markets for agricultural commodities also force farmers to accept a price level that is lower than the market determined price level. Hence, given the prices of nonagricultural products, the farmers' purchasing power has been deteriorating. Moreover, the share as well as the growth rate of farm employment hinges directly on agricultural production. The share of farm employment in the total private and public sector employment has declined from 7.3 percent in 1992 to 5.11 and 4.93 per cent in 1997 and 1999 respectively (BHOLE and DASH, 2002).

Table 5: Industrial Proposed Investment and Employment, 1995 to 2000

Year	Proposed Investment (LOIs + IEM) (Crores)	Proposed Employment (LOIs + IEM) (Nos.)
1995	139774	1205588
1996	103210	876873
1997	61907	617667
1998	60659	547541
1999	129719	494483
2000	73374	442114

NOTE:
LOIs indicates Letter of Intents and IEM indicates Industrial Entrepreneur Memorandum.
SOURCE: Same as in Table 1.

Table 6: Annual Average Compound Growth Rate of Agricultural Production (%)

	1980-81 to 1989-90	1990-91 to 2000-01
All Crops	3.19	1.73
Total Food Grains	2.85	1.66
Rice	3.62	1.79
Wheat	3.57	3.04
Coarse Cereals	0.40	0.06
Pulses	1.52	-0.58
Non-Food Grains	3.77	1.86

SOURCE: Same as in Table 1.

The poor agricultural performance coupled with high food prices has worsened the industrial production during the later half of the 1990s. The rural income elasticity of demand can be divided into (1) income elasticity of food demand and (2) income elasticity of non-food demand. Given the level of disposable income, a certain proportion of income is spent on non-food products. If food prices increase the rural poor are bound to shift their demand away from non-food to food articles. This has happened in India because of the policy of curbing the subsidy bill. The Composite Price Index of Agricultural Production has risen faster than both the Consumer Price Index of Industrial Workers and General Wholesale Price Index. The Price Index of Agricultural Production has risen by 124 percent between 1990-91 and 2000-01 whereas Wholesale Price Index has risen by 111.17 percent during the same time period. This has also led to poor off-take of food grains when food stocks have been the highest. The total food stock in India increased to 58.0 million tonnes by January 2002 (32.4 and 25.6 million tonnes of wheat and rice respectively), whereas the minimum food stock norm is only 16.8 million tonnes of food grains (8.4 million tonnes of wheat and rice each).

The decline in rural poverty has been arrested, there has been a widening of rural-urban income disparity, and the annual growth rate of rural per capita expenditure has declined during 1990s. The rural poverty ratio had declined to 33.70 per cent in 1989-90 from 45.65 per cent in 1983, but it has increased to and remained at about 38 per cent during 1990s. On the other hand, the urban poverty ratio has declined to about 34 percent in 1990s from 36 percent in 1989-90 (GUPTA, 1999). The widening rural-urban income disparity is a matter of serious concern. A myriad of factors like low agricultural growth rate, a rise in relative prices of food, a decline in developmental public expenditure, a decline in nonagricultural employment, low investment in rural roads and agricultural R & O are relevant in this context (SEN, 1996 and FAN et al 1999).

The industrial growth rate has also declined because of the type of economic reforms in general and the trade reforms in particular which have been carried out since 1991. The trade reforms consisting of freer access to foreign capital and technology, abolition of import licensing on most of the tradables, phased reduction of tariffs, and removal or reduction of quantitative restrictions on imports have been carried out. The demand for industrial products comprise domestic and external demand. Any change in industrial production can be either on account of a change in domestic demand or external trade or a combination of both. A change in either export or import of any industrial product can have some impact on the domestic production and employment of the respective industry. An import of a machine reduces the activity not only in a machine-making industry but also in other industries which supply inputs to that industry. The degree and the speed with which this happens depends on the strength of industrial linkages. Nambiar et al (1999) have estimated the effect of import liberalisation on value added and employment in manufacturing sector in India. According to them, trade has been one of the root causes for crippling Indian industry. The industrial production has not only declined but also its composition has undergone a drastic change in the recent past. The share of capital and intermediate goods sector in total industrial production has declined from

68.63 per cent in 1960-66 to 28.15 per cent in 1990-98 and that of consumer goods sector has increased from 31.38 per cent in 1960-66 to 52.45 per cent in 1990-98 (CHAUDHURY, 2002).

The gradual removal of quantitative restrictions on imports of various items through Open General Licence (OGL) system due to Indo-US agreement has adversely affected many small-scale and tiny industries, which have either closed down, or running with low capacity utilisation, or have switched over to other kinds of activities, or have reduced the number of working shifts. Jaina Time industry which had a turnover of 9 crores and had employed 900 workers has been closed down. Other units that have already been closed down include Bifora, Allwyn, Timestar, and Action. The current capacity utilisation in watch and toy industries has come down to 25 per cent. All small-scale and tiny industries which were producing wall clocks, alarm clocks, watches have switched over to importing smuggled watches, fixing glasses on them, encasing them and selling them in the grey market. Jewel Plastics which was previously working three shifts is currently operating only one shift. All these can be attributable to dumping, under-invoicing of imports, price and quantity differentiation, and smuggled imports that are, in fact, the result of import liberalisation. The growth rate of the number of units of small-scale industries has declined from 7.9 per cent in 1992-93 to 5.0 per cent in 1999-2000. The growth rate of exports of small-scale industrial sector has dwindled to 5.0 percent in 2000-01 from 14.8 per cent in 1994-95. The growth rate of output of small-scale industries that had shown an initial increase from 7.1 per cent in 1993-94 to 11.3 per cent in 1996-97 has declined to 8.1 per cent in 2000-2001. Similarly its .growth rate of employment that had shown an initial increase from 4.1 per cent in 1993-94 to 4.8 percent in 1996-97 has declined to 4.0 per cent in 2000-01 (ECONOMIC SURVEY, 2001-2002).

The growth rates of both the workers (who are employed in the manufacturing process, or any other kind connected with the manufacturing process) and total persons employed (workers. working proprietors and those who hold supervisory or managerial position), respectively, have declined in the latter half of the 1990s (See Table 8). India is a country with surplus labour. Therefore, it is desirable that labour-intensive industries should grow and the wage inequality should decline. But the share of labour-intensive industries in the aggregate value added and employment, respectively, has gone down in 1991-98 as compared to 1990-91. The growth rate of output (value added) of capital-intensive sector has been higher than that of the labour intensive sector (CHAUDHURY, 2002). There has also been a marginal widening of wage differential between skilled and unskilled workers (NAMBIAR et al, 1999). The rise in capital intensity i.e. rise in real net fixed capital stock per worker can occur either because of technological upgradation or the substitution of capital for labour. But in India, in a number of sectors accounting for more than half of the total output, an increase in capital intensity between 1990-91 and 1997-98 has occurred due to the substitution of capital for labour rather than a general technological upgradation. It is well-known that in the cotton textile industry, the mill owners have been cutting production costs by reducing employment (DHANRAJ, 2001).

Table 7: Indices of Agricultural Production (Base: Triennium Ending 1981-82= 100)

	1995-96	1997-97	1997-98	1998-99	1990-2000	2000-2001
All Commodities	160.7	175.7	165.3	177.9	175.6	163.9
Food Grains	(-2.6)	(9.3)	(-5.9)	(7.6)	(-1.3)	(-6.6)
	146.1	160.9	155.7	165.2	169.7	157.5
Rice	(-6.2)	(10.1)	(-3.2)	(6.1)	(2.7)	(-7.2)
	154.8	164.4	166.0	173.0	180.3	170.7
Wheat	(-5.9)	(6.8)	(0.9)	(4.2)	(4.2)	(-5.3)
	176.4	197.0	188.5	202.5	217.0	195.4
Coarse Cereals	(-5.6)	(11.7)	(-4.3)	(7.4)	(7.2)	(-9.9)
	100.2	118.2	104.9	108.1	104.8	109.0
Pulses	(-2.9)	(17.9)	(-11.2)	(3.05)	(-3.05)	(4.0)
	121.0	140.1	126.9	145.8	132.1	105.4
Non-Food	(-11.9)	(15.8)	(-9.4)	(14.9)	(-9.4)	(-20.2)
Grains	185.4	200.9	181.6	199.4	185.6	174.8
	(2.5)	(8.4)	(-9.6)	(9.8)	(-6.9)	(-5.8)

NOTE: Figures in brackets indicate growth rate over the previous year.

SOURCE: Same as in Table 1.

Table 8: ASI Manufacturing Registered Sector Employment

Year	No. of Workers	Annual Growth Rate	Total Persons Employed	Annual Growth Rate
1989-90	5517800	-	7096492	-
1990-91	5500907	-0.31	7126099	0.42
1991-92	5513561	0.23	7176184	0.70
1992-93	5816352	5.49	7624563	6.25
1993-94	5797102	-0.33	7612797	-0.15
1994-95	6033669	4.08	7890907	3.65
1995-96	6603790	9.45	8719814	10.50
1996-97	6526360	-1.17	8502192	-2.50
1997-98	6521534	-0.07	8462263	-0.47
1998-99	6242983	-4.27	8403551	-0.69

SOURCE: Chaudhuri (2002).

The trends in and the structure of employment-unemployment, and the real wage rate during the reform period need to be examined. The National Sample Survey Organisation (NSSO) provides employment-unemployment data according to activity status: Usual Status, Current Weekly Status, and Daily Status. The employment rate, i.e., the number of persons per one thousand population, has declined in each of the above categories in rural, urban and all-India categories during the 1990s. The share of self-employed and regular wage earners has declined and the casualisation of workers has increased during the 1990s (BHOLE and DASH, 2002).

(3) The contraction in industrial growth rate can also be attributable to the co-ordination failure among economic agents like households, corporates, banks, and the government. Co-ordination among economic agents depends on confidence and expectations about the future economic activity which, in turn, depends on a myriad of factors like industrial structure, past performance of the industrial production, nature of technical knowledge, and the policy environment. Writers like Keynes, Lavington, Pigou, and Taussig have laid great stress on expectations in explaining various phases of business cycle. In contrast to Arrow-Debrew's model of co-ordination success in a competitive environment, coordination failure is very much prevalent in the present uncertain milieu. Under such circumstances, the most desirable strategies become riskier and economic agents either fail or become powerless. At the same time they are concerned about their individual behaviour and are guided by the existing trade-off between risk and returns. As a result, a risk-dominated sub-optimal, instead of Pareto-optimal equilibrium is attained. The Pareto-preferred outcome is not obtained in an uncertain environment because the individual economic agents cannot internalise the externalities. (COOPER, 1999).

Let us see how the co-ordination failure has emerged among economic agents in India in the latter half of the 1990s. The households and the corporates have misdirected the flows of funds from the most productive sectors to Information Technology, Telecommunications, and Entertainment (ICE) stocks. The share of market capitalisation of a few ICE stocks in the total capital marketisation has increased from 8.6 percent in 1998 to around 50.0 percent in 2000. This implies that the money has been circulated among only a few ICE stocks in the secondary market at the cost of capital formation. On the other hand, the growth rate of bank deposits has declined from 19.0 per cent in 1997-98 to 17.9 and 13.4 per cent in 1998-99 and 1999-2000, respectively.

Freedom for portfolio diversification and price determination given to the financial intermediaries in the wake of financial liberalisation has given them wider choice in portfolio selection. In the pre-liberalisation era, banks were required to invest a certain proportion of their deposits in government securities under SLR obligations. The SLR has now been reduced from 35 to 25 percent to increase the liquidity of banks. But the investment-deposit ratio (which includes investment in both government and other approved securities) has remained, on an average, at 38 to 40 percent. On the other hand, the credit-deposit ratio has declined consistently throughout the period of economic contraction (from 58.0 percent in 1995-96 to 55.1 percent in 1996-97, 54.1 per cent in 1997-98, and 51.6 percent in 199899). The annual rate of growth of bank credit, on an average, has declined from 9.4 percent in 1970s and 5.8 percent in 1980s to 5.3 per cent in 1990s (See Fig. 4). This has happened due to both demand and supply factors. According to the industrialists, the high cost of credit has discouraged them from borrowing from the banks and financial institutions. At the same time, it is also true that banks and financial institutions have shown reluctance to lend to sectors such as agriculture, small-scale industries, rural and small borrowers. This is reflected in the change in the structure of bank credit that has occurred during 1990s. The share of agriculture in total bank credit declined from 13 per cent at the end of March 1994 to 9.3 per cent at the end of March 2000. Likewise the share of artisans, village industries and all other small-scale industries in the total bank credit has declined from 12 per cent in 1994 to 10.6 per cent in 2000. Put it differently, the share of all institutional categories constituting the 'household sector' (i.e., other than the public sector and private corporate sector) in the total bank credit has significantly declined from 54 per cent in March 1994 to 37 per cent in March 2000. Thus, a decline in the credit-deposit ratio and a change in the structure of credit might have contributed to the industrial recession.

Conclusions and Policy Suggestions

The recession appears to have been caused by low farm employment, low agricultural production, high food prices, income inequality, large non-farm unemployment, change in the composition of industrial production in favour of consumer durables and against basic and intermediate products, closing down of many small-scale and tiny industries, substitution of capital for labour, trade reforms in general and import liberalisation in particular, and co-ordination failure among the economic agents because of an increase in risk and uncertainty. It is unlikely that interest rate has been a significant causal factor behind industrial recession.

The potential output in the industrial sector can be produced in a sustainable manner if both the farm and non-farm employment opportunities increase to a much greater extent. By encouraging the off-farm activities like agro-based as well as small and medium industries which are highly labour-intensive, employment opportunities can be created for the rural poor to a much greater extent. The agricultural growth potential can be harnessed by undertaking public investment in irrigation, power, transportation, and agricultural research. Similarly, adequate institutional credit needs to be provided to small and marginal farmers. Some institutional reforms like the redistribution of land in favour of the landless and marginal and small farmers are needed as the existing agrarian structure is not conducive to the utilisation and development of productive potential in agriculture in a sustained way. The capital and intermediate goods industries need to be given a priority on account of their large linkage effects on income and employment. There is also an urgent need to improve the state of expectations and confidence (business optimism) by taking appropriate policy measures to reduce the risk and uncertainty so that the co-ordination failure among the economic agents can be minimised.

The interest rate reduction alone cannot revive the Indian economy. In fact, further interest rate cuts may have a number of adverse effects, viz., it may reduce the gross domestic capital formation by reducing savings and net capital inflows, enhance financial instability through portfolio readjustment in favour of speculative financial assets, increase inequity in the returns on various financial assets, have adverse impact on exchange rate management, reduce the purchasing power of medium, low, and fixed income earners, and initiate the reversal in price stability. It may be remembered that a continuous interest rate reduction in the past four years has had little favourable impact on the performance of the industrial sector in India.

References

ATHUKORALA, P. (1998), "Interest Rates, Savings and Investment: Evidence from India", Oxford Development Studies, Vol. 26, No. 2, pp. 153-169.

BHOLE, L. M. (1998), "Indirect Vs Direct Systems of Business Finance: Theory and Evidence", International Journal of Development Banking, Vol. 16, No. 2, pp. 13-27.

BHOLE, L. M. (1999), Financial Institutions and Markets, Third Edition, Tata McGraw-Hill Publishing Company Limited, New Delhi.

BHOLE, L. M. and DASH, P. (2002), "Employment and Unemployment in India During 1970s to 1990s", The Indian journal of Labour Economics (Communicated).

BRAHMANANDA, P. R. (2000), "Washington Consensus-II; Fall out of Interest Rates, Trade Policies", The Business Line, October 28.

CHAUDHURI, S. (2002), "Economic Reforms and Industrial Structure in India" Economic and Political Weekly, Jan 12, pp. 155-162.

COOPER R. W. (1999), Coordination Games Complementarities and Macroeconomics, Cambridge University Press, Cambridge.

DHANRAJ, P. P. (2001), "Impact of Trade Unions, Employment and Technology on Wages", Economic and Political Weekly, December 29, pp. 4846-4850.

EPW Research Foundation. (2001), "Structural Deterioration of Banking Development" Economic and Political Weekly, November 24, pp. 4330-4336.

FAN, S. et. al. (1999), "Linkages Between Government Spending, Growth. and Poverty in Rural India", Research Report No. 110, International Food Policy Research Institute, Washington D.C.

GANGOPADHYA, S. (1994), "Some Issues in Interlinked Agrarian Markets", in Kausik Basu (Eds), Agrarian Questions, Oxford University Press, New Delhi.

GOYAL, A. (1997), "Financial Reforms: Why Interest Rates Must Be Kept Low", International Journal of Development Banking, Vol.15, No. 2, July 1997, pp. 15-26.

GOVERNMENT OF INDIA, Economic Survey, Various Issues.

GULATI, A. and BATHLA, S. (2001), "Capital Formation in Indian Agriculture", Economic and Political Weekly, May 19, pp. 1697-1708.

GUPTA, K. L. (1986), "Financial Development and Economic Growth in India and South Korea", Journal of Economic Development, Vol. 11, No. 2, pp.41-62.
GUPTA, S. P. (1999), "Trickle Down Theory Revisited: The role of Employment and Poverty", V. B. Singh Memorial Lecture, 41st Annual Conference of the Society of Labour Economics, IGIDR, Mumbai, Nov. 18-20.
HABERLER, G. (1964), Prosperity and Depression, George Allen and Unwin Limited, London.
KEYNES, J. M. (1936), General Theory of Employment, Interest and Money, Macmillan, London.
KOYCK, L. M. and Maria J. Hooft-Welvaars (1966), "Economic Growth, Marginal Productivity of Capital, and the Rate of Interest", in F. H. HAHN and F. P. R. BRECHLING (eds.), The Theory of Interest Rates, Macmillan, New York.
LANYI, A. and R. SCACAGLU (1983), "Interest Rate Policies in Developing Countries", Occasional Papers, No-22, IMF, Washington D.C.
MATTHEWS R. C. O. (1960), "The Rate of Interest in Growth Models", Oxford Economic Papers, Volume 12, pp. 249-268.
Nambiar, R. G. et al. (1999), "Is Import Liberalisation Hurting Domestic Industry and Employment?" Economic and Political Weekly, February 13, pp. 417-424.
PATNAIK, P. (1994), "Disproportionality Crises and Cyclical Growth: A Theoretical Note", in Deepak Nayaar (Eds.) Industrial Growth and Stagnation, Oxford University Press, Bombay.
PATNAIK, P. (1999), "The Performance of the Indian Economy in the 1990s", Social Scientists, Vol.27, No. 5-6, May-June, pp. 3-16.
RADHAKRISHNA, R. (2002), "Agricultural Growth, Employment and Poverty", Economic and Political Weekly, Jan. 19, pp. 243-250.
RAJ, K. N. (1994), "Growth and Stagnation in Industrial Development", in Deepak Nayaar (Eds.) Industrial Growth and Stagnation, Oxford University Press, Bombay.
Rangarajan. R. (1988), "Agricultural Growth and Industrial Performance in India", Research Report 33, International Food Policy Research Institute. Washington D.C.
RESERVE BANK OF INDIA, Handbook of Statistics on Indian Economy, 2000, Mumbai, 2001.
___, Monthly Bulletin, Various Issues.
___, Private Corporate Business Sector in India Selected Financial Statistics from 1950-51 to 1997-98, Mumbai. 2000.
SEN, A. K. (1971), "Interest, Investment and Growth" in Amartya Sen (eds.), Growth Economics, Penguin Books, Harmondsworth.
SEN, Abhijit. (1996), "Economic Reforms, Employment and Poverty: Trends and Options", Economic and Political Weekly, Vol. 31, Nos. 35, 36, and 37, pp. 2459-2477.
SUNDARAM, K. (2001), "Employment-Unemployment Situation in the Nineties", Economic and Political Weekly, March 17, pp. 931-940.
VAIDYANATHAN, A. (1994), "Constraints on Growth and Policy Options" in Deepak Nayaar (Eds) Industrial Growth and Stagnation, Oxford University Press, Bombay.

[17]

Anti-Inflationary Policy in India[*]

Introduction

Price stability was mentioned as .one at the major objectives in the Fourth Five Year Plan in India. Various measures like increasing agricultural production, building up of sizeable buffer stacks, additional mobilization of internal resources etc. were to be taken to "stabilize food-grain prices and the price level in general". Actually, however, the price situation became the worst in the Fourth Five Year Plan, especially in its last two years. A rise in the price level at an unprecedented rate of 25 to 30 per cent per annum has induced many people to analyse inflationary process in India afresh. While there is a general agreement even among economists on the consequences of inflation, their approach to causes and cures of inflation has generally been absolutist. Moreover, one finds that there are certain factors which have been either completely ignored or have not been duly emphasized by them. The purpose of this article is to try to provide a wider perspective for understanding the phenomenon of inflation in India. This would also naturally involve reviewing certain measures which have been suggested so far for fighting the menace of inflation.

In the ultimate analysis, price stability can be attained by maintaining a balance between the supply of and demand for commodities and services. Increase in production, efficient distribution of available goods and services, and the maintenance of high level of home availability of goods and services through proper export-import policy, are necessary far the regulation of the supply side. Similarly the action on the demand side involves control over total National Expenditure. This in turn can be done through measures like rationalisation of public expenditure, financial discipline, fiscal and monetary policy and the blocking of liquid assets etc.

[*] Paper published in *Industrial India – Silver Jubilee Annual*, December 1975.

Production and Prices

There is no doubt that the best way to halt and reverse the march of inflation, and to maintain the price stability afterwards is to increase sufficiently the production of commodities and services. But it is necessary to guard against the danger of overemphasizing the usefulness of this measure, especially in the short run. There are obvious difficulties in raising the production of all commodities and services simultaneously at the required rate. The mere attempt to build up the whole range of productive capacities would create concurrent and competing claims on foreign exchange and disposable capital resources. Further, the increase in production per se would not ease inflationary pressures because the faulty export policy may hinder the corresponding increase in the level of internal availability of goods and services.

The Role of Exports

This brings us to one of the neglected but really important factors behind inflation in India viz., export promotion. As a result of blind belief in "foreign exchange barrier" in the growth process, and due to the vested interests in earning of foreign exchange, an extreme zeal has been shown for promoting exports by hook or crook. How perverse our policies have become is shown by the attempt to export commodities by the Khadi and Village Industries Commission. Too much emphasis an increasing exports has made it difficult to achieve other plan objectives like raising the standard of living of the masses, maintaining price stability, increasing employment opportunities etc. The average annual rate of growth of exports during the Fourth Five Year Plan has been so much above the combined annual average rate of growth of agricultural production and industrial production, that there is a prima facie case to believe that increasing exports have accentuated inflationary pressures in India. It is estimated that, on an average, exports during the Fourth Plan increased at a rate of more than 12 % per annum, while the targeted rate of growth during the same period was only 7 % per annum. During the two years (1972-73 and 1973-74) of very high price rise, exports increased by about 22 % per year. In the still recent past, the Commerce Minister is reported to have disclosed that India's exports during April-August of the financial year 1974-75 have increased by 48.5 %, thus providing a base for 35 % rise in exports during the full year. On the other hand, industrial production has increased at an average rate of 5.1 % per year during 1969-73. It is well known that the growth rate of industrial production has decelerated towards the end of the Fourth Five Year Plan. Similarly, during the same period the average rate of growth of agricultural production, including that of foodgrains, has hardly crossed 3 % level, notwithstanding much fanfare regarding the so called "green revolution". The implications for the general price level of such disproportionate increase in exports, when compared to the increase in production are obvious.

Though the correlation between the general price level and exports may be thought to be a little obscure, there is no doubt that in the case of food articles like certain varieties of rice, sugar, meat, meat products, fish, fruits like mangoes and bananas, spices, onions, and even in case of investment and other goods like cement, woolen products, etc., the price situation has taken the worst turn due to the callous increase in exports of these commodities. In 1973, Maharashtra State alone exported 1.5 lakh tonnes of sugar i.e. more than the total quantity exported by the country as a whale during 1972. These sugar exports have added to the scarcity of sugar and the consequent rise in its price on the home market. Similarly, the business in India has taken the advantage of buoyancy in the world market for meat and meat products. During October-November 1973, exports of these products jumped to Rs. 66 lakhs from Rs. 27 lakhs in the corresponding period in 1972. This export boom has been accompanied by the spurt in meat prices on the Indian market. Similarly, at present, of the total woolen hosiery production in India, hardly 10 % goes to meet internal consumption, including defence requirements. No wonder, prices of woolen goods have been increasing fast in India.

It may be objected here that while studying the impact of increase in exports on the level of prices, one has to take into account the likely increase in internal availability of goods through imports. The recent changes on the imports-front, however, suggest the unlikelihood of imports having eased the price pressures guaranteed by increasing exports. Firstly, the annual average rate of growth of imports during the Fourth Five Year Plan has been 6.7 % compared to 12% annual rate of growth of exports during the same period. The rate of growth of imports during 1972-73 was merely 0.1 %, while the exports increased by 22% during the same year. It is true that the increase in imports outpaced the increase in exports during 1973-75. But this has been mainly due to the jump in the import bill on account of crude imports. For example, crude and petroleum products and fertilizers only would account far Rs. 1900 crores (i.e. almost 50 %) in the total imports of Rs. 4000 crores in 1974-75. Secondly, the terms of trade are increasingly becoming unfair to developing countries like India. A study by the Indian Institute of Foreign Trade has shown that the terms of trade have proved to be more favourable for the developed countries. The quantity index moved to 266 and 440 far developing and developed countries respectively in 1970; while the index of value realised was 279 and 597 respectively during the same period. For India in particular, while the unit value of major exports have at best gone up by 50 %, there has been a steep rise in the import costs by 80 % to 400 %. As for individual commodities, apart from a very steep hike in the oil prices, prices of imported non-ferrous metals, newsprint, plastics, chemicals, synthetic fibres have risen by 100 % or more. Similar price increases have occurred for fertilizers, steel and alloy steels etc. This means that the country has been forking out more dollars without getting proportionate increase in supplies in return.

Therefore, one of the constituents of the anti-inflationary policy in India has to be the rationalization of our export policy. We have to get rid of the present "export illusion" or "export mania" and have to reconcile as far as possible to the earning of foreign exchange from the proved exportable surpluses only. It is imperative that export promotion through various incentives etc. does not create acute internal shortages, thereby accentuating the price pressures. This measure obviously requires a concurrent change in the desired direction in the development strategy, in the policy of importing commodities like oil, and contracting fresh debts for this purpose. For the immediate future, there would also be a need for rescheduling our past debts. In the absence of such a bold and unconventional approach, the increase in home production at feasible rates will hardly help to contain the price rise.

Public Distribution and All That

The next point in anti-inflationary action on the supply side is the creation of an appropriate environment for the free and fair distribution of the available commodities and services. There seems to be a general feeling that the public distribution system would take care of this distributional problem. It is true that if all the parts of the country, all the vulnerable sections of the community, and all the essential and near-essential commodities are brought within the fold of the public distribution system and if the efficient procurement of commodities to be distributed is ensured, the public distribution would help to hold the price line. It should however be obvious that all these are too big "ifs" to make the measure operationally feasible. The very size of India's land and population renders the effective implementation of this measure impracticable. In order to grasp the significance of this "size-barrier", one just needs to note that both in terms of population and the volume of foodgrains, the coverage of the present public distribution system is woefully inadequate. The statutory rationing covered only 16 million people by the end of 1972. Similarly, the quantity of foodgrains distributed annually has so far remained around 8 to 9 million tonnes. As against this, it has been estimated that at least more than 20 million tonnes need to be channelised through the public distribution system even for meeting the minimum requirements of only the low income groups. On the other side of the problem, it is to be noted that the Government has miserably failed to procure sufficient amount of foodgrains from the home production. It is well known that State after State has repeatedly slashed the targets for procurement of different foodgrains in the recent past. The reality is that we simply do not have the tradition of efficient, sincere, honest and devoted administration to implement efficiently the public distribution system on the "size" required. Given our social and political set-up, very little faith can be put in the public distribution system for solving the problem of inflation. Short of full and efficient coverage, the Government's marginal tinkering with the distributional channels creates an atmosphere and psychology which encourages black-marketing in commodities, and ends up with worsening the price situation. Therefore, it is necessary to free the market mechanism from the restrictive Government intervention as also from the grip of "mercantile and speculative capital".

Dismantling of Price Controls

Such minimization of restrictive Government intervention is necessary with regard to the price controls also. In India, prices of food articles, and other agricultural commodities like cotton, sugarcane, oil seeds etc., and the prices of "basic" commodities like coal, steel, cement, chemicals, petroleum etc. have been regulated, controlled or fixed by the Government. It is surprising that in the conventional analysis of inflation, it has been generally overlooked that inflation in India is not the result of free and unregulated movements of prices alone. It has become a serious problem in spite of, nay partly because of the policy of price controls adopted by the Government. The substantial part of inflation in India throughout the entire period, more so in the recent past, has been due to the "marking up" of prices either by the Authorities themselves, and/or by the private sector with the permission from or the connivance of the authorities. It is to be noted that quite often, the allowed "mark up" has been quite out .of proportion to the one dictated either by costs conditions or demand conditions. This is evident from the price fixation of commodities like sugar, steel, cement etc. The indices of sugar prices clearly show that all the controls in prices of sugarcane and sugar, and also the increase in production of these commodities, have failed to check the continuous rise in the price of sugar. More recently, the raising of prices of products like kerosene, cooking gas twice or thrice in a single year or so must have contributed to the inflationary pressure. The very significant increase in the procurement prices of almost all crops in 1973 (when the harvest position was relatively good) against the advice of the Agricultural Prices Commission, and the upward revision of issue prices of rice, wheat, vanaspati, controlled cloth, milk, bread etc. must have given a further fillip to the inflationary process. Again, the frequent hikes in freight rates and the prices of materials like coal and coke must have helped in the price spiral. As Prof. Gyanchand has stated, "while it is true that overexpansion of currency and credit has been the initiating factor in upward movement of prices, ... the mounting spiral of prices has also been generated and aggravated by our measures of control and regulation of prices.... The process at work in fixation of prices of many commodities has itself contributed significantly to the generation and intensification of inflationary trends" (The Menace of Inflation, p. 114 and 144). If the Government chooses every time to surrender to the compulsions of inflationary situation, what is the use of maintaining a facade of elaborate controls and regulations?

Investment and Prices

It is necessary here to examine the role of investment in the current inflationary situation in India. Some people feel that it is the so-called stagnation in investment which has led to the current economic crisis. As such, in order to pull the economy out of the present crisis, it is necessary to raise the rate of capital formation in the economy. Depending on their ideological leaning, they advocate that the investment needs to be pushed up mainly in the public sector or in the private sector. Any measure suggested to deal with money supply is branded as "erroneous" or "dangerous" by both of them. They feel that "an obsession with keeping down the rate of growth of money supply and curbing Government expenditure to contain the budgetary deficit will in the end have the effect of further reducing investment."

We feel that this analysis of the growth process in general and the inflationary process in particular springs mare from the ideological preferences, and is less in conformity with the economic realities in our country. It is just not true that those who ask to curb excessive growth in money supply treat inflation as an "essentially monetary phenomenon". Their perspective of the situation is much broader than that of their critics.

The "package programme" which has been suggested by same of them for fighting inflation bears testimony to this. They do however insist correctly that undue increase in money supply, especially arising from large and continuous deficits is one of the very important factors behind inflation, and as such it needs to be properly controlled. And if some people still feel that money supply is really a minor factor, and it is really the level of investment which is of far greater importance in this context, they can also be very well charged with treating inflation as an "essentially investment phenomenon". It must be said that though the importance of investment in the growth process cannot be denied, there are many more things to the investment process which are neglected or which are not cited by the investment enthusiasts. It is generally agreed that a mere increase in the rate of investment hardly ensures the "stable growth". Firstly, there is no reason to believe that high level of investment by itself ensures high level of output. Therefore, it is very much possible that the high rate of investment unaccompanied by the corresponding increase in output will accentuate inflationary pressures rather than ease them. As K.N. Raj mentions in his booklet, Planning and Prices in India, "most of the planned increases in the rate of investment have been based hitherto on the assumption that output in the economy will grow at a very rapid rate and that savings in the public sector will also increase rapidly. Neither has in reality materialised, and it would be a serious mistake to ignore these unpalatable facts" (p. 20). Further, the increase in the level of investment may not help to control inflation because the commodities far which there is an increase in demand immediately, may not be those whose production increases as a result of the said investment programme. In short, when we think of increasing investment, if we do not take care of the time lag between the investment expenditure and the supply of goods, pattern of investment, and the sources utilized for financing investment expenditure, we may be helping to generate cumulative inflationary pressures rather than to control them.

Experience from the Past

This has been shown by the experience in India in all the years since 1957 onwards. There is no evidence from this period to show that increasing Government expenditure and mounting budgetary deficits to finance it have created conditions favourable for "stable growth". Annual average of budgetary deficit increased from Rs. 189.6 crores in the Second-Five-Year Plan to Rs.750.00 crores in the Fourth-Five-Year Plan. It has been admitted by investment enthusiasts themselves that out of the high level of Government expenditure, developmental expenditure formed sixty per cent or more before 1965-66. Similarly, the share of capital formation expenditure in the total expenditure of the Central Government was around 47 % during the Third Five Year Plan. One would then like to ask as to why inflation was still a problem during the Second and Third Five Year Plans in spite of the high level of Government expenditure, and relatively high ratio of developmental and capital formation expenditure? Surely, it is not only during the last two years that we are encountering the problem of inflation. No doubt, inflation has reached serious proportions during the recent past partly as a result of unfortunate increase in the non-developmental expenditure. But it would be a serious mistake to forget that the present outburst of high prices is also the legacy of the investment policy followed since the beginning of the Second Five-Year Plan. Incidentally, there is also no evidence to show that the investment in the private sector has been or is being badly affected by the lack of monetary resources. In fact, the very people who complain against the reduction in investment, but who have preference for the public sector, point out that the rate of capital formation in the private sector has declined not due to the lack of finance but because the businessmen find it lucrative to produce less, and still earn higher profits by selling dear.

A Change in the Strategy Required

Therefore, without denying the importance of the higher level of investment and the financial discipline, we maintain that unless we change our development strategy and correspondingly alter the pattern of investment, we would not be in a position to solve any of our urgent problems, including inflation. It is high time we redefine our "basic" Sectors, and eschew over-ambitious and very costly programmes which impel us to resort to an unduly high degree of inflationary and external financing.

Perhaps this point would be better appreciated if we draw people's attention to the emerging trend in thinking in this context in the developed world itself. After the energy crisis, H.T. Odum, a Professor of environmental engineering, studied the relative casts of using alternative energy sources. By using complicated techniques involving computer models, he developed the concept of "net energy" and showed that the exploitation of the alternative sources of energy may not be an economic proposition after all. On the basis of his study, his conclusions with regard to inflation and growth are: Inflation is caused primarily by the pursuit of high economic growth using ever mare costly fuels. The future holds continued inflation and other economic distress unless man changes the pattern of his energy use. What is the way out? In Odum's words, in future, "the principal economic activity would be labour-intensive and land-intensive agriculture, with a minimum of machines and artificial fertilizers". The long term basis of this pastoral system would be "the use of the effective self-organizing solar converters: the forests, ecosystems, and the lower-energy agricultural patterns that have long been with us" (Newsweek, Jan. 20, 1975, p. 48).

Monetary and Fiscal Measures

Various monetary and fiscal measures adopted by the Government during the last one or two years for controlling inflation have to be assessed in the light of the analysis presented so far. The hike in the Bank rate from 6 % to 9 % in two stages, restricting dividend payments beyond a certain proportion for two years by the joint stock companies, compulsory deposit requirements imposed upon different classes in the society, all these have to be deemed as right steps for regulating the total National Expenditure. We feel that much of the criticism advanced against these measures is misplaced, and is inspired by the parochial interests. It may be true that compulsory deposits would involve some hardship for the wage earners and the salaried class. But as the saying goes, we cannot eat the cake and also have it. No section in the community should grudge some sacrifice for the time being in order to tackle the urgent problem of inflation. Similarly, there is no need to change the policy of dear money and restriction on dividend distribution. Some people have been asking for such a change because they believe that investment and production would be the "casualty" of such a policy. We have already discussed the severe limitations of this "investment-refrain" in controlling inflation. In addition, we have to make a distinction between the decline in fixed investment and decline in inventory investment. To the extent that the above mentioned measures bring about the decline in excess inventory investment, they would be helpful rather than detrimental for containing inflation. The creation of fixed assets at a moderate level is unlikely to suffer because there are no restrictions on the use of funds which the companies would collect as a result of restriction on dividend payments. The needs for genuine fixed capital formation have never suffered due to the lack of resources. Further, there is a substantial scope for increasing production from the existing unutilised productive capacity. The financial discipline is as much required in the private sector as in the public sector.

The real limitations of these measures lie in the fact that although they would help to arrest the further increase in prices, they are unable to reverse the present price-trends, and to stabilise them thereafter. They operate in a given milieu of priorities, and in the absence of radical changes in planning strategy, exports policy, interventionist policy etc., they will be unable by themselves to usher in an era of continued or uninterrupted stable growth. These measures are supplementary, albeit important, not basic to the problem of controlling inflation in India.

[18]

The Role of Interest Rate in Exchange Rate Management in India[*]

Introduction

As a part of the acceptance of the policy of Structural Adjustment Programme (SAP) and Stabilization Programme (SP), India has adopted a "Managed Floating" or "Managed Flexible" exchange rate system since March 1993. In the aftermath of the adoption of such a policy, the external value of the rupee has substantially depreciated in terms of major currencies, and the rupee exchange rate has now become far more volatile than in the past (See Table 1 and Figure 1). As it has been argued, "capital movements have rendered exchange rates significantly more volatile than before". (MOHAN, 2004, p. 95)

As it is natural, the exchange rate management has become one of the major tasks of the monetary authorities under the "managed float" system of exchange rate. The objective of exchange rate management or exchange rate policy has been to maintain the stability of exchange rate, or to target orderly movements in exchange rate changes, or to avoid excessive volatility or sharp changes in the behavior of exchange rate. The exchange rate policy in India does not allow the rupee to appreciate freely in line with market trends, or to depreciate significantly, nor does it target its "calculated volatility". In the words of the former Governor of the RBI, "the RBI does not have a fixed 'target' for the exchange rate which it tries to defend or pursue over time; the RBI is prepared to intervene in the market to dampen excessive volatility as and when necessary ..." (JALAN, 2003, pp. 16).

Table 1: Variability of Exchange Rates in India

Exchange Rates / Year	US Dollar	Pound Sterling	Deutsch Mark	Japanese Yen	NEER (Trade based weights)	NEER (Export based weights)
1992-1997	2.02	4.15	2.05	3.65	2.50	2.39
1997-2005	3.44	6.80	11.85	4.20	1.58	1.60
1991-2005	6.54	11.58	14.15	5.56	3.36	3.39

NOTE: Variability has been measured by standard deviation.

Figure 1:
Exchange Rate of the Indian Rupee Vis-à-vis Some Major Foreign Currencies

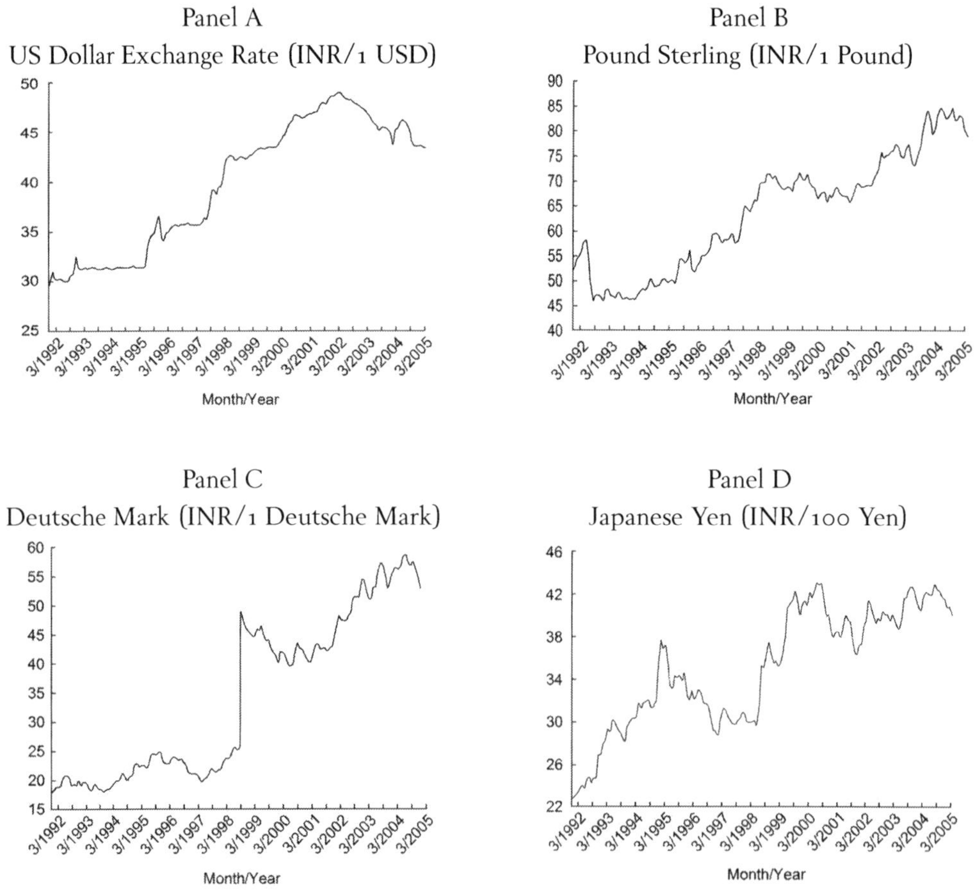

Source: Reserve Bank of India, Handbook of Statistics on the Indian Economy, 2004-05

Apart from direct market intervention in the form of buying and selling of foreign currencies by the RBI, the authorities have to use other techniques of monetary policy in their efforts to contain wide swings in the exchange rate. Given the RBI's preference for indirect or market-oriented techniques of monetary policy as a part of financial sector reforms, the use of interest rates as an instrument to achieve certain objectives, including the stability of exchange rate, has assumed great importance. The RBI has already been using interest rate policy to contain the volatility of the exchange rate in India. For example, as it has been stated, "the Reserve Bank responded promptly through measures like the bank rate, repo rate ... to curb destabilizing speculative activities during these episodes of volatility while allowing an orderly correction in the value of the rupee" (RBI, 2002-03, p.204). The use of interest rates policy effectively to dampen excessive volatility of the Indian exchange rate requires systematic knowledge about the precise nature of relationship between the interest rate and exchange rate, or the extent of impact of changes in the rate of interest on the behavior of the exchange rate.

The objective of this paper is, therefore, to try to find out empirically whether and how far the exchange rate is determined by the interest rate in India by using the advance econometric techniques. Apart from a study by Pattanaik and Mitra (2001), there is hardly any other major study on this theme in India. The present study therefore assumes greater relevance and importance. It improves on the study just mentioned by taking a much longer period for analysis, by improving the model specification, and by conducting the period analysis. The paper estimates the relationship between the rate of interest and exchange rate for 3 periods: (i) January 1991 to December 2005 (the entire reform period). (ii) January 1991 to March 1997 (high interest rates period). (iii) April 1997 to December 2005 (low or "Soft" interest rates period).

The paper is structured as follows: Section I presents a brief review of literature on interest rate and exchange rate relationship. The methodology and model used in this Paper is discussed in Section II. Section III discusses the empirical findings. The conclusions are presented in Section IV.

I. A Brief Review of Literature

A variety of patterns of interrelationships between the exchange rate and interest rate has been visualized in economic literature. For example, the uncovered interest parity theory implies that domestic interest rate is the sum of world interest rate and expected depreciation of home currency. In other words, the interest rate differential between domestic country and the rest of the world is equal to the expected change in the domestic exchange rate. Assuming the world interest rate (i^*) to be exogenously determined, the relationship between domestic interest rate and exchange rate depends on how expected exchange rate responds to changes in interest rates. For example, in Dornbusch's over shooting model (1976), expected exchange rate appreciates more than the spot rate that prevails before raising interest rates to equalize the returns on domestic assets and foreign assets. Therefore, there is a negative relationship between interest rate and exchange rate, i.e., a high interest rate policy is associated with exchange rate appreciation.

According to Sargent and Wallace (1981) a high interest rate policy may lead to a reduction in demand for money and increase in price level because an increase in interest rate implies an increase in government debt, which, in turn, would be financed by seinorage. As a result there will be exchange rate depreciation. Similarly, an increase in interest rate may adversely affect the future export performance which would reduce foreign exchange reserves and thereby, lead to depreciation of currency (Furman and Stiglitz, 1998). They have further argued that there are two important channels through which exchange rates are likely to be affected by the increase in interest rates namely, the risk of default and risk premium. The high interest rate policy may decrease the probability of repayment and increase the risk premium on domestic assets. Therefore, an increase in interest rate may lead to exchange rate depreciation via increase in capital outflow.

Another view in this context has been that in the atmosphere of political stability and perfect information, a temporary increase in interest rate can lead to exchange rate stability because it will induce investors to believe that there will be exchange rate appreciation (Drazen, 2001). According to Bensaid and Jeanne (1997), over a period of time, the cost of an interest rate defense of the currency may get reflected in financial fragility of banks and financial institutions, deterioration of the fiscal position of the government, reduction in the share of export in national income, all of which may lead to the depreciation of currency.

The nature of relationship between the rate of interest and exchange rate has been studied by some researchers abroad empirically also. For example, Goldfajn and Baig (1998) have studied the linkage between real interest rate and real exchange rate for the Asian countries during July 1997 to July 1998 by using Vector Autoregression (VAR) based on the impulse response function of the daily interest rates and exchange rates. They were not able to arrive at any strong conclusion regarding the relationship between interest rate and exchange rate. Goldfajn and Gupta (1999) have examined 80 currency crisis episodes between 1980 and 1998. By using fixed effect panel regression, they have concluded that an increase in interest rate is associated with an appreciation of nominal exchange rate. Kraay (1998) has examined whether an interest rate policy can be used to defend the speculative attack on currency by using monthly data for 75 developed and developing countries over the period 1960-99 and found that the high interest rates policy is not effective in defending the currencies against speculative attacks. Furman and Stiglitz (1998) have examined the effect of an increase in interest rate on the exchange rate for 9 developing countries during 1992-98. They found that the high interest rate was associated with a subsequent depreciation of nominal exchange rate but the effect was more pronounced in low inflation country than in high inflation country.

The spot exchange rate not only depends on monetary variables but also other factors (non-monetary variables). Some studies have attempted to control the influence of factors other than domestic monetary policy so that the effect of monetary policy on exchange rate can be isolated. Basurto and Ghosh (2000) have used this procedure for Indonesia, Republic of Korea, Thailand, and Mexico during 1990s. They found that the tight monetary policy was associated with an appreciation of exchange rate.

Gould and Kamin (2000) examined the interest rate and exchange rate relationship by studying the effect of interest rate, risk premium, and default probabilities on the exchange rates for Indonesia, South Korea, Malaysia, Philippines, Thailand, and Mexico. They found that the exchange rates in these countries were not influenced by interest rates. In India a study by Pattanaik and Mitra (2001) found that one standard deviation shock to the call rate leads to rupee appreciation by about 8 paise in the second month, but subsequently the exchange rate depreciates more than offsetting the initial impact of the hike in interest rates.

II. The Model and Methodology

Before we present the model, and methodology used by us for econometric estimation of the extent of influence of interest rate on the exchange rate, let us form a preliminary view of this relationship with the help of graphical analysis. Figures 2 and 3 present the relative behavior of interest rate and exchange rate, respectively by using monthly data for the 15 year period of 1991-2005. While Figures 2 and 3 present the relative behaviour of interest rates (call money rate and 91-day Treasury Bills rate, respectively) and rupee-dollar exchange rate, Figure 4 presents the said exchange rate and the interest rate differential (measured as 91-day Treasury Bills Rate in India minus 3-month Treasury Bills Rate in U.S.A).

Figure 2:
Nominal Exchange Rate and Call Money Rate in India, January 1991 to December 2005

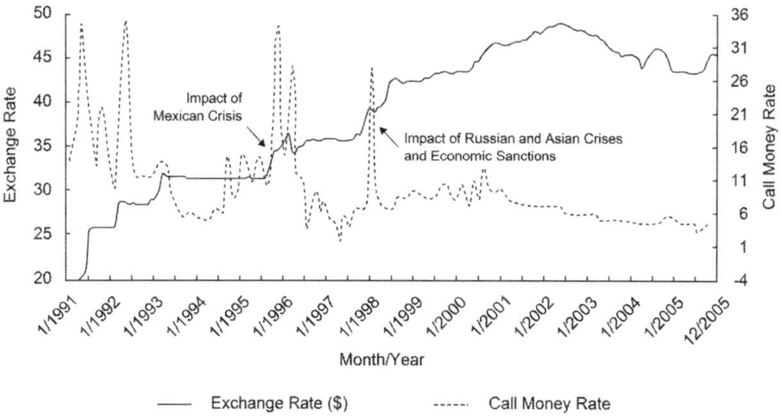

Source: Same as in Figure 1.

Figure 3:
Nominal Exchange Rate and 91-day Treasury Bills Rate in India, January 1991 to December 2005

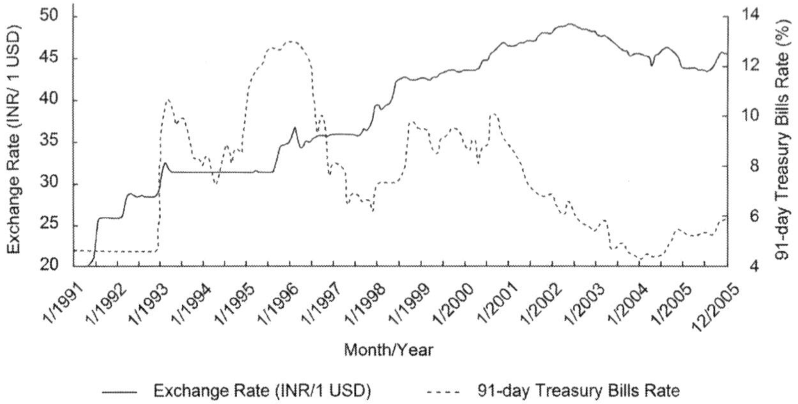

Source: Same as in Figure 1.

Figure 4:
Interest Rate Differential and Exchange Rate in India, January 1991 to December 2005

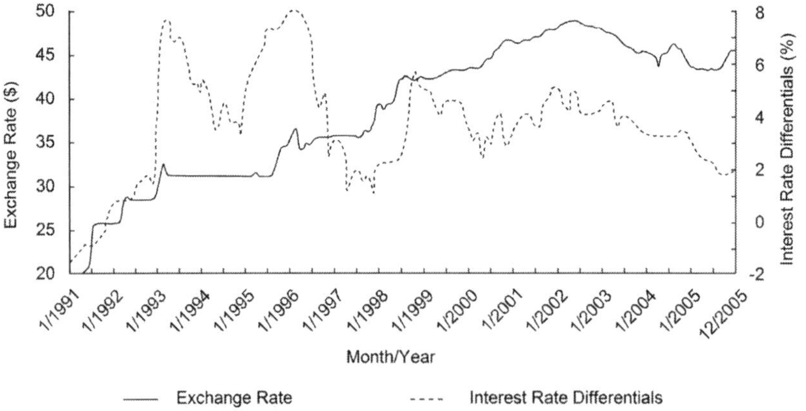

NOTE:
Interest rate differential is equal to 91-day Treasury bills rate in India minus 3-month Treasury bills rate in US.
SOURCE: Same as in Figure 1.

It can be observed from these figures that, on the whole, over the entire period under study, while the Indian exchange rate has increased (i.e. rupee has depreciated), the interest rates have first increased and then declined. The year-wise analysis would reveal that increases in interest rates have been associated with increases in exchange rate i.e. interest rate and exchange rate have been positively related in many periods such as January 1991 to February 1993, and so on. On the other hand, they have been negatively related in many other periods. It may be carefully noted here that the exchange rate is defined as so many units of rupee per unit of foreign currency, say the dollar. Therefore, an increase in exchange rate represents a depreciation of the rupee, and when accompanied by an increase in interest rate, the exchange rate and interest rate can be said to be positively related. In other words, if it is found that interest rate and exchange rate are positively related, it means that increases (decreases) in interest rates have led to depreciation (appreciation) of the rupee.

Let us now turn to the further analysis of the interest rate-exchange rate relationship with the help of co-integration technique.

On the basis of a study of theoretical and empirical literature on the relationship between interest rate and exchange, we hypothesize that the exchange rate is a function of interest rate, money supply, gross domestic product, inflation rate differential, and net intervention. The rationale behind this hypothesis is as follows:

The impact of changes in domestic interest rate on exchange rate could be either positive (i.e., depreciation) or negative (i.e. appreciation). Other things remaining constant, a higher domestic nominal interest rate reduces demand for real balances. Given the quantity of money, the reduced demand for real money balances leads to a rise in price level. A rise in domestic price level causes exchange rate to depreciate to maintain purchasing power parity. The same effect of interest rate may occur through another channel. An increase in domestic interest rates may imperil the ability of the domestic firms and banks to pay back the external debt. As a result, risk of default increases which causes capital outflows and the depreciation of the currency. According to another view, higher nominal interest rates strengthen the value of domestic currency because they induce capital inflows reflected in a rising capital account surplus that requires a domestic currency appreciation to assure external balance.

An increase in money supply at home, *ceteris paribus*, can be expected to lead to exchange rate depreciation because a higher money supply causes an increase in price level and in order to maintain purchasing power parity, the exchange rate has to depreciate.

The impact of changes in domestic output on exchange rate could be either positive (i.e., depreciation) or negative (i.e. appreciation). The domestic output may have negative effect on exchange rate via transaction demand for money. Other things remaining constant, an increase in domestic output increases the transaction demand for money, which, in turn, leads to a decline in price level, and, therefore, to an exchange rate appreciation to maintain purchasing power parity. According to another view, other things being equal, a rise in home income raises import spending and hence worsens the current account results in the depreciation of exchange rate to assure external balance.

The exchange rate and the inflation rate differential between the home country and the rest of the world are expected to be positively related. An increase in domestic inflation as compared to world inflation may increase the domestic demand for foreign commodities and reduce the foreign demand for domestic commodities, which, in turn, would lead to the depreciation of domestic currency.

What could be the effect of net intervention, i.e., the difference between the purchases and sales of foreign currency assets by the monetary authorities on the exchange rate? Intervention is of two types: sterilized and nonsterilized intervention. Nonsterilized intervention increases domestic money supply and depreciates the exchange rate. On the other hand, sterilized intervention can have either positive or negative impact on the exchange rate. According to former channel, a sterilized intervention may induce agents in the economy to anticipate that the monetary authorities are committed to lowering the value of domestic currency and may depreciate the exchange rate. According to latter channel, a sterilized intervention increases the amount of domestic bonds. Given the domestic interest rate, it attracts more capital inflow and appreciates the exchange rate.

Thus, the relationship between exchange rate and interest rate can be studied with the help of the following exchange rate function:

$$ER_t = C + \alpha_1 IRDIFF_t + \alpha_2 Ml + \alpha_3 GDP + \alpha_4 INFDIFF_t + \alpha_5 INTER_t + U_t \quad (1)$$

Where ER = Exchange Rate, IRDIFF = Interest Rate Differential between domestic and foreign countries, M1 = Money Supply, GDP = Gross Domestic Product, INFDIFF = Inflation Differential between domestic and foreign countries, INTER = Net intervention by the Central Bank, C = constant, and t is time period.

The regression coefficients in the above equation are expected to have the following signs:

$$\alpha_1 > \text{or} < 0,\ \alpha_2 > 0,\ \alpha_3 > \text{or} < 0,\ \alpha_4 > 0,\ \alpha_5 < 0$$

We have estimated this equation by using Co-integration, and Impulse Response Techniques (Enders, 1995; Hamilton, 1994). All variables are expressed in the level form. The required data for the purpose of estimation have been obtained from the various publications of Reserve Bank of India and the International Monetary Fund. The study uses monthly data from January 1991 to December 2005. The exchange rate is measured as the units of Indian rupee vis-a-vis US dollar.

Interest rate differential is measured as the difference between domestic 91-day Treasury Bill Rate and US 3-months Treasury Bill Rate. Money supply is measured as domestic narrow money supply. General Index of Industrial Production has been used as proxy for Gross Domestic Product because the monthly data for the latter variable are not available. Inflation differential is measured as the difference between domestic inflation rate (measured in terms of Wholesale Price Index (1980-81 = 100)), and US inflation rate (measured in terms of Producer Price Index (1980-81 = 100). Net intervention is represented by the monthly net purchases of foreign currency by the RBI in terms millions of US dollars.

The assumptions of the classical linear regression model require that both the dependent and independent variables are stationary. In the presence of nonstationary variables, there might be what Granger and Newbold (1974) call a spurious regression. A spurious regression has a high R^2, significant t-statistics, but the results are without any economic meaning. Therefore, the first econometric step we have taken is to test the null hypothesis that the series are random walk or non-stationary by using Augmented Dickey-Fuller (1979, 1981) tests. To test if a series contains a unit root, the following three equations are considered.

$$\Delta Y_t = \alpha + \beta t + \gamma Y_{t-1} + \alpha \sum_{i=1}^{m} \Delta Y_{t-1} + \varepsilon_t \tag{2}$$

$$\Delta Y_t = \alpha + \gamma Y_{t-1} + \alpha \sum_{i=1}^{m} \Delta Y_{t-1} + \varepsilon_t \tag{3}$$

$$\Delta Y_t = \gamma Y_{t-1} + \alpha \sum_{i=1}^{m} \Delta Y_{t-1} + \varepsilon_t \tag{4}$$

The first equation includes both an intercept and a deterministic trend. The second equation excludes the deterministic trend, whereas the third equation excludes both the drift and the deterministic terms. In each case the null hypothesis is that $\gamma = 0$, that is, there is a unit root. Comparing the resulting t-statistics with the appropriated value reported in the Dickey-Fuller tables allows to determine whether to accept or reject the null hypothesis $\gamma = 0$. The critical values are denoted by τ_τ τ_μ τ for equations 1, 2, and 3, respectively.

Since the true data generating process is not known, we have followed a sequential procedure suggested by Doldado, Jenkinson, and Sosvila-Rivero (1990) to test for a unit root. Such a procedure is important because if we inappropriately omit the intercept or time trend, the power of the test can go to zero. On the other hand, extra regressors increase the absolute value of the critical values so that we may fail to reject the null of a unit root.

If the variables were found to be non-stationary, we have tested the possibility of one or more co-integrating relationships using the Johansen and Juselius (1990, 1992) methodology in the form of two test statistics namely, the trace test and the maximal eigen value during the above-mentioned three time periods. The impact of stationary exogenous variables on exchange rate has been studied with the help of error correction model (ECM) (Sargan, 1984; Engle and Granger, 1987). The interrelationship between exchange rate and interest rate differential has been captured by the Impulse Response Function Analysis which traces the response of exchange rate to one standard deviation change in interest rate. When the off-diagonal elements of the correlation coefficient matrix of the error terms are found to be greater than 0.2, Cholesky Decomposition has been followed in the ordering of the variables to make the errors contemporaneously uncorrelated (Sims, 1980; Enders, 1995).

III. Empirical Results

Table 2 presents the ADF unit root test results for all variables. The variables like money supply, inflation rate differential, industrial production, exchange rate, interest rate differential are found to be non-stationary, whereas the net intervention is found to be stationary in level form.

Table 2: Unit Root Test Statistic

Variables	Null: γ = 0 in equation 3 τ_τ	Null : γ = 0, β = 0, in equation 3 ϕ_3	Null: γ = 0 in equation 2 τ_μ	Null: γ = 0, α= 0, In equation 2 ϕ_1	Null: γ = 0 in equation 1 τ	Results*
MI (4)	1.84	13.30				Yes**
INFDIFF (2)	-2.65	3.72	-2.20	2.45	-1.67	Yes**
Gnp (4)	-2.61	4.56	1.10	8.84		Yes**
ER (2)	2.07	5.28	-3.11	8.42		Yes*
INTDIFF (1)	2.76	4.67	-2.46	4.16	-1.05	Yes**
INTER (0)	-7.90					No*
CV at 5%	-3.43	6.34	-2.88	4.63	-1.95	
CV at 1%	-3.99	8.27	-3.46	6.52	-2.48	

Note:
(1) CV denotes critical values.
(2) * and ** indicate significance at 1 % and 5 % level respectively.
(3) Numbers in brackets indicate lag length.

The optimal lag length or order of the VAR was found to be 2 by the Akaike Information Criterion (AIC), Schwarz Bayesian Criterion (SBC) for the entire reform period and for the high interest rates period but the optimal lag length was found to be one for the low interest rates period. It has been found that the data shows the existence of linear trend. This implies that the underlying VAR model does not contain deterministic trend but contains unrestricted intercept. The maximal eigen value and the trace statistics strongly rejected the null hypothesis that there is no co-integrating relationship between the variables (i.e., r = 0), and they showed that there is one co-integrating relationship between the variables (i.e., r = 1) for the entire reform period, high interest rates period, and low interest rates period (See Tables 3 and 4). The model selection criteria like AIC and SBC also suggested the existence of one cointegrating relationship between the variables (results have not been reported here). The normalized co-integrating vectors for the exchange rate have been presented in Table 5.

As expected, the coefficient of money supply has positive sign in both high interest rate and low interest rate periods but has negative sign in the entire reform period. Similarly, in-

Table 3: Cointegration LR Test Based on Maximal Eigen value of the Stochastic Matrix for Nominal Interest Rates

Ho:	H1:	Statistics	Critical values		Results
			95 %	90 %	
Exchange Rate = f (Money Supply, Inflation Rate Differential, GIIP, Interest Rate Differential) Order of VAR = 2 Time Period: January 1991 to December 2005					
r = 0	r = 1	44.61	33.64	31.02	Reject Null Hypothesis
r ≤ 1	r = 2	22.06	27.42	24.99	Accept Null Hypothesis
r ≤ 2	r = 3	17.09	21.12	19.02	Accept Null Hypothesis
r ≤ 3	r = 4	8.77	14.88	12.98	Accept Null Hypothesis
r ≤ 4	r = 5	1.38	8.07	6.50	Accept Null Hypothesis
Exchange Rate = f (Money Supply, Inflation Rate Differential, GIIP, Interest Rate Differential) Order of V AR = 2 Time Period: January 1991 to March 1997					
r = 0	r = 1	39.90	33.64	31.02	Reject Null Hypothesis
r ≤ 1	r = 2	17.59	27.42	24.99	Accept Null Hypothesis
r ≤ 2	r = 3	6.05	21.12	19.02	Accept Null Hypothesis
r ≤ 3	r = 4	3.90	14.88	12.98	Accept Null Hypothesis
r ≤ 4	r = 5	1.08	8.07	6.50	Accept Null Hypothesis
Exchange Rate = f (Money Supply, Inflation Rate Differential, GIIP, Interest Rate Differential, Net Intervention) Order of VAR = 1 Time Period: April 1997 to December 2005					
r = 0	r = 1	62.26	33.64	31.02	Reject Null Hypothesis
r ≤ 1	r = 2	25.54	27.42	24.99	Accept Null Hypothesis
r ≤ 2	r = 3	6.65	21.12	19.02	Accept Null Hypothesis
r ≤ 3	r = 4	5.72	14.88	12.98	Accept Null Hypothesis
r ≤ 4	r = 5	0.89	8.07	6.50	Accept Null Hypothesis

Note: r is the order of cointegration.

flation rate differential has influenced positively exchange rate in the whole period and low interest rate period. This implies that the pass-through effect of inflation rate differential to exchange rate. The coefficient of industrial production has positive sign in all equations except the low interest rate period. Since the coefficient of interest rate differential has positive sign in the whole period and in the low interest rate period, it implies that an increase in interest rate differential has caused depreciation of exchange rate in India in the just mentioned time periods. But an increase in interest rate differential resulted in appreciation of exchange rate in the high interest rate period, as the coefficient of interest rate differential has negative sign.

The same result has also been obtained by some other studies (PATTNAIK and MITRA, 2001). The coefficient of stationary exogenous variable like net intervention has been obtained from the error correction model. The effect of net market intervention on exchange rate was found to be negative.

The dynamic interaction between the variables can be captured by the Impulse Response Function Analysis which traces the response of a given variable to one standard deviation change in any other variable. Here, the impulse responses of exchange rate to interest rate differential have been studied in three time periods (See Figures 5, panel a, b, and c). In order to draw useful structural information, some sort of restrictions that are consistent with economic theory should be imposed on the error correction model. Following Cholesky type of identifying restrictions, the order of the variables chosen here is money supply, inflation rate differential, industrial production, exchange rate, and interest rate differential. If money supply increases, the aggregate demand increases, which, in turn, increases the price level and industrial production, which again, causes depreciation of exchange rate and the RBI increases interest rate to stabilise exchange rate.

Table 4: Cointegration LR Test Based on Trace Statistics of the Stochastic Matrix for Nominal Interest Rates

Ho:	H1:	Statistics	Critical values		Results
			95 %	90 %	
Exchange Rate = f (Ml, Inflation Differential, GIIP, Interest Rate Differential) Order of VAR = 2 Time Period: January 1991 to December 2005					
$r = 0$	$r \geq 1$	93.93	70.49	66.23	Reject Null Hypothesis
$r \leq 1$	$r \geq 2$	49.31	48.88	45.70	Reject Null Hypothesis
$r \leq 2$	$r \geq 3$	27.25	31.54	28.78	Accept Null Hypothesis
$r \leq 3$	$r \geq 4$	10.15	17.86	15.75	Accept Null Hypothesis
$r \leq 4$	$r = 5$	1.38	8.07	6.50	Accept Null Hypothesis
Exchange Rate = f (Ml, Inflation Differential, GIIP, Interest Rate Differential) Order of V AR = 2 Time Period: January 1991 to March 1997					
$r = 0$	$r \geq 1$	68.53	70.49	66.23	Reject Null Hypothesis
$r \leq 1$	$r \geq 2$	28.63	48.88	45.70	Accept Null Hypothesis
$r \leq 2$	$r \geq 3$	11.03	31.54	28.78	Accept Null Hypothesis
$r \leq 3$	$r \geq 4$	4.98	17.86	15.75	Accept Null Hypothesis
$r \leq 4$	$r = 5$	1.08	8.07	6.50	Accept Null Hypothesis
Exchange Rate = f (M1, Inflation Differential, GIIP, Interest Rate Differential, Net Intervention) Order of VAR = 1 Time Period: April 1997 to December 2005					

$r = 0$	$r \geq 1$	101.05	70.49	66.23	Reject Null Hypothesis
$r \leq 1$	$r \geq 2$	38.78	48.88	45.70	Accept Null Hypothesis
$r \leq 2$	$r \geq 3$	13.24	31.54	28.78	Accept Null Hypothesis
$r \leq 3$	$r \geq 4$	6.58	17.86	15.75	Accept Null Hypothesis
$r \leq 4$	$r = 5$	0.85	8.07	6.50	Accept Null Hypothesis

NOTE: Same as in Table 4.6.

Table 5: Co-integrating Coefficients of Exchange Rate

Variables	January 1991 to December 2005	January 1991 to March 1997	April 1997 to December 2005
Money Supply (Ml)	- 0.00017 (0.00003)	0.00025 (0.00006)	0.00075 (0.00072)
Inflation Rate Differential	0.9185 (0.3435)	- 0.7577 (0.2603)	1.2915 (1.4553)
GIIP	1.0871 (0.1827)	- 0.8454 (0.2701)	4.3951 (4.1307)
Interest Rate Differential	1.0076 (0.4571)	-0.0421 (0.2816)	1.5676 (2.0461)
Net Intervention**	-	-	- 0.00014 (0.00002)

NOTE:
(a) Figures in brackets are standard errors.
(b) **Coefficients have been obtained from the error correction model.

It is found that one standard deviation change (around 0.60 percentage increase) in interest rate differential caused exchange rate depreciation by 3.5 paise in the whole time period (Figure 5, panel a). On the other hand, a 0.74 percentage increase in interest rate differential resulted in exchange rate appreciation by 1.5 paise in the fourth month and later on depreciated a little but the overall impact was net appreciation by 0.87 paise (Figure 5, panel b). But the exchange was found to be depreciated by 0.041 paise due to change (around 0.43 percentage increase) in interest rate differential in the low interest rate differential (Figure 5, panel c).

Figure 5: Impulse Response of Exchange Rate due to One Standard Deviation Change in Interest Rate Differential

Panel a:
Response of Exchange Rate

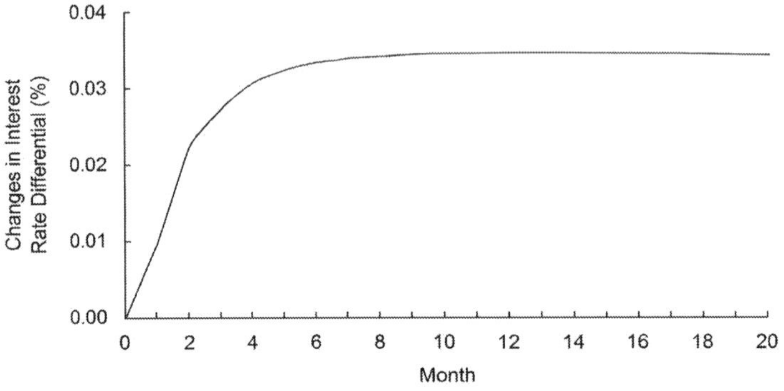

Panel b:
Response of Exchange Rate

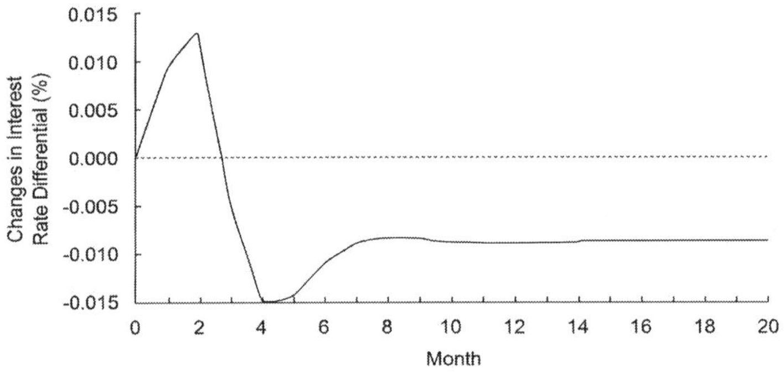

Panel c:
Response of Exchange Rate

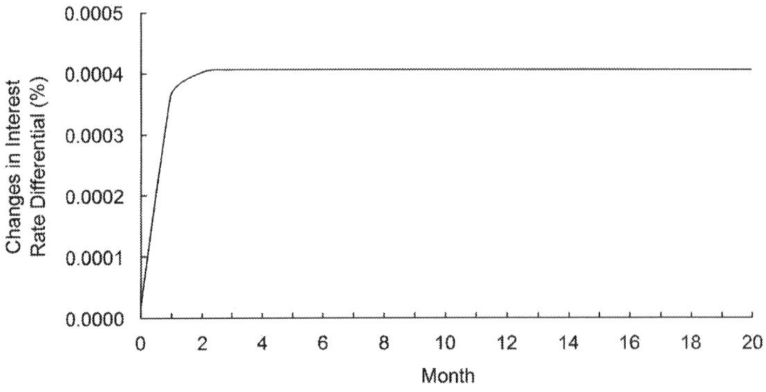

IV. Summary and Conclusions

The monetary authorities in India have taken several steps to liberalize capital account transactions and to make exchange rate more flexible to maximize gains from foreign capital. But free capital mobility very often causes many adverse economic consequences like sharp exchange rate depreciation, or sudden fall in foreign exchange reserve, or both. The external value of the rupee has become volatile as the Indian economy has been opened up progressively. Apart from direct intervention, the Reserve Bank of India has been using interest rate policy to reduce volatility of the Indian rupee.

In this context, the present Paper has attempted to find out empirically the role of interest rate in determining the exchange rate in India by using cointegration technique based on vector autoregression model during January 1991 to December 2005, January 1991 to March 1997 (high interest rate phase), and April 1997 to December 2005 (low interest rate phase). The results show that the industrial production, money supply, interest rate differential, and inflation rate were positively related with the exchange rate during 1991-2005 and 1997-2005, while they were negatively related with the exchange rate during 1991-1997. The impulse response technique shows that the over all exchange rate appreciation was 0.87 paise due to one standard deviation change (around 0.74 percentage increase) in interest rate differential during 1991-97, whereas the exchange rate was found have depreciated by 0.041 paise due to one standard deviation change (around 0.43 percentage increase) in interest rate differential during 1997-2005. These results imply that the impact of interest rate changes on the exchange rate is not uniform or consistent in all the periods, and, therefore, there are limitations on the effective use of interest rate as a monetary policy instrument for stabilizing the external value of rupee. It also means that the further liberalization of the capital account transactions in India may not be advisable at least in the near future.

References

Basurto, G. and Ghosh, A. (2000), „The Interest Rate-Exchange Rate Nexus in Currency Crises", IMF Staff Papers, Vol. 47, Special Issue, pp. 99-120.

Bensaid, B. and Jeanne O. (1997), „The Instability of Fixed Exchange Rate Systems When Raising the Nominal Interest Rate is Costly" European Economic Review, Vol. 41, No. 8, pp. 1461-1478.

Branson, W. H. (1976), „Asset Markets and Relative Prices in Exchange Rate Determination" Institute for International Economic Studies, Seminar Paper No. 66, Stockholm.

Dickey, D. A. and Fuller, W. A. (1979), „Distribution of the Estimators for Autoregressive Time Series with a Unit Root", Journal of the American Statistical Association, No. 74, pp. 427-31.

DOLDADO, J., JENKINSON, T, and SOSVILA-RIVERO, S, (1990) „Co-integration and Unit Roots", Journal of Economic Surveys, 4, pp. 249-73.

DORNBUSCH, R. (1976), „Expectations and Exchange Rate Dynamics", Journal of Political Economy, 84 (6), December, pp. 1161-76.

DRAZEN, A. (2001), „Interest Rate Defense against Speculative Attack As a Signal: A Primer" University of Maryland, Department of Economics, College Park, Md.

ENDERS, W. (1995), „Applied Econometric Time Series", John Wiley & Sons, Inc., New York.

ENGLE, R. F. and GRANGER, C. W. J. (1987) „Co-integration and Error Correction: Representation, Estimation and Testing," Econometrica, Vol. 55, pp. 251-276.

FLEMING, J. M. (1962), „Domestic Financial Policies under Fixed and Floating Exchange Rate Systems", IMF Staff Papers, Vol. 9, pp. 369-379.

FRANKEL, J. A. (1979), „On the Mark: A Theory of Floating Exchange Rates Based on Real Interest Differentials" American Economic Review, No. 69, pp. 6101-22.

FURMAN, J. and STIGLITZ J. E. (1998), „Economic Crises: Evidence and Insights From East Asia" Brooking Papers on Economic Activity, No. 2, Brooking Institution, Washington D.C.

GOLDFAJN, I. and BAIG, T. (1998), „Monetary Policy in the Aftermath of Currency Crises: The Case of Asia", International Monetary Fund Working Paper, WP/98/170, Washington D. C.

GOLDFAJN, I. and GUPTA, P. (1999), „Does Monetary Policy Stabilize the Exchange Rate Following a Currency Crisis?" International Monetary Fund Working Paper, WP/99/42, Washington D. C.

,GOLDSTEIN, M. (1998), „The Asian Financial Crises: Causes, Cures, and Systemic Implications", Institute for International Economics, Washington D. C.

GOODHART, C.A.E. (1989), Money, Information, and Uncertainty, Second Edition, The Macmillan Press Ltd., London.

GOULD, D. M. and KAMIN, S. B. (2000), „The Impact of Monetary Policy on Exchange Rates during Financial Crisis", International Finance Discussion Paper 669, Board of Governers of the Federal Reserve System, Washington D.C.

GRANGER, C. W. J. (1969), „Investing Causal Relations by Econometric Models and Cross-Spectral Methods" Econometrica, Vol. 37, pp.424-295.

GRANGER, C. W. J. (1986), „Developments in the Study of Co-integrated Economic Variables", Oxford Bulletin of Economics and Statistics, Vol.48, pp.226-46.

HAMILTON, J. (1994), Time Series Analysis, Princeton University Press, Princeton.

JALAN, B. (1993), „Exchange Rate Management: An Emerging Consensus?" presented at the 14th National Assembly of Forex Association of India, August 14, Mumbai.

JOHANSEN, S. and JUSELIUS, K. (1992), „Testing Structural Hypothesis in A Multivariate Co-integration Analysis of PPP and the UIP for UK", Journal of Econometrics, 53, pp. 211-44.

___ (1990), „Maximum Likelihood Estimation and Inference on Co-integration with Applications to the Demand for Money", Oxford Bulletin of Economics and Statistics, 52, pp. 169-209.

KEMINSKY, G. and SCHUMULKLER, S. (1998), „The Relationship Between Interest Rates and Exchange Rates in Six Asian Countries" World Bank, Development Economics and Office of the Chief Economist, Washington, D.C.

KOURI, P. J. K. (1976), „The Exchange Rate and the Balance of Payments in the Short-run and in the Long-run: A Monetary Approach", Scandinavian Journal of Economics, Vol. 78, pp. 280-304.

KRAAY, A. (1998), „Do High Interest Rates Defend Currencies against Speculative Attacks?", Policy Research Working Paper 2267, World Bank, Development Research Group, Macroeconomics and Growth, Washington D.C.

MUNDELL, R. A. (1963), „Capital Mobility and Stabilization Policy under Fixed and Flexible Exchange Rates", Canadian Journal of Economics and Political Sciences, Vol. 29, pp. 475-485.

MOHAN, R. (2004), „Challenges to Monetary Policy in a Globalizing Context", RBI Bulletin, January, pp. 81-102.

PATTNAIK, S. and MITRA, A. K. (2001), „Interest Rate Defence of Exchange Rate: Tale of the Indian Rupee", Economic and Political Weekly, November 24, pp. 4418-4427.

RESERVE BANK OF INDIA (2002-03), Report on Currency and Finance.

___ (2004-05), Handbook of Statistics on Indian Economy, 2002, Mumbai.

___ Monthly Bulletin, Various Issues.

SARGAN, J. D. (1984) „Wages and Prices in the United Kingdom: A Study of Econometric Methodology" in K. F. WALLIS and D. F. HENDRY (Eds.) „Quantitative Economics and Econometric Analysis", Basil Blackwell, Oxford.

SARGENT, T. J. and WALLACE, N. (1981), „Some Unpleasant Monetarist Arithmetic", Federal Reserve Bank of Minneapolis Quarterly Review, No. 5, Fall, pp 1-17.

[19]

Responsiveness of Investment and Other Expenditures to Changes in Techniques of Monetary Control in India, 1950-51 to 1977-78[*]

Introduction

After achieving political independence, India launched a planned, programme of economic development with accelerated rate of increase in national income, social justice, reduction in unemployment, and price stability as its principal objectives. In reality, we have suffered from ratcheting upwards of inflation and unemployment accompanied by stagnant output. Why has this happened?

In order to solve this riddle and to ensure that the economy performs creditably in future, it is necessary, among other things, to know much more than we do about how different branches of economic policy work and what kind of inter-relationship exists between them. Therefore, we undertook an in-depth theoretical and empirical analysis of the various aspects, including its relationship with fiscal policy, of the working of monetary policy in India during the period 1951 to 1978.

Monetary policy influences economic activity by operating on different margins, *viz.*, marginal efficiency of capital, time preference, and liquidity preference. Accordingly, after discussing the indicators, theoretical basis, and the evolution of techniques of monetary control, we have analysed the impact of monetary policy on

(i) investment of different types, and in different sectors and industries,
(ii) private consumption expenditure,
(iii) government consumption expenditure,
(iv) government borrowing,

[*] Paper published in *ICSSR Research Abstracts Quarterly*, July-December, 1986.

(v) demand for money,
(vi) money supply, and
(vii) trade credit.

In addition, the implications of financial innovation which have occurred in the Indian financial system over the past thirty years for the working of monetary policy have also been discussed. The empirical evidence is generated with the help of econometric, trend, ratio, and graphical analyses. The important findings and policy suggestions are summarized below.

Theory And Effectiveness of Monetary Policy In India

The principal objectives of monetary policy have been faster and just economic growth, price stability, and reduction in unemployment. Its theoretical basis has rightly been eclectic. A number of indicators such as money supply (in its narrow as well as broad sense), volume and seasonal return flow of bank credit, interest rates, volume of RBI refinance, level of inventories, etc., were employed in its formulation and implementation. It is creditable that the tendency towards singularization of the target/indicator of policy was avoided in view of the complex nature of interrelationships in the monetary system.

The RBI possesses all the major traditional techniques of monetary control and it is vested with enough of legal authority for their effective use. It has experimented and innovated considerably in respect of the form and application of these techniques. However, they have not been used sufficiently, actively, and boldly for the purpose of economic stabilization. The number and range of variations in the important tools such as the Bank rate and Cash Reserve Ratio, (CRR) have been very small indeed. The RBI has shown reluctance to change the Bank rate in a straightforward manner since 1960 itself. With the passage of time, this technique has suffered more and more from atrophy. It is remarkable that techniques of monetary control (not only OMO but also others) were increasingly used 'as techniques of distribution' of financial resources –distribution between the public and private sectors, and between different subsectors of the latter. This resulted in the removal of a larger and larger part of flows of finance from the scope of regulatory mechanism with serious consequences for its effectiveness. Subject to this, one can discern a shift from the 'cost effect' to 'availability effect' as a channel of monetary policy. This was achieved through increasing reliance on direct rationing of and discretionary control over the volume of both bank credit and RBI refinance.

Monetary Policy And Investment

The objectives of authorities' investment policy were, to minimize investment in inventories, to discourage inessential fixed investment, and to increase its productivity. The achievement or otherwise of these objectives is reflected in relative growth rates of investment, output, employment, and capacity utilization. Now, there is no evidence to show that the growth of investment was repressed by monetary restraint. The annual average rates of fixed and inventory capital formation in both nominal and real terms increased quite substantially in each successive quinquennium. The rate of real fixed capital formation was higher than its nominal rate till about the middle of 1970s, which shows that the alleged deterioration in investment activity probably occurred only in the latter half of 1970s. On the other hand, all other indicators – the high and increasing capital – output ratio, the high level of and widespread idle capacity, the higher rate of increase in fixed investment than that of employment, etc. – point towards the lack of success of monetary policy in attaining its proximate objectives.

Econometric analysis showed that the acceleration principle explained the behaviour of fixed but not inventory investment. Tax incentives emerged as a major determinant of fixed investment. Similarly, price expectations had a significant influence on inventory decisions. [1] Monetary policy variables such as the rate of interest and a measure of availability of credit were not totally irrelevant in investment decisions. While none of the types of affixed investment in any of the sectors was amenable to their influence, they did have a significant impact on inventory investment. Its elasticity with respect to them was about -0.7 and 0.8 respectively. However, many times, the extent of explained variance in it on account of only these variables was not high. Generally, credit availability was shown to be a more potent investment factor than the rate of interest [2], but monetary authorities should not renounce the use of either of them. If the rate of interest is to play an effective role, it must rise faster than prices and wage cost. Investment functions did not appear to be stable. [3]

The efforts of the RBI to restrict bank credit and accumulation of inventories as per the recommendations of Dehejia and Tandon Committees did not meet with success. The actual levels of inventories of medium and large corporate business units were often higher than the prescribed norms, and yet, the supply of bank credit to them was "greater than what it was desired to be. Similarly, bank credit against sensitive commodities covered under selective credit controls often increased substantially in spite of their stagnant or decreasing production, resulting in flaring up of their prices. Further, the availability of credit enjoyed by industries which deal in these commodities was higher than that of other industries and the average for all industries.

Monetary Policy And Consumption Expenditure

Income emerged as the most important determinant of private consumption expenditure, and the marginal propensity to consume was around 0.8 for private total consumption and 0.2 for non-essential consumption. While the rate of interest had significant influence on the former with the elasticity coefficient of -0.16, it was positively (but not always significantly) related to the latter, which shows that in this case the income effect of interest rate over-swamped its cost effect. Inflationary expectations also had a significant influence on consumption decision but its elasticity coefficient was quite small (0.03). Surprisingly, the demographic variable had a negative relationship with the consumption expenditure, which may reflect an adverse effect of population growth on the development process, and consequently, on the standard of living. Given the fact that the private consumption expenditure accounts for about 70 to

80 per cent of the aggregate expenditure in the Indian economy, there appears to be a good potential for monetary policy to regulate the level of aggregate effective demand.

Monetary Policy And Public Finance

A study of the Central and State governments' finances showed that the proportion of tax revenue to total revenue has not increased materially with the tightness of monetary policy. The share of non-development expenditure in the total expenditure has been high and it has increased over the period of time. The lack of financial discipline is further evident from an increase in the total deficit financing, the existence of deficits on States' revenue account, and a decline in the revenue account surplus of the Centre. The rate of interest was negatively but weakly related to the government consumption expenditure, but it explained variations in Government market borrowings reasonably well. In short, the behaviour of fiscal sector so far has not been conducive to the effectiveness of monetary policy, but there is a potential for reducing the conflict between them provided certain appropriate measures are adopted.

Monetary Policy And Demand For Money

Sectoral studies of demand for money showed that banks' cash holdings were substantially influenced by the rate of interest and CRR. An increase in interest rate did not lead to any consistent decline in cash holdings of the Central and State governments. The corporate sector's demand for money was significantly affected by the rate of interest which had an elasticity coefficient of about -0.6. However, as in case of the government, since the corporate sector has only a marginal share in the aggregate demand for money, the destabilizing effect of its behaviour in this context can be ignored. The behaviour of demand for money of the household sector is of crucial importance as it forms about 85 per cent of the aggregate demand for money. The determinants of demand for money in both of these cases were very similar. Price expectations and the rate of interest emerged as the most significant determinants which had elasticity coefficients of about -0.25 and 3.0 respectively. This means that an increase in interest rates would definitely lead to a decline in expenditure *via* increase in demand for money provided reasonable price stability is maintained. Otherwise, the interest rate effect would partially be offset by the price expectations effect. The demand for money functions appeared to lack stability.

Monetary Supply And Monetary Policy

Money supply was found to affect the level of general as well as consumer goods prices but not of real national income. The elasticity of prices with respect to money supply was around 0.6. The proportion of narrowly defined money (M_1 = currency plus demand deposits) to total money supply ($M_2 = M_1$ plus time deposits) declined during the period under study, but it still continued to be the major part (60 per cent) up to 1975-76. The ratio of M_1 to M_2 declined by 27 percentage points in 27 years (1950-51 to 1975-76), but thereafter, it declined by as many as

19 percentage points in just 5 years (1975-76 to 1980-81). A part of this rapid decline was due to a change in the scheme of classifying banks' saving deposits into demand and time deposits. These qualifications notwithstanding, the fact remains that slowly but surely, the character of money supply in India has undergone such a material change that it would now be inadequate to control only M_1 for controlling economic activity.

Is money supply exogenous in India? No, it is not. That the authorities cannot have a rigid and full control over it is shown by our findings about the behaviour of demand for money by the banking, corporate, and household sectors. But it is not completely demand-determined either. The authorities-both the Central Bank and the Government together – can influence the stock of money by employing appropriate policy tools. It is to be emphasized that the Central Bank alone, without the active help and cooperation of the fiscal authority, is not in a position to control money supply completely.

The important explanatory factors of money supply changes were government borrowings, availability of credit, and foreign exchange assets with elasticity coefficients of about 1.0, 0.8, and 0.08 respectively. Deficit financing and interest rate were positively but weakly related to the supply of money.

The rate of interest played a complex role in the process of money supply determination. Its effect worked through many channels which were not unidirectional. Firstly, it led to an increase in money supply *via* reduction in banks' cash ratio. Secondly, it did not result in the reduction of demand for credit by the public, as a result of which, it was found to be positively related to money supply. This was most probably due to the fact that increase in interest rates was not stiff enough. Finally, it must have indirectly helped in reducing money supply *via* its effect on government borrowings.

Trade Credit And Monetary Policy

Trade credit as an autonomous source of financing expenditures needs to be closely watched over. Its volume has increased substantially and is as important a source of funds as bank credit. Generally, while the government, foreign, and private limited companies have used it mainly out of business or transactions motive, the finance motive has been very much present in its use by all types of public limited companies. Since the latter group of companies accounts for about 40 per cent of the total trade credit of the corporate sector, it is necessary to ensure that it does not circumvent monetary control through its trade credit decisions.

In the case of public limited companies, the restriction on availability of bank credit and increase in interest rate have resulted in an increase in the volume of trade dues and a lengthening of the payment period. Unlike other countries, the adverse effect of trade credit in India has worked through own accounts of the above-mentioned companies rather than through redistribution of bank credit and readjustment of asset-holdings. A study of trade credit also has shown that monetary authorities would not be successful in controlling the level of expenditures only through the control of monetary base or money supply.

Implications of Financial Innovations

The Indian monetary system has experienced a number of institutional, organizational and banking innovations during the past thirty years, which have favourable, as well as adverse implications for monetary control. For instance, the creation and growth of many term lending financial institutions and guarantee organizations have resulted in an increase in the supply of cheap finance and a reduction of risk in the loan business which has helped to increase investment expenditures. Further, this innovation has helped the government to conceal large budget deficits by privatising what otherwise would have been included as budget deficit. Similarly, the spread of public ownership in the financial system has demoted the principles of liquidity and profitability in the functioning of financial institutions. Further, an increase in the banking habit, a reduction in the currency ratio, and an increase in the time to total deposits ratio which have resulted from the geographical spread of banking have contributed significantly to changes in the stock of money and its composition. Next, the process innovations which have already taken place and which are in the making in the business and banking sectors have reduced the liquidity needs of commercial banks and their customers. As a result, in comparison with the past, there would now be a larger increase in expenditures for a given increase in purchasing power. Finally, the monetary system has become much more integrated now than any time in the past. On the one hand, this has increased the ability of banks and other financial institutions to meet the demand for finance by using idle resources from wherever they exist in the system, and without approaching RBI as the lender of last resort. On the other, it has created favourable conditions for the quick and widespread transmission of the effect of actions initiated by the authorities.

Methodologically, the large-scale econometric exercises showed that, as it is well-known, the estimation of multiple regression functions is beset with frustrating multi-collinearity problems. The estimation of functions with lagged, and trend-removed data did not necessarily improve the results. Among the functional forms used, generally, the linear-nominal form yielded the best fits. Many times, there was either reduction in the value of R^2 or increase in auto-correlation when other functional forms were used.

Reasons For Ineffectiveness of Monetary Policy

Why has the monetary policy performed as it actually did in respect of achieving its proximate and ultimate objectives? What is the potential for its assuming an effective role in future? What suggestions one can give to make it more effective?

(1) One wonders whether the authorities had sufficient information on the composition of investment, and if they had, whether they used it satisfactorily for conducting their policy. Their efforts were primarily directed to the regulation of inventory investment in general, and in the private corporate sector in particular. Now, although this was certainly necessary, it was clearly not sufficient. When fixed investment happens to be 80 to 95 per cent of total investment, the policy which treats it as *ipso facto* valuable and, therefore, for all practical purposes,

outside its regulatory scope, is bound to be stymied. That such an approach to investment activity was not necessary can now be said with the benefit of hindsight. There is a scope for bringing even fixed investment under the ken of restrictive monetary policy. Since 60 per cent of fixed investment is in the form of construction investment, such a policy would help to curb conspicuous construction and excessive expenditures on townships, etc. The existence of idle capacity and high capital-output ratio (this ratio is very high indeed in certain industries like mining, electricity generation and supply, and transport and communication) indicates the scope for reducing fixed investment without affecting output adversely, and with desirable effect on employment.

It is also not correct to be preoccupied with investment in and financing of corporate sector alone, and to be passive spectator of the happenings in this regard in the public and household sectors because each of them now accounts for about 40 to 45 per cent of gross investment in the Indian economy. Further, the household sector finances not only its own investment almost entirely but also a very large part (about 50 per cent) of investment in the public and private corporate sectors. Let it be recalled that it also accounts for a major part of the aggregate demand for money and consumption expenditure. In short, the success of monetary policy in India very much hinges on its willingness to regulate fixed investment, and on its ability to influence saving and investment decisions in the household and public sectors. The importance of this truth has been grievously missed so far.

It is, however, not simple to control these sectors. Each of them has some unique features which would require a fresh approach to monetary management and appropriate innovations in the techniques of monetary control for its efficacy. The public sector is monolithic, there is an aura of social utility in its working, and it depends largely on budgetary sources for its financial requirements. Similarly, the decision making units in the household sector are small, numerous, geographically widely spread, and mostly self-sufficient financially.

(2) In spite of an apparent increase in interest rates and the restraint on credit availability, a number of indicators show that essentially the credit policy in India has remained quite liberal.

(i) The cost as well as availability of credit to the public, small-scale industrial, agricultural exports, and other priority sectors has been quite easy. The major portion of bank credit in each year was being loaned at quite a low rate of interest. For example, in 1974-75, the year of the so-called unprecedented tight money policy, when the minimum rate of interest was fixed to be 12.5 per cent, while about 19 per cent of bank credit was supplied at interest rates up to 12 per cent, about 48 per cent of credit was advanced at interest rates of 14 to 16 per cent. At the highest rate of interest of 18 per cent, hardly 2 per cent of bank credit was supplied.

The compulsory direction of bank credit at low or concessional rates of interest to the government and priority sectors shielded them from rising interest rates and contracted the scope of regulatory mechanism. This blunted the cutting edge of restrictive policy and redistributed the burden of such a policy on to other sectors which form only a small part of the control field. In other words, the conflict between 'control' and 'distributional' or 'promotional' objectives resulted in the helplessness of the RBI as a regulatory institution.

(ii) Except during the first half of 1950s, the real rate of interest has remained far below the nominal rate of interest. The average real rate of interest was -1.79 per cent during 1956-57 to 1960-61, less than 1.0 per cent during 1961-62 to 1970-71, and about 2.5 per cent during 1971-72 to 1977-78.

(iii) The degree of tightness of credit is conventionally indicated by the levei of credit-deposit ratio. In addition, it is useful to study variations in the combined ratio of credit-deposit and banks' investment ratios for gauging the state of financial conditions in the economy as a whole. This ratio apparently declined from 107.5 % in 1955-56 to 91.2 % in 1979-80. This decline however, was mainly due to the fact that in later years, banks invested more funds in 'other approved securities' which do not form a part of the investment ratio. If these securities are also included, the above-mentioned decline in the combined ratio was much smaller, and it was always more than 100. We must also take into account the supply of finance from term lending institutions to realize the existence of easy availability of funds in India during the period under study.

(3) The interface between monetary policy and fiscal policy also has positively hindered the effectiveness of the former in the following manner.

(i) Tax incentives and liberal depreciation allowances have proved more important than monetary variables as determinants of investment. Again with the benefit of hindsight, it can be said that there is no need to continue the liberal fiscal policy in respect of capital formation. The policy of requiring business units to pay taxes on a certain minimum portion of their profits introduced in 1983-84 budget is, therefore, very much in the right direction. It is instructive to note in this context that in a country like Sweden, just as fixed investment is encouraged by tax measures, if necessary, it is also subjected to investment tax.

(ii) The most important factor behind the weak performance of monetary policy was the management of government finances in general and the public debt in particular. The public debt policy has resulted in an atrophy of more than one technique of monetary control, and it has drastically diminished the RBI control over money supply. Because of government's borrowing programmes, the normal goal of economic stabilization has almost been given up, and the RBI is using all its powers and techniques to support the, market for government securities in order to ensure the government's ability to borrow huge quantities of funds at low and stable interest rates.

This situation in India is akin to the one which exists today in the UK and which existed in the USA in the early post-War years. In the latter case, the Federal Reserve System became increasingly restive at the continued restrictions on its freedom to assume its normal role in the task of economic stabilization. Finally, the bond support policy was ended with Treasury-Federal Reserve Accord in March 1951. There is a need for similar assertion by the RBI, the recognition of the wisdom of such a stance of RBI by the government, and a formal accord between the two. If interest rates on the government debt are increased, banks and other financial institutions would automatically invest in government securities by their own volition, and then there would be no need for subterfuges such as the SLR, etc. It is once again a happy thing that a small beginning, has been made in this regard in the past two years. This new policy ought to be consolidated and continued further.

(4) The RBI has been performing a purely supplementary role in the matter of economic stabilization. Can it play its role more forcefully and as an equal partner? We are inclined to think that it can. Let us examine this important matter closely.

One comes across a view that in a mixed economy such as ours, the existence and growth of the public sector restricts the Central Bank's freedom to act and thereby weakens its policy. Now, it is true that this is what has happened so far, but it is not inherent that this should always happen. If properly interpreted, given the cheap and easy availability of funds, investment decisions in the public sector can be said to have been quite rational. Similarly, the control which is exercised over the use of funds by the public sector as a result of constant consultations within the official set-up cannot be deemed to be non-existent because not much is known about such consultations. Further, monetary policy is inadequate for curing depression in a purely private sector economy. The public sector provides certain minimum support to economic activity which can be used advantageously for enhancing the effectiveness of monetary policy. In short, the presence of the public sector normally should not weaken monetary policy unless it is insisted that the provision of cheap and easy finance to it is a must whatever the cost of such a policy to the stabilization objective and an over-all efficiency of the system.

Let us take the question of control of money supply also. The fiscal policy has been its predominant determinant so far, but it is possible to improve substantially the RBI control over it. The RBI credit to the government accounts for about 75 per cent of changes in the reserve money and about 40 to 50 per cent of changes in the money supply. If so, the question which can be legitimately raised is, if the RBI cannot control its own credit, can it be expected to control anything at all? Would it not be ironical to accept the 'monetary authority' does not have authority to control its own supply of funds? Add to this the fact that the share of bank credit to the commercial sector (another variable which is very much under RBI control) in the supply of money has increased over the period of time and now it is about one-third, and one would then grasp the reality of the potential which exists for the RBI control over money supply.

Structurally, it is interesting and important to note that now the volume of commercial bank credit and investment is about equal to the volume of total disbursements by the Central and all State Governments. If we take into account the RBI credit to the government and commercial sectors also, the size of monetary sector becomes much larger than that of the fiscal sector. Therefore, if the RBI manages money, finance, and securities in accordance with the sound principles of monetary control and financial management, there is no reason why it should continue to play a second fiddle to the fiscal policy.

This is not to say that the fiscal policy is unimportant or subordinate, and that money supply can become exogenous in India. The institutional realities here require that the choice of either fiscal policy or monetary policy is unreal. What we need is continuous co-ordination, concomitance, and compatibility between the two so that their functioning becomes mutually redounding.

(5) The discussion so far implies that the following changes ought to be introduced in the interest rates policy of the RBI.

(i) The atrophy condition of the Bank rate must be changed and its role as a signal of the authorities' intentions and the state of credit in the economy must be restored. The practice of its backdoor increases and prescribing multiple refinance rates must be replaced by that of changing it in a straightforward manner and using it more vigorously and actively. Although we understand why the authorities have refrained from doing this so far, the unhappy experience of the extant policy shows that it would not be wise to continue it in future.

(ii) The present policy of 'administering' interest rates needs to be discarded, and interest rates should be raised to a higher level. At present, almost all interest rates in India are fixed by fiat. [4] This policy has rendered interest rates useless as indicators of credit situation and people's expectations. While it is a right policy not to rely on money supply alone as the indicator of monetary policy, the RBI has turned the most important of other variables inefficacious as an indicator of monetary policy.

It is also anomalous that the belief in the theory of Bank rate should coexist with the policy of pegging banks' deposit and loan rates of interest. Under the system of administered low interest rates, the working of Bank rate mechanism has been undermined at every stage.

Similarly, when interest rates are administered, since there is no homogeneity in the fixation of ceilings in case of different sources of funds, and since certain sources of funds are under the direct control of RBI, while others are not, the purpose of control over the former was defeated, and there was an inequitable distribution of cost-bearing by different types of borrowers. It was found that in 1980-81, whereas interest cost as percentage of value added was about 14 per cent for large companies with gross fixed assets of Rs.10 crore or more, it was as high as 32.6 per cent for companies with gross fixed assets of Rs. 1 crore or less. [5]

Further, interest rate ceilings have begotten non-market credit controls or quantitative credit ceilings as a means of controlling inflationary pressures. The latter measure suffers from the following shortcomings in comparison with the use of interest rates. [6] Firstly, the imposition of loan ceilings is a conspicuous and uncertain way of reducing aggregate demand. They may appear to have been effective in achieving their objective of curtailing credit to some private sector borrowers, but it is doubtful whether they have succeeded in curtailing real expenditures. Secondly, there is no guarantee that rationed out units are the ones which are the least productive. Monetary authorities' request to banks that only productive loans be made does not guarantee that only such loans would be made. An increase in interest rates, on the other hand, ensures that unproductive expenditure is reduced and credit is used for relatively greater productive purposes. Thirdly, there is also a likelihood that rationed out units find their way around loan ceilings. If credit ceilings persist for a long period, they tend to drive credit flows through less efficient channels of financial intermediation. The phenomenal growth of deposits with business units in India proves this point. It is hard to reconcile the existence of this type of control with the objective of creating an efficient financial mechanism. Finally, their prolonged use places a terrible strain on the happy cooperative as distinct from legalistic relationship which exists between the Central Bank and commercial banks. It is not an efficient system in which one side is continually looking for loopholes in the control mechanism while the other side is continually trying to plug them.

This does not mean that there is no place for quantitative credit ceilings at all. When the loan markets are characterized by imperfections, and when severe credit restraint is called for, their use may become temporarily necessary. Similarly, sometimes in the short-run, in the absence of such controls, changes in interest rates needed would be quite sharp and disruptive of financial markets. Barring such situations, an excessive shift from the use of interest rates to a disproportionately heavy reliance on credit rationing, as it has happened in India in the past few years, must be avoided or corrected.

(iii) There is also a need for the simplification of interest rates structure in India. Too many interest rates have come to prevail now and this has happened through policy prescriptions. Interest rates differ depending on the size and type of banks, the purpose, size, security and area of loans, etc. When interest rates are freed and are allowed to be market determined, the simplification mentioned above would be greatly achieved. It is heartening that the RBI has already taken some steps in this connection in 1980-81. [7]

(iv) It is high time that the anomaly of long-term interest rates persistently being lower than short-term rates is also removed. The long-term lending rates of banks and other financial institutions have usually been lower than even the minimum short-term rates of banks, let apart their ceiling rates. In view of our findings about fixed investment activity, this anomaly should be corrected by raising long-term rates and not by lowering short-term rates.

(6) The rationalization of interest rates policy should be accompanied by certain reforms in the use of other techniques of monetary control.

Firstly, the technique of CRR has so far remained largely unused in India. It was used only in 3 or 4 years (1973-76 and 1981), and it reached the maximum level of only 8 per cent as against the legally permissible maximum of 15 per cent. It is quite an effective technique (the experience of its use in 1982 showed this); its increase directly and surely reduces bank credit and money supply while an increase in interest rates, if it is mild, would compound the difficulties of monetary authorities by increasing money supply rather than decreasing it. The SLR as the so-called supplementary technique has created an euphoria in this context. It is now accepted officially also that the SLR is not a tool of monetary control at all, and that it merely distributes available resources between the private and public sectors. Our earlier discussion on government finances and public debt management strongly suggests the desirability of minimizing the use of this technique. Instead, the use of CRR should be preferred.

Secondly, different techniques should not be employed in a mutually defeating manner. For example, when the bank rate was raised in 1974, the CRR and marginal CRR were lowered. Similarly, when the CRR is increased, banks should not be allowed to expand credit by borrowing more from the RBI. The function of the Central Bank as the lender of last resort is basically for protecting banks from collapse and not for enabling them to expand credit when the Central Bank wants to tighten credit screws.

Thirdly, the experimentation in the application of different techniques has often resulted in the loss of simplicity of traditional techniques. The intricate manner in which some of them have come to be used has increased the administrative difficulties, loopholes, leakages, and lags in their working. The quota-cum-slab rate and the NLR systems of employing bank rate technique, and the existence of a large number of concessions multiple and differentiated margins, ceilings, and interest rates in respect of selective credit controls illustrate this point. In certain years, three different ratios, SLR, NLR, CRR, simultaneously existed with differences in definitions of assets and liabilities for calculating each of them. Simplicity is a virtue which enhances the utility of techniques of monetary control.

Major Conclusions

The final impression which this study has led us to form about the role of monetary policy in India is one of hope and encouragement. The period in which it has operated so far was a special period in which a young nation was preoccupied with and was in a hurry to accomplish the task of socialist development. It was, therefore, perhaps natural that the monetary policy was almost entirely geared to the achievement of goals of growth and distribution. Announcements notwithstanding, the stabilization objective received attention only in so far as it supposedly did not undermine the former two objectives. In other words, the conduct of monetary policy was subject to notions and ideology which were not necessarily conducive to its effectiveness in the area of stabilization. [8] We also did not know much about the functioning of the monetary system which was still in the process of evolution. Therefore, it has been primarily a learning period.

Yet, monetary policy variables affected many intermediate key variables in the right direction, although the effect was usually weak. With certain changes indicated earlier, it is possible for them to play a more significant role. The structure of monetary system is also favourable for the effective role of monetary policy. Certain changes such as increase in interest rates on government debt, reduction in tax incentives for fixed investment, subjecting public sector loans and food procurement credit to Credit Authorization Scheme augur well for the effectiveness of monetary policy in future provided there is no backtracking on them.

But monetary policy in India is not to be understood in the 'monetarist' sense. Money supply alone does not determine the level of economic activity, nor is it exogenous in India. To pose a choice as either fiscal policy or monetary policy is unrealistic. Both of them together can achieve price stability through demand management. However, it is doubtful how vital their contribution can be in determining the level of real national income. [9]

Notes and References

1. This variable had a great relevance in consumption and money demand decisions also.
2. A similar result was obtained in respect of the determination of money supply and trade credit also.
3. The need for increase in interest rates faster than prices and the lack of stability were discovered while studying demand for money also.
4. L. M. BHOLE, *Financial Markets and Institutions,* Tata McGraw-Hill Co., New Delhi, 1982, pp. 345-46.
5. *Economic and Political Weekly,* June 5, 1982, p. 924.
6. See A. D. BAIN, 'Monetary Control Methods in the United Kingdom', in G. Clayton, and others (eds.) , *Monetary Theory and Policy in the 1970's,* Oxford University Press, Oxford, 1971; J. KARKEN, 'Appraisal of Monetary Management', and Bank of England, 'Monetary Management in the United Kingdom', in H. G. JOHNSON (ed.), *Readings in British Monetary Economics,* Oxford University Press, Oxford, 1972; and E. S. SHAW, *Financial Deepening and Economic Development,* Oxford, University Press, London, 1973.
7. RESERVE BANK OF INDIA, *Report on Currency and Finance, 1980-81, Vol. 1,* p. 106.
8. Incidentally, there was no success in achieving growth and distribution objectives also. Does not this mean that the conventional wisdom that there is a conflict between different goals of monetary policy may not be true after all ?
9. L. M. BHOLE, Impacts of Monetary Policy, Himalaya Publishing House, Bombay, 1985.

[20]

*Some Aspects of the Past Evolution and Future Prospects of Monetary Policy in India**

Introduction

The Reserve Bank of India completed half-a-century of its functioning as a Central Banking authority in 1985. The monetary policy in India in its various aspects has undergone a sea change in these fifty years. It is believed that a historical perspective greatly helps in better understanding of the future. The twin objectives of this paper, therefore, are to present a brief overview of the past evolution of monetary policy and to discuss only some aspects of its future prospects. The paper has three sections. In Section I, a brief outline of the evolution of the theory, objectives, techniques, etc. of monetary policy, and its performance over the past fifty years is presented. In Section II, some important factors which might have contributed to changes in and performance of monetary policy are discussed. In Section III, certain implications of the previous analysis for the future conduct of monetary policy are indicated. The focus of the whole paper is on the political economy of the past and future of monetary policy.

I. The Evolution of Indian Monetary Policy

The Reserve Bank of India was set up in April 1935 and it remained as a shareholders' bank till 1949. During the early years (1935-1950), the main regulatory objectives of the Bank were management of foreign exchange, maintenance of exchange rate, and control of inflation. No great promotional role was envisaged for the Bank at the time of its creation. It did not attempt much experimentation in the sphere of monetary policy in its early years. It had mainly

* Paper published in *The Indian Economic Association Conference Volume*, December 1987.

two instruments of monetary control namely, the Bank Rate and Open Market Operations (OMO). While the Bank rate was used only once (in November 1935 when it was reduced from its initial level of 3.5 per cent to 3 per cent) during the period mentioned above, OMO, after being used somewhat actively for sometime (1335-39), became reoriented towards debt management thereafter. [1] It appears that coming events were casting their shadows before in the sphere of techniques of monetary control. By virtue of its organization and leadership, the Bank's policies had not become completely subservient to the Government policies in spite of a high degree of po1itico-economic instability and exigencies till 1950. Unfortunately, this was to change slowly but greatly with the passage of time during the post-1950 period.

The monetary policy has evolved to a stage of maturity during the era of planned economic developments. [2] During this era, as it is well-known, both the promotional and regulatory objectives came to be equally emphasized. Accordingly, the monetary policy has been geared to the achievement of the acceleration of economic development, social justice, increase in employment, price stability, and the development of the appropriate financial system. It is obvious and it has been recognized that while the last two objectives constitute the core of monetary policy, it can play only a contributory role in respect of the first three goals. The proverbial trade-off in this context has been recognized by expressing the task of monetary policy as one of "controlled expansion" or "disinflation without deflation." Over the period of time, the scope of policy has been widened from the growth of industrial output to that of agricultural output also. In financial terms, the objective of monetary policy is said to be the controlled expansion of bank credit and money supply with special attention being paid to the seasonal aspects of these variables. With the passage of time, the achievement of the desired distribution of credit has become as much a concern as the regulation of the volume of aggregate credit. It may even be argued that the distribution rather than level of total credit has received greater attention in the later period, i.e., after the beginning of 1970s. [3]

The theoretical basis of policy has throughout been, and rightly so, an eclectic one. It has been a discretionary policy rather than a policy by any rigid or semi-rigid monetary rule. It is held that money matters but it alone does not matter, and that other factors such as bank credit, structural and institutional realities, and investment play an important role in the transmission mechanism of monetary policy. Accordingly, money supply, aggregate bank credit, seasonal return flow of bank credit, fixed and inventory investment, the rate of growth of deposits (resources) of banks and their being in the "credit bind", volume of RBI refinance have all been used as targets/indicators of monetary policy. The bank credit has been regarded as a particularly important variable, and the control of money supply has been attempted mainly through the control of bank credit. However, the singularization of the target/indicator of policy has been wisely avoided in view of the complex nature of inter-relationships in the monetary system.

The RBI has used a large number of techniques of monetary policy – the traditional ones, their variants, and the new ones – during the period of study. The list of its instruments include (i) Open Market Operations (OMO), (ii) Moral Suasion, (iii) Bank Rate, (iv) Discretionary Control of Refinance from RBI, (v) Ceilings on RBI Refinance, (vi) Regulation of interest rates on commercial bank, deposits and loans, and other interest rates, (vii) Cash Reserve Ratio (CRR), (viii) Statutory Liquidity Ratio (SLR), (ix) Quantitative Ceilings on or Direct Allocation (rationing) of the volume and direction of bank credit, (x) Fixation of average and marginal credit-deposit ratio, (xi) Selective Credit Controls (SCC), (xii) Credit Authorization Scheme, and (xiii) Formulation of credit budgets or plans.

It is obvious that it is not possible to describe and discuss in details the chronological changes, developments, evolution, and working of all these techniques here. [4] We can highlight here only some significant features of the trends and developments in this respect in a summary fashion.

A study of techniques would reveal that a number of innovations in their use has been introduced over the period of time. The traditional techniques have been considerably modified as a result of which they have tended to lose their simplicity and directness of effect. This perhaps has not been conducive to the administration of these techniques. It may have worsened the problems such as lags, leakages, loopholes, and even injustices from which the working of instruments of monetary policy usually tend to suffer. The use of quota-cum-slab Rate (QCSR) and Net Liquidity Ratio (NLR) systems instead of direct variations in the Bank rate is one of the examples in this context. Different techniques, viz. Bank rate, control of RBI refinance, CRR had come to be directly linked with each other through QCSR, NLR and SLR systems.

The monetary techniques have not been used sufficiently actively and boldly for the purpose of economic stabilization. The number, extent, and range of variations in the important tools such as the Bank rate and CRR have been very small indeed. The Bank bas shown reluctance to change the Bank rate in a straight-forward or direct manner very many times. With the passage of time, the Bank rate technique has suffered more and more from atrophy. This has required the introduction of the system of administered interest rates with the components of direct fixation of interest rates in the economy, keeping these rates at unnaturally low levels, and direct and discretionary quantitative allocation of RBI refinance and bank credit. This system of administered interest rates has played havoc with the efficacy of monetary policy. [5] The CRR technique also remained almost completely unutilized till 1973 although it has been used quite actively thereafter.

We have also witnessed the shift from the cost-effect to the availability or direct and discretionary non-price-rationing effect in the regulation of refinance from the RBI, and the bank credit. Over the period of time, the use of not only OMO but also Bank rate, SLR, etc. has come to be influenced by the considerations of Government finances and debt management. It is noteworthy that many a technique of monetary control has been increasingly used as techniques of distribution of financial resources – distribution between the public and private sectors, and between different sub-sectors of the latter. This has resulted in the insulation of a larger and larger part of flows of finance from the impact of regulatory mechanism.

What can we say about the performance of monetary policy? Although it is really difficult to answer such a complex question, a rough and broad answer may be attempted here to complete this survey of the evolution of monetary policy. Let us take one of the major concerns of monetary policy namely, the control of investment activity. The Central Bank's objectives in this respect were to minimize investment in inventories, to discourage inessential fixed investment, and to increase the productivity of investment. The achievement or otherwise of these objectives is reflected in the relative growth rates of investment, output, employment, and capacity utilization. Then the high and increasing capital-output ratio, the high level of and widespread existence of idle capacity, the excess of rate of growth of investment over the rates of growth of employment and output, and unduly high levels of inventory investment reflect the lack of success of monetary policy in attaining its proximate objectives. Similarly one has to admit that the performance of monetary policy cannot be adjudged to have been creditable if one looks at its major ultimate goals. The real national income has increased at an annual average rate of about 3 to 3.5 percent over the period of study. The annual average rate of change in wholesale prices was – 2.45 per cent during 1950-51 to 1954-55, and 6.19, 5.75, 7.05, 12.54 per cent respectively in each successive five-year period thereafter till about 1980. The number of chronically unemployed persons increased from 1.42 million in 1961 to 3.61 million in 1971 and 4.37 million in 1978. Thus, the economy clearly suffered from ratcheting upwards of the rates of inflation and unemployment accompanied by a stagnant rate of growth of output. It has been a unique characteristic of the Indian economy that instead of experiencing "trade offs" between different economic objectives, there has been a deterioration on all fronts in spite of high rates of saving and investment.

II. Explanation of Evolution

What explains the evolution of choice of techniques, and the performance of monetary policy in India? Why did the Central Banking authority formulate and implement the monetary policy in the way it did? Three primary factors, *inter alia*, help to explain the actual working of monetary policy in India.

There is evidence to show that various decisions in the sphere of monetary policy in USA and UK are greatly influenced by the fashionable ideas or fashions in ideas which are shaped by the academic economists and experts. The policy makers are said to be prone to fashions in ideas and academics are well-placed to shape these fashions. Some of the most significant policy changes in recent years such as the acceptance of monetarism in UK, USA, and Europe, the choice of operating procedures and indicators/targets in USA, the adoption of the policy of Competition and Credit Control in 1971 in UK are explicable in terms of the influence of academics and fashions in ideas. [7] Can we say that policy changes in India also were due to the facts that economists were thinking about money and Central Banking in new ways and that their ideas were widely communicated to and accepted by the policy makers? Although we lack a systematic study and detailed documentation in this regard, it would be difficult to hold that the way monetary policy evolved in India was the result of influence of any particular academic theories, thoughts, ideas. It has been already stated that the basis of monetary policy in India has been an eclectic one; and we are not aware of any major work which has advocated, for example, the systems of administered interest rates or quantitative credit rationing, and an overemphasis on the, distribution of credit at the cost of economic stability and quality of credit.

The students of monetary policy abroad have increasingly emphasized the importance of the role of financial innovations in shaping the evolution of monetary policies there. [8] There is no doubt that the Indian monetary system also has experienced many institutional, organizational, banking innovations during the past thirty-five years. [9] However, although they naturally had many significant implications for the conduct of monetary policy, particularly two points about their impact on monetary policy which are relevant in the present context should be noted. Firstly, the financial innovations have influenced the monetary policy in both ways i.e. they have created difficulties as well as favourable conditions for its effectiveness. Secondly, they do not appear to have necessitated the changes in the choice of' techniques and the perception of the task of monetary policy which have actually occurred. For example, it is hard to relate the atrophy of the Bank rate and OMO or the change from the greater reliance on interest rates mechanism to that of CRR to anyone or a group of financial innovations.

This brings us to the political economy of monetary policy as the major explanation of changes which we have experienced. Faced with the continuing crises of inflation, unemployment, exchange rate instability etc., students of monetary policy have been increasingly forced to deemphasize purely technical approaches and turn to political factors also while analysing the functioning and evolution of monetary policies in various countries. [lo] In essence, this concept states that the reaction functions of Central Banking authority, its particular monetary policy actions or decisions, and its choices of instrument arc directly and indirectly (via fiscal, budgetary and debt policies of the Government) determined more by the State's political goals, constraints, considerations, forces or the electoral politics, interest-group politics, ideological politics or the State's populist stance or the power of big business than by economic factors, structural changes, and technical requirements of financial markets and institutions. It is suggested here that the most of the major changes in and the performance of monetary policy in India are explicable mainly in terms of such a concept of political economy of monetary policy.

There is a good scope for research in and documentation of the political nature of monetary policy decision-making by taking specific episodes, stages, changes in monetary policy in India. It, however, does appear to us that the conduct of monetary policy in this country has been increasingly determined by the political forces to a degree which is not permissible or which is not implied in the concepts of even "monetary authorities" and "mixed economy." It is to be noted that the term "monetary authorities" implies two (independent) decision making centres and not one. However, over the period of time, Government intervention, and fiscal policy considerations have become overwhelmingly so important that we no longer seem to have two authorities formulating monetary policy; the Fiscal Authority, appears, so to say, to have swallowed the Central Banking Authority. With this, the reign of political forces in the conduct of monetary policy has become well-established. The manner of use of OMO, the atrophy of the Bank rate, the system of administered interest rates, quantitative credit allocations, the overwhelming importance of RBI credit to Government in determining the volume of reserve money supply, administered prices, etc. reflect the reality of the political economy of monetary policy. The lowering of interest rates structure in April 1987 (along with the liberalized tax policy) in the face of very serious resources crunch, the unprecedented level of deficit financing, the rising cost of living, the contrary recommendations of the Committee to Review the Working of Monetary Policy (which, incidentally, the Government have accepted), and the loss involved for the small saver, are the most recent examples of the political economy of monetary policy in India.

III. Monetary Policy In Coming Years

Having discussed the past of monetary policy so far, we now indicate two or three changes which, if introduced, would make monetary policy a more effective instrument of achieving the constitutional objectives in future.

It follows from the previous discussion that there is a need for and a lot to gain from rethinking, reviewing, reassessing the extent of the role of the State in the economy. The hope about the future of monetary policy hinges on the capacity of the Indian society to reduce drastically the centralization of decision making and to minimize the role of predominantly political, ideological, and populist considerations in the conduct of monetary policy. It is quite acceptable that in a planned economy, monetary policy has to be consistent with the priorities laid down in the plans. This, however, does not necessitate that the monetary policy be converted, be rendered purely as an adjunct, as a subserving subsidiary of the political process. Planning by nature is not an entirely political activity; it is supposed to be based on rational thinking and expert inputs too. It is also to be remembered that the concept of the mixed economy is the outcome of the dissatisfaction with not only laissez-faire economy but also centralized or command economy. It is also to be recalled with benefit that the economists have always perceived that the Central Banking authority should be independent at least "within" the Government if not independent "of" the Government. The concept of mixed economy is consistent with the concept of indicative planning. Therefore, the movement towards indicative planning would help creating a more congenial environment and framework for the working of monetary policy in future.

Assuming that the political economy of monetary policy can change appropriately, what should be and what should not be the future thrust areas of monetary policy? The Committee to Review the Working of the Monetary System [11] and the Governor of the RBI [12] have recently pointed out the following future thrust areas of monetary policy; (i) To mobilise and expand the pool of savings of the community. (ii) To promote price stability. (iii) To promote efficiency of the payment system. and of the allocation of savings. (iv) To improve credit delivery system, quality of lending, and recycling of funds. (v) To meet in adequate measure the resource needs of the Government.

The emphasis on price stability, efficiency of allocation of savings, and quality of credit is quite appropriate. The problems of industrial sickness, overdues, and recovery of loans to borrowers in the priority sectors are bound to require a lot of attention of the Central Banking authority in the near future. However, we would like to suggest that the time has come to modify the first and the fifth of the above-mentioned tasks. In view of the facts over a long period of time that in spite of a secular and high increase in the rates of saving, investment, Government expenditure, Government debt, deficit financing, the performance of the economy in all vital respects has been miserable, we must rethink about the role of these variables as development factors, and accordingly, redefine the tasks of monetary policy.

It is suggested here that the future task of monetary policy should be to maintain the rate of saving rather than to increase it, and that it should bother more about the type, quality, efficiency of investment rather than about ever increasing rate of investment. The operation of monetary policy (and all other economic policies too), for too long, has been burdened with the conventional wisdom about the wholesome qualities of investment. If it is realized that what counts is not what is spent but what is produced, it would be easily possible to deal with the traditional bugbears of monetary policy namely, Government expenditure, Government debt, deficit financing, and external debt. In fact, the only sure way to deal with them is to deemphasize investment.

There are many sound considerations why we should free ourselves from the investment fetish. [13] For example, why should economists who believe in the law of diminishing returns take the view that when it comes to investment, more must always be better? Is not our history of planning replete with monstrous examples of misdirected and wasted investment? Instead of always increasing investment; would it not be better if we stop and try to fathom the true value of the capital stock that is of low quality and unused? It is also necessary to realized that it is possible for private investment, just like Government spending, to be wasted. Making the right investment is more important than making more investment. The policies designed to promote investment often tend to stimulate replication of those investments that already exist and may be redundant. The fact that investment is defined not on the basis of what is produced but on the basis of by whom it is bought should suggest 'the more the better' is not always the right rule for investment. The policy to produce capital goods which produce still more capital goods *ad infinitum* i.e. the policy of investment for investment's sake in faulty. In a sense, the Government deficits, public debt, etc. are unreal issues; they can be meaningfully dealt with only when the public recognizes and consents to material reductions in real military spending and all kinds of unnecessary investments. It is a mistake to think that the way out of such problems is more and more borrowings/aid from abroad. As long as the nation is committed to spend more in real resources than what we are able to produce, the problems engendered by public debt, deficit financing, etc. are not going to be solved by the monetary policy. These variables represent the absence of discipline in national spending and also the ethical and societal issues which clamour for urgent attention of the nation. The monetary policy can deliver goods in the coming era only to the extent that the wider issues posed in this Section are successfully tackled.

Notes and References

1. See Reserve Bank of India, History of the Reserve Bank of India, Bombay, 1970.
2. See various articles in the Reserve Bank of India Bulletin, viz. "Recent Evolution of Monetary policy in India", Bulletin, April 1966; "Recent Monetary Policy Measures", Bulletin, May 1973; "Some Thoughts on Monetary and Credit policy", Bulletin, February 1979; "The Current Inflation and Monetary Policy", Bulletin, December 1979; and "Monetary Policy for Dynamic Growth", Bulletin, December 1985. Also see RBI, Report of the Committee to Review the Working of the Monetary System, Bombay, 1985.
3. This and certain other parts of the formulation in this paper draw heavily from the author's book, Impacts of Monetary Policy, Himalaya Publishing House, Bombay, 1985.
4. For such a treatment, see L. M. Bhole, Impacts of Monetary Policy, *op. cit*, pp. 16-27 and pp. 295-322.
5. For the full discussion of this system, see L. M. Bhole, "Administered Interest Rates in India", Economic and Political Weekly, June 2l-29, 1985.
6. For evidence on these indicators, see L. M. Bhole, Impacts of Monetary Policy, op. cit., pp. 28-58.
7. Moran, M., The Politics of Banking, Macmillan, London, 1986, pp. 33-39.
8. See, for example, Silber, W. L. (ed.), Financial Innovation, Lexington Books, London, 1975; Hester, D. D., "Innovations and Monetary Control", Brookings. Papers on Economic Activity, 1, 1681.
9. The topic of financial innovations vis-a-vis monetary policy has been discussed in L. M. Bhole, Impacts of Monetary Policy, *op.cit.*, pp.240-262.
10. See Hodgman, D. R. (ed.), The Political Economy of Monetary Policy: National and International Aspects, Federal Reserve Bank of Boston, Proceedings of the Conference held at Perugia, Italy, 1983; and Moran, M., op. *cit.*
11. RBI, Report of the Committee to Review the Working of the Monetary System, *op.cit.*, p. 298.
12. Malhotra, R. N., "Monetary Policy for Dynamic Growth", RBI Bulletin, December 1985.
13. The elaboration of this point is heavily based on the Discussion paper by A. M. Wojnilower in Federal Reserve Bank of Boston, The Economics of Large Governmental Deficits, Proceedings of a Conference held in 1983, pp. 99-111.

[21]

*International Aspects of Monetary Policy in India**

Introduction

Until about two decades ago, an analysis of the conduct of monetary policy everywhere normally used to be made under the implicit or explicit assumption of a closed economy. With the growth of integration or internationalization of different national economies, the scholars abroad have been paying greater attention to the international aspects of monetary policy. As a result, the literature on this subject has grown rapidly in the recent past.

Much of this literature, however, is mathematical, abstract and highly specialized, using difficult technical tools and highly austere, professional style. It has been developed by referring to largely artificial or hypothetical or assumed conditions or circumstances. It can be understood only with a great effort even by the academics, not to speak of the policy-makers. As has been rightly pointed out, such a literature has made communication between the academics and policy-makers more difficult, instead of bridging the gap between them. [1]

In India, the theme of monetary policy in an open economy continues to be conspicuously absent in discussions on monetary policy even today. The facts about the external sector or balance of payments (BOP) do not appear to be taken into account while deciding on a particular stance or instrument of monetary policy. It is interesting to note that even the Chakravarty Committee has made absolutely no reference to the implications of an open economy for the working of the Indian monetary system. It is felt by some that the treatment of the external sector in various Reserve Bank of India (RBI) publications is "clinical or coldly detached presentation", and that the RBI has not deemed it necessary to regard continuous pressure on BOP as a major challenge or a priority area for attention in monetary management. [2]

* Paper published in *International Journal of Development Banking*, January, 1991.

It is in this context that the present paper seeks to describe and analyze certain relevant facts and relationships which are vital inputs for the effective conduct of monetary policy in the international setting.

The RBI regards price stability to be its major goal or responsibility. It has been stated that "... of the various objectives, price stability is perhaps the one that can be pursued most effectively by monetary policy.... Stress on price stability as the most important objective of monetary policy does not mean that it cannot contribute to the attainment of other objectives... Monetary policy, however, is able to make a more effective contribution to the achievement of the objective of price stability than other objectives". [3] Incidentally, it is interesting to note that the central bankers in many other countries also view price stability as their main task. For example, the Governor of the Bank of England also has stated that "... the first and overriding goal must, of course, be the establishment and maintenance of price stability. This is one of the greatest service that finance can render industry-or at any rate, instability is certainly the greatest disservice". [4]

Similarly, money supply is undoubtedly regarded as a major proximate control variable. The RBI continuously monitors and seeks to control changes in different monetary aggregates, reserve money and liquidity in the economy. The international aspects of inflation and money supply process, and the related matter of capital movements, therefore, have been selected for a study in this paper. [5]

The plan of the paper is as follows: Section I provides a background wherein various indicators of the internationalization of the Indian economy are described. How far inflation in India is caused by the external shocks is analyzed in Section II. The money supply process in an open economy is studied in Section III. The interest rates in India, as a part of the structure of world interest rates, and the interest sensitivity of capital-movements, are discussed in Section IV. Section V presents lessons and conclusions.

I. Is India an Open Economy?

The need for adopting an open economy paradigm for the analysis of monetary policy depends on the extent of openness of a given economy. In this respect, India apparently appears to be in a different category than countries such as USA, UK, Germany, Japan, Tunisia, Phillippines, Zaire, etc. which have a high degree of participation in the world trade and finance. There is a view that India should be categorized either as a 'closed economy' or a 'very small open economy' on the basis of the share of her external trade in her national income or in the total world trade. The aggregate of her imports and exports in relation to GDP was about 14 per cent in 1951, 13 per cent in 1961, 9 per cent in 1971, 17 per cent in 1981, and 14 per cent in 1986. Her external trade was about 1 per cent of total world trade in the 1980s. In comparison, the external trade has usually accounted for at least 20 per cent to 25 per cent of GDP in the above mentioned countries. [6]

However, trade figures alone do not give a correct idea regarding the degree of openness of a given economy, particularly from the point of view of the working of monetary policy. For this, we specially need to look at the indicators of financial integration also. If we do so, the picture of the Indian economy which emerges is quite different. The net inflow of foreign resources was about 3 per cent of GDP while the savings of the public sector and private corporate sector were about 2 per cent and 1.5 per cent of GDP, respectively, in the 1980s. The external sources have financed as much as 10 per cent to 35 per cent of the public sector plan outlays in India. The external debt (including private debt) as percentage of GNP is quite high and it has increased from 15.2 per cent in 1970 to 18.8 per cent in 1987. The total external debt was about Rs.70000 crore in 1988-89; if we add the short-term debt and accrued interest of FCNR deposits, it was more than Rs.100000 crore in that year. The Flow-of-Funds tables show that the share of foreign claims in the total claims has increased from 8 per cent during 1951-52 to 1955-56 to 14 per cent during 1976-77 to 1980-81. All Indian banks now have about 122 branches in 25 countries; similarly, 24 foreign banks have 150 branches and they account for 3 per cent of total banking business in India.

Many developments are taking place which reflect growing international integration of the Indian financial system. For example, India has started participating in international financial innovations such as using Note Issuance Facility (NIF), Revolving Underwriting Facility (RUF), and Euro-Commercial Paper (ECP), all of which help to reduce risk arising from the volatility of interest rates and exchange rates. Similarly, Indian financial institutions such as the Industrial Development Bank of India (IDBI), Export-Import Bank of India (EXIM bank) are now participating in the international swap market. [7] Further, in the recent past, many financial institutions, instruments, schemes and incentives have been introduced to attract funds from abroad. India Fund and India Growth Fund started by the UTI and the measures to attract NRI funds are some of the examples in this respect. Of late, there has also been an increase in the direct borrowings in the private capital markets abroad by financial institutions, banks, private companies and public sector units. The amount of commercial borrowings has increased from a little less than Rs. 1000 crore in 1980-81 to a little more than Rs. 2000 crore in 1987-88. The NRI deposit liabilities have grown from Rs. 3819 crore in 1985 to Rs. 14154 crore in 1989 which means that they accounted for about 20 per cent of the total long-term external debt and about 10 per cent of deposits of the scheduled commercial banks in that year. Finally, a significant increase in the number of foreign collaborations in Indian industry has taken place during 1980s. Out of 10,981 foreign collaboration agreements approved during 1948-86, 4911 agreements have been approved during 1980-86.

II. International Influences on Inflation

Having shown that India is no longer an insulated economy, we now turn to gauge the extent of external causes of inflation in India. Table 1 and Figures la & 1b show the rate and nature (structure) of inflation in India during 1970-71 to 1988-89. [8] Apart from a persistent and high annual rate of increase, inflation in India is characterized by certain interesting and notable structural features. The consumer price index (CPI) for industrial workers has almost always been higher than the wholesale price index (WPI) and, since 1980, the rate of increase of the former has been substantially higher than that of the latter. Similarly, the food index of CPI (CPIF) has been higher and it has increased at a faster rate than that of the food index of WPI (WPIF). The weighted contribution of the prices of wage goods to the general inflation has steadily increased over the period of time. How far did the international factors contribute to the extent and nature of the inflation just described?

Table 1: Measures of Prices Inflation in India (%)

Year	WPI (1970-71-100)	WPIF (1970-71-100)	CPI Industrial Workers (1960-100)
	(1)	(2)	(3)
1971-72	6.00	1.10	3.22
1972-73	9.62	9.79	7.81
1973-74	20.22	23.42	20.77
1974-75	25.19	25.54	26.8
1975-76	-1.08	-4.65	-1.26
1976-77	2.08	-5.48	-3.83
1977-78	5.20	12.25	7.64
1978-79	0.00	-1.14	2.16
1979-80	17.11	8.72	8.76
1980-81	18.24	11.22	11.38
1981-82	9.32	12.98	12.46
1982-83	2.63	6.38	7.76
1983-84	9.45	13.20	12.55
1984-85	7.08	4.94	6.39
1985-86	5.73	7.07	6.52
1986-87	5.31	6.50	8.70
1987-88	7.59	8.44	9.19

Source: RBI, *Report on Currency and Finance*, various issues.

Figure 1a:
Movements in Consumer Price Index (CPI) and Wholesale Price Index (WPI) Numbers: 1970-71 to 1988-89 (Common Base: 1980-81 = 100)

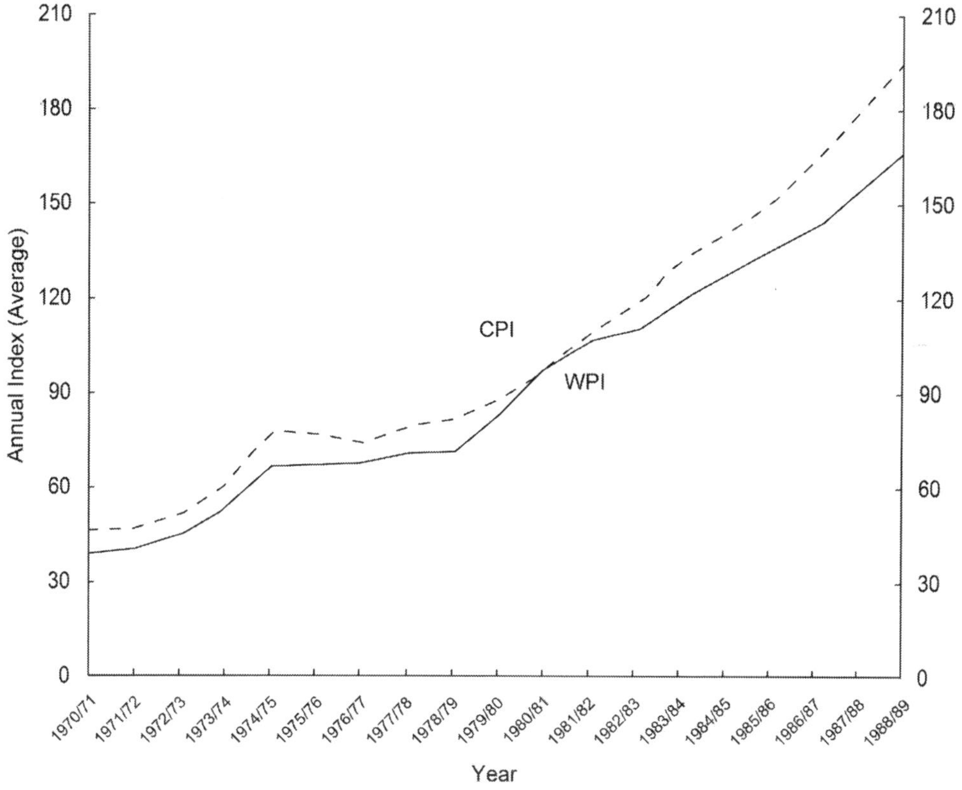

Three channels of transmission of world inflation into the domestic economy have usually been identified. Firstly, changes in import prices induce producers and traders to change domestic prices. Secondly, changes in exports affect the demand for country's output which means that an increase (decrease) in exports would lead to an increase (decrease) in domestic prices. Thirdly, an inflation abroad generates a surplus in the country's BOP and increases its monetary base and money supply *via* increases in international reserves. This contributes to an increase in domestic prices. [9]

While the third channel which is an indirect one will be discussed in the next section, the other two are studied in this section. There is evidence to say that the extent and nature of inflation in India are partially explained by changes in import prices, and by the changing structure of foreign trade in general and exports in particular. Exports have increased rapidly over the period without a corresponding increase in the proved exportable surpluses. The high rates of increase in exports have created conditions of shortages in the domestic markets. The exports in 1987-88 were 10 times the exports in 1970-71 in value terms. The quantum index of total exports (1968-89 = 100) also has more than doubled from 106.0 in 1970-71 to 242.00 in 1987-88. The structure of foreign trade has changed such that while the volume of imports has declined, the volume of exports has more than doubled. Similarly, while the exports of food articles and other wage goods have increased substantially in both value and volume terms, agricultural production in those terms on a per capita basis has not increased much. Individually, exports of fish and fish preparations, meat and meat products, fruits and vegetables, spices, etc. also have increased phenomenally in the recent past. Finally, import prices have increased more than four times in the 1970s and 1980s.

Figure 1b:
Movements in Food Index (WPI and CPI):
1980-81 to 1988-89 (Common Base: 1980-81 = 100)

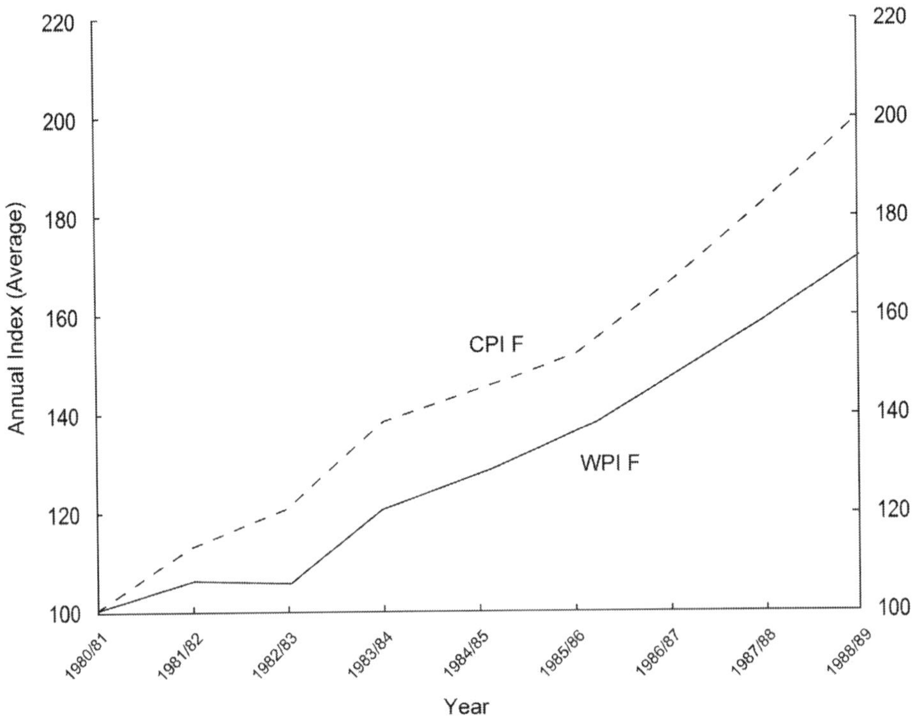

In order to further study this problem, we have constructed and tested a simple econometric model of inflation in India. In this model, the independent variables are the per capita real gross domestic product (PCRGDP), the index (1969-70 = 100) of agricultural production (AP), narrow money supply (M), the quantum index (1968-69 = 100) of total exports (TEX-PO), the quantum index (1968-69 = 100) of exports of food articles (FEXPO), the exchange rate (ER) measured as so many rupees per unit of dollar, and the unit value index (1968-69 = 100) of imports (IMPP). Inflation, the dependent variable, is measured alternatively by the wholesale price index (1970-71 = 100) for all commodities (WPI), the wholesale price index (1970-71=100) for food articles (WPIF), and the consumer price index (1960 = 100) for the industrial workers (CPI). The OLS method and the double-log functional form have been used to estimate the model for the period, 1970-71 to 1987-88. The estimated regression equations are reproduced in Table 2. The figures in brackets in Table 2 are t-values.

Table 2: International Determinants of Inflation in India, 1970-71 to 1987-88

(1) $WPI = 4.25 - 0.359\ PCRGDP + 0.61\ M - 0.15\ TEXPO + 0.254\ IMPP$

(0.809) (5.27) (0.915) (3.485)

$\bar{R}^2 = 0.986$; D.W. = 1.988; SEE = 0.0527

(2) $WPI = 8.57 - 0.987\ PCRGDP + O.864\ M - 0.112\ ER$

(1.58) (10.54) (0.359)

$\bar{R}^2 = 0.973$; D.W. = 1.811; SEE = 0.072

(3) $WPIF = 3{:}83 - 0.152\ AP + 0.524\ M - 0.479\ FEXPO + 0.33\ IMPP$

2 (0.632) (8.71) (2.76) (3.844)

$\bar{R}^2 = 0.979$; D.W. = 2.166; SEE = 0.0578

(4) $WPIF = 0.927 + 0.279\ AP + 0.563\ M + 0.004\ ER$

(0.968) (5.873) (0.015)

$\bar{R}^2 = 0.960$; D.W. = 1.484; SEE = 0.0812

(5) $CPI = 2.57 + 0.104\ PCRGDP + 0.593\ M - 0.426\ TEXPO + 0.289\ IMPP$

(0.25) (5.46) (2.73) (4.225)

$\bar{R}^2 = 0.986$; D.W. = 2.1347; SEE = 0.0495

(6) $CPI = 3.93 - 0.114\ AP + 0.556\ M - 0.407\ FEXPO + 0.299\ IMPP$

(0.546) (10.67) (2.71) (4.024)

$\bar{R}^2 = 0.986$; D.W. = 2.119; SEE = 0.0498

(7) $CPI = 6.71 - 0.654\ PCRGDP + 0.692\ M + 0.24\ ER$

(1.04) (8.427) (0.767)

$\bar{R}^2 = 0.971$; D.W. = 1.834; SEE = 0.072

(8) $CPI = 1.45 + 0.263\ AP + 0.598\ M + 0.012\ ER$

2 (1.02) (7.0) (0.049)

$\bar{R}^2 = 0.971$; D.W. = 1.424; SEE = 0.0724

The fits are quite good insofar as $\overline{R}^2$ is very high and there is an absence of serial correlation. Money supply is with the correct sign and high statistical significance in all the equations without an exception; its elasticity coefficient is typically around 0.6. The variable, import prices, also is always with the correct sign and statistical significance, and its elasticity coefficient is typically around 0.3. The other independent variables, however, have not performed well. The supply variable is with the correct sign (negative) in five out of eight functions but it lacks statistical robustness. The performance of the export variable is the most unexpected, and the poorest. It always has the wrong sign. That this may be due to multi-colinearity is indicated by the fact that in simple regression functions (not reproduced here), this variable was always with the correct sign, and it was always highly significant statistically. In the case of exchange rate, it was hypothesized that the exchange rate depreciation would be positively related with the domestic prices *via* its effects in the form of increase in exports and import prices. Actually, this variable does have a correct sign in all but one function, but every time the value of its elasticity coefficient is rather small and it is never significant statistically. In conclusion, inflation in India has a significant imported content. The direct influence of external factors on domestic prices works through import prices and exports, while the indirect influence works through money supply changes.

Our earlier study of inflation for the period, 1950-51 to 1975-76 had also shown that exports were a consistently significant determinant of prices in India; that the export elasticity of prices was about 0.3; that money supply was a significant determinant of prices with an elasticity coefficient of about 0.5; and that the supply of output had influenced prices in the expected direction but this relationship lacked statistical robustness. [10]

Another study of Indian inflation for two different periods, viz., 1956-1972 and 1956-76, has also shown that inflation in prices of imported or traded goods preceded, and significantly and disproportionately aggravated domestic inflation through cost-push pressures. [11]

III. Money Supply Process in an Open Economy

It is not intended to undertake in this section a full study of all the determinants of money in India. We have carried out such a study for the period 1951-52 to 1979-80 in an earlier work, where it was found that the government market borrowing was the most important determinant of money supply and reserve money; that the deficit financing, availability of credit, interest rate, and foreign exchange assets also significantly affected changes in money supply and reserve money. [12] Here, our attention is focused only on two issues: how far international factors determine changes in reserve money and money supply, and whether money supply changes are 'sterilized' and 'offset' in India.

The volume of reserve money and money supply has increased by 11 times and 8 times, respectively, between 1970-71 and 1987-88. Table 3 shows that the annual rate of change in money supply and reserve money has widely fluctuated, and that the volume of foreign exchange assets has been an important source of change in the reserve money. The contribution of foreign exchange assets to the growth of reserve money also has fluctuated widely in the range of 5 per cent to 41 per cent (column 5). Has the RBI 'sterilized' changes in foreign exchange assets by changing the volume of its domestic claims in the opposite direction? The columns 3 and 4 show that this does not appear to have happened because the foreign and domestic claims have moved substantially in the same direction in many years. If the 'sterilization' occurs, there would be a strong negative correlation between the two types of claims just mentioned. The actual correlation coefficient between these claims during the period 1970-71 to 1987-88 was found to-be 0.48475, which strongly refutes the notion of 'sterilization' in India.

Table 3: Changes in Money Supply, Reserve Money and Sources of Reserve Money (%)

Year	M	H	FEA	DA	FEAIH
	(1)	(2)	(3)	(4)	(5)
1971-72	14.08	12.50	5.66	22.27	10.37
72-73	16.04	11.11	-7.14	14.36	8.66
73-74	14.89	21.66	29.42	16.96	9.20
74-75	7.40	1.36	-41.81	8.00	5.28
75-76	12.93	4.05	175.70	6.63	14.00
76-77	19.84	23.37	135.58	6.82	26.76
77-78	-8.28	14.73	78.28	-0.01	41.58
78-79	19.44	25.68	21.49	7.14	40.14
79-80	15.69	21.16	-2.14	52.59	31.93
80-81	16.58	16.86	-11.37	28.16	24.23
81-82	6.89	8.24	-43.32	24.39	12.86
82'83	14.91	10.00	-36.10	8.71	7.36
83-84	16.14	24.67	-6.07	20.08	5.55
84-85	19.63	9.37	87.43	12.06	9.52
85-86	10.10	20.31	9.82	24.94	8.70
86-87	17.43	18.20	37.42	17.49	10.26
87-88	12.69	18.97	14.69	16.65	9.94

NOTATION:
M - Narrow money supply; H - Reserve Money; FEA - Net Foreign Exchange Assets of RBI; DA - Domestic claims of RBI.

SOURCE: RBI, *Report on Currency and Finance*, various issues.

These issues were further studied by estimating a simple money supply determination model by using OLS method and the double-log functional form. Money supply (M) or high powered money (H) were regressed on the foreign exchange assets of the RBI (FEA), the domestic assets of the RBI (DA), and the foreign exchange reserves (FER) of the country, either separately or in certain combinations. The coefficient of FEA or FER would show the money multiplier associated with changes in foreign reserves. If it were found to be positive and significantly different from zero, it would mean that changes in foreign reserves or BOP had a significant impact on domestic money supply, and that the monetary authorities were unwilling or unable to 'sterilize' this impact.

Approaching this problem somewhat differently, we regressed DA on FEA and FEA on DA also to obtain 'sterilization' and 'offset' coefficients. While the 'sterilization' coefficient shows, as said earlier, that whenever international reserves change independently, such changes are 'sterilized' by changing domestic assets in the opposite direction, the 'offset coefficient' shows that whenever domestic assets change independently or autonomously, such changes are 'offset' by changing foreign assets in the opposite direction. Both these coefficients are expected to have values between 0 and -1. Table 4 presents the results of estimation of money supply determination model.

Figures in brackets are t-values.

Again, the fits are mostly good except the fact that simple regressions are marred by auto correlation. Without going into further details of interpretation of these results, it can be concluded that: (a) money supply process in India is significantly influenced by international factors, and (b) the monetary authorities in India do not or cannot follow the policy of either 'sterilization' or 'offsetting'. The elasticity coefficient of foreign reserves is quite high (0.5 to 0.8) in simple regressions but it is about 0.1 to 0.2 in multiple regressions. In our earlier study also, this coefficient was found to be around 0.1.

While studying international influences on the domestic money supply, a relevant question which arises is: what has caused changes in international reserves? To what extent were reserve changes due to changes in the trade balance and capital flows, respectively? The variations in reserves due to capital flows are the result of monetary factors which are of more immediate concern for monetary policy. In India, while the trade balance has almost always been negative, the capital account has mostly been positive. Thus, it is mainly changes in capital inflows which help to explain changes in reserves and money supply in India. This leads us to a study of capital movements in the next section.

Table 4: International Determinants of Reserve Money and Money Supply, 1970-71 to 1987-88

(I) $H = 3.22 + 0.601\ FEA$; $\bar{R}^2 = 0.517$; $DW. = 0.265$;
(4-.385) $SEE = 0.532$

(2) $H = 2.25 + 0.79\ FER$; $\bar{R}^2 = 0.803$; $DW. = 0.314$
(8.38) $SEE = 0.339$

(3) $H = 0.445 + 0.135\ FEA + 0.827\ DA;\ \bar{R}^2 = 0.994;\ DW. = 1.796;$
$(6.35) \quad (34\text{-}.61) \quad SEE = 0.0611$

(4) $H = 0.55 + 0.202\ FER + 0.743\ DA;\quad \bar{R}^2 = 0.995;\ D.W. = 1.457;$
$SEE = 0.06$

(5) $M = 3.83 + 0.49\ FEA;\quad \bar{R}^2 = 0.484;\ D.W. = 0.255$
$(4.119) \quad SEE = 0.461$

(6) $M = 3.00 + 0.655\ FER;\quad \bar{R}^2 = 0.784;\ D.W. = 0.312$
$(7.91) \quad SEE = 0.299$

(7) $M = 1.43 + 0.084\ FEA + 0.715\ DA;\quad \bar{R}^2 = 0.989;\ D.W. = 1.39$
$(3.78) \quad (27.91) \quad SEE = 0.065$

(8) $M = 1.51 + 0.141\ FER + 0.651\ DA;\quad \bar{R}^2 = 0.992;\ D.W. = 1.463$
$(4.62) \quad (19.95) \quad SEE = 0.058$

(9) $FEA = 0.819 + 0751\ DA;\quad \bar{R}^2 = 0.39;\ D.W. = 0.432$
$SEE = 0.736$

(10) $DA = 3.35 + 0.566\ FEA;\quad \bar{R}^2 = 0.39;\ D.W. = 0.243$
$SEE = 0.639$

IV. Capital Movements and the Structure of World Interest Rates

International capital movements are an important element in the world transmission of economic fluctuations and inflation because they not only affect changes in money supply but also bring about complex linkages of monetary conditions between countries. It is, therefore, necessary to discuss in this section: (a) the extent to which interest rates in India and abroad are correlated and how the interest rate differential between India and other countries has behaved, and (b) what is the nature of, and how far capital movements have been sensitive to, changes in interest rates. A knowledge of these aspects would also enable us to gauge the extent of integration of the Indian economy with the world economy and the extent of loss of autonomy of monetary policy.

It may be noted at the outset that interest rates in India are administered and they are administered to a degree far higher than in many other countries. As a result, the correlation between Indian interest rates and world interest rates can be expected to be weak and the causal link between the foreign and domestic rates would be through a policy reaction to changes in external rates and other external monetary variables.

Figures 2 and 3 portray the level and changes in the money market rates and the long-term interest rates in five countries, namely, India, USA, UK, West Germany and Japan during 1971-88. Similarly, Table 5 presents temporal variations in the short-term as well as long-term interest rates differentials between India and each of the other four countries. Table 6 gives the correlation of the short-term and long-term interest rates in India with the respective rates in each of the other four countries. The important points which emerge from this evidence are as follows:

(1) The short-term rate of interest in India has usually been higher than the similar rate in other countries, especially West Germany and Japan. There does not exist a clear increasing or decreasing trend in the differential between the Indian and world short-term rates.

(2) The long-term rate of interest in India has been mostly lower than the similar rate in other countries except during the years after 1985. The positive long-term interest rate differential in favour of India after 1985 has arisen more because of a sharp decline in the world rates than a sharp increase in the Indian rate during these years.

The evidence of a different nature also supports the point that the long-term rate of interest in India has lagged behind the similar rate in other countries. It has been estimated that while the mean domestic nominal interest rate on time deposits of six months and above during 1971-80 was 6.79 per cent, the average foreign interest rate adjusted for expected changes in exchange rates during the same period was 11.25 per cent. [13]

Figure 2:
World Money Market Rates

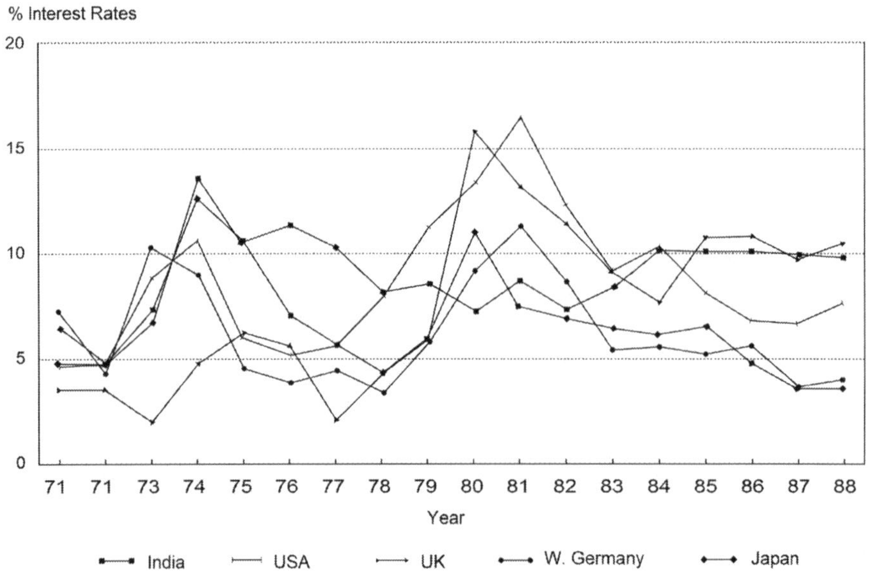

Figure 3:
World Long-Term Interest Rates

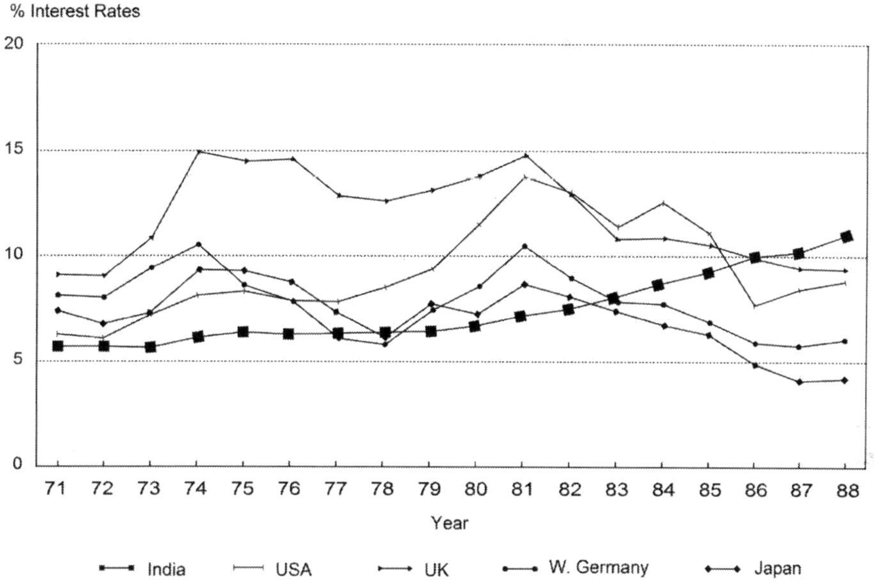

(3) Both the short-term and long-term interest rates abroad have fluctuated more than those rates in India. The flexibility and volatility of all interest rates in other countries have been far greater than in India. The short-term rate of interest has been more volatile than the long-term rate of interest in all the countries including India.

(4) The correlation between interest rates in India and those in other countries except Japan has been very low (see Table 6). Subject to this, the correlation between the long-term rates in India and abroad has been relatively higher than the correlation between the shgrt-term rates, and while the former has mostly been negative, the latter has mostly been positive. In contrast, the correlation of interest rates among the four countries other than India has been high and positive in respect of the short-term rates, and low and negative in respect of the long-term rates. It is interesting to note that while the short-term interest rates in the-world are positively correlated, the long-term rates are negatively correlated.

Interest rates in India are clearly out of alignment with those in other countries, and the relationship between interest rates in India and other countries is clearly of a different type or nature in comparison with the relationship of interest rates among developed countries. This may be due to the system of pervasive and closely administered interest rates and exchange control in India.

All this had two types of effects on capital movements in India. Firstly, interest rates have played only a marginal role in determining whatever capital inflows have taken place, at least until recently. Secondly, it has induced capital outflows abroad. It is well known that an illicit

Table 5: Interest Rates Differentials: India and Other Countries

Year	Money Market Rate				Long-term Rate			
	1	2	3	4	5	6	7	8
1970-71	1.64	2.85	-0.85	1.58	-0.48	-3.26	-2.36	-1.64
71-72	0.26	1.24	0.39	-0.03	-0.36	-3.25	-2.25	-1.05
72-73	-2.09	4.72	-3.55	-0.52	-1.47	-5.07	-3.65	-1.61
73-74	3.02	8.89	4.65	0.98	-2.02	-8.73	-4.36	-3.22
74-75	4.58	4.32	5.99	-0.27	-1.84	-8.04	-2.15	-2.85
75-76	6.23	5.74	7.39	4.30	-1.58	-8.14	-1.51	-2.43
76-77	4.64	8.05	6.04	4.50	-1.35	-6.41	0.12	-1.01
77-78	0.12	3.76	4.69	3.69	-2.12	-6.10	0.57	0.28
78-79	-2.73	2.46	2.60	2.61	-2.88	-6.54	-0.95	-1.24
79-80	-6.12	-8.38	-1.82	-3.69	-4.68	-7.08	-1.79	-0.51
80-81	-7.77	-4.51	-2.65	1.18	-6.57	-7.59	-3.23	-1.51
81-82	-4.99	-4.09	-1.40	0.33	-5.33	-5.29	-1.36	-0.47
82-83	-0.79	-0.79	2.94	1.91	-3.35	-2.82	0.10	0.57
83-84	-0.28	2.33	4.40	3.85	-3.83	-2.24	0.87	1.84
84-85	1.90	-0.78	4.81	3.54	-1.75	-1.40	2.35	2.38
85-86	3.16	-0.71	4.40	5.18	2.27	0.08	4.03	5.01
86-87	3.25	0.25	6.19	6.40	1.77	0.67	4.31	5.94
87-88	2.11	-0.59	5.71	6.10	2.12	1.61	4.87	6.70

NOTATION:
1, 5: India-US; 2, 6: India-UK; 3, 7: India-West Germany; 4, 8: India-Japan. Source: IMF, *International Financial Statistics*, various issues.

Table 6: Correlation of Interest Rates in India with those in Other Countries, 1970-71 to 1987-88

Country	Short-rate	Long-rate
USA	0.027	0.302
UK	0.0119	-0.431
W. Germany	-0.129	-0.083
Japan	0.422	-0.736

export of capital, gold smuggling, and even official export of capital have been continuously occurring on a vast scale in India. Apart from exchange, trade, and gold controls, the low domestic interest rates can be said to have been a significant contributing factor behind this phenomenon.

A study of the nature and structure of capital flows in India would enable us to understand this relationship between interest rates and capital movements. Table 7 presents net capital flows under various heads of capital account in India. It can be seen that it is only on the official loan account that there has always been a net inflow of capital, and that this net inflow has increased substantially over a period of time. Insofar as interest rate is not an important consideration while sanctioning official loans, an increase in the net inflow of capital on official account cannot be said to have occurred in response to changes in interest rates. The interest sensitivity of this very major component of capital inflow is almost nil.

Table 7: Net (Inflow-Outflow) Capital Flows in India (Rs. Crore)

Year	Private (Long-term)	Banking	Official			Total
			Loans	Amortization	Misc.	
	(1)	(2)	(3)	(4)	(5)	(6)
1970-71	-29	-8	656	-188	-29	400
1971-72	-3	9	616	-210	154	565
1972-73	-7	-17	586	-245	-65	250
1973-74	-37	-I	891	-1992	131	-1010
1974-75	-26	-47	1554	-237	-294	948
1975-76	-53	27	1326	-284	-445	5570
1976-77	-7	117	879	-316	-474	194
1977-78	-75	68	631	-417	-522	-165
1978-79	-22	-8	583	-408	99	239
1979-80	-40	-82	895	-476	296	593
1980-81	77	13	1664	-611	-227	916
1981-82	118	-13	1257	-576	-278	492
1982-83	208	68	1689	-611	-539	825
1983-84	697	182	1782	-693	219	2187
1984-85	1093	-193	3034	-726	184	3390
1985-86	2292	186	3683	-1152	85	4891
1986-87	2257	-70	6462	- 2588	-172	5899

NOTE: Figures are rounded off.

SOURCE: Y.U.K. Sarma, "India's Balance of Payments-1948-49 to 1984-85: *Survey*", *Journal of the Indian School of Political Economy*, July-Dec. 1989, pp 283-289.

As far as the private account is concerned, there was a net outflow of capital on this account till 1979-80 after which there has been a substantial increase in the net capital inflow. A major part of this increased inflow, however, has been in the form of NRI investments and deposits which have been induced by a package of policy measures of which fixing the attractive and very flexible interest rates, especially for these deposits, has been one measure. In a bid to encourage deposits by NRIs in order to meet pressures on BOP, the authorities have been fixing rates of interest on these deposits which are higher than the domestic rates as well as the prevailing interest rates in the international markets, and these interest rates have been changed very frequently in keeping with interest rate changes in international capital markets. The recent changes in the private capital account are, therefore, suggestive of what can be achieved by an appropriate interest rate policy.

There have been net capital outflows in many years on the banking and the official miscellaneous accounts also. Needless to add that the unofficial capital outflows are not reflected in Table 7.

V. Lessons and Conclusions

The Indian economy or the Indian monetary system is not very closely integrated with the world system. But it is not an isolated or a closed economy either. There has been an increase in the internationalization of the Indian financial system in the past many years. As a result, the monetary policy in India cannot be conducted in a totally autonomous manner, particularly if we take a futuristic view.

The money supply in India is affected by our exchange with other countries which means that it cannot be treated as an exogenous variable, and that there are limitations on conducting monetary policy by making money supply as the only target or indicator of monetary policy. Academic notions such as 'sterilization' and 'offsetting' of money supply changes have no practical relevance or use in the conduct of monetary policy in India. Where the inflow of foreign capital is consciously and actively encouraged to meet partially the savings gap or the financial resources crunch in the domestic economy, where capital inflows are accompanied by an increase in deficit financing, and where the open market operations are not extensively undertaken, changes in capital inflows or foreign exchange reserves, instead of being 'sterilized', must have a direct and immediate effect on the domestic money supply.

International factors have directly and indirectly contributed to the inflationary pressures in India, and monetary authorities would find it difficult to achieve the goal of price stability unless these factors are taken care of. To the extent that an increase in import prices and exports contributes to inflation, it appears that even the goal of price stability is not within the full control of the central bank.

The behaviour of interest rates or the interest rates policy in India has encouraged capital outflows rather than capital inflows, except in the case of remittances by NRIs in the recent past. This, once again, suggests the potential for achieving the perceived goals through an appropriate interest rate policy provided the system of administered interest rates is systematically dismantled. Like NRIs, domestic savers also deserve and ought to be rewarded adequately. The increase in domestic interest rates would help in better allocation of resources, raising domestic savings, increasing efficiency of investment, and thereby reduce the need for capital inflows. [14] Such a policy would help a lot in tackling the problem of internal as well as external debt burden or debt trap. To pay higher interest rates on domestic savings or domestic debt is preferable to paying higher interest rates on foreign savings because while the interest income on the former remains within the country, the interest income on the latter constitutes a drain on the economy.

While monetary policy is no doubt constrained by the international factors and considerations, it does not mean that the conduct of monetary policy is to be dominated by external considerations or that monetary policy has lost autonomy totally or that it has become useless. As has been rightly pointed out, the national economic policies will continue to remain preoccupied with essentially national concerns, and that even in economies where the international sector is relatively much greater than in a country like India, the national sector is always bigger than the international sector. [15] The import of our discussion is different from the monetarist stand that the domestic monetary policy is useless on account of 'offsetting' capital flows or 'sterilization' effect. In fact, by upholding or substantiating the thesis of imported inflation, we are again rejecting the concept of 'sterilization' and thereby assigning an important role, albeit a more difficult one, to the domestic monetary policy.

Notes

1. Bryant, 1980, p. xix.
2. Banerji, 1989.
3. Rangarajan, 1989, pp. 3-4.
4. Robin, 1989, p. 4.
5. The other aspects of monetary policy which also could have been discussed relate to the target/indicator choice, the relationship between interest rate and exchange rate policies, the multilateral relationship between inflow of foreign savings, government deficits, and money supply.
6. All such information in the paper is based on publications of the RBI, CSO, Government of India, and other official sources.
7. For details see Bhatt, 1989, pp. 1464-65.
8. Figure 1 has been reproduced from RBI, Annual Report, 1988-89, p. 65.
9. Brunner, 1974, pp. 192-193.
10. Bhole, 1985(a), pp. 291-294.
11. Bhalla, 1981, pp. 143-152.
12. Bhole, *op cit.*, Chapter 9.

13. Khatkhate, 1988, p. 1429.
14. Bhole, 1985(b).
15. Llewellyn, 1980, p. 5.

References

ALIBER, R. Z. (ed.), *National Monetary Policies and the International Financial System,* The University of Chicago Press, Chicago, 1974.

ANDO, Albert and others, *Monetary Policy in Our Times,* The MIT Press Massachusetts 1985.

BANERJI, Arun, "Balance of Payments: Evading the Real Issues" *Economic* & *Politic* Weekly, March 11, 1989.

BERGSTRAND, J.H., "Short-run Domestic Monetary Control in an International Money Market", *New England Economic Review,* Federal Reserve Bank of Boston, July-August 1984.

BHALLA, Surjit, S., "India's Closed Economy and World Inflation", in W.R., Cline, and Associates, *World Inflation and the Developing Countries,* The Brookings Institution, Washington, 1981.

BHATT, V. V., "On Participating in the International Capital Market", *Economic* & *Political Weekly,* July 1, 1989.

BHOLE, L. M., *Impacts of Monetary Policy,* Himalaya Publishing House, Bombay, 1985(a).

___, "Administered Interest Rates in India", *Economic* & *Political Weekly,* June 22-29, 1985(b).

BILSON, J. F. O., and Marston, R.C. (eds.), *Exchange Rate Theory and Practice,* National Bureau of Economic Research, Massachusetts, 1984.

BRUNNER, Karl, "Money Supply Process and Monetary Policy in an Open Economy" in A.K. Swoboda (ed), *International Trade and Money,* London, 1973.

___, "Monetary Management, Domestic Inflation and Imported Inflation", in R. Z. ALIBER (eds.), *op. cit.*

BRYANT, R. C., *Money and Monetary Policy in interdependent Nations,* The Brookings Institution, Washington, 1980.

BRYANT, R. C., and others (eds.), *Empirical Macroeconomics for Interdependent Economies,* The Brookings Institution, Washington, 1988.

CAVES, R. E., and H. JOHNSON (eds.), *Readings in International Economics,* R. Irwin, Homewood, Illinois, 1988.

CLAASEN, E. and P. SALIN (eds.), *Stabilization Polities in Open Economies,* North Holland, Amsterdam, 1972.

COOPER, R. N. (ed.), *International Finance,* Penguin, 1969.

FEDERAL RESERVE BANK OF BOSTON, *International Aspects of Stabilization Policies,* Conference Proceedings, 1974.

___, *Key Issues in International Banking,* Conference Proceedings, 1977.

___, *The Political Economy of Monetary Policy: National and International Aspects*, Conference Proceedings, 1983.

HERIN, J., and others (eds.), *Flexible Exchange Rates and Stabilization Policy*, Macmillan, London, 1977.

KHATKHATE, D. R., "Assessing the Level of Interest Rates in Less Developed Countries", *Economic & Political Weekly*, July 9, 1988.

Kurgman, P.R., "International Aspects of US Monetary and Fiscal Policy", in Federal Reserve Bank of Boston, *The Economics of Large Government Deficits*, Conference Proceedings, 1983.

LEIGH-PEMBERTON, Robin, "Europe 1992: Some Monetary Policy Issues", *Economic Review*, Federal Reserve Bank of Kansas City, September-October 1989.

LLEWELLYN, D. T., *International Financial Integration*, Macmillan, London, 1980.

LOMBRA, R. E., and WITTE, W. E., "Political Economy of International and Domestic Monetary Relations", Iowa State University Press, Ames, 1982.

MORRIS, F. E., "The Changing World of Central Banking", *New England Economic Review*, Federal Reserve Bank of Boston, March-April, 1986.

MUNDELL, R.A, and AK. Swoboda (eds.), *Monetary Problems of the International Economy*, University of Chicago Press, Chicago, 1969.

MUNDELL, R.A, *Monetary Theory: Inflation, Interest, and Growth in the World Economy*, Goodyear, Pacific Palisades, 1971.

OECD, *Exchange Rate Management and the Conduct of Monetary Policy*, Paris, 1985.

RANGARAJAN, C., "Issues in Monetary Management", *The Indian Economic Journal*, January-March, 1989.

TAYLOR, Lance, *Varieties of Stabilization Experience*, Clarendon Press, Oxford, 1988.

WILLIAMSON, John, *The Open Economy and the World Economy*, Basic Books. 1983.

[22]

*Recent Changes in the Theory and Policy of Cash Reserves Ratio and Statutory Liquidity Ratio: A Critical Appraisal**

Introduction

A number of financial reforms has been recently introduced in India as a part of trade and industrial policy liberalization. The *reduction* in the Cash Reserves Ratio (CRR) and the Statutory Liquidity Ratio (SLR) is being posed as an important part of these financial reforms. The Committee on the Financial System (Narasimham Committee) had recommended that the SLR should be *reduced* in a phased manner to 25 per cent over a period of about five years, and that the Reserve Bank of India (RBI) should consider *reducing* the CRR progressively from its level existing in 1991. The Committee had argued that given the government's resolve to reduce the fiscal deficit to a level consistent with macro-economic stability, and given the deregulation of interest rates, there would be a greater scope for using Open Market Operations (OMO), and, correspondingly, there would be a less need for using the CRR for controlling the secondary expansion of bank credit (RBI, 1991).

The authorities have accepted these recommendations. The RBI, accordingly, announced the discontinuation of the incremental CRR of 10 per cent in April 1992, and a reduction in SLR for 38.5 per cent to 37.75 per cent in October 1992 (to be effected in three phases). The monetary policy for the first half of 1993-94 further reduced the SLR from 37.75 per cent to 36.75 per cent (to be effected in four phases), and the CRR from 15 per cent to 14 per cent (to be effected in two phases), with the major *objective of enlarging the availability of credit to the commercial sector.*

Following these changes, the Governor of the RBI has said that, as a part of financial sector reforms, a start has been made to reduce the reserves requirements, and that the RBI *is com-*

* Paper published in *Vikalpa*, October-December, 1993.

mitted to a reduction in the levels of pre-emptions in the forms of CRR and SLR (Rangarajan, 1993). The medium-term commitment is to *reduce* the CRR from its effective level of 16.5 per cent in 1991 to 10 per cent in 1997, and to *reduce* the SLR from 38.5 per cent in 1991 to 25 per cent in 1996.

The objective of this paper is to critically examine the primary purpose of and the arguments behind this (medium term) *commitment to reduce* the CRR and SLR. In the process, it offers some reflections on the theory of choice of techniques of monetary control from the point of view of this effectiveness. The paper is organized as follows. In Section I, the reserves requirements system in India, as it has evolved over the past many years, is described briefly (Bhole, 1992; Gupta, 1979; RBI Report, 1985). This is followed by a critical analysis of the reserves requirements policy in Section II. Subsequently, an approach to a more effective or superior monetary policy has been outlined in Section III. Summary and Conclusions are presented in Section IV.

I. Reserves Requirements System in India

The variable primary and secondary (supplementary) reserves requirements have been one of the few main weapons of discretionary monetary policy in many countries. Such legal reserves requirements place an upper limit on deposit creation by banks and thereby help Central Banks to control directly the growth of bank credit and money supply. The RBI has also been having the power to use this weapon ever since 1956. Between 1956 and 1962, there were separate CRRs in respect of demand liabilities and time liabilities of the banks. In 1962, they were merged and a single minimum CRR of 3 per cent of total demand and time liabilities of banks was fixed. Thereafter, the RBI was empowered to change the CRR beyond 3 per cent with respect to total deposit liabilities (called the average CRR), and/or with respect to incremental deposit liabilities after a specified date (called the marginal or incremental CRR). Till recently, changes in the average CRR and the marginal CRR were subject to the ceiling of 15 per cent and 100 per cent, respectively.

The RBI is empowered to impose and vary penal interest rates on banks in respect of their shortfalls (defaults) in the prescribed CRR. Similarly, the RBI can pay, at its discretion, interest on that portion of cash reserves which is the difference between the prescribed CRR and the minimum CRR of 3 per cent, provided the bank has not defaulted in respect of maintaining the prescribed CRR. The RBI has frequently used these powers.

From the point of view of the degree of active use of the CRR, the period since 1956 can be sub-divided as follows:

- 1956 to 1972 when virtually no use of this technique was made. The average CRR remained at the level of 3 per cent throughout this period.
- 1973 to 1991 when it was used very actively in both the directions. On the whole, the average CRR was raised from 3 per cent to 15 per cent during this period.
- November 1991 onwards when the authorities have committed to *reduce* the CRR, and, as said above, have started reducing it.

The Chakravarty Committee had found that the CRR was a highly effective and a very useful instrument of inflation control and monetary regulation because of its quick and predictable impact, and that it was particularly suited for Indian conditions where a sudden rise in the price level by 15-20 per cent has occurred every few years since the middle of 1960s. Its active use as the primary weapon since 1973 was dictated by a sharp increase in inflationary pressures, the large and continuous budgetary deficits, a significant decline in currency-deposit ratio contributing to a higher value of the money multiplier, the limited scope for OMO, the low levels of refinance which had already been achieved resulting in little scope for its further curtailment, and the continued popularity of fixed deposits with banks as a mode of financial savings.

As to the future, assuming that the Indian monetary system would be restructured as it had recommended, the Committee had suggested that:

- The practice of prescribing the marginal CRR be adopted very sparingly for short durations, and only in special circumstances requiring drastic remedies.
- When the incremental CRR was imposed or stipulated, it should be converted to an average CRR at an appropriate time.
- There should be a less need for resorting to variations in the average CRR as a primary tool of monetary policy.

It ought to be noted that the Chakravarty Committee had not recommended a *reduction* in the CRR, and that its suggestion to use the CRR cautiously and sparingly was contingent on the restructuring of the monetary system. However, not much progress has been made in this regard. Moreover, most of the conditions which had led to the active use of the CRR after 1973 still exist in India. The recognition of these realities, and the felt need that the CRR may have to be *raised* and used actively in the coming years had possibly made the authorities to get the Parliament's approval for raising the maximum permissible CRR from 15 per cent to 20 per cent, around the time the Narasimham Committee submitted its report. The sudden reversal of thinking on the role of CRR during the post-June 1991 period, therefore, needs to be examined closely and understood properly.

The RBI has been empowered since 1949 to vary the SLR also. It can increase the SLR up to the level of 40 per cent of the total demand and time liabilities of the commercial banks. While defaults by banks in maintaining the prescribed SLR do not invite penal interest payments or the loss of interest on cash reserves, they do result in restrictions on banks' access to refinance facilities from the RBI, and in the higher cost of such refinance.

The objectives of the SLR have been:

- to impose financial discipline on banks
- to provide protection to deposit-holders
- to create/support/provide a captive market for government securities
- to allocate directly total bank credit between the government sector and the private commercial sector
- to help in monetary regulation.

The SLR works as an instrument of monetary control indirectly by affecting:

- government borrowings from the RBI
- banks' freedom to sell government securities or to borrow from the RBI against those securities
- banks' scope to offset the impact of changes in the CRR by liquidating their government securities holdings.

From the point of view of how actively the SLR has been used, the period since 1949 can be sub-divided as follows:

- 1950 to 1963 when the SLR remained constant at the level of 20 per cent.
- 1964 to 1969 during which it was raised to 25 per cent in 1964, and it remained at that level till 1969.
- 1970 to 1991 when it was actively used and it reached the level of 38.5 per cent in 1990.
- November 1991 onwards when it is slate for a significant *reduction*.

Incidentally, the Chakravarty Committee had not recommended for such a reduction in the SLR.

Thus, the CRR and the SLR control system in India has consisted of the powers of the Central Bank:

- to change the CRR between 3 and 15 per cent
- to change the SLR up to 40 per cent
- to impose incremental CRR up to 100 per cent
- to pay interest on the CRR between 3 and 15 per cent
- to impose interest and/or penalty on defaults in the prescribed CRR and SLR.

In operating this system, unlike in the US, there has been no discrimination among scheduled commercial banks on the basis of either the size or the location. However, there has been a difference in the treatment of commercial banks and cooperative banks; the latter are required to maintain the CRR and the SLR at much lower levels. Similarly, the NRI deposit accounts bear lower levels of these ratios as compared to residents' deposit accounts with commercial banks.

The control system under discussion certainly appears to have been designed, developed and deployed for regulatory, safety, liquidity and distributive purposes; credit distribution between the public and private sectors has never been its only or even primary objective.

II. A Critical Analysis of the Present Policy

Are Global Trends Relevant for India?

Of late, there has been a change in the thinking on reserves ratio technique in many Western countries where the reserves requirements are being either reduced drastically or eliminated completely. For example, the Federal Reserve System in the US has recently reduced such requirements on transactions deposits, and eliminated them on time deposits. The Central Banks in Switzerland, New Zealand, Australia, Canada and Germany have also implemented such a policy (WEINER,

1992). Following these trends, it has been argued that the Indian financial system also should prepare itself for a similar major change in the system of monetary control (TARAPORE, 1993).

The cross-country experiences and trends can prove to be useful in modeling the domestic policy only if cross-country differences in economic conditions, institutional realities, technical details, feasibility difficulties and diversity of prescription are thoroughly examined in respect of their comparability with indigenous situation. This does not appear to have happened while formulating the present reserves requirements policy in India. As will be discussed shortly, the current economic and financial conditions in India are not propitious for a substantial reduction in reserves requirements, particularly because it is not feasible, at least in the medium-term, to harness effectively the other techniques of monetary control for the purpose of stabilization.

Similarly, the manner of application of reserves ratio technique in India has been different from the one abroad. In many countries abroad, different and separate levels of reserves ratio are prescribed for demand deposits and time deposits; and even after its recent reduction, the ratio against demand deposits is still quite high (10 to 12 per cent) in countries like the US and Germany. A really significant reduction in the reserves ratio against demand deposits has occurred only in Canada. Therefore, the policy of a significant reduction in the CRR can be adopted in India only after examining the question whether we need to go back to our own old system of separate CRRs for demand deposits and time deposits, respectively.

Further, the reduction/elimination of reserves ratio in other countries has been effected gradually over a long period of about 20 years, while in India, it is to be effected within a period of about 5 years. The destabilizing consequences of such a swift shift should not be overlooked. It must also be kept in mind that notwithstanding the current foreign "fashion" in this context, there are also competing or alternative viewpoints there which have emphasized the use of "reserves strategy" and "control through reserves and assets ratios" for a better working of monetary policy, and for encouraging competition in the financial system.

In view of these multiple considerations, and in view of the recognition or admission by the authorities themselves that the contemporary reserves requirements policy abroad may be a "fashion of the time" and that such a policy in India would attenuate monetary control, a serious rethinking of the commitment to reduce the CRR and the SLR is certainly called for.

Untenability of "Reserves Tax" Argument

The drastic reduction/elimination of the CRR is allegedly advocated in order to ease the financial burden on banks and other depository institutions, and to improve their competitiveness and profitability. In countries like the US, Canada and Germany, there is no payment of interest on compulsory or required reserves of the banks. It is, therefore, argued that the interest forgone on involuntarily held reserves is, in effect, a tax, called a "Reserves Tax" on either the banks or their shareholders or their customers. The tax takes the form of either lower profitability or lower dividends, or lower interest rates on deposits or higher interest rates on bank loans. The "Reserves Tax" like any other selective tax, is said to distort the allocative process; it takes banks less competitive and it channelizes more funds to institutions which are not required to hold cash reserves compulsorily. The measure of "Reserves Tax" is said to be equal to interest forgone when no interest is paid on reserves (either the whole amount of required reserves or the amount of minimum reserves), or it would be equal to interest forgone when interest is paid but is lower than the market rate of interest.

The "Reserves Tax" argument has been advanced by many in India also. However, it is not tenable for the following reasons:

- In India, the compulsory reserves on which no interest is paid are only 3 per cent of demand and time liabilities of the banks. It would be impossible to maintain that had the CRR not existed, banks would have lent even these reserves and earned an income on them. Even in the absence of the CRR, banks would have had to hold some reserves to meet liquidity requirements. One has absolutely no idea whether the reserves thus held would have been 3 per cent or more or less. However, it can safely be argued that the CRR of 3 per cent does not impose a "Reserves Tax" on banks because it can be treated as if it is held voluntarily. In other words, interest forgone on the CRR of 3 per cent can be called a tax only if one can be sure that banks would not have voluntarily maintained even that amount of reserves, and yet they would have functioned in a smooth, stable and viable manner.
- As to the CRR beyond 3 per cent, banks in India are paid a fairly high rate of interest, and, if needed, this rate of interest can be raised further. The Narasimham Committee itself had recommended that ultimately this rate of interest should be raised to banks' average cost of deposits. In general, it may be in the interests of economic stability to pay suitable interest on compulsory reserves where no interest is paid or to pay higher interest where the existing rate is thought to be low by certain standards. The "Reserves Tax" argument is based on the rejection, without further systematic analysis, of this alternative.
- The argument regarding the competitive disadvantage of banks vis-à-vis other financial institutions also does not have much force in the present context. Firstly, to the extent that interest is paid or can be paid on reserves, the banks' disadvantage is reduced. Secondly, the so called "Reserves Tax" cannot be said to have been a determining factor behind the reduction in the share of banks in the total financial savings in the economy. The bank deposits to financial savings ratio and the CRR do not appear to be negatively correlated. There is no reason for such a negative correlation in India. The crucial factor in this context has been the low rates of interest on bank deposits. Deposit rates have been administratively fixed at unreasonably low levels, and the CRR had nothing to do with such a fixation. We have had a simultaneous reduction in the bank deposits rates and the CRR in the recent past. Perhaps, the concern over a decline in the share of banks in savings mobilization is not genuine because many systematic policy efforts have been undertaken over many years to development the so called equity culture in the country. In short, for improving the competitiveness of banks, and for correcting distortions in resource mobilization and allocation process, what is needed is attractive interest rates on bank deposits and not reduction in reserves requirements.

• The current thinking on the CRR abroad and in India cannot be justified even if we accept, for the sake of argument, that it imposes a "Reserves Tax" on banks. It is not possible to avoid taxation if the economy is to be managed well. If we are to eliminate the CRR for tax reasons, we, perforce, will have to eliminate all taxes in the economic system. Similarly, strictly speaking, it is not only the technique of the CRR which can be said to involve a "tax element". The use of other techniques of monetary control in place of the CRR would also involve cost or burden or "tax" of some kind or other.

• It is also very pertinent to remember that reduction/elimination of the "Reserves Tax" may result in the imposition of a higher "instability tax" or "inflation tax" on the economy. The role of techniques of monetary control has to be viewed positively rather than negatively. These techniques help to stabilize the economic system, and since instability is a greater evil than the inconvenience or financial "loss" incidental to the use of these techniques, the latter cannot really be called a "tax". The "Reserves Tax" argument as the basis of CRR policy provides for *shifting* the cost of economic management on to economic units which are more vulnerable to inflationary and other types of economic instability. It is, therefore, iniquitous and undermines the goal of social justice.

The CRR, Privatization and Credit Control

On account of all the weaknesses of the "Reserves Tax" argument, one wonders whether "improving bank profitability" is the real objective or purpose behind the current CRR policy. As far as the SLR is concerned, significant increase in coupon rates on government bonds, effected in the past few years, had already begun to render the profitability argument largely irrelevant. This is particularly so because, of late, the risk-adjusted average rate of interest on the portfolio of commercial and other private loans has not been significantly above the rate of interest on government securities. It is a matter of conjecture only that if the SLR had been lower, the banks would not have invested much in government securities for reasons of profitability. Apart from the rate of return earned on them, the investments in government securities may help to improve bank profitability indirectly also by absorbing fluctuations in the demand for commercial or industrial credit.

The present CRR and SLR policy, therefore, appears to be primarily inspired by the resurrection and celebration of the ideology of privatization. The multi-purpose role of reserves requirements is now being transformed into a single-purpose role of channelizing more and more funds to be private industrial, commercial and business sectors. It appears that one more technique of credit control is now being converted purely into a technique of credit distribution – credit distribution in favour of the organized private sector. To put it differently, perhaps the reserves requirements technique is now being used to achieve the "reverse crowding out" effect. Let us elaborate on this theme.

Historically, reserves requirements, in the beginning, were primarily meant to ensure the liquidity, viability and stability of banks by restraining the greedy and profit-hungry bankers from overlending bank resources. In a sense, therefore, even at this stage, the CRR played a regulatory role. Subsequently, the regulatory role of the CRR came to be extended for controlling the volume of credit and money supply. At a still later juncture, the distribution of financial resources between the public and private sector got incorporated as an explicit objective of monetary policy in many countries including India. However, so far, the CRR has nowhere been used for the purpose of sectoral credit distribution. It is the other techniques – secondary reserves requirements and direct credit allocation in foreign countries; and these techniques plus the bank rate and OMO in India (Bhole, 1985) – which have been mostly used for this purpose.

While the monetary policy in India continues to play a distributive role, the present reserves requirements policy differs from the earlier one in two respects. Firstly, the new policy seeks to make the CRR also as an instrument of credit distribution. Secondly, it seeks to use both the CRR and the SLR for channelizing more credit to the private sector instead of the public sector. The favoured sector of the monetary policy has now changed from the public sector to the private sector.

The official policy statements clearly reflect this shift. The CRR, along with the SLR, is now perceived primarily as a technique of "pre-empting resources" or "enabling banks to provide large amounts of credit at their discretion" or "enlarging availability of credit to the commercial sector." It was stated recently that "... we are committed to a reduction in the levels of pre-emptions in the form of CRR and SLR ...," that "an objective of credit policy during 1993-94 is to enlarge the availability of credit to commercial sector ...," and that "... the one per cent point reduction in SLR and CRR requirements, would ... augment bank's total lendable resources ..." (Rangarajan, 1993). Would it not be more correct to say that the CRR result in the *immobilization or impounding* or resources and not in their *pre-emption*?

This new perception would unfortunately undermine the stabilization role of the CRR and the SLR. It appears quite clear that the monetary policy implications of a reduction in reserves ratios have not been weighted adequately, otherwise the authorities would not have committed for such a reduction before the real, concrete, significant, actual improvement in the fiscal stance itself. From the viewpoint of its stabilization role, there cannot be any definite and advance medium-term commitment to reduce the CRR, because changes in it must occur in the light of economic conditions obtaining in each (short) period. To make such a commitment is to jettison one of the major advantages of monetary policy vis-à-vis fiscal policy, namely, its flexibility.

It, therefore, appears quite certain that the new policy has been predominantly influenced by ideological considerations. In a mixed economy, to say that what can be potentially lent to the private sector along constitutes an "augmentation of lendable resources of banks" is not convincing. Further, if reduction in the budget deficit and in the SLR is said to be necessary for economic stability, then how can it be said, without involving a serious contradiction, that an increase in credit availability to the private commercial sector, through a reduction in the CRR and the SLR would contribute to stabilization? Is it the case that while government expenditure is inflationary, private expenditure is not? If economic stabilization is the goal, the supply of credit to *both* public and private sectors needs to be restricted; and to achieve this, what is needed, among other things, is to increase the CRR, and not to reduce it. The claims that a reduction in the CRR and SLR is necessary for restoring macro-economic stability and that such a reduction constitutes a financial sector reform can be believed only if one believes in the virtues of privatization and in the need for "reverse crowding out" as a matter of faith.

Objectively speaking, just as captive and cheap supply of funds to the government through the mechanism of the SLR was incorrect, so also an insistent redirection or diversion of funds to the private sector by reducing the CRR and the SLR is not in the interests of the economy. The present directive to *reduce* the SLR, like the earlier directive to *increase* it, is against the spirit of liberalization, autonomy and flexibility in the working of banks. The level of SLR targeted under the present policy may prove to be quite restrictive; it may very easily come in the way of free, efficient and economic management of their assets-portfolios by the banks.

The rational approach to policy demands that the cost and availability of funds to *both* public and private sectors must be determined after keeping in view their genuine, prudent and productive requirements, the overall scarcity of funds in the economy and the general economic conditions in the country. The CRR and the SLR policy under such dispensation would be quite different from the present policy of *necessarily reducing* these ratios. It is undoubtedly a worthwhile and desirable objective that the conduct of monetary policy be freed from the pendulum-like swings between the public and the private sector, the swings which are dictated by changes in the political ideology. The monetary policy in India ought to be conducted keeping in mind the wider or general requirements and conditions in the economy as a whole, and not by giving the "most favoured sector" treatment to either of the two sectors under discussion. The present policy lacks holistic character in this sense.

Have Economic Conditions Really Improved?

The present CRR and SLR policy has been justified on the grounds that the fiscal and monetized deficit has now declined, and that inflation has been brought under control. However, there has been a great confusion between the normative and the actual in this respect; the policy has been planned and executed by taking for granted that the intentions of the authorities in these matters have actually been fulfilled. The facts are quite different.

The actual budget deficit was Rs. 12657 crore against the deficit target of Rs.5389 crore and against the revised deficit estimate of Rs. 7207 crore in 1992-93. In its Annual Report for 1992-93, the RBI has stated that its credit to the centre stood at Rs.16245 crore and the Centre's budget deficit stood at Rs. 21065 crore as on August 20, 1993, against the targeted deficit of Rs. 4314 crore for the whole of 1993-94. Inflation in 1992-93 and 1993-94 cannot be said to have been brought under control; the actual public experience in this regard has been quite different from the cleverly worked out reduction in the wholesale price indices. Moreover, the direction of changes in various major determinants of inflation does not indicate the likelihood of a decline in the rate of inflation in these years.

The low rate of growth of industrial output over the past two- three years; the high rate of growth of 14.13 per cent in M_3 , 11.32 per cent in net bank credit to government, 14.93 per cent in bank credit to commercial sector, 11.49 per cent in reserve money, and 1741 per cent in net foreign exchange assets of banking sector – all in 1992-93 (RBI Bulletin, 1993); and the excessive increase in RBI credit to the centre and budget deficit in 1993-94 so far, clearly indicate that the current monetary, credit and budgetary conditions in India are not favourable to a reduction in the CRR and the SLR.

Are Other Techniques Superior?

The present policy of de-emphasizing the role of the CRR and the SLR is based on the expectation that the RBI (Central Banks) would be able to replace them by other techniques of monetary control, especially OMO. This raises certain very important and relevant questions. Are other techniques definitely superior to the reserves ratios technique? Is the shift to other techniques feasible in India? Is it not possible that the CRR technique possesses some important advantages which indicate that it should be retained rather than discarded? We discuss these issues in the present and next two sections.

As to the superiority of other techniques, it may be noted that OMO, for example, are useful in quickly influencing changes in bank credit and money supply; but it is so only when there is a well-developed and active money market and government securities market existing in the country. They can be used with felicity and can be reversed easily only under such conditions. Further, OMO may have to be conducted simply to offset some "outside" factors (such as a seasonal inflow of currency and changes in treasury's cash balances) which are only remotely related to monetary policy considerations. There is also a feeling that OMO, often, are not of much help because they are so unobtrusive and are used either two frequently or infrequently (Ritter and Silber, 1977; Coats, 1980). Similarly, changes in the discount rate may not be effective because they may follow rather than precede changes in money markets. In addition, interest rates are also susceptible to changes for reasons other than the monetary policy.

Moreover, the success of OMO and discount rate techniques hinges on changes in the demand side rather than the supply side of reserves and credit. For example, when the discount rate is changed, how far will it affect the volume of bank reserves, bank credit and money supply will depend upon the decision of the banks to borrow from the Central Bank, and the decision of the commercial sector to borrow from the banks. All such factors tend to limit the effectiveness and usefulness of these techniques.

Unfeasibility of Shifting to Other Techniques

Apart from the absence of unconditional theoretical superiority of other techniques, the scope for substituting them for the CRR in practice, particularly in Indian conditions, is quite limited. It is quite well known that OMO in India will not be used so far to any significant extent as a technique of monetary control during the long 55-year history of the Indian Central Bank.

This also been so for reasons of death management, and the underdeveloped nature, in terms of breadth, width and depth, of the government securities market. Neither are the conditions conducive nor is there any worthwhile experience in India for using OMO wisely, effectively and with finesse for the purpose of regulation. Even a country like the UK has not made much use of their technique so far for regulatory process. It would take many more years for it to become a substitute, either completely or in a major way, for the CRR in the user of which RBI has gained substantial and valuable experience by now.

The situation with regarded to the discount rate ad other interest rates is similar. Interest rates in India has remained administered over a long period of time, and the bank rate technique has not been used for a decade now. The bold efforts towards making interest rates policy simple, free and flexible, unfortunately, has met with only a limited success. The reversal of the bold and appropriate interest rates policy introduced in October 1991, by reducing interest rates thrice within a matter of past few months should convince anyone that the immediate shift from the CRR to the interest rates technique is very difficult indeed. If the CRR is not used sufficiently, RBI would be left without any major instrument of monetary control.

In Defence of Reserves Requirements

The policy under discussion also disregards the merits of the reserves ratio technique. Some experts feel that this technique has certain theoretical beauty, viz., the reserves concept can easily be structured to control fairly precisely the movements of any single monetary aggregate, and changes in reserves ratio have an extremely widespread, powerful, immediate, and even "blunt" impact on bank reserves and money supply (Morris, 1972). Its "bluntness" should not be regarded as its drawback because, in situations of sudden and wide fluctuations, it would prove to be a great blessing. In less severe conditions, its 'bluntness" can be softened and its "lumpiness' partially reduced, by using it cautiously or by fine-tuning it suitably.

On the basis of experience, many Central Banks and economists feel that the control of bank reserves is necessary and important if money supply is to be controlled as a part of anti-inflationary programme. Therefore, even when they are making a case for the greater use of other techniques, they are, simultaneously, devising operating procedures and implementing strategies (reserves strategies) which would regulate reserves effectively. In India, where the scope for using other techniques is rather limited, the direct control of reserves through changes in the CRR would have to remain an essential or integral part of the regulatory mechanism for quite some time to come.

In other words, the belief in the theory of money multiplier, and the importance given to controlling money supply, do indicate the continued need for using the reserves ratio technique. The key result of the money multiplier framework is that the monetary control would suffer greatly if reserves requirements are drastically reduced or eliminated. The current official policy, therefore, is inconsistent with the authorities' chosen theoretical model of the monetary policy.

It is sometimes argued that if we go beyond the money multiplier framework, if we de-emphasize money supply control, and if we make interest rates as the principal "intermediate target," it may be possible to reduce or eliminate reserves requirements. However, this is also not strictly correct because even then the reserves requirements would retain its useful role by becoming a vehicle for facilitating control over short-term interest rates, instead of being a vehicle for controlling money stock directly (Weiner, 1992).

In this context, a reference to a discussion on the reform of regulatory mechanism which took place in the UK some years back is quite relevant at this juncture. Like in India, the monetary control system in the UK consisted of administered interest rates, credit ceilings, credit rationing, etc. for a long period of time during 1960s. Discussing how to reform this system with a view to improve the working of regulatory mechanism, to encourage competition and to create even playing fields, it was proposed that:

- the CRR should be used
- the interest should be paid on cash reserves
- all financial institutions should be required to hold public debt in some minimum proportion to their liabilities (Bain, 1971).

III. Towards a More Effective Monetary Policy

The above discussion is not meant to claim that the reserves ratio technique is superior to other techniques, and therefore, it alone would be sufficient for the purpose of regulation. It is not an infallible instrument; it also has its own limitations. For example, a given level of free reserves is compatible with many different levels of bank credit and money supply; and it is quite possible that the volume of free reserves may vary within the same limits over a long period of time, while money supply and bank credit may grow considerably during that period.

Some important lessons can be derived from the working of monetary policy across various countries in different periods of time which are as follows:

Each of the techniques of monetary control has its own limitations; in spite of this, economists have heatedly argued for the superiority of one technique or the other.

The Central Banks have also mostly pursued a single-technique policy; this has greatly reduced the effectiveness of monetary policy which, in turn, has given it a bad name and lowered its prestige.

Monetary policy has to be conducted within a particular framework of institutions, markets and economic conditions which provide opportunities for and create constraints on its working.

No given technique or target is superior to others in terms of all the criteria of comparison, viz., liquidity of banks, efficiency in neutralizing cyclical fluctuations, allocative efficiency, administrative ease, technical characteristics and implications for long-run capital accumulation and growth. No technique or target, therefore, can be said to be dispensable. The phenomenon of monetarists favouring money supply and downgrading interest rates, or the Keynesians favouring interests rates and downgrading money supply, or the Central Bankers now downgrading reserves requirements and favouring OMO, is unfortunate indeed.

As said above, in practice also, there has been a singularization in deploying techniques of monetary control; the monetary policies usually have been single-technique policies during the post-Second World War period. It was OMO in the US, direct credit rationing or bank rate in the UK and bank rate or CRR in India. This has naturally led to an overuse of one technique and disuse of other techniques. It has also resulted in a drastic reduction in the number of instruments of policy in relation to the number of policy goals. The effectiveness of techniques in general has tended to suffer on these counts.

An ideal approach to monetary policy formulation would, therefore, be to develop a multi-technique policy in which more than one technique would be used suitably, optimally and in a well-coordinated manner. Just as there is a need to coordinate and mix monetary policy and fiscal policy appropriately, so also there is a need to coordinate and mix different techniques of monetary policy suitably. This approach would have its own difficulties, but it would be more rational and better suited to deal with complex and diverse economic reality. It would avoid overuse or disuse or extreme (desperate, immoderate) use of techniques, and would lend far greater flexibility to their use. In consequence, monetary policy would certainly gain in effectiveness.

In India, this approach would involve an effective control of money supply, rejuvenation of the bank rate, allowing interest rates to vary in a wider band, making a beginning towards reducing the burden of debt management on OMO and using reserves requirements flexibly and optimally.

A policy package of this nature has been suggested by Dr. I.G. Patel, the former governor of the RBI. Since his views are of great relevance and importance, we give them here *in extenso*. He has argued that, given his contention that the practice of monetary targeting can be moderately useful, and given his disinclination to endorse a very active use of the interest rate weapon, he would certainly not advocate giving up all quantitative and direct controls such as those exercised through reserves requirements for banks. According to him, a flexible use of reserves requirements can help in minimizing the secondary impact of excessive fiscal deficits, and it can also help stave off private speculative boom. However, what should be used flexibly is the CRR and SLR which must be kept stable over long periods to reflect its longer-term rationale of prudential reserves and a legitimate share for the government in the longer-term savings. Further, marginal reserves requirements would have a greater impact in the short-run; but there is often an undesirable tendency to keep them on for ever or to translate them into average terms. The device of making marginal reserves requirements time bound is worthy of consideration (PATEL).

IV. Summary and Conclusions

We have presented in this paper a detailed examination of the Indian policy makers' medium-term commitment to drastically *reduce* the CRR and the SLR. It has been argued by us that the issues involved in the use of CRR and the SLR are far more complex than the one-dimensional perception which appears to underlie such a commitment. The choice of techniques of monetary policy has to depend upon economic conditions obtaining in different periods of time, and therefore, it is improper to make an advance and definite commitment to change a technique in a particular or specific direction, beyond a very short period. To pose such a commitment as a part of financial reforms is not very convincing either. The present CRR and the SLR policy has undermined the regulatory or stabilization role of these techniques by trying to make them primarily instruments of distribution of bank resources of favour of the private commercial sector. The present economic conditions in India and the expected future scenario do not warrant substantial reduction in the CRR and the SLR. Since the "Reserve Tax" argument is not tenable and since a major or complete shift to techniques such as the discount rate and OMO is neither theoretically justifiable nor practically feasible, the present policy under discussion has to be called erroneous. Such a policy appears to be predominantly inspired by the trends (fashions) abroad whose relevance for India has not been adequately examined as well as politico-ideological considerations. In a complex and multi-objective world, a flexible and well-coordinated multi-technique world, a flexible and well-coordinated multi-technique monetary policy would definitely prove to be superior to a rigid and single-technique monetary policy. It can be predicted with quite a high degree of certainty that the deteriorating credit, money supply, prices and fiscal conditions in India would soon compel the authorities to reverse their current reserves requirements policy.

References

BAIN, A. D. (1971). "Monetary Control Methods in the United Kingdom" in G. Clayton et al (eds.). *Monetary Theory and Policy in the 1970s.* London: Oxford University Press, pp. 165-175.

BHOLE, L. M. (1985). *Impacts of Monetary Policy.* Bombay: Himalaya, p. 27.

___ (1992). *Financial Institutions and Markets* (Second Edition). New Delhi: Tata McGraw-Hill, pp. 74-89.

COATS, W. L. (1980). "The Use of Reserves Requirements in Developing Countries," in W. L. COATS, Jr. and D. R. LJATLJATE (eds.) *Money and Monetary Policy in Less Developed Countries.* New York: Pergamon, p. 417.

GUPTA S. B. (1979). *Monetary Planning in India.* New Delhi: Oxford University Press, pp. 118-132 and 158-167.

MORRIS, F. E. (1972). "RPDs as the Target" in Federal Reserve Bank of Boston, *Controlling Monetary Aggregates II: The Implementation.*

PATEL, I. G. "Monetary Policy Revisited" in Bankers' Training College, Advanced Central Banking and Management Programme, Bombay, Mimeo.

RANGARAJAN, C. (1993). "The Inter-Relationship between Fiscal Policy and Monetary Policy and Financial Sector Reform," *Discount and Finance*, May 22, p. 6.

RESERVE BANK OF INDIA (1985). *Report of the Committee to Review the Working of the Monetary System* (Chakravarty Committee), Bombay, pp 246-256.

___ (1991). *Report of the Committee on the Financial System*, Bombay, November, pp. 4-5.

___ (1993). *Bulletin*, July.

RITTER, L. S. and SILBER, W. L. (1977). *Money*. New York: Basic Books, pp. 118-119.

TARAPORE, S. S. (1993). "The Future Course of Monetary Policy," *RBI Bulletin*, April, p. 599.

WEINER, S. E. (1992). "The Changing Role of Reserve Requirements in Monetary Policy," *Economic Review*, Federal Reserve Bank of Kansas City, Fourth Quarter, p. 45.

Made in the USA
Monee, IL
05 November 2026

67849407R00213